FEEL FREE

FEEL FREE

Essays

Zadie Smith

HAMISH HAMILTON
an imprint of
PENGUIN BOOKS

HAMISH HAMILTON

UK | USA | Canada | Ireland | Australia
India | New Zealand | South Africa

Hamish Hamilton is part of the Penguin Random House group of companies
whose addresses can be found at global.penguinrandomhouse.com.

First published 2018
002

Copyright © Zadie Smith, 2018

The picture credits on page 437 and the acknowledgements on
pages 438–44 constitute an extension of this copyright page.

The moral right of the author has been asserted

Set in 12.5/16 pt Fournier MT Std
Typeset by Jouve (UK), Milton Keynes
Printed in Great Britain by Clays Ltd, St Ives plc

A CIP catalogue record for this book is available from the British Library

HARDBACK ISBN: 978–0–241–14689–7
TRADE PAPERBACK ISBN: 978–0–241–14690–3

www.greenpenguin.co.uk

Penguin Random House is committed to a
sustainable future for our business, our readers
and our planet. This book is made from Forest
Stewardship Council® certified paper.

For Kit and Hal
and
For Robert B. Silvers, *in memoriam*

'People can be slave-ships in shoes.'

— Zora Neale Hurston

'The eyes are not windows. There are nerve impulses, but no one reads them, counts them, translates them, and ruminates about them. Hunt for as long as you want, there's nobody home. The world is contained within you, and you're not there.'

— Daniel Kehlmann

CONTENTS

Contents

FOREWORD

I was having dinner with old friends in Rome when one of them turned to me and said: 'But of course your writing so far has been a fifteen-year psychodrama.' Everybody laughed – so did I – but I was a little stung by it, and worried at the idea for a few weeks. Now here I am bringing it up in this foreword. It's true that for years I've been thinking aloud – and often wondering if I've made myself ludicrous in one way or another. I think the anxiety comes from knowing I have no real qualifications to write as I do. Not a philosopher or sociologist, not a real professor of literature or film, not a political scientist, professional music critic or trained journalist. I'm employed in an MFA programme, but have no MFA myself, and no PhD. My evidence – such as it is – is almost always intimate. I feel this – do you? I'm struck by this thought – are you? Essays about one person's affective experience have, by their very nature, not a leg to stand on. All they have is their freedom. And the reader is likewise unusually free, because I have absolutely nothing over her, no authority. She can reject my feelings at every point, she can say: 'No, I have never felt that' or 'Dear Lord, the thought never crossed my mind!'

Writing exists (for me) at the intersection of three precarious, uncertain elements: language, the world, the self. The first is never wholly mine; the second I can only ever know in a partial sense; the third is a malleable and improvised response to the previous two. If my writing is a psychodrama I don't think it is because I have, as the Internet would have it, *so many feels*, but because the correct balance and weight to be given to each of these three elements is never self-evident to me. It's *this* self – whose boundaries are uncertain, whose language is never pure, whose world is in no way 'self-evident' – that I try to write from and to. My hope is for a reader who, like the author, often wonders how free she really is, and who takes it for granted that reading involves all the same liberties and exigencies as writing.

A note: I realize my somewhat ambivalent view of human selves is wholly out of fashion. These essays you have in your hands were written in England and America during the eight years of the Obama presidency and so are the product of a bygone world. It is of course hardly possible to retain any feelings of ambivalence – on either side of the Atlantic – in the face of what we now confront. Millions of more or less amorphous selves will now necessarily find themselves solidifying into protesters, activists, marchers, voters, firebrands, impeachers, lobbyists, soldiers, champions, defenders, historians, experts, critics. You can't fight fire with air. But equally you can't fight for a freedom you've forgotten how to identify. To the reader still curious about freedom I offer these essays – to be used, changed, dismantled, destroyed or ignored as necessary!

Zadie Smith

New York

18 January 2017

IN THE WORLD

North-west London Blues

Last time I was in Willesden Green I took my daughter to visit my mother. The sun was out. We wandered down Brondesbury Park toward the high road. The 'French Market' was on, which is a slightly improbable market of French things sold in the concrete space between the pretty turreted remnants of Willesden Library (1894) and the brutal red-brick beached cruise ship known as Willesden Green Library Centre (1989), a substantial local landmark that racks up nearly five hundred thousand visits a year. We walked in the sun down the urban street to the concrete space – to market. This wasn't like walking a shady country lane in a quaint market town ending up in a perfectly preserved eighteenth-century square. It was not even like going to one of these farmers' markets that have sprung up all over London at the crossroads where personal wealth meets a strong interest in artisanal cheeses.

But it was still very nice. Willesden French Market sells cheap bags. It sells CDs of old-time jazz and rock and roll. It sells umbrellas and artificial flowers. It sells ornaments and knick-knacks and doodahs, which are not always obviously French in theme or nature. It sells water pistols. It sells French breads and pastries for not much more than you'd pay for the baked goods in Greggs down Kilburn High Road. It sells cheese, but of the decently priced and easily recognizable kind – Brie, goat's, blue – as if the market has travelled unchanged across the Channel from some run-down urban suburb of Paris. Which it may have done for all I know. The key thing about Willesden's French Market is that it accentuates and celebrates this concrete space in front of Willesden Green Library Centre, which is at all times a meeting place, though never quite so much as it is on market day. Everybody's just standing around, talking, buying or not buying cheese, as the mood takes them. It's really pleasant. You could almost forget Willesden High Road was ten yards away. This matters. When you're standing in the market you're not going to work, you're not going to school, you're not waiting for a bus. You're not heading for the Tube or shopping for necessities. You're not on the high road where all these activities take place. You're just a little bit off it, hanging out, in an open-air urban area, which is what these urban high streets have specifically evolved to stop people from doing.

Everybody knows that if people hang around for any length of time in an urban area without purpose they are likely to become 'antisocial'. And indeed there were four homeless drunks sitting on one of the library's strange architectural protrusions, drinking Special Brew. Perhaps in a village they would be sitting under a tree, or have already been driven from the area by a farmer with a pitchfork. I do not claim to know what happens in villages. But here in Willesden they were sitting on their ledge and the rest of us were congregating for no useful purpose in the unlovely concrete space, simply standing around in the sunshine, like some kind of community. From this vantage point we could look ahead to the turrets, or left to the Victorian police station (1865), or right to the half-ghostly façade of the Spotted Dog (1893).

We could have a minimal sense of continuity with what came before. Not so much as the people of Hampstead must have, to be sure, or the folk who live in pretty market towns all over the country, but here and there in Willesden the past lingers on. We're glad that it does. Which is not to say that we are overly nostalgic about architecture (look at the library!) but we find it pleasant to remember that we have as much right to a local history as anyone, even if many of us arrived here only recently and from every corner of the globe.

On market day we permit ourselves the feeling that our neighbourhood, for all its catholic mix of people and architecture, remains a place of some beauty that deserves minimal preservation and care. It's a nice day out, is my point. Still, there's only so long a toddler will stand around watching her grandmother greet all the many people in Willesden her grandmother knows. My daughter and I took a turn. You can't really take a turn in the high road so we went backwards, into the library centre. Necessarily backwards in time, though I didn't – couldn't – bore my daughter with my memories: she is still young and below nostalgia's reach. Instead I will bore you. Studied in there, at that desk. Met a boy over there, where the phone boxes used to be. Went, with school friends, in there, to see *The Piano* and *Schindler's List* (cinema now defunct), and afterward we went in there, for coffee (café now defunct), and had an actual argument about art, an early inkling that there might be a difference between a film with good intentions and a good film.

Meanwhile my daughter is running madly through the centre's esplanade, with another toddler who has the same idea. And then she reverses direction and heads straight for Willesden Bookshop, an independent shop that rents space from the council and provides – no matter what Brent Council may claim – an essential local service. It is run by Helen. Helen is an essential local person. I would characterize her essentialness in the following way: 'Giving the people what they didn't know they wanted.' Important category.

Different from the concept popularized by Mr Murdoch: 'Giving the people what they want.' Everyone is by now familiar with the Dirty Digger's version of the social good – we've had thirty years of it. Helen's version is different and necessarily perpetrated on a far smaller scale.

Helen gives the people of Willesden what they didn't know they wanted. Smart books, strange books, books about the country they came from, or the one that they're in. Children's books with children in them that look at least a bit like the children who are reading them. Radical books. Classical books. Weird books. Popular books. She reads a lot, she has recommendations. Hopefully, you have a Helen in a bookshop near you and so understand what I'm talking about. In 1999 I didn't know I wanted to read David Mitchell until Helen pointed me to *Ghostwritten*. And I have a strong memory of buying a book by Sartre here, because it was on the shelf and I saw it. I don't know how I could have known I wanted Sartre without seeing it on that shelf – that is, without Helen putting it there. Years later, I had my first book launch in this bookshop and when it got too full, mainly with local friends of my mother, we all walked up the road to her flat and carried on over there.

And it was while getting very nostalgic about all this sort of thing with Helen, and wondering about the possibility of having another launch in the same spot, that I first heard of the council's intention to demolish the library centre, along with the bookshop and the nineteenth-century turrets and the concrete space and the ledge on which the four drunks sat. To be replaced with private luxury flats, a greatly reduced library, 'retail space', and no bookshop. (Steve, the owner, could not afford the commercial rise in rent. The same thing happened to his Kilburn Bookshop, which closed recently after thirty years.) My mum wandered in, with some cheese. The three of us lamented this change and the cultural vandalism we felt it represented. Or, if you take the opposite view, we stood around pointlessly, like the Luddite, fiscally ignorant liberals we are, complaining about the inevitable.

A few days later I got back on a plane to New York, where I teach for a part of each year. Logically it should be easier, when a person is far away from home, to take bad news from home on the chin, but anyone who has spent time in a community of ex-pats knows the exact opposite is true: no one could be more infuriated by events in Rome than the Italian kid serving your cappuccino on Broadway. Without the balancing setting of everyday life all you have is the news, and news by its nature is generally bad. Quickly you become hysterical. Consequently I can't tell whether the news coming out of my home is really as bad as it appears to be, or whether objects perceived from three thousand miles away are subject to exaggerations of size and colour. Did a Labour-run council really send heavies into Kensal Rise Library, in a dawn raid, to strip the place of books and Mark Twain's wall plaque? Are the people of Willesden Green seriously to lose their bookshop, be offered a smaller library (for use by more patrons from other libraries Brent has closed), an ugly block of luxury flats – and told that this is 'culture'?

Yes. That's all really happening. With minimal consultation, with bully-boy tactics, secrecy and a little outright deceit. No doubt the local councillors find themselves in a difficult position: the percentage cuts in Brent are among the highest in the country, mandated by the central government. But the chronic mismanagement of finances is easily traced back to the previous Labour government, and so around and around goes the baton of blame. The Willesden Green plan as it stands so obviously gives the developers an extremely profitable land deal – while exempting them from the need to build social housing – that you feel a bit like a child pointing it out. In this economy who but a child would expect anything else?

Reading these intensely local stories alongside the national story creates another effect that may be only another kind of optical illusion: mirroring. For here in the Leveson Inquiry into the 'ethics of the British press' you find all the same traits displayed, only writ large. Minimal consultation, bully-boy tactics, secrecy, outright deceit. Are some of the largest decisions of British political life really being made at the private dinner tables of a tiny elite? Why is Jeremy Hunt, the secretary of state 'for culture, Olympics, media and sport', texting Murdoch? What did Rebekah promise the prime minister and the prime minister promise Rebekah in that pretty little market town of Chipping Norton? During another period of ex-pat existence, in Italy, I sat at a Roman café table in a Renaissance square rolling my eyes at the soap opera of Italian political life: wiretapped politicians and footballers and TV stars, backroom media deals, glaring conflicts of interest, tabloid culture run riot, politicians in the pockets of newspapers. I used to chuckle over *La Repubblica* and tease my Italian friends about the kind of problems we didn't have in our basically sound British parliamentary democracy.

And so I recognize myself to be an intensely naive person. Most novelists are, despite frequent pretensions to deep sociopolitical insight. And I retain a particular naivety concerning the British state, which must seem comical to many people, particularly younger people. I can only really account for it by reaching back again, briefly, into the past. It's a short story about debt – because I owe the state, quite a lot. Some people owe everything they have to the bank accounts of their parents. I owe the state. Put simply, the state educated me, fixed my leg when it was broken, and gave me a grant that enabled me to go to university. It fixed my teeth (a bit) and found housing for my veteran father in his dotage. When my youngest brother was run over by a truck it saved his life and in particular his crushed right hand, a procedure that took half a year, and which would, on the open market – so a doctor told me at the time – have cost a million pounds. Those were the big things, but there were also plenty of little ones: my subsidized sports centre and my doctor's office, my school music lessons paid for with pennies, my university fees. My NHS glasses aged nine. My NHS baby aged thirty-three. And my local library. To steal another writer's title: England made me. It has never been hard for me to pay my taxes because I understand it to be the repaying of a large, in fact, an almost incalculable, debt.

Things change. I don't need the state now as I once did; and the state is not what it once was. It is complicit in this new, shared global reality in which states deregulate to privatize gain and re-regulate to nationalize loss. A process begun with verve by a Labour government is now being perfected by David Cameron's Tory–Lib Dem coalition. The charming tale of benign state intervention described above is now relegated to the land of fairy tales: not just naive but actually fantastic. Having one's own history so suddenly and abruptly made unreal is an experience of a whole generation of British people, who must now wander around like so many ancient mariners boring foreigners about how they went to university for free and could once find a National Health dentist on their high street.

I bore myself telling these stories. And the thing that is most boring about defending libraries is the imputation that an argument in defence of libraries is necessarily a social-liberal argument. It's only recently that I had any idea that how a person felt about libraries – not schools or hospitals, libraries – could even represent an ideological split. I thought a library was one of the few sites where the urge to conserve and the desire to improve – twin poles of our political mind – were easily and naturally united. Besides, what kind of liberal has no party left to vote for, and feels not so much gratitude to the state as antipathy and, at times, fear?

The closest I can find myself to an allegiance or a political imperative these days is the one expressed by that old social democrat Tony Judt: 'We need to learn to *think* the state again.' First and foremost I need to become less naive. The money is gone, and the conditions Judt's generation inherited and my generation inherited from Judt's are unlikely to be replicated in my lifetime, if ever again. That's the bad news from home. Politically all a social liberal has left is the ability to remind herself that fatalism is only another kind of trap, and there is more than one way to be naive. Judt again:

> We have freed ourselves of the mid-20th-century assumption – never universal but certainly widespread – that the state is likely to be the *best* solution to any given problem. We now need to liberate ourselves from the opposite notion: that the state is – by definition and always – the *worst* available option.

What kind of a problem is a library? It's clear that for many people it is not a problem at all, only a kind of obsolescence. At the extreme pole of this view is the technocrat's total faith: with every book in the world online, what need could there be for the physical reality? This kind of argument thinks of the library as a function rather than a plurality of individual spaces. But each library is a different kind of problem and 'the Internet' is no more a solution for all of them than it is their universal death knell.

Each morning I struggle to find a seat in the packed university library in which I write this, despite the fact that every single student in here could be at home in front of their MacBook browsing Google Books. And Kilburn Library – also run by Brent Council but situated, despite its name, in affluent Queen's Park – is not only thriving but closed for refurbishment. Kensal Rise is being closed not because it is unpopular but because it is unprofitable, this despite the fact that the friends of Kensal Rise Library are willing to run their library themselves (if All Souls College, Oxford, which owns the library, will let them). Meanwhile it is hard not to conclude that Willesden Green is being mutilated not least because the members of the council see the opportunity for a sweet real-estate deal.

All libraries have a different character and setting. Some are primarily for children or primarily for students or the general public, primarily full of books or microfilms or digitized material or with a café in the basement or a market out front. Libraries are not failing 'because they are libraries'. Neglected libraries get neglected, and this cycle, in time, provides the excuse to close them. Well-run libraries are filled with people because what a good library offers cannot be easily found elsewhere: an indoor public space in which you do not have to buy anything in order to stay.

In the modern state there are very few sites where this is possible. The only others that come readily to my mind require belief in an omnipotent creator as a condition for membership. It would seem the most obvious thing in the world to say that the reason why the market is not an efficient solution to libraries is because the market has no use for a library. But it seems we need, right now, to keep restating the obvious. There aren't many institutions left that fit so precisely Keynes's definition of things that no one else but the state is willing to take on. Nor can the experience of library life be re-created online. It's not just a matter of free books. A library is a different kind of social reality (of the three-dimensional kind), which by its very existence teaches a system of values beyond the fiscal.

I don't think the argument in favour of libraries is especially ideological or ethical. I would even agree with those who say it's not especially logical. I think for most people it's emotional. Not logos or ethos but pathos. This is not a denigration: emotion also has a place in public policy. We're humans, not robots. The people protesting the closing of Kensal Rise Library love that library. They were open to any solution on the left or on the right if it meant keeping their library open. They were ready to Big Society the hell out of that place. A library is one of those social goods that matter to people of many different political attitudes. All that the friends of Kensal Rise and Willesden Library and similar services throughout the country are saying is: these places are important to us. We get that money is tight, we understand that there is a hierarchy of needs, and that the French Market or a Mark Twain plaque are not hospital beds or classroom size. But they are still a significant part of our social reality, the only thing left on the high street that doesn't want either your soul or your wallet.

If the losses of private companies are to be socialized within already struggling communities, the very least we can do is listen to people when they try to tell us where in the hierarchy of their needs things like public space, access to culture, and preservation of environment lie. 'But I never use the damn things!' says Mr Notmytaxes in the letters page. Sir, I believe you. However. British libraries received over 300 million visits last year, and this despite the common neglect of the various councils that oversee them. In north-west London people are even willing to form human chains in front of them. People have taken to writing long pieces in newspapers to 'defend' them. Just saying the same thing over and over again. Defend our libraries. We like libraries. Can we keep our libraries? We need to talk about libraries. Pleading, like children. Is that really where we are?

Postscript: not long after this piece was published in the *New York Review of Books*, the library and bookshop were torn down. But the collective fuss made by activists had an effect: the library built in its place is a functioning one, with fewer books, it's true, but plenty of students, families and readers filling its shelf-light spaces, while on its second floor, a small but beautiful local museum took a few thousand square feet of prime real estate from the developers.

Elegy for a Country's Seasons

There is the scientific and ideological language for what is happening to the weather, but there are hardly any intimate words. Is that surprising? People in mourning tend to use euphemism; likewise the guilty and ashamed. The most melancholy of all the euphemisms: 'The new normal.' It's the new normal, I think, as a beloved pear tree, half drowned, loses its grip on the earth and falls over. The train line to Cornwall washes away – the new normal. We can't even say the word 'abnormal' to each other out loud: it reminds us of what came before. Better to forget what once was normal, the way season followed season, with a temperate charm only the poets appreciated.

What 'used to be' is painful to remember. Forcing the spike of an unlit firework into the cold, dry ground. Admiring the frost on the holly berries, en route to school. Taking a long, restorative walk on Boxing Day in the winter glare. Whole football pitches crunching underfoot. A bit of sun on Pancake Day; a little more for the Grand National. Chilly April showers, Wimbledon warmth. July weddings that could trust in fine weather. The distinct possibility of a Glastonbury sunburn. At least, we say to each other, at least August is still reliably ablaze – in Cornwall if not at Carnival. And it's nice that the Scots can take a little more heat with them when they pack up and leave.

Maybe we will get used to this new England, and – like the very young and recently migrated – take it for granted that April is the time for shorts and sandals, or that the New Year traditionally announces itself with a biblical flood. They say there will be butterflies appearing in new areas, and birds visiting earlier and leaving later – perhaps that will be interesting, and new, and not, necessarily, worse. Maybe we are misremembering the past! The Thames hasn't frozen over for generations, and the dream of a White Christmas is only a collective Dickensian delusion. Besides, wasn't it always a wet country?

It's amazing the side roads you can will yourself down to avoid the four-lane motorway ahead. England was never as wet as either its famous novels suggest or our American cousins presume. The weather has changed, is changing, and with it so many seemingly small things – quite apart from train tracks and houses, livelihoods and actual lives – are being lost. It was easy to assume, for example, that we would always be able to easily find a hedgehog in some corner of a London garden, pick it up in cupped hands, and unfurl it for our children – or go on a picnic and watch fat bumblebees crawling over the mouth of an open jam jar. Every country has its own version of this local sadness. (And every country has its version of our arguments, when it comes to causation. Climate change or cars? Climate change or cell-phone sites?) You're not meant to mention the minor losses, they don't seem worth mentioning – not when compared to the visions of apocalypse conjured by climate scientists and movie directors. And then there are all those people who believe that nothing much is happening at all.

Although many harsh words are said about the childlike response of the public to the coming emergency, the response doesn't seem to me very surprising, either. It's hard to keep apocalypse consistently in mind, especially if you want to get out of bed in the morning.

What's missing from the account is how much of our reaction is emotional. If it weren't, the whole landscape of debate would be different. We can easily imagine, for example, a world in which the deniers were not deniers at all, but simple ruthless pragmatists, the kind of people who say: 'I understand very well what's coming, but I am not concerned with my grandchildren; I am concerned with myself, my shareholders, and the Chinese competition.' And there are indeed a few who say this, but not as many as it might be reasonable to expect.

Another response that would seem natural aligns a deep religious feeling with environmental concern, for those who consider the land a beauteous gift of the Lord should, surely, rationally, be among the keenest to protect it. There are a few of these knocking around, too, but again, not half as many as I would have assumed. Instead the evidence is to be 'believed' or 'denied' as if the scientific papers are so many Lutheran creeds pinned to a door. In America, a curious loophole has even been discovered in God's creation, concerning hierarchy. It's argued that because He placed humans above 'things' – above animals and plants and the ocean – we can, with a clean conscience, let all those things go to hell. (In England, traditional Christian love of the land has been more easily converted into environmental consciousness, notably among the country aristocrats who own so much of it.)

But I don't think we have made matters of science into questions of belief out of sheer stupidity. Belief usually has an emotional component; it's desire, disguised. Of course, on the part of our leaders much of the politicization is cynical bad faith, and economically motivated, but down here on the ground, the desire for innocence is what's driving us. For both 'sides' are full of guilt, full of self-disgust – what Martin Amis once called 'species shame' – and we project it outwards. This is what fuels the petty fury of our debates, even in the midst of crisis.

During Superstorm Sandy, I climbed down fifteen floors, several months pregnant, in the darkness, just so I could get a Wi-Fi signal and email a climate-change-denying acquaintance with this fresh evidence of his idiocy. And it only takes a polar vortex for one's inbox to fill up with gleeful counter-narratives from right-leaning relatives – as if this were all a game, and the only thing hanging in the balance is whether or not you or your crazy uncle in Florida are 'alarmists' or 'realists'. Meanwhile, in Jamaica, where Sandy first made landfall, the ever more frequent tropical depressions, storms, hurricanes, droughts and landslides do not fall, for Jamaicans, in the category of ontological argument.

Sing an elegy for the washed away! For the cycles of life, for the saltwater marshes, the houses, the humans – whole islands of humans. Going, going, gone! But not quite yet. The apocalypse is always usefully cast into the future – unless you happen to live in Mauritius, or Jamaica, or the many other perilous spots. According to recent reports, 'if emissions of global greenhouse gases remain unchanged', things could begin to get truly serious around 2050, just in time for the seventh birthday party of my granddaughter. (The grandchildren of the future are frequently evoked in elegies of this kind.) Sometimes the global, repetitive nature of this elegy is so exhaustively sad – and so divorced from any attempts at meaningful action – that you can't fail to detect in the elegists a fatalist liberal consciousness that has, when you get right down to it, as much of a perverse desire for the apocalypse as the evangelicals we supposedly scorn.

Recently it's been possible to see both sides leaning in a little closer to hear the optimistic arguments of the technocrats. Some sleight of hand has occurred by which we begin to move from talk of combating and reversing to discussion of carbon capture and storage, and higher sea walls, and generators on the roof, and battening down the hatches. Both sides meet in failure. They say to each other: 'Yes, perhaps we should have had the argument differently, some time ago, but now it is too late, now we must work with what we have.'

This will no doubt look very peculiar to my seven-year-old granddaughter. I don't expect she will forgive me, but it might be useful for her to get a glimpse into the mindset, if only for the purposes of comprehension. What shall I tell her? Her teachers will already have explained that what was happening to the weather, in 2014, was an inconvenient truth, financially, politically – but that's perfectly obvious, even now. A global movement of the people might have forced it on to the political agenda, no matter the cost. What she will want to know is why this movement took so long to materialize. So I might say to her: look, the thing you have to appreciate is that we'd just been through a century of relativism and deconstruction, in which we were informed that most of our fondest-held principles were either uncertain or simple wishful thinking, and in many areas of our lives we had already been asked to accept that nothing is essential and everything changes – and this had taken the fight out of us somewhat.

And then also it's important to remember that the necessary conditions of our lives – those things that seem to us unavoidably to be the case – are not only debated by physicists and philosophers but exist, irrationally, in the minds of the rest of us, beneath contempt intellectually, perhaps, but we still experience them as permanent facts. The climate was one of those facts. We did not think it could change. That is, we always knew we could do a great deal of damage to this planet, but even the most hubristic among us had not imagined we would ever be able to fundamentally change its rhythms and character, just as a child who has screamed all day at her father still does not expect to see him lie down on the kitchen floor and weep. Now, do you think that'll get me off the hook with my (slightly tiresome and judgemental) future granddaughter? I worry.

Oh, what have we done! It's a biblical question, and we do not seem able to pull ourselves out of its familiar – essentially re-ligious – cycle of shame, denial, and self-flagellation. This is why (I shall tell my granddaughter) the apocalyptic scenarios did not help – the terrible truth is that we had a profound, historical at-traction to apocalypse. In the end, the only thing that could create the necessary traction in our minds was the intimate loss of the things we loved. Like when the seasons changed in our beloved little island, or when the lights went out on the fifteenth floor, or the day I went into an Italian garden in early July, with its owner, a woman in her eighties, and upon seeing the scorched yellow earth and withered roses, and hearing what only the really old people will confess – *in all my years I've never seen anything like it* – I found my mind finally beginning to turn from the elegiac *what have we done?* to the practical *what can we do?*

Fences: A Brexit Diary

Back in the old neighbourhood in north-west London after a long absence, I went past the local primary school and noticed a change. Many of my oldest friends were once students here, and recently – when a family illness returned us to England for a year – I enrolled my daughter. It's a very pretty red-brick Victorian building, and was for a long time in 'special measures', a judgement of the school inspection authority called Ofsted, and the lowest grade a state school can receive. Many parents, upon reading such a judgement, will naturally panic and place their children elsewhere; others, seeing with their own eyes what Ofsted – because it runs primarily on data – cannot humanly see, will doubt the wisdom of Ofsted and stay put. Still others may not read well in English, or are not online in their homes, or have never heard of Ofsted, much less ever considered obsessively checking its website.

In my case I had the advantage of local history: for years my brother taught here, in an after-school club for migrant children, and I knew perfectly well how good the school is, has always been, and how welcoming to its diverse population, many of whom are recently arrived in the country. Now, a year later, Ofsted has judged it officially 'good', and if I know the neighbourhood, this will mean that more middle-class, usually white, parents will take what they consider to be a risk, move into the environs of the school, and send their kids here.

If this process moves anything like it does in New York, the white middle-class population will increase, keeping pace with the general gentrification of the neighbourhood, and the boundaries of the 'catchment area' for the school will shrink, until it becomes, over a number of years, almost entirely homogeneous, with dashes of diversity, at which point the regulatory body will award its highest rating at last. But none of this has happened in the old neighbourhood yet and perhaps will never happen – given its lengthy and proud history of every conceivable form of diversity – and this was anyway not the change I noticed when I passed by.

At the time my particular brand of liberal paranoia was focused elsewhere: I noticed the fence. For this Victorian school, which, for a hundred years, has found cast-iron railings sufficient to mark its periphery, had now added what looked like tall bamboo slats between the bars, as well as six feet of plant life climbing these slats, blocking the view of the playground from the street and therefore of the children as they played. I went home and sent an intemperate email to a couple of parent governors:

> I walked past the school for the first time since I came home (yesterday) and noticed the wooden veil – for lack of a better word – that has gone up around the school. It made me so sad. I've lived in this area forty years. I saw a wall go up outside the Jewish school ten years ago and then a few years ago at the Muslim school. But I never thought I'd see one up outside ——. I'm very curious as to how it came about, who asked for it, how it was decided, whether the parents are happy with it and what – officially – is its purpose? 'Security'? 'Privacy'? Or something else?

An intemperate email, filled with liberal paranoia. By contrast the reply I received was sane and polite. 'Privacy and pollution' were the given reasons, pollution in particular being 'a huge thing at the moment' that the school had been asked to address by the local council. Plus the playground has a lot of concrete, the vegetation softened the look of the area, and in truth it hadn't occurred to the parent governors that the new arrangement might look in any way defensive or strange to passers-by. I reread my email and felt ashamed to have sent it. What state of mind had led me to interpret a simple cosmetic change so negatively?

I'm used to change: around here change is the rule. The old grammar school up the hill became one of the largest Muslim schools in Europe; the old synagogue became a mosque; the old church is now a private apartment building. Waves of immigration and gentrification pass through these streets like buses. But I suppose this local school, in my mind, was a kind of symbol. And if we've found one thing to be true in Britain recently it's that we, the British, can find ourselves behaving strangely when we allow material realities to turn into symbols.

I valued this little school especially, symbolically, as a mixed institution in which the children of the relatively rich and the poor, the children of Muslims, Jews, Hindus, Sikhs, Protestants, Catholics, atheists, Marxists and the kind of people who are religious about Pilates, are all educated together in the same rooms, play together in the same playground, speak about their faiths – or lack of them – to each other, while I walk by and often look in, and thus receive a vital symbolic reassurance that the world of my own childhood has not yet completely disappeared. These days the Jewish school looks like Fort Knox. The Muslim school is not far behind it. Was our little local school also to become a place behind a fence, separated, private, paranoid, preoccupied with security, its face turned from the wider community?

Two days later the British voted for Brexit. I was in Northern

Ireland, staying with my in-laws, two kindly, moderately conservative Northern Irish Protestants with whom I found myself, for the first time in our history, on the same side of a political issue. The shock I'd felt at the school gates I now felt in front of their enormous telly, as together we watched England fence itself off from the rest of Europe, with hardly a thought about what this meant for its Scottish and Irish cousins in the north and the west.

Much has been written since about the shockingly irresponsible behaviour of both David Cameron and Boris Johnson, but I don't think I would have been so entirely focused upon Boris and Dave if I had woken up in my own bed, in London. No, then my first thoughts would have been essentially hermeneutic. What does this vote mean? What was it really about? Immigration? Inequality? Historic xenophobia? Sovereignty? EU bureaucracy? Anti-neoliberal revolution? Class war?

But in Northern Ireland it was clear that one thing it certainly wasn't about, not even slightly, was Northern Ireland, and this focused the mind on the extraordinary act of solipsism that has allowed this long-brutalized little country to become the collateral damage of an internal rift within the Conservative Party. And Scotland! It's hard to credit. That two supposedly well-educated men, who have presumably read their British history, could with such utter recklessness throw into hazard a hard-won union of three hundred years' standing – in order to satisfy their own professional ambitions – appeared that morning a larger crime, to me, than the severing of the decades-long European pact that actually prompted it all.

'Conservative' is not the right term for either of them any more: that word has at least an implication of care and the preservation of legacy. 'Arsonist' feels like the more accurate term. Michael Gove and Nigel Farage meanwhile are the true right-wing ideologues, with clear agendas toward which they have been working for many years. The first had his sights on the Trojan horse of 'sovereignty', from inside of which empty symbol an unfettered deregulated financial sector was supposed to leap. The second, who resigned on 4 July 2016, seemed to be in the grip of a genuine racial obsession, combined with a determination to fence off Britain from the European mainstream not only on the question of freedom of movement but on a range of issues from climate change to gun control to repatriation of immigrants.*

A referendum magnifies the worst aspects of an already imperfect system – democracy – channelling a dazzlingly wide variety of issues through a very narrow gate. It has the appearance of intensification – Ultimate democracy! Thumbs up or thumbs down! – but in practice delivers a dangerously misleading reduction. Even many who voted Leave ended up feeling that their vote did not accurately express their feelings. They had a wide variety of motives for their vote, and much of the Remain camp was similarly splintered.

Some of the reasoning was almost comically removed from the binary question posed. A friend whose mother still lives in the neighbourhood describes a conversation over the garden fence, between her mother and a fellow north London leftist, who explained to my friend's mother that she herself had voted Leave in order 'to

---

* Farage believes that the Arctic Sea ice cap is growing back and that reports of its disappearance are deliberate overstatement, forged in conspiracy by Green activists in cahoots, naturally, with 'EU federalists'. He thinks that the strict gun laws put in place after the massacre at Dunblane should be repealed, and he feels that the 'basic principle' of Enoch Powell's 'rivers of blood' speech – in which he said the proposed immigration and antidiscrimination legislation would lead to violence – was correct.

get rid of that bloody health secretary!' Ah, like so many people across this great nation I also long to be free of the almost perfectly named Jeremy Hunt, but a referendum turns out to be a very ineffective hammer for a thousand crooked nails.

The first instinct of many Remain voters on the left was that this was only about immigration. When the numbers came in and the class and age breakdown became known, a working-class populist revolution came more clearly into view, although of the kind that always perplexes middle-class liberals, who tend to be both politically naive and sentimental about the working classes. Throughout the day I phoned home and emailed and tried to process, along with much of London – or at least the London I know – our enormous sense of shock. 'What have they done?' we said to each other, sometimes meaning the leaders, who we felt must have known what they were doing, and sometimes meaning the people, who, we implied, didn't.

Now I'm tempted to think it was the other way around. Doing something, anything, was in some inchoate way the aim: the notable feature of neoliberalism is that it feels like you can do nothing to change it, but this vote offered up the rare prize of causing a chaotic rupture in a system that more usually steamrolls all in its path. But even this most optimistic leftist interpretation – that this was a violent, more or less considered reaction to austerity and the neoliberal economic meltdown that preceded it – cannot deny the casual racism that seems to have been unleashed alongside it, both by the campaign and by the vote itself.

To the many anecdotal accounts I will add two reported by my Jamaican-born mother. A week before the vote a skinhead ran up to her in Willesden and shouted '*Über Alles Deutschland!*' in her face, like a memory of the late seventies. The day after the vote, a lady shopping for linens and towels on the Kilburn High Road stood near my mother and the half-dozen other people originally from other places and announced to no one in particular: 'Well, you'll all have to go home now!'

What have you done, Boris? What have you done, Dave? Yet within this tale of our solipsistic leaders, thoughtlessly lighting a fuse, there is contained a less pleasing story of our own Londoncentric solipsism, which seems to me equally real, and has formed a different kind of veil, perhaps just as hard to see through as the blinding personal ambition of a man like Boris. The profound shock I felt at the result – and which so many other Londoners seem to have experienced – suggests at the very least that we must have been living behind a veil, unable to see our own country for what it has become.

The night before I left for Northern Ireland, I had dinner with old friends, north London intellectuals, in fact exactly the kind of people the Labour MP Andy Burnham made symbolic reference to when he claimed that the Labour Party had lost ground to UKIP because it was 'too much Hampstead and not enough Hull', although of course, in reality, we were all long ago priced out of Hampstead by the bankers and the Russian oligarchs. We were considering Brexit. Probably every dinner table in north London was doing the same. But it turned out we couldn't have been considering it very well because not one of us, not for a moment, believed it could possibly happen. It was so obviously wrong, and we were so obviously right – how could it?

After settling this question, we all moved on to bemoaning the strange tendency of the younger lefty generation to censor or silence speech or opinions they consider in some way wrong: no-platforming, safe spaces, and the rest of it. We were all right about that, too. But then, from the corner, on a sofa, the cleverest among us, who was at that moment feeding a new baby, waited till we'd all stopped bloviating and added: 'Well, they got that habit from us. We always wanted to be seen to be right. To be on the right side of an issue. More so even than doing anything. Being right was always the most important thing.'

In the days following the result I thought about this insight a lot. I kept reading pieces by proud Londoners speaking proudly of their multicultural, outward-looking city, so different from these narrow xenophobic places up north. It sounded right, and I wanted it to be true, but the evidence of my own eyes offered a counter-narrative. For the people who truly live a multicultural life in this city are those whose children are educated in mixed environments, or who live in genuinely mixed environments, in public housing or in a handful of historically mixed neighbourhoods, and there are no longer as many of those as we like to believe.

For many people in London right now the supposedly multicultural and cross-class aspects of their lives are actually represented by their staff – nannies, cleaners – by the people who pour their coffees and drive their cabs, or else the handful of Nigerian princes you meet in the private schools. The painful truth is that fences are being raised everywhere in London. Around school districts, around neighbourhoods, around lives. One useful consequence of Brexit is to finally and openly reveal a deep fracture in British society that has been thirty years in the making. The gaps between north and south, between the social classes, between Londoners and everyone else, between rich Londoners and poor Londoners, and between white and brown and black, are real and need to be confronted by all of us, not only those who voted Leave.

Amid all the hysterical characterization of those Leavers in the immediate aftermath – not least my own – I paused and thought of a young woman I had noticed in the playground the year my daughter spent in that school in special measures. She was a mother, like the rest of us, but at least fifteen years younger. After walking behind her up the hill to my house a few times I figured out she lived in the same housing estate in which I myself grew up. The reason I noticed her at all was because my daughter happened to be deeply enamoured of her son. A playdate was the natural next step.

But I never took that next step and neither did she. I didn't know how to penetrate what I felt was the fear and loathing she seemed to have for me, not because I was black – I saw her speaking happily with the other black mothers – but because I was middle class. She had seen me open the shiny black door to the house opposite her estate, just as I had seen her enter the estate's stairwell each day. I remembered these fraught episodes from childhood, when things were the other way around. Could I ask the girl in the big fine house on the park into our cramped council flat? And later, when we moved up to a perfectly nice flat on the right side of Willesden, could I then visit my friend in a rough one on the wrong side of Kilburn?

The answer was, usually, yes. Not without tension, not without occasional mortifying moments of social comedy or glimpses of domestic situations bordering on tragedy – but still it was yes. Back then, we were all still willing to take the 'risk', if 'risk' is the right word to describe entering into the lives of others, not merely in symbol but in reality. But in this new England it felt, to me at least, impossible. To her, too, I think. The gap between us has become too large.

The tall, narrow Victorian house I bought fifteen years ago, though it is exactly the same kind of house my middle-class friends owned when I was growing up, is now worth an obscene amount of money, and I worried that she might think I had actually paid that obscene amount of money to own it. The distance between her flat and my house – though it is, in reality, only two hundred yards – is, in symbol, further than it has ever been. Our prospective playdate lay somewhere over this chasm, and never happened, as I never dared ask for it.

Extreme inequality fractures communities, and after a while the cracks gape so wide the whole edifice comes tumbling down. In this process everybody has been losing for some time, but perhaps no one quite as much as the white working classes who really have nothing, not even the perceived moral elevation that comes with acknowledged trauma or recognized victimhood. The left is thoroughly ashamed of them. The right sees them only as a useful tool for its own personal ambitions. This inconvenient working-class revolution we are now witnessing has been accused of stupidity – I cursed it myself the day it happened – but the longer you look at it, you realize that in another sense it has the touch of genius, for it intuited the weaknesses of its enemies and effectively exploited them. The middle-class left so delights in being right! And so much of the disenfranchised working class has chosen to be flagrantly, shamelessly wrong.

We have a history of ridiculing the poor, in Britain, for 'shafting themselves', for 'voting against their interests'. But no less has the neoliberal middle and upper middle class shafted itself, living in its gilded London prisons. If you think that's an exaggeration, go up to Notting Hill and watch the private security vehicles, paid for by residents, slowly patrolling up and down the streets, in front of all those £20 million residences, nervous perhaps of the council house residents still clinging on, the other side of the Portobello Road. Or go up to the Savoy and have a gander at the vintage cocktail list on which the cheapest drink on offer goes for £100 (the priciest is something called the Sazerac – which claims to be the most expensive cocktail in the world – coming in at £5,000). Strange times.

Of course that cocktail list is only another stupid symbol, but it is of its time and place. There has been a kind of money madness in London for some time and for the rest of us looking on it's hard to find in such symbols any sign of a beautiful, harmonious, or even happy life (what kind of happy person needs to be seen ordering a £5,000 cocktail?), though at least when you are this rich you can comfortably fool yourself that you are happy, utilizing what the old north London Marxists used to call your 'false consciousness'. That crusty standby won't work any more for describing the economically and socially disenfranchised of this nation: they are struggling, deeply unhappy, and they know it.

I do believe that, putting aside the true ideological believers on the right, and the high-minded leftists who object to the EU as a tool of global capitalism, the majority of those who voted Leave did so out of anger and hurt and disappointment, helped along by years of calculated political and press manipulation of certain low feelings and base instincts. As painful as it is to write it, when Google records large numbers of Britons googling 'What is the EU?' in the hours after the vote, it becomes very difficult to deny that a significant proportion of our people were shamefully negligent in their democratic duty on 23 June 2016.

However people vote, we have to listen to them, but ignorance at the ballot box shouldn't be celebrated or disingenuously defended. And beyond ignorance, it is simply wrong to take a serious action without seriously considering its consequences for others, in this case, for entire sovereign nations to the north and west of you, never mind the rest of Europe. But I don't find the people who voted Leave to be in any way exceptional in having low motives.

While we loudly and rightly condemn the misguided racial attitudes that led to millions asking 'them' to leave 'us', to get out of our jobs and public housing and hospitals and schools and country, we might also take a look at the last thirty years and ask ourselves what kind of attitudes have allowed a different class of people to discreetly manoeuvre, behind the scenes, to ensure that 'them' and 'us' never actually meet anywhere but in symbol. Wealthy London, whether red or blue, has always been able to pick and choose the nature of its multicultural and cross-class relations, to lecture the rest of the country on its narrow-mindedness while simultaneously fencing off its own discreet advantages. We may walk past 'them' very often in the street and get into their cabs and eat their food in their ethnic restaurants, but the truth is that more often than not they are not in our schools, or in our social circles, and they very rarely enter our houses – unless they've come to work on our endlessly remodelled kitchens.

Elsewhere in Britain people really do live cheek-by-jowl with the recently migrated, and experience the undercutting of their wages by newcomers. They really do have to fight for resources under an austerity government that makes it all too easy to blame your unavailable hospital bed on the migrant family next door, or on an oblique bureaucracy across the Channel, which the nitwit demagogues on the TV keep telling you is the reason there's not enough money in the NHS. In this atmosphere of hypocrisy and deceit, should the working-class poor have shown themselves to be the 'better man' when all around them is corruption and venality? When everyone's building a fence, isn't it a true fool who lives out in the open?

Right now the news cycle is moving so fast that it feels the wheels might come off, and there is much talk of a second referendum, which would of course reinforce the fundamental suspicions of many of the disenfranchised that it is only we, the well-to-do Remainers with the right views, whose decisions truly count. No: here is our bed, and it appears that we must lie in it. But to say we have all played our part is not to obscure those who have played the central role of conductor at this shameful last night at the Proms. Cameron and Johnson have already fallen and/or been pushed on to their swords, and Gove has followed, but fatally ineffectual Jeremy Corbyn – despite dozens of knives in the back – refuses to budge. If it is indeed true that he was not just ineffective in the Remain campaign but engaged in 'deliberate sabotage' of it – as has been claimed by Phil Wilson, an MP and the parliamentary chair of Labour In For Britain – then Corbyn has profoundly betrayed the youth vote that so recently swept him into power.* He must go.

When we put a school in special measures in England some of the more optimistic middle-class mums – in which group I include myself – will murmur over morning coffee: 'Well, special measures is a good thing really, because now they'll have to do something about it.' Britain is now in special measures – the crisis that was always there has been revealed – and rather than pull another veil over the mess we might as well start trying to build from where we are. The first item on the agenda being replacing the 'head' – as any failing school knows – and then preparing what's left of the left for a fight. The rights and protections provided for the British people, however imperfectly, by Europe, must not now be replaced by this

---

* Jonathan Freedland, 'The Young Put Jeremy Corbyn In, but He Betrayed Them over Brexit', *Guardian*, 27 June 2016.

nonsensical Faragian vision of British sovereignty, in which a maimed Saint George, with two of his limbs lopped off, picks up his sword and hobbles off to battle the EU dragon to renegotiate, from a far weaker position, all the terms we spent these last decades putting in place.

As I began this essay Farage was spotted triumphant in a pair of Union Jack shoes, at a private garden party, with Rupert Murdoch and Alexander Lebedev, whose son owns the *Evening Standard* and the *Independent*, and Liam Fox – then running for Conservative leader – discussing public matters behind closed doors. By the time I was finishing it, Farage had resigned, saying, 'I want my life back.' In Britain, Nigels come and go, but Ruperts are for ever. My life and the lives of my fellow Britons are at all times at least partially governed by a permanent, unelected billionaire class, who own the newspapers and much of the TV, and through which absurd figures like Farage are easily puffed up, thus swinging elections and shaping policy. Another very useful lesson: the post-war British compact between government and people is not guaranteed, and it can be collectively unravelled, or trampled over by a few malign actors. Therefore the civilizing liberal arguments that established a universal health care system, state education and public housing out of the ruins of war now need a party willing to make those arguments afresh in a new age of global capitalism, though whether that party will still even bear the name 'Labour' remains to be seen.

The recently migrated have come to this country precisely because of this patrimony – for the housing, the education, and the health care – and some have come merely to exploit it, no doubt. But the great majority have come to participate: they enrol their kids in our state schools, they pay their British taxes, they try to make their way. It is certainly not a crime or a sin to seek a better life abroad, or to flee from countries riven by wars, many of which we ourselves had a hand in. Whether we still know, in Britain, what a better life is, what its necessary conditions are and how to achieve them, is what's now in doubt.

A few days after the vote I came to France, to teach my NYU students in their Paris summer programme, something that I suppose will not be so easy to do very soon. Straight off the train, I headed to dinner and sat down in a restaurant opposite one of my colleagues, the Bosnian-born writer Aleksandar Hemon, ordered a drink, and pronounced Brexit, melodramatically, 'a total disaster'. Novelists are prone to melodrama. Hemon sighed, smiled sadly, and said: 'No: just "a disaster". War is the total disaster.' Living through Yugoslavia's bloody sovereignty implosion gives a man a sense of proportion. A European war on that scale is something Britain has avoided intimately experiencing for more than half a century now, and in defence against which the EU was in part formed. Whether we go any further down the road marked 'disaster' is up to us.

On Optimism and Despair

First I would like to acknowledge the absurdity of my position. Accepting a literary prize is perhaps always a little absurd, but in times like these not only the recipient but also the giver feels some sheepishness about the enterprise.* But here we are. President Trump rises in the West, a united Europe drops below the horizon on the other side of the ocean – but here we still are, giving a literary prize, receiving one. So many more important things were rendered absurd by the events of 8 November that I hesitate to include my own writing in the list, and only mention it now because the most frequent question I'm asked about my work these days seems to me to have some bearing on the situation at hand.

The question is: 'In your earlier novels you sounded so optimistic, but now your books are tinged with despair. Is this fair to say?' It is a question usually posed in a tone of sly eagerness – you will recognize this tone if you've ever heard a child ask permission to do something she has in fact already done. Sometimes it is put far more explicitly, like so: 'You were such a champion of "multiculturalism". Can you admit now that it has failed?' When I hear these questions I am reminded that to have grown up in a homogeneous culture in

* This essay is the text of a talk I gave in Berlin on 10 November on receiving the 2016 *Welt* Literature Prize.

a corner of rural England, say, or France, or Poland, during the seventies, eighties or nineties, is to think of oneself as having been simply alive in the world, untroubled by history, whereas to have been raised in London during the same period, with, say, Pakistani Muslims in the house next door, Indian Hindus downstairs, and Latvian Jews across the street, is thought of, by others, as evidence of a specific historical social experiment, now discredited.

Of course, as a child I did not realize that the life I was living was considered in any way provisional or experimental by others: I thought it was just life. And when I wrote a novel about the London I grew up in, I further did not realize that by describing an environment in which people from different places lived relatively peaceably side by side, I was 'championing' a situation that was in fact on trial and whose conditions could suddenly be revoked. This is all to say I was very innocent, aged twenty-one. I thought the historical forces that had taken the black side of my family from the west coast of Africa, through slavery to the Caribbean, through colonialism and post-colonialism to Britain were as solid and real as the historical forces that, say, purged a small Italian village of its Jews and, by virtue of its physical distance from Milan, kept that village largely white and Catholic in the same years my little corner of England turned racially pluralistic and multi-faith. I thought my life was as contingent as the lives lived out in a rural Italian village and that in both cases historical time was moving in the only direction it can: forward. I did not understand that I was 'championing' multiculturalism simply by depicting it, or by describing it as anything other than incipient tragedy.

At the same time I don't think I ever was quite naive enough to believe, even at twenty-one, that racially homogeneous societies were necessarily happier or more peaceful than ours simply by virtue of their homogeneity. After all, even a kid half my age knew what the ancient Greeks did to each other, and the Romans, and the seventeenth-century British, and the nineteenth-century Americans. My best friend during my youth – now my husband – is himself from Northern Ireland, an area where people who look absolutely identical to each other, eat the same food, pray to the same God, read the same holy book, wear the same clothes and celebrate the same holidays have yet spent four hundred years at war over a relatively minor doctrinal difference they later allowed to morph into an all-encompassing argument over land, government and national identity. Racial homogeneity is no guarantor of peace, any more than racial heterogeneity is fated to fail.

I find these days that a wistful form of time travel has become a persistent political theme, both on the right and on the left. On 10 November *The New York Times* reported that nearly seven in ten Republicans prefer America as it was in the fifties, a nostalgia of course entirely unavailable to a person like me, for in that period I could not vote, marry my husband, have my children, work in the university I work in, or live in my neighbourhood. Time travel is a discretionary art: a pleasure trip for some and a horror story for others. Meanwhile some on the left have time-travel fancies of their own, imagining that the same rigid ideological principles once applied to the matters of workers' rights, welfare and trade can be applied unchanged to a globalized world of fluid capital.

But still the question of a failed project – as it applies to the tiny unreal world of my fiction – is not entirely wrong-headed. It's true enough that my novels were once sunnier places and now the clouds have rolled in. Part of this I chalk up simply to the experience of middle age: I wrote *White Teeth* as a child, and have grown up alongside it. The art of mid-life is surely always cloudier than the art of youth, as life itself gets cloudier. But it would be disingenuous to pretend it is only that. I am a citizen as well as an individual soul and one of the things citizenship teaches us, over the long stretch, is that there is no perfectibility in human affairs. This fact, still obscure to the twenty-one-year-old, is a little clearer to the woman of forty-one.

As the departing president well understood, in this world there is only incremental progress. Only the wilfully blind can ignore that the history of human existence is simultaneously the history of pain: of brutality, murder, mass extinction, every form of venality and cyclical horror. No land is free of it; no people are without their bloodstain; no tribe entirely innocent. But there is still this redeeming matter of incremental progress. It might look small to those with apocalyptic perspectives, but to she who not so long ago could not vote, or drink from the same water fountain as her fellow citizens, or marry the person she chose, or live in a certain neighbourhood, such incremental change feels enormous.

Meanwhile the dream of time travel – for new presidents, literary journalists and writers alike – is just that: a dream. And one that only makes sense if the rights and privileges you are accorded currently were accorded to you back then, too. If some white men are more sentimental about history than anyone else right now, it's no big surprise: their rights and privileges stretch a long way back. For a black woman the expanse of liveable history is so much shorter. What would I have been and what would I have done – or more to the point, *what would have been done to me* – in 1360, in 1760, in 1860, in 1960? I do not say this to claim some pedestal of perfect victimhood or historical innocence. I know very well how my West African ancestors sold and enslaved their tribal cousins and neighbours. I don't believe in any political or personal identity of pure innocence and absolute rectitude.

But neither do I believe in time travel. I believe in human limitation, not out of any sense of fatalism but out of a learned caution, gleaned from both recent and distant history. We will never be perfect: that is our limitation. But we can have, and have had, moments in which we can take genuine pride. I took pride in my neighbourhood, in my childhood, back in 1999. It was not perfect but it was filled with possibility. If the clouds have rolled in over my fiction it is not because what was perfect has been proved empty but because what was becoming possible – and is still experienced as possible by millions – is now denied as if it never did and never could exist.

I realize as I write this that I have strayed some way from the happiness that should rightly attend accepting a literary prize. I am very happy to accept this great honour – please don't mistake me. I am more than happy – I am amazed. When I started to write I never imagined that anyone outside of my neighbourhood would read these books, never mind outside of England, never mind 'on the continent', as my father liked to call it. I remember how stunned I was to embark on my very first European book tour, to Germany, with my father, who had last been here in 1945, as a young soldier in the reconstruction. It was a trip filled, for him, with nostalgia: he had loved a German girl, back then, and one of his great regrets, he admitted to me on that trip, was not marrying her and instead coming home, to England, and marrying first one woman and then another, my mother.

We made a funny pair on that tour, I'm sure: a young black girl and her elderly white father, clutching our guidebooks and seeking those spots in Berlin that my father had visited almost fifty years earlier. It is from him that I have inherited both my optimism and my despair, for he had been among the liberators at Belsen and therefore seen the worst this world has to offer, but had, from there, gone forward, with a sufficiently open heart and mind, striding into one failed marriage and then another, marrying both times across various lines of class, colour and temperament, and yet still found in life reasons to be cheerful, reasons even for joy.

He was, I realize now, one of the least ideological people I ever met: everything that happened to him he took as a particular case, unable or unwilling to generalize from it. He lost his livelihood but did not lose faith in his country. The education system failed him but he still revered it and placed all his hopes for his children in it. His relations with women were mostly disastrous but he did not hate women. In his mind he did not marry a black girl, he married 'Yvonne', and he did not have an experimental set of mixed-race children, he had me and my brother Ben and my brother Luke.

How rare such people are! I am not so naive even now as to believe we have enough of them at any one time in history to form a decent and tolerant society. But neither will I ever deny their existence or the possibility of lives like his. He was a member of the white working class, a man often afflicted by despair who still managed to retain a core optimism. Perhaps in a different time under different cultural influences living in a different society he would have become one of the rabid old angry white men of whom the present left is so afeared. As it was, born in 1925 and dying in 2006, he saw his children benefit from the civilized post-war protections of free education and free health care, and felt he had many reasons to be grateful.

This is the world I knew. Things have changed, but history is not erased by change, and the examples of the past still hold out new possibilities for all of us, opportunities to remake, for a new generation, the conditions from which we ourselves have benefited.

Neither my readers nor I are in the relatively sunlit uplands depicted in *White Teeth* any more. But the lesson I take from this is not that the lives in that novel were illusory but rather that progress is never permanent, will always be threatened, must be redoubled, restated and *reimagined* if it is to survive. I don't claim that it's easy. I do not have the answers. I am by nature not a political person and these are the darkest political times I have ever known. My business, such as it is, concerns the intimate lives of people. The people who ask me about the 'failure of multiculturalism' mean to suggest that not only has a political ideology failed but that human beings themselves have changed and are now fundamentally incapable of living peacefully together despite their many differences.

In this argument it is the writer who is meant to be the naive child, but I maintain that people who believe in fundamental and irreversible changes in human nature are themselves ahistorical and naive. If novelists know anything it's that individual citizens are internally plural: they have within them the full range of behavioural possibilities. They are like complex musical scores from which certain melodies can be teased out and others ignored or suppressed, depending, at least in part, on who is doing the conducting. At this moment, all over the world – and most recently in America – the conductors standing in front of this human orchestra have only the meanest and most banal melodies in mind. Here in Germany you will remember these martial songs; they are not a very distant memory. But there is no place on earth where they have not been played at one time or another. Those of us who remember, too, a finer music must try now to play it, and encourage others, if we can, to sing along.

41

IN THE AUDIENCE

Generation Why?

How long is a generation these days? I must be in Mark Zuckerberg's generation – there are only nine years between us – but somehow it doesn't feel that way. This despite the fact that I can say (like everyone else on Harvard's campus in the fall of 2003) that 'I was there' at Facebook's inception, and remember Facemash and the fuss it caused; also that tiny, exquisite movie star trailed by fanboys through the snow wherever she went, and the awful snow itself, turning your toes grey, destroying your spirit, bringing a bloodless end to a squirrel on my block: frozen, inanimate, perfect – like the Blaschka glass flowers. Doubtless, years from now I will misremember my closeness to Zuckerberg, in the same spirit that everyone in sixties Liverpool met John Lennon.

At the time, though, I felt distant from Zuckerberg and all the kids at Harvard. I still feel distant from them now, ever more so, as I increasingly opt out (by choice, by default) of the things they have embraced. We have different ideas about things. Specifically we have different ideas about what a person is, or should be. I often worry that my idea of personhood is nostalgic, irrational, inaccurate. Perhaps Generation Facebook have built their virtual mansions in good faith, in order to house the People 2.0 they genuinely are, and if I feel uncomfortable within them it is because I am stuck at Person 1.0. Then again, the more time I spend with the tail end of Generation

Facebook (in the shape of my students) the more convinced I become that some of the software currently shaping their generation is unworthy of them. They are more interesting than it is. They deserve better.

In *The Social Network* Generation Facebook gets a movie almost worthy of them, and this fact, being so unexpected, makes the film feel more delightful than it probably, objectively, is. From the opening scene it's clear that this is a movie about 2.0 people made by 1.0 people (Aaron Sorkin and David Fincher, forty-nine and forty-eight respectively). It's a *talkie*, for goodness' sake, with as many words per minute as *His Girl Friday*. A boy, Mark, and his girl, Erica, sit at a little table in a Harvard bar, zinging each other, in that relentless Sorkin style made famous by *The West Wing* (though at no point does either party say, 'Walk with me' – for this we should be grateful).

But something is not right with this young man: his eye contact is patchy; he doesn't seem to understand common turns of phrase or ambiguities of language; he is literal to the point of offence, pedantic to the point of aggression. ('Final clubs,' says Mark, correcting Erica, as they discuss those exclusive Harvard entities, '*Not* Finals clubs.') He doesn't understand what's happening as she tries to break up with him. ('Wait, wait, this is real?') Nor does he understand *why*. He doesn't get that what he may consider a statement of fact might yet have, for this other person, some personal, painful import:

Erica: I have to go study.
Mark: You don't have to study.
Erica: *How do you know I don't have to study?!*
Mark: *Because you go to BU!*

Simply put, he is a computer nerd, a social 'autistic': a type as recognizable to Fincher's audience as the cynical newshound was to Howard Hawks's. To create this Zuckerberg, Sorkin barely need brush his pen against the page. We came to the cinema expecting to meet this guy and it's a pleasure to watch Sorkin colour in what we had already confidently sketched in our minds. For sometimes the culture surmises an individual personality, collectively. Or thinks it does. Don't we all know why nerds do what they do? To get money, which leads to popularity, which leads to girls. Sorkin, confident of his foundation myth, spins an exhilarating tale of double rejection – spurned by Erica and the Porcellian, the Finaliest of the Final Clubs, Zuckerberg begins his spite-fuelled rise to the top. Cue a lot of betrayal. A lot of scenes of lawyers' offices and miserable, character-damning depositions. ('Your best friend is suing you!') Sorkin has swapped the military types of *A Few Good Men* for a different kind of all-male community in a different uniform: GAP hoodies, North Face sweats.

At my screening, blocks from NYU, the audience thrilled with intimate identification. But if the hipsters and nerds are hoping for Fincher's usual pyrotechnics they will be disappointed: in a lawyer's office there's not a lot for Fincher to *do*. He has to content himself with excellent and rapid cutting between Harvard and the later court cases, and after that, the discreet pleasures of another, less remarked upon Fincher skill: great casting. It'll be a long time before a cinema geek comes along to push Jesse Eisenberg, the actor who plays Zuckerberg, off the top of our nerd typologies. The passive-aggressive, flat-line voice. The shifty boredom when anyone, other than himself, is speaking. The barely suppressed smirk. Eisenberg even chooses the correct nerd walk: not the sideways corridor shuffle (the *Don't Hit Me!*), but the puffed-chest vertical march (the *I'm not 5'8", I'm 5'9"!*).

With rucksack, naturally. An extended four-minute shot has him doing exactly this all the way through the Harvard campus, before he lands finally where he belongs, the only place he's truly comfortable, in front of his laptop, with his blog:

> Erica Albright's a bitch. You think that's because her family changed their name from Albrecht or do you think it's because all BU girls are bitches?

Oh, yeah. We know this guy. Overprogrammed, furious, lonely. Around him Fincher arranges a convincing bunch of 1.0 humans, by turns betrayed and humiliated by him, and as the movie progresses they line up to sue him. If it's a three-act movie it's because Zuckerberg screws over more people than a two-act movie can comfortably hold: the Winklevoss twins and Divya Narendra (from whom Zuckerberg allegedly stole the Facebook concept), and then his best friend, Eduardo Saverin (the CFO he edged out of the company), and finally Sean Parker, the boy-king of Napster, the music-sharing program, although he, to be fair, pretty much screws himself. It's in Eduardo – in the actor Andrew Garfield's animate, beautiful face – that all these betrayals seem to converge, and become personal, painful. The arbitration scenes – which should be dull, being so terribly static – get their power from the eerie opposition between Eisenberg's unmoving countenance (his eyebrows hardly ever move; the real Zuckerberg's eyebrows *never* move) and Garfield's imploring disbelief, almost the way Spencer Tracy got all worked up opposite Fredric March's rigidity in another courtroom epic, *Inherit the Wind*.

Still, Fincher allows himself one sequence of (literal) showboating. Halfway through the film, he inserts a ravishing but quite unnecessary scene of the pretty Winklevoss twins (for a story of nerds, all the men are surprisingly comely) at the Henley Regatta. These two blond titans row like champs. (One actor, Armie Hammer, has been digitally doubled. I'm so utterly 1.0 that I spent an hour of the movie trying to detect any difference between the twins.) Their arms move suspiciously fast, faster than real human arms, their muscles seem outlined by a fine pen, the water splashes up in individual droplets as if painted by Caravaggio, and the music! Trent Reznor, of Nine Inch Nails, commits exquisite brutality upon Edvard Grieg's already pretty brutal 'In the Hall of the Mountain King'. All synths and white noise. It's music video stuff – the art form in which my not-quite generation truly excels – and it demonstrates the knack for hyperreality that made Fincher's *Fight Club* so compelling while rendering the real world, for so many of his fans, always something of a disappointment. Anyway, the twins lose the regatta, too, by a nose, which allows Fincher to justify the scene by thematic reiteration: sometimes very close is simply not close enough. Or as Mark pleasantly puts it across a conference table: 'If you guys were the inventors of Facebook you'd have invented Facebook.'

All that's left for Zuckerberg is to meet the devil at the crossroads: naturally he's an Internet music entrepreneur. It's a Generation Facebook instinct to expect (hope?) that a pop star will fall on his face in the cinema, but Justin Timberlake, as Sean Parker, neatly steps over that expectation: whether or not you think he's a shmuck, he sure plays a great shmuck. Manicured eyebrows, sweaty forehead, and that coked-up, wafer-thin self-confidence, always threatening to collapse into paranoia. Timberlake shimmies into view in the third act to offer the audience, and Zuckerberg, the very same thing, essentially, that he's been offering us for the past decade in his videos: a vision of the good life.

This vision is also wafer-thin, and Fincher satirizes it mercilessly.

Again, we know its basic outline: a velvet rope, a cocktail waitress who treats you like a king, the best of everything on tap, a special booth of your own, fussy tiny expensive food ('Could you bring out some things? The lacquered pork with that ginger confit? I don't know, tuna tartare, some lobster claws, the foie gras and the shrimp dumplings, that'll get us started'), appletinis, a Victoria's Secret model date, wild house parties, fancy cars, slick suits, cocaine and a 'sky's the limit' objective: 'A million dollars isn't cool. You know what's cool? . . . A *billion* dollars.' Over cocktails in a glamorous nightclub, Parker dazzles Zuckerberg with tales of the life that awaits him on the other side of a billion. Fincher keeps the thumping Euro house music turned up to exactly the level it would be in real life: the actors have to practically scream to be heard above it. Like many a nerd before him, Zuckerberg is too hyped on the idea that he's in heaven to notice he's in hell.

Generation Facebook's obsession with this type of 'celebrity lifestyle' is more than familiar. It's pitiful, it pains us, and we recognize it. But would Zuckerberg recognize it, the real Zuckerberg? Are these really *his* motivations, *his* obsessions? No – and the movie knows it. Several times the script tries to square the real Zuckerberg's apparent indifference to money with the plot arc of *The Social Network* – and never quite succeeds. In a scene in which Mark argues with a lawyer, Sorkin attempts a sleight of hand, swapping an interest in money for an interest in power:

> Ma'am, I know you've done your homework and so you know that money isn't a big part of my life, but at the moment I could buy Harvard University, take the Phoenix Club and turn it into my ping-pong room.

But that doesn't explain why the teenage Zuckerberg gave away his free app for an MP3 player (similar to the very popular Pandora, as it recognized your taste in music), rather than selling it to Microsoft. What power was he hoping to accrue to himself in high school, at seventeen? Girls, was it? Except the girl motivation is patently phoney – with a brief interruption Zuckerberg has been dating the same Chinese-American, now a medical student, since 2003, a fact the movie omits entirely. At the end of the film, when all the suing has come to an end ('Pay them. In the scheme of things it's a parking ticket'), we're offered a Zuckerberg slumped before his laptop, still obsessed with the long-lost Erica, sending a 'Friend request' to her on Facebook, and then refreshing the page, over and over, in expectation of her reply . . . Fincher's contemporary window-dressing is so convincing that it wasn't until this very last scene that I realized the obvious progenitor of this wildly enjoyable, wildly inaccurate biopic. Hollywood still believes that behind every mogul there's an *idée fixe*: Rosebud meet Erica.

If it's not for money and it's not for girls – what is it for? With Zuckerberg we have a real American mystery. Maybe it's not mysterious and he's just playing the long game, holding out: not a billion dollars but 100 billion dollars. Or is it possible *he just loves programming*? No doubt the film-makers considered this option, but you can see their dilemma: how to convey the pleasure of programming – if such a pleasure exists – in a way that is both cinematic and comprehensible? Movies are notoriously bad at showing the pleasures and rigours of art-making, even when the medium is familiar.

Programming is a whole new kind of problem. Fincher makes a brave stab at showing the intensity of programming in action ('He's wired in,' people say to other people to stop them disturbing a third person who sits before a laptop wearing noise-reducing earphones) and there's a 'vodka-shots-and-programming' party in Zuckerberg's dorm room that gives us some clue of the pleasures. But even if we spent half the film looking at those busy screens (and we do get glimpses), most of us would be none the wiser. Watching this movie, even though you know Sorkin wants your disapproval, you can't help feel a little swell of pride in this 2.0 generation. They've spent a decade being berated for not making the right sorts of paintings or novels or music or politics. Turns out the brightest 2.0 kids have been doing something else extraordinary. They've been making a world.

World-makers, social network-makers, ask one question first: How can I do it? Zuckerberg solved that one in about three weeks. The other question, the ethical question, he came to later: Why? Why Facebook? Why this format? Why do it like that? Why not do it another way? The striking thing about the real Zuckerberg, in video and in print, is the relative banality of his ideas concerning the 'Why?' of Facebook. He uses the word 'connect' as believers use the word 'Jesus', as if it were sacred in and of itself: 'So the idea is really that, um, the site helps everyone connect with people and share information with the people they want to stay connected with . . .' Connection is the goal. The quality of that connection, the quality of the information that passes through it, the quality of the relationship that connection permits – none of this is important. That a lot of social networking software explicitly encourages people to make weak, superficial connections with each other (as Malcolm Gladwell has recently argued)* and that this might not be an entirely positive thing, seems never to have occurred to him.

He is, to say the least, dispassionate about the philosophical

---

* See 'Small Change: Why the Revolution Will Not Be Tweeted', *New Yorker*, 4 October 2010.

questions concerning privacy – and sociality itself – raised by his ingenious program. Watching him interviewed I found myself waiting for the verbal wit, the controlled and articulate sarcasm of that famous Zuckerberg kid – then remembered that was only Sorkin. The real Zuckerberg is much more like his website, on each page of which, once upon a time (2004), he emblazoned the legend: *A Mark Zuckerberg Production.* Controlled but dull, bright and clean but uniformly plain, non-ideological, affectless.

In Zuckerberg's *New Yorker* profile it is revealed that his own Facebook page lists, among his interests, minimalism, revolutions, and 'eliminating desire'.* We also learn of his affection for the culture and writings of ancient Greece. Perhaps this is the disjunct between real Zuckerberg and fake Zuckerberg: the movie places him in the Roman world of betrayal and excess, but the real Zuckerberg may belong in the Greek, perhaps with the Stoics ('eliminating desire'?). There's a clue in the two Zuckerbergs' relative physiognomies: real Zuckerberg (especially in profile) is Greek sculpture, noble, featureless, a little like the Doryphoros (only facially, mind – his torso is definitely not seven times his head). Fake Mark looks Roman, with all the precise facial detail filled in. Zuckerberg, with his steady relationship and his rented house and his refusal to get angry on television even when people are being very rude to him (he sweats instead), has something of the teenage Stoic about him. And of course if you've eliminated desire you've got nothing to hide, right?

It's *that* kind of kid we're dealing with, the kind who would never screw a groupie in a bar toilet – as happens in the movie – or leave his

* See Jose Antonio Vargas, 'The Face of Facebook: Mark Zuckerberg Opens Up', *New Yorker*, 20 September 2010.

doctor girlfriend for a Victoria's Secret model. It's this type of kid who would think that giving people *less* privacy was a good idea. What's striking about Zuckerberg's vision of an open Internet is the very blandness it requires to function, as Facebook members discovered when the site changed their privacy settings, allowing more things to become more public, with the (unintended?) consequence that your Aunt Dora could suddenly find out you joined the group Queer Nation last Tuesday. Gay kids became un-gay, partiers took down their party photos, political firebrands put out their fires. In real life we can be all these people on our own terms, in our own way, with whom we choose. For a revealing moment Facebook forgot that. Or else got bored of waiting for us to change in the ways it's betting we will. On the question of privacy, Zuckerberg informed the world: 'That social norm is just something that has evolved over time.' On this occasion, the world protested, loudly, and so Facebook has responded with a site revamp that will allow people to divide their friends into 'cliques', some who see more of our profile and some who see less.

How this innovation will work alongside 'Facebook Connect' remains to be seen. Facebook Connect is the 'next iteration of Facebook Platform', in which users are 'allowed' to ' "connect" their Facebook identity, friends and privacy to any site'. In this new, open Internet, we will take our real identities with us as we travel through the Internet. This concept seems to have some immediate stoical advantages: no more faceless bile, no more inflammatory trolling: if your name and social network track you around the virtual world beyond Facebook, you'll have to restrain yourself and so will everyone else. On the other hand, you'll also take your likes and dislikes with you, your tastes, your preferences, all connected to your name, through which people will try to sell you things.

Maybe it will be like an intensified version of the Internet I already live in, where ads for dental services stalk me from pillar to post and I am continually urged to buy my own books. Or maybe the whole Internet will simply become like Facebook: falsely jolly, fake-friendly, self-promoting, slickly disingenuous. For all these reasons I quit Facebook about two months after I'd joined it. As with all seriously addictive things, giving up proved to be immeasurably harder than starting. I kept changing my mind: Facebook remains the greatest distraction from work I've ever had, and I loved it for that. I think a lot of people love it for that. Some work-avoidance techniques are onerous in themselves and don't make time move especially quickly: smoking, eating, calling people up on the phone. With Facebook, hours, afternoons, entire days went by without my noticing.

When I finally decided to put a stop to it, once and for all, I was left with the question bothering everybody: Are you ever truly removed, once and for all? In an interview on the *Today Show*, Matt Lauer asked Zuckerberg the same question, but because Matt Lauer doesn't listen to people when they talk, he accepted the following answer and moved on to the next question: 'Yeah, so what'll happen is that none of that information will be shared with anyone going forward.'

You want to be optimistic about your own generation. You want to keep pace with them and not to fear what you don't understand. To put it another way, if you feel discomfort at the world they're making, you want to have a good reason for it. Master programmer and virtual-reality pioneer Jaron Lanier (b. 1960) is not of my generation, but he knows and understands us well, and has written a short and frightening book, *You Are Not a Gadget*, which chimes with my own discomfort, while coming from a position of real knowledge and insight, both practical and philosophical. Lanier is interested in the ways in which people 'reduce themselves' in order to make a computer's description of them appear more accurate. 'Information systems,' he writes, 'need to have information in order to run, but information *underrepresents reality*' (my italics). In Lanier's view, there is no perfect computer analogue for what we call a 'person'. In life, we all profess to know this, but when we get online it becomes easy to forget. In Facebook, as it is with other online social networks, life is turned into a database, and this is a degradation, Lanier argues, which is 'based on [a] philosophical mistake . . . the belief that computers can presently represent human thought or human relationships. These are things computers cannot currently do.' We know the consequences of this instinctively; we feel them. We know that having two thousand Facebook friends is not what it looks like. We know that we are using the software to behave in a certain, superficial way toward others. We know what we are doing 'in' the software. But do we know, are we alert to, what the software is doing to us? Is it possible that what is communicated between people online 'eventually becomes their truth'? What Lanier, a software expert, reveals to me, a software idiot, is what must be obvious (to software experts): software is not neutral. Different software embeds different philosophies, and these philosophies, as they become ubiquitous, become invisible.

Lanier asks us to consider, for example, the humble file, or rather, to consider a world without 'files'. (The first iteration of the Macintosh, which never shipped, didn't have files.) I confess this thought experiment stumped me about as much as if I'd been asked to consider persisting in a world without 'time'. And then consider further that these designs, so often taken up in a slapdash, last-minute fashion, become 'locked in', and, because they are software, used by millions, too often become impossible to adapt, or change.

MIDI, an inflexible, early-eighties digital music protocol for connecting different musical components, such as a keyboard and a computer, takes no account of, say, the fluid line of a soprano's coloratura; it is still the basis of most of the tinny music we hear every day – in our phones, in the charts, in elevators – simply because it became, in software terms, too big to fail, too big to change.

Lanier wants us to be attentive to the software into which we are 'locked in'. Is it really fulfilling our needs? Or are we reducing the needs we feel in order to convince ourselves that the software isn't limited? As Lanier argues: 'Different media designs stimulate different potentials in human nature. We shouldn't seek to make the pack mentality as efficient as possible. We should instead seek to inspire the phenomenon of individual intelligence.' But the pack mentality is precisely what Open Graph, a Facebook innovation of 2008, is designed to encourage. Open Graph allows you to see everything your friends are reading, watching, eating, so that you might read and watch and eat as they do. In his *New Yorker* profile, Zuckerberg made his personal 'philosophy' clear: 'Most of the information that we care about is things that are in our heads, right? And that's not out there to be indexed, right? . . . It's, like, hardwired into us in a deeper way: you really want to know what's going on with the people around you.'

Is that really the best we can do online? In the film, Sean Parker, during one of his coke-fuelled 'Sean-athon monologues', delivers what is intended as a generation-defining line: 'We lived on farms, then we lived in cities and now we're gonna live on the Internet.' To this idea Lanier, one of the Internet's original visionaries, can have no profound objection. But his sceptical interrogation of the 'Nerd reductionism' of Web 2.0 prompts us to ask a question: What kind of life?* Surely not this one, where 500 million connected people all decide to watch the reality-TV show *Bride Wars* because their friends are? 'You have to be somebody,' Lanier writes, 'before you can share yourself.' But to Zuckerberg sharing your choices with everybody (and doing what they do) *is* being somebody.

Personally I don't think Final Clubs were ever the point; I don't think exclusivity was ever the point; nor even money. *E pluribus unum* – that's the point. Here's my guess: he wants to be like everybody else. He wants to be liked. Those 1.0 people who couldn't understand Zuckerberg's apparently ham-fisted PR move of giving the school system of Newark $100 million on the very day the movie came out – they just don't get it. For our self-conscious generation (and in this, I and Zuckerberg, and everyone raised on TV in the eighties and nineties, share a single soul), *not being liked* is as bad as it gets. Intolerable to be thought of badly for a minute, even for a moment. He didn't need to just get out 'in front' of the story. He had to get right on top of it and try to stop it breathing. Two weeks later, he went to a screening. Why? Because everybody liked the movie.

When a human being becomes a set of data on a website like Facebook, he or she is reduced. Everything shrinks. Individual character. Friendships. Language. Sensibility. In a way it's a transcendent experience: we lose our bodies, our messy feelings, our desires, our fears. It reminds me that those of us who turn in disgust

* Lanier: 'Individual web pages as they first appeared in the early nineties had the flavor of personhood. MySpace preserved some of that flavor, though a process of regularized formatting had begun. Facebook went further, organizing people into multiple-choice identities, while Wikipedia seeks to erase point of view entirely.'

from what we consider an overinflated liberal-bourgeois sense of self should be careful what we wish for: our denuded networked selves don't look more free, they just look more owned.

With Facebook, Zuckerberg seems to be trying to create something like a Noosphere, an Internet with one mind, a uniform environment in which it genuinely doesn't matter who you are, as long as you make 'choices' (which means, finally, purchases). If the aim is to be liked by more and more people, whatever is unusual about a person gets flattened out. One nation under a format. To ourselves, we are special people, documented in wonderful photos, and it also happens that we sometimes buy things. This latter fact is an incidental matter, to us. However, the advertising money that will rain down on Facebook – if and when Zuckerberg succeeds in encouraging 500 million people to take their Facebook identities on to the Internet at large – this money thinks of us the other way around. To the advertisers, we are our capacity to buy, attached to a few personal, irrelevant photos.

Is it possible that we have begun to think of ourselves that way? It seemed significant to me that on the way to the cinema, while doing a small mental calculation (how old I was when at Harvard; how old I am now), I had a Person 1.0 panic attack. Soon I will be forty, then fifty, then soon after dead; I broke out in a Zuckerberg sweat, my heart went crazy, I had to stop and lean against a litter bin. Can you have that feeling, on Facebook? I've noticed – and been ashamed of noticing – that when a teenager is murdered, at least in Britain, her Facebook wall will often fill with messages that seem not quite to comprehend the gravity of what has occurred. You know the type of thing: *Sorry babes! Missin' you!!! Hopin' u iz with the Angles. I remember the jokes we used to have LOL! PEACE xxxxx*

When I read something like that, I have a little argument with myself: 'It's only poor education. They feel the same way as anyone would, they just don't have the language to express it.' But another part of me has a darker, more frightening thought. Do they genuinely believe, because the girl's wall is still up, that she is still, in some sense, alive? What's the difference, after all, if all your contact was virtual?*

Software may reduce humans, but there are degrees. Fiction reduces humans, too, but bad fiction does it more than good fiction, and we have the option to read good fiction. Jaron Lanier's point is that Web 2.0 'lock-in' happens soon; is happening; has to some degree already happened. And what has been 'locked in'? It feels important to remind ourselves, at this point, that Facebook, our new beloved interface with reality, was designed by a Harvard sophomore with a Harvard sophomore's preoccupations. What is your relationship status? (Choose one. There can be only one answer. People need to know.) Do you have a 'life'? (Prove it. Post pictures.) Do you like the right sort of things? (Make a list. Things to like will include: films, music, books and television, but not architecture, ideas or plants.)

But here I fear I am becoming nostalgic. I am dreaming of a Web that caters to a kind of person who no longer exists. A private person, a person who is a mystery, to the world and – which is more

---

* Perhaps the reason why there has not been more resistance to social networking among older people is because 1.0 people do not use Web 2.0 software in the way 2.0 people do. An analogous situation can be found in the way the two generations use cell phones. For me, text messaging is simply a new medium for an old form of communication: I write to my friends in heavily punctuated, fully expressive, standard English sentences – and they write back to me in the same way. Text-speak is unknown between us. Our relationship with the English language pre-dates our relationships with our phones.

important – to herself. Person as mystery: this idea of personhood is certainly changing, perhaps has already changed. Because I find I agree with Zuckerberg: selves evolve.

Of course, Zuckerberg insists selves simply do this by themselves and the technology he and others have created has no influence upon the process. That is for techies and philosophers to debate (ideally techie-philosophers, like Jaron Lanier). Whichever direction the change is coming from, though, it's absolutely clear to me that the students I teach now are not like the student I once was or even the students I taught seven short years ago at Harvard. Right now I am teaching my students a book called *The Bathroom* by the Belgian experimentalist Jean-Philippe Toussaint – at least I used to *think* he was an experimentalist. It's a book about a man who decides to pass most of his time in his bathroom, yet to my students this novel feels perfectly realistic; an accurate portrait of their own denuded selfhood, or, to put it neutrally, a close analogue of the undeniable boredom of urban twenty-first-century existence.

In the most famous scene, the unnamed protagonist, in one of the few moments of 'action', throws a dart into his girlfriend's forehead. Later, in the hospital, they reunite with a kiss and no explanation. 'It's just between them,' said one student, and looked happy. To a reader of my generation, Toussaint's characters seemed, at first glance, to have no interiority – in fact theirs is not an absence but a refusal, and an ethical one. *What's inside of me is none of your business.* To my students, *The Bathroom* is a true romance.

Toussaint was writing in 1985, in France. In France philosophy seems to come before technology; here in the Anglo-American world we race ahead with technology and hope the ideas will look after themselves. Finally, it's the *idea* of Facebook that disappoints. If it were a genuinely interesting interface, built for these genuinely different 2.0 kids to live in, well, that would be something. It's not that. It's the Wild West of the Internet tamed to fit the suburban fantasies of a suburban soul. Lanier:

> These designs came together very recently, and there's a haphazard, accidental quality to them. Resist the easy grooves they guide you into. If you love a medium made of software, there's a danger that you will become entrapped in someone else's recent careless thoughts. Struggle against that!

Shouldn't we struggle against Facebook? Everything in it is reduced to the size of its founder. Blue, because it turns out Zuckerberg is red–green colour-blind. 'Blue is the richest color for me – I can see all of blue.' Poking, because that's what shy boys do to girls they are scared to talk to. Preoccupied with personal trivia, because Mark Zuckerberg thinks the exchange of personal trivia is what 'friendship' *is*. A Mark Zuckerberg Production indeed! We were going to live online. It was going to be extraordinary. Yet what kind of living is this? Step back from your Facebook Wall for a moment: Doesn't it, suddenly, look a little ridiculous? *Your* life in *this* format?

The last defence of every Facebook addict is: *But it helps me keep in contact with people who are far away!* Well, email and Skype do that, too, and they have the added advantage of not forcing you to interface with the mind of Mark Zuckerberg – but, well, you know. We all know. If we *really* wanted to write to these faraway people, or see them, we would. What we actually want to do is the bare minimum, just like any nineteen-year-old college boy who'd rather be doing something else, or nothing.

At my screening, when a character in the film mentioned the early blog platform LiveJournal (still popular in Russia), the audience laughed. I can't imagine life without files but I can just about imagine a time when Facebook will seem as comically obsolete as LiveJournal. In this sense, *The Social Network* is not a cruel portrait of any particular real-world person called 'Mark Zuckerberg'. It's a cruel portrait of us: 500 million sentient people entrapped in the recent careless thoughts of a Harvard sophomore.

The House That Hova Built

It's difficult to know what to ask a rapper. It's not unlike the difficulty (I imagine) of being a rapper. Whatever you say must be considered from at least three angles, and it's an awkward triangulation. In one corner you have your hard-core hip-hop heads; the type for whom the true Jay-Z will forever be that gifted twenty-five-year-old with rapid-fire flow, trading verses with the visionary teenager Big L – 'I'm so ahead of my time, my parents haven't met yet!' – on a 'rare' (easily dug up on YouTube) seven-minute freestyle from 1995. Meanwhile, over here stands the pop-rap fan. She loves the Jiggaman with his passion for the Empire State Building and bold claims to 'Run This Town'. Finally, in the crowded third corner, stand the many people who feel rap is not music at all but rather a form of social problem. They have only one question to ask a rapper, and it concerns his choice of vocabulary. (Years pass. The question never changes.) How to speak to these audiences simultaneously? Anyway: I'm at a little table in a homey Italian restaurant on Mulberry Street waiting for Mr Shawn Carter, who has perfected the art of triangulation. It's where he likes to eat his chicken parms.

He's not late. He's dressed like a kid, in cap and jeans, and if he said he was thirty you wouldn't doubt him. (He's forty-two.) He's overwhelmingly familiar, which is of course a function of his fame – rap superstar, husband of Beyoncé, minority owner of the

Nets, whose new home, the Barclays Center in Brooklyn, will open this month – but also of the fact he's been speaking into our ears for so long. No one stares. The self-proclaimed 'greatest rapper alive' is treated like a piece of the furniture. Ah, but there's always one: a preppy white guy discreetly operating his iPhone's reverse-camera function. It's an old hustle; it makes Jay chuckle: 'They think they're the first one who's ever come up with that concept.'

He likes to order for people. Apparently I look like the fish-sandwich type. Asked if he thinks this is a good time for hip-hop, he enthuses about how inclusive hip-hop is: 'It provided a gateway to conversations that normally would not be had.' And now that rap's reached this unprecedented level of cultural acceptance, maybe we're finally free to celebrate the form without needing to continually defend it. 'Say that I'm foolish I only talk about jewels/ Do you fools listen to music or do you just skim through it?' He's not so sure: 'It's funny how you can say things like that in plain English and then people still do it.' He is mildly disappointed that after publishing *Decoded*, his 2010 memoir, people still ask the same old questions. The flippancy annoys him, the ease with which some still dismiss rap as 'something that's just this bad language, or guys who degrade women, and they don't realize the poetry and the art'. This is perhaps one downside to having the 'flow of the century'.

With Tupac, you can hear the effort, the artistry. And Biggie's words first had to struggle free of the sheer bulk of the man himself. When Jay raps, it pours right into your ear like water from a tap.

The fish sandwich arrives. Conversation turns to the schoolboy who was shot to death, Trayvon Martin – 'It's really heartbreaking, that that still can happen in this day and age' – and, soon after, to Obama: 'I've said the election of Obama has made the hustler less relevant.' When he first made this point, 'People took it in a way that

I was almost dismissing what I am. And I was like: no, it's a good thing!' He didn't have Obama growing up, only the local hustler. 'No one came to our neighbourhoods, with stand-up jobs, and showed us there's a different way. Maybe had I seen different role models, maybe I'd've turned on to that.' Difficult to keep these two Americas in your mind. Imagine living it – within one lifetime!

In *Decoded*, Jay-Z writes that 'rap is built to handle contradictions', and Hova, as he is nicknamed, is as contradictory as they come. Partly because he's a generalist. Biggie had better boasts, Tupac dropped more knowledge, Eminem is – as 'Renegade' demonstrated – more formally dexterous. But Hova's the all-rounder. His albums are showrooms of hip-hop, displaying the various possibilities of the form. The persona is cool, calm, almost frustratingly self-controlled: 'Yeah, 50 Cent told me that one time. He said: "You got me looking like Barksdale" ' – the hot-blooded drug kingpin from HBO's *The Wire* – ' "and you get to be Stringer Bell!" ' – Barksdale's level-headed partner. The rapper Memphis Bleek, who has known Jay-Z since Bleek himself was fourteen, confirms this impression: 'He had a sense of calm way before music. This was Jay's plan from day one: to take over. I guess that's why he smiles and is so calm, 'cause he did exactly what he planned in the nineties.' And now, by virtue of being forty-two and not dead, he can claim his own unique selling proposition: he's an artist as old as his art form. The two have grown up together.

Jay-Z, like rap itself, started out pyrotechnical. Extremely fast, stacked, dense. But time passed and his flow got slower, opened up. Why? 'I didn't have enough life experience, so what I was doing was more technical. I was trying to impress technically. To do things that other people cannot do. Like, you can't do this' – insert beat-box and simultaneous freestyle here – 'you just can't do that.' Nope. Can't even think of a notation to demonstrate what he just did. Jay-Z in technician mode is human voice as pure syncopation. On a track like 'I Can't Get with That', from 1994, the manifest content of the music is never really the words themselves; it's the rhythm they create. And if you don't care about beats, he says, 'You've missed the whole point.'

Plenty did, hearing only a young black man, boasting. 'I got watches I ain't seen in months / Apartment at the Trump I only slept in once.'

But asking why rappers always talk about their stuff is like asking why Milton is forever listing the attributes of heavenly armies. Because boasting is a formal condition of the epic form. And those taught that they deserve nothing rightly enjoy it when they succeed in terms the culture understands. Then something changed: 'As I started getting life experiences, I realized my power was in conveying emotions that people felt.' He compared himself to a comedian whose jokes trigger this reaction: 'Yo, that's so true.' He started storytelling – people were mesmerized. 'Friend or Foe' (1996), which concerns a confrontation between two hustlers, is rap in its masterful, full-blown, narrative form. Not just a monologue, but a story, complete with dialogue, scene setting, characterization. Within its comic flow and light touch – free from the relentless sincerity of Tupac – you can hear the seeds of 50 Cent, Lil Wayne, Eminem, so many others. 'That was the first one where it was so obvious,' Jay noted. He said the song represented an important turning point, the moment when he 'realized I was doing it'.

At times he restricts himself formally, like the Oulipo, that experimental French literary group of the sixties. In the song '22 Twos', from 1996, we get twenty-two delicious plays on the words 'too' and 'two'.

Ten years later, the sequel, '44 Fours', has the same conceit, stepped up a gear. 'Like, you know, close the walls in a bit smaller.' Can he explain why? 'I think the reason I still make music is because of the challenge.' He doesn't believe in relying solely on one's natural gifts. And when it comes to talent, 'You just never know – there is no gauge. You don't see when it's empty.'

In the years since his masterpiece, 'Reasonable Doubt', the rapper has often been accused of running on empty, too distant now from what once made him real. In *Decoded*, he answers existentially: 'How distant is the story of your own life ever going to be?' In the lyrics, practically: 'Life stories told through rap/Niggas actin' like I sold you crack/Like I told you sell drugs, no, Hov' did that/So hopefully you won't have to go through that.' But can't a rapper insist, like other artists, on a fictional reality, in which he is somehow still on the corner, despite occupying the penthouse suite? 'Out hustlin', same clothes for days/I'll never change, I'm too stuck in my ways.' Can't he still rep his block? For Jay-Z, pride in the block has been essential and he recognized rap's role in taking 'that embarrassment off of you. The first time people were saying: I come from here – and it's okay.' He quotes Mobb Deep: 'No matter how much loot I get I'm staying in the projects!' But here, too, he sees change: 'Before, if you didn't have that authenticity, your career could be over. Vanilla Ice said he got stabbed or something, they found out he was lying, he was finished.' I suggested to him that many readers of this newspaper* would find it bizarre that the reputation of the rapper Rick Ross was damaged when it was revealed a few years ago that he was, at one time, a prison guard. 'But again,' Jay says, 'I think

* This essay appeared in the 6 September 2012 edition of *The New York Times* magazine.

hip-hop has moved away from that place of everything has to be authentic. Kids are growing up very differently now.'

Sure are. Odd Future. Waka Flocka Flame. Chief Keef. Returning to what appear to be the basic building blocks of rap: shock tactics, obscenity, perversely simplistic language. After the sophistication of Rakim, Q-Tip, Nas, Lupe Fiasco, Kanye West and Jay himself, are we back on the corner again? 'Yeah, but Tupac was an angel compared to these artists!' He shakes his head, apparently amused at himself. And it's true: listening to a Tupac record these days feels like listening to a pleasant slice of Sinatra. But Jay-Z does not suffer from nostalgia. He loves Odd Future and their punk-rock vibe. He sees their anger as a general 'aversion to corporate America', particularly as far as it has despoiled the planet. 'People have a real aversion to what people in power did to the country. So they're just lashing out, like: "This is the son that you made. Look at your son. Look at what you've done." '

But surely another thing they're reacting against, in the Harold Bloom 'anxiety of influence' sense, is the gleaming $460 million monument of Hova himself.

Years ago, Martin Amis wrote a funny story, 'Career Move', in which the screenwriters live like poets, starving in garrets, while the poets chillax poolside, fax their verses to agents in Los Angeles and earn millions off a sonnet. Last year's *Watch the Throne*, a collaboration with Kanye, concerns the coming to pass of that alternative reality. 'Hundred stack/How you get it?' Jay-Z asks Kanye on 'Gotta Have It'. The answer seems totally improbable, and yet it's the truth: 'Layin' raps on tracks!' Fortunes made from rhyming verse. Which is what makes *Watch the Throne* interesting: it fully expresses black America's present contradictions. 'It's a celebration of black excellence/Black tie, black Maybachs/Black excellence, opulence, decadence.' But it's also a bitter accounting of the losses in a long and unfinished war. Kanye raps: 'I feel the pain in my city wherever I go/314 soldiers died in Iraq/509 died in Chicago.' Written by a couple of millionaire businessmen on the fly ('Like "New Day", Kanye told me that – the actual rap – last year at the Met Ball, in my ear at dinner'), it really shouldn't be as good as it is. But somehow their brotherly rivalry creates real energy despite the mammoth production. And in one vital way the process of making it was unusually intimate: 'Most people nowadays – because of technology – send music back and forth.' But this was just two men 'sitting in a room, and really talking about this'. At its most sublime – the ridiculously enjoyable 'Niggas in Paris' – you feel a strong pull in both men toward sheer abandon, pure celebration. Didn't we earn this? Can't we sit back and enjoy it? It's a song that doesn't want to be responsible, or to be asked the old, painful questions. Who cares if they're keeping it real? Or even making sense? Check that beat! Then there's *that* word. 'It's a lot of pain and a lot of hurt and a lot of things going on beyond, beneath that.' He offers an analogy: 'If your kid was acting up, you'd be like, "What is wrong with you?" If they have a bellyache – "Oh, you ate all the cotton candy." You'd make these comparisons, you'd see a link. You'd psychoanalyse the situation.'

Rappers use language as a form of asymmetrical warfare. How else to explain George W. Bush's extraordinary contention that a line spoken by a rapper – 'George Bush doesn't care about black people' – was 'one of the most disgusting moments in my presidency'? But there have always been these people for whom rap language is more scandalous than the urban deprivation rap describes. On 'Who Gon Stop Me', Jay-Z asks that we 'please pardon all the curses' because 'when you're growing up worthless', well, things come out that way. Black hurt, black self-esteem. It's the contradictory pull of the 'cipher', rap terminology for the circle that forms around the kind of freestyling kid Jay-Z once was. What a word! Cipher (noun): 1. A secret or disguised way of writing; a code. 2. A key to such a code. 3. A person or thing of no importance. *Watch the Throne* celebrates two men's escape from that circle of negation. It paints the world black: black bar mitzvahs, black cars, paintings of black girls in MoMA, all black everything, as if it might be possible in a single album to peel back thousands of years of negative connotation. Black no longer the shadow or the reverse or the opposite of something but now the thing itself. But living this fantasy proves problematic: 'Only spot a few blacks the higher I go/ What's up to Will? Shout-out to O/That ain't enough, we gon' need a million more/Kick in the door, Biggie flow/I'm all dressed up with nowhere to go. You're 1 per cent of the 1 per cent.' So what now? 'Power to the people, when you see me, see you!' But that just won't do. It's Jay-Z who's in Paris, after all, not the kids in the Marcy Houses, the housing project in Brooklyn where he grew up. Jay-Z knows this. He gets a little agitated when the subject of Zuccotti Park comes up: 'What's the thing on the wall, what are you fighting for?' He says he told Russell Simmons, the rap mogul, the same: 'I'm not going to a park and picnic, I have no idea what to do, I don't know what the fight is about. What do we want, do you know?'

Jay-Z likes clarity: 'I think all those things need to really declare themselves a bit more clearly. Because when you just say that "the 1 per cent is that", that's not true. Yeah, the 1 per cent that's robbing people, and deceiving people, these fixed mortgages and all these things, and then taking their home away from them, that's criminal, that's bad. Not being an entrepreneur. This is free enterprise. This is what America is built on.'

It's so weird watching rappers becoming elder statesmen. 'I'm out for presidents to represent me.' Well, now they do – and not only on dollar bills. Heavy responsibility lands on the shoulders of these unacknowledged legislators whose poetry is only, after all, four decades young. Jay-Z's ready for it. He has his admirable Shawn Carter Scholarship Foundation, putting disadvantaged kids through college. He's spoken in support of gay rights. He's curating music festivals and investing in environmental technologies. This October, his beloved Nets take up residence in their new home – the Barclays Center. And he has some canny, forward-looking political instincts: 'I was speaking to my friend James, who's from London, we were talking about something else, I just stopped and I was like, "What's going to happen in London?" This was maybe a month before the riots. He was like, "What?" I said: "The culture of black people there, they're not participating in changing the direction of the country. What's gonna happen there?" He actually called me when it blew up, he was like, "You know, I didn't really understand your question, or the timing of it, until now." '

But still I think 'conscious' rap fans hope for something more from him; to see, perhaps, a final severing of this link, in hip-hop, between material riches and true freedom. (Though why we should expect rappers to do this ahead of the rest of America isn't clear.) It would take real forward thinking. Of his own ambitions for the future, he says: 'I don't want to do anything that isn't true.' Maybe the next horizon will stretch beyond philanthropy and Maybach collections.

Meanwhile, back in the rank and file, you still hear the old cry go up: Hip-hop is dead! Which really means that our version of it (the one we knew in our youth) has passed. But nothing could be duller than a nineties hip-hop bore. Lil Wayne? Give me Ol' Dirty Bastard.

Nicki Minaj? Please. Foxy Brown. Odd Future? WU-TANG CLAN 4EVAH. Listening to Jay-Z – still so flexible and enthusiastic, ears wide open – you realize you're like one of these people who believes jazz died with Dizzy. The cheque comes. You will be unsurprised to hear the Jiggaman paid. At the last minute, I remembered to ask after his family, 'Oh, my family's amazing.' And the baby? 'She's four months.' 'Marcy raised me, and whether right or wrong/Streets gave me all I write in the song.' But what will TriBeCa give Blue? 'I actually thought about that more before she was born. Once she got here I've been in shock until maybe last week?' Her childhood won't be like his, and this fact he takes in his stride. 'We would fight each other. My brother would beat me up,' he says, but it was all in preparation for the outside. 'I was going to have to fight, I was going to have to go through some things, and they were preparing me.' He smiles: 'She doesn't have to be tough. She has to love herself, she has to know who she is, she has to be respectful, and be a moral person.' It's a new day.

Brother from Another Mother

The wigs on *Key & Peele* are the hardest-working hairpieces in show business. Individually made, using pots of hair clearly labelled – 'Short Black/Brown, Human', 'Long Black, Human' – they are destined for the heads of a dazzling array of characters: old white sportscasters and young Arab gym posers; rival Albanian/Macedonian restaurateurs; a couple of trash-talking, church-going, African-American ladies; and the President of the United States, to name a few. Between them, Keegan-Michael Key and Jordan Peele play all these people, and more, on their hit Comedy Central sketch show, now in its fourth season. (They are also the show's main writers and executive producers.) They eschew the haphazard whatever's-in-the-costume-box approach – enshrined by Monty Python and still operating on *Saturday Night Live* (*SNL*)– in favour of a sleek, cinematic style. There are no fudged lines, crimes against drag, wobbling sets, or corpsing. False moustaches do not hang limply: a strain of yak hair lends them body and shape. Editing is a three-month process, if not longer. Subjects are satirized by way of precise imitation – you laugh harder because it looks like the real thing. On one occasion, a black actress, a guest star on the show, followed Key into his trailer, convinced that his wig was his actual hair. (Key – to steal a phrase from Nabokov – is 'ideally bald'.) 'And she wouldn't leave until she saw me take my hair off, because she

thought that I and all the other guest stars were fucking with her,'
he recalled. 'She's, like, "Man, that *is* your hair. That's your hair.
You got it done in the back like your mama would do." I said, "I
promise you this is glued to my head." And she was squealing with
delight. She was going, "Oh! This is crazy! This is crazy!" She just
couldn't believe it.' Call it method comedy.

The two men are physically incongruous. Key is tall, light brown,
dashingly high-cheekboned and LA fit; Peele is shorter, darker,
more rounded, cute like a teddy bear. Peele, who is thirty-five, wears
a nineties slacker uniform of sneakers, hoodie and hipster specs. Key
is fond of sharply cut jackets and shiny shirts – like an ad exec on
casual Friday – and looks forty-three the way Will Smith looked
forty-three, which is not much. Before he even gets near hair and
make-up, Key can play black, Latino, South Asian, Native American,
Arab, even Italian. He is biracial, the son of a white mother and a
black father, as is Peele. But though Peele's phenotype is less
obviously malleable – you might not guess that he's biracial at
all – he is so convincing in voice and gesture that he makes you see
what isn't really there. His Obama impersonation is uncanny, and
it's the voice and hands, rather than the make-up lightening his skin,
that allow you to forget that he looks nothing like the president. One
of his most successful creations – a nightmarish, overly entitled
young woman called Meegan – is an especially startling transformation: played in his own dark-brown skin, she somehow still
reads as a white girl from the Jersey Shore.

Between chameleonic turns, the two men appear as themselves,
casually introducing their sketches or riffing on them with a cosy
intimacy, as if recommending a video on YouTube, where they are
wildly popular. A sketch show may seem a somewhat antique format,
but it turns out that its traditional pleasures – three-minute scenes,

meme-like catchphrases – dovetail neatly with online tastes. Averaging 2 million on-air viewers, Key and Peele have a huge second life online, where their visually polished, byte-size, self-contained skits – easily extracted from each twenty-two-minute episode – rack up views in the many millions. Given these numbers, it's striking how little online animus they inspire, despite their aim to make fun of everyone – men and women, all sexualities, any subculture, race or nation – in repeated acts of equal-opportunity offending. They don't attract anything approaching the kind of critique a sitcom like *Girls* seems to generate just by existing. What they get, Peele conceded, as if it were a little embarrassing, is 'a lot of love'. Partly, this is the licence we tend to lend to (male) clowns, but it may also be a consequence of the antic freedom inherent in sketch, which, unlike sitcom, can present many different worlds simultaneously.

This creative liberty took on a physical aspect one warm LA morning in mid-November, as *Key and Peele* requisitioned half a suburban street in order to film two sketches in neighbouring ranch houses: a domestic scene between Meegan and her lunkhead boyfriend, Andre (played by Key), and a genre spoof of the old Sidney Poitier classic *Guess Who's Coming to Dinner*. 'One of our bits makes you laugh? We have you, and you will back us up,' Peele suggested, during a break in filming. 'And, if something offends you, you will excuse it.' Sitting at a trestle table in the overgrown back garden of 'Meegan's Home', he was in drag, scarfing down lunch with the cast and crew, and yet – for a man wearing a full face of make-up and false eyelashes – he seemed almost anonymous among them, speaking in a whisper and gesturing not at all. On set, Peele is notably introverted, as mild and reasonable in person as he tends toward extremity when in character. Looking down at his cleavage, he murmured, 'You often hear comments, as a black man, that there's something emasculating about putting on a dress. It may be technically true, but I've found it so fun. It's not a downgrade in any way.'

When Key sat down beside Peele, he, too, seemed an unlikely shock merchant, although for the opposite reason. Outgoing, exhaustingly personable, he engages frenetically with everyone: discussing fantasy football with a cameraman, rhapsodizing about the play *An Octoroon* with his PR person and ardently agreeing with his comedy partner about the curious demise of the short-lived TV show *Freaks and Geeks* ('ahead of its time'), the present sociohistorical triumph of nerd culture, and a core comic principle underpinning many of their sketches. ('It's what we call "peas in a pod": two characters who feel just as passionate about the same thing.')

Peele loves 'a comedy scene that makes you cry' – like the last episode of Britain's *The Office* – and cites Ricky Gervais's creation Regional Manager David Brent as a personal touchstone. Key loves Gervais, too, though his 'favourite performer of all time ever' is another Brit, Peter Sellers. 'Because it's all pathos, pathos, pathos.' When considering these matters, the two men laugh at each other's jokes and finish each other's sentences, apparently free of the double-act psychodrama made infamous by such toxic pairings as Martin and Lewis, Crosby and Hope, and Abbott and Costello. Like their Comedy Central stablemates Abbi Jacobson and Ilana Glazer, from the sitcom *Broad City*, they pull off the unusual trick of wringing laughs out of amity. One of the network's original concepts for the show was 'Key versus Peele', which was soon abandoned when the two stars couldn't find enough topics on which to disagree, even comically.

Both men have an improv background, and improv's culture of mutual support suffuses their material. (Faced with an empty stage,

Key explained, 'If I bump into a "desk", then he walks into the room five minutes later and walks around that "desk". You don't act, you react.') From their enthusiastic LA valets, avid fans of the actor they call 'Liam Neesons' (catchphrase: 'Liam Neesons is my shit!'), to the two homoerotic Arabic gentlemen who frot each other while supposedly admiring passing hotties in full burkas ('You saw ankle bone?'), a natural chemistry – the product of a genuine relationship – is being turned up to eleven. 'We're brothers,' Peele said. 'It's not even best friends. It's a total brother understanding.'

Twenty minutes later, Key and Peele had a nine-alarm fight – as Andre and Meegan. Andre was attempting to break up with Meegan, and Meegan was refusing to let him. She sat on a plush white sofa, surrounded by reality-TV-show-inspired furnishings, filing her nails and becoming, despite a veil of self-help language, increasingly incensed. ('Can I ask why? Because I'm doing a lot of, like, growth work on myself.') Peele played it perfectly, but the camera angle was awkward and his wrist hair kept escaping the cuffs of Meegan's pink velour tracksuit. As they reset, Peele subtly extemporized. The moment in which Meegan demands an explanation – 'Grown adults give reasons!' – morphed into 'Grown individuals present examples!' – a lift in register that proved unaccountably funnier. In response, a hapless Andre could only bellow and writhe in frustration.

'Meegan and Andre' is one of Key and Peele's most popular recurring sketches, and plays to their strengths: Peele's pitch-perfect ear for verbal tics and Key's long-limbed physical comedy. As the sophistic, motor-mouthed Meegan, Peele gets to the core of what contemporary entitlement looks like – concern with one's personal rights combined with non-interest in one's duties – managing to place Meegan in that comedy sweet spot where girl power meets good old-fashioned narcissism. Key, meanwhile, uses all his native brio to embody an amiable jock, utterly dominated and forever perplexed as to why. 'I was almost out the door,' Andre said twice to himself, as Meegan, satisfied that the break-up had been averted, grew bored and wandered off into the kitchen. Key put his head in his hands and arranged his body in the manner of a man drained of hope. This improvised gesture solved the problem of an explosive scene that seemed to dribble away, and Key carried it off with a sincerity that tipped the scale gently from comic toward tragic.

A little later, on a raised wooden deck at the back of the house, Key and Joel Zadak – who manages both Key and Peele – sat on high stools watching the footage. It was clear that Key had expanded Andre from the confused putz of previous seasons to something close to an emotionally abused person. If the depth Key brings to comic moments is unexpected, the bigger surprise is that he's doing comedy at all: he intended to be a classical actor. After attending the University of Detroit Mercy, he got an MFA from the Pennsylvania State University School of Theater, and claims to have been a tad put out when, in 1997, he was invited to become a member of the Second City Detroit: 'I've got an MFA! A Mother-Fucking-A! I took total umbrage!' (He still has dreams of playing the Dane, although, given his age and his schedule, he may have to wait for Lear. ' "Remember that night you said you'd do *Hamlet?*" ' he said wistfully, quoting a Chicago actor friend's recent query. 'I was, like, "Call me in 2017." ') But it is the mixture of the classical and the contemporary in him – the voice that sounds as natural saying 'umbrage' as saying 'mother-fucking' – that provides much of his comic charm.

Perhaps because of this background in dramatic theatre, Key is the showman, the all-rounder, while there is a detail and a level of delicacy to Peele's craft that require just the right frame to set it off.

Beyond *Key and Peele*, it's hard to imagine Peele in any vehicle not constructed around a comic character of his own devising, just as the *Pink Panther* series was essentially an elaborate showcase for the marvel that was Peter Sellers's Inspector Clouseau. By contrast, you can envision Key in a variety of projects: off Broadway as Hamlet, but also presenting the Oscars, floating in space next to Sandra Bullock, or putting his hand on Tom Hanks's shoulder, delivering some bad news. Whatever scene you set, Key will give you everything he's got. But the same qualities that make Key such an easy and pleasant presence on set – amiability, flexibility, absence of dogma – also make him hard to pin down as a personality. He's so good at reacting, so attuned to other people's feelings, that it's not always easy to assess what he feels. 'I very often don't know what's fuelling my passion,' he confessed, while someone fussed with Andre's ludicrous ducktail. 'I'm just being practical with the skill set that I have.'

That afternoon, during the Poitier sketch, which featured only Key, Peele unburdened himself of Meegan, re-dressed as himself and sat down beneath the dappled light of an orange tree, where he considered his career: 'Fifteen, twenty years ago, I decided I wanted to be a sketch performer.' Not an unusual dream, perhaps, for a funny kid raised on the Upper West Side, a mile and a half from the *Saturday Night Live* studios, although few would have pursued it with Peele's single-minded persistence. While at PS 87, the Metropolitan Opera did a workshop with his fifth-grade class; Peele was given the shy kid's job of assistant stage manager, the duties of which included being understudy to one of the leads. When that actor called in sick, Peele filled in for several performances, playing the part of a 'cool guy' (black leather jacket, sunglasses, chain), and discovering, in the process, how much he liked having an audience.

Later, as a student at Sarah Lawrence – where he had intended to study puppeteering – he joined an improv troupe, which soon became his main concern; two years in, he dropped out of college entirely to form a comedy partnership with his college room-mate and fellow troupe member Rebecca Drysdale, who's now a writer on *Key and Peele*. (He realized, he has said, that he had no need of puppets. He would use himself: 'the most intricate puppet of all'.) Drysdale and Peele called themselves 'Two White Guys', although they were – as the publicity made explicit – 'a black guy and a white Jewish lesbian,' and went on to perform two well-received sketch shows at Chicago's ImprovOlympic Theater before the rest of Peele's Sarah Lawrence class had even graduated. Soon afterwards, Peele joined Boom Chicago, an improv troupe based in Amsterdam, which has a remit to create comedy that 'addresses Dutch, American and world social and political issues', although Peele made his mark playing Ute, a vapid Danish supermodel and an occasional presenter of the Eurovision Song Contest. (She had a Eurotrash accent and said things like 'Yes, because, like, if you have English as a second language it's hard to make your head talk!')

Becoming other people: this is Peele's gift. The small scraps online of his forays into stand-up reveal a man who doesn't quite know who to be onstage – there's no persona he's happy to be stuck in – and Peele, recognizing this, abandoned the form early. 'The one thing that you don't figure out as an improviser or a sketch performer is "What am I?" ' he observed. The essence of his talent is multi-vocal, and he has, in the past, attributed this to his childhood anxiety at having the wrong voice, which, in his case, meant speaking like his mother – that is, speaking 'white'. ('It cannot be a coincidence that I decided to go into a career where my whole purpose is altering the way I speak and experiencing these different characters and maybe proving in my soul that the way someone speaks has nothing to do with who they are,' he told Terry Gross, on *Fresh Air*.) In improv, the question of authenticity becomes irrelevant: the whole point is to fake it.

To watch the afternoon's filming, I walked next door, into a modern living room disguised as a late-fifties interior, complete with sideboard and drinks cabinet and cut-glass tumblers half filled with fake whiskey. Key was struggling through an awkward meal with his white girlfriend and her parents, who he believes dislike him because he's black. It's only when he stands up, affronted, and prepares to walk out – 'There's no point in trying to reason with people who can't appreciate the differences in others' – that we see that he has a great big tail (to be added in post-production). The mother says, 'I cannot *believe* you brought a black man into our house!' A moment later, the camera pulls back for the punchline: everybody has a tail. During a pause in filming – as the crew discussed the timing of the tail reveal – Bonnie Bartlett, the actress playing the mother, who is in her mid-eighties, turned to Key and murmured, 'It must have been interesting to be *your* mother, because you're so . . .' She touched her own – pink – face. A moment later, perhaps worried that she'd given offence, Bartlett looked stricken, but Key smiled kindly. 'I think that's a fair statement of the case,' he said. 'Now, where are you from, Bonnie?' 'Illinois.' 'You're kidding me!' The actress, encouraged, began to tell her story: 'My hometown was settled by men taken there to work . . . these Swedish men . . .' She faded. '*Really*,' Key persisted, with great warmth. 'That's such an interesting story.' The crew reset the cameras. This time, when Bartlett's line came around, she said, 'I can't believe you would bring a dark man into this house.' Cut. Bartlett looked stricken once more: 'I can't believe I said "dark"! But we didn't say "black" in those days . . .' Key turned anthropological, objectively curious: 'What did you say? Did you say "Negro?" ' Bartlett, relieved, considered the question: ' "Colored", I think . . .' Key thanked her for the smart correction: they went with 'colored'.

Key and Peele met – as Key recently told Jimmy Kimmel – in 2003, when they 'fell in comedy love' while performing on consecutive nights in Chicago, at the Second City Theater. Peele was visiting with Boom Chicago, doing his Ute bit; Key was playing a sociopathic high-school gym instructor called Coach Hines, who 'inspires' his teenage students by regularly enumerating all the ways in which he will violently murder them if they do anything wrong. Improv is not a world overburdened with people of colour, but neither man felt territorial when, soon after, they each auditioned for Fox's raucous, satirical sketch show *Mad TV*. In the end, they were both hired, and quickly put to work, mainly impersonating black celebrities – Ludacris, Bill Cosby, Snoop Dogg – but also doing some of the kind of detailed fictional work they would later develop on *Key and Peele*. Coach Hines became a recurring spot, while Peele turned an impersonation of the rapper 50 Cent into a character study, in which Key, as Fifty's manager, phones the rapper to tell him of the chart dominance of his rival Kanye West. 50 Cent, heartbroken, sings a maudlin song called 'Sad 50 Cent'. (Sample lyric: 'I walk around my prostitute garden, and my carousel. Nothing seems to make me smile today.' The song was nominated for an Emmy in 2008.) The humour on *Mad TV* was broad – and too reliant on celebrity subjects – but it was a great place to hone your sketch-writing skills, and made both men, especially Peele, usefully hunger for a time when a joke wouldn't have to pass through a dozen producers to get on the air.

Toward the end of their five-season stint, a big-eared, biracial senator began to make headlines and, a short while later, became president. *SNL* needed an impersonator. This was, for Peele, 'the dream. That was what I set out to do.' But when the call came he was under contract to *Mad TV*. He was devastated that a legal matter was screwing him up, especially when he had, he felt, 'strategized everything perfectly'. Watching the other Obamas on *SNL* was a 'strange, strange little period' in his life, but also motivating: 'I think the strategist in me went, "All right, well what does this mean? This means there's gotta be something that I can put these skills into; there's gotta be a reason I'm not doing this, ultimately." ' When Peele was freed from his *Mad TV* contract, in 2009 – and after a pilot for Fox went nowhere – he and Key began discussing a sketch show, and a young director named Peter Atencio immediately came to mind.

Key had met Atencio when they made a Web series on a green screen in the 'crappy one-bedroom apartment in Hollywood' that Atencio describes himself as living in at the time ('It was for MySpace, which dates how long ago that was'), having moved from Boulder, Colorado, at nineteen, in the hope of making movies. They liked each other and kept in touch; Key introduced Peele to Atencio. Only thirty-one now, he was twenty-seven when Key and Peele managed to persuade Comedy Central to accept him after the studio's first choice for director dropped out. With a small team of eight writers and four producers, the first season was written over thirteen weeks, creating two hundred and sixty sketches that were later pared down to fifty-four. Atencio has directed every episode of *Key and Peele*, until this current season. After the network put in for a double order of episodes, post-production on the first half began overlapping with the filming of the second; unwilling to relinquish control of colour and sound mixing, Atencio conceded a third of the season to a trio of directors. But, even when he's not himself directing, he's a frequent visitor wherever *Key and Peele* is filming, which, on the day we spoke, happened to be a standard-issue black box of a set, deep within the Universal Studios complex.

Extras were filing through the sun-baked parking lot to play the crowd at a basketball game, and Atencio stood in the studio's doorway like a benign house spirit, watching them pass, nodding at producers and then walking across the room to greet Key and Peele, where they sat 'courtside', having their wigs tweaked. Tall and lumbering, with a soft, pale, pouchy face partly obscured by thick geek glasses and a baseball cap, he was dressed in baggy streetwear, all of it a little lopsided on his large frame, and looked more like a visiting weed dealer than the man who usually runs the show. Back outside, he blinked moleishly in the sun. 'I live within it,' he said, speaking of the series. 'It is my life. It's definitely the only way I know how to do it. It's probably the only way it could be done.'

From the outset, Atencio wanted *Key and Peele* to have a distinct look. He recalled that his pitch was to 'make every sketch the funniest set piece in a movie'. Rather than resorting to the kind of verbal exposition on which so much sketch comedy relies, he suggested using 'visual information, editing cues, things that kind of set the tone and the mood so that you don't have to do it in the writing'. A goofy scene concerning the frustration of holding a 'Group 1' boarding card as various groups file on to the plane right in front you – 'Uniformed military personnel . . . People in wheelchairs. Any priests, nuns, rabbis, imams. Any old people in wheelchairs with babies. Any old religious people with military babies. Jason Schwartzman. Anyone with a blue suitcase' – culminates with Key, still clutching his ticket, sitting amid the movie-grade wreckage of a commercial airliner. It looks so epic and expensive it draws gasps as well as laughs but was shot relatively cheaply by Atencio on the *War of the Worlds* set at Universal Studios.

Comedy Central promoted the first season with the tagline 'If you don't watch this show, you're a racist,' but *Key and Peele* rarely resorts to the kind of binary racial humour so appreciated by Homer Simpson – *black people do this, white people do that* – and the colour line is far from being its sole concern. (Nor is it all pathos, pathos, pathos. One sketch ponders the eternal question 'What if names were farts?') Where the comedy is racial, the familiar, singular 'race card' is switched for something more like the whole pack fanned out, with the focus on what Peele has called 'the absurdity of race'. 'I always look back at standardized tests,' he said, as he sat in Hair and Make-up, submitting to a small but significant wig transition from 'sports announcer' to 'sportscaster'. 'They make you say what race you are, where you check out, and I think that's ultimately an unhealthy tradition.' His eyes, naturally rather narrow, widened dramatically. 'It is *crazy* that as a kid we're taught, "What is your identity?" We're *asked* that!' Key, who sat at the other end of the trailer, going from having hair to being bald to having hair again, is similarly struck by the irrational nature of racial categories. 'The limbic system is alive and well,' he said. 'And it's going, "*I need to find a category. I need to find a category. If I don't find a category, I'm not safe.*" '

He seemed to be referring to a neurological theory according to which the limbic system is responsible for our primal reactions – such as recognizing membership within a certain tribe – because it looks for visual equivalences between things, whereas our prefrontal cortex, which developed later, is able to make complex cognitive decisions. 'So the thing is: the limbic system is still kicking it, hard,' he continued. 'And people are going to fight it, but naturally try to categorize themselves. Because when all we had was a limbic system people were, like, "Dude, there's us and those fucking sabre-toothed tigers, *so we all have to stick together.*" ' This led to a discussion of how tiny differences in phenotype – the relative 'flatness' of Peele's nose compared with the higher bridge of Key's – can create differences in people's lives, both in the way that we are comprehended by others and in the way, especially as children, we comprehend ourselves.

> Key: 'Jordan and I are . . . we're biracial.'
> Peele: 'Yes. Half black, half white.'
> Key: 'And because of that we find ourselves particularly adept at lying, er, because on a daily basis we have to adjust our blackness.'

This moment occurs onstage, in the first episode of *Key and Peele*, while they are out of character, speaking to a live studio audience, and it has some of stand-up's confessional feel. Sometimes, they explain, this adjustment has to happen simply to 'terrify white people'. (Without it, 'we sound whiter than the black dude in the college a cappella group. We sound whiter than Mitt Romney in a snowstorm.') But it may also be a way of seeking approval from the other side of the line. 'When we're around other brothers and sisters,' Peele says, with a sly smile, 'you gotta dial it up.' This leads to a demonstration of blackness dialled up ('You know what I'm talking about, brother – and you know I know what you're talking about; and you know I know you know; no doubt no doubt no doubt . . .'), complete with physical gestures, which aren't the familiar, supposedly 'black' gestures of TV comedy (no gang signs or exaggerated side-to-side head bopping) but are still, of course, stereotypical. The heads move, but the movement is far more closely, accurately, observed, and then expanded upon: Peele's little shuffling dance of joy, the way Key closes his eyes to signify assent. I would describe it as a fond imitation.

The skit alerts us to a shared trait that we may not have noticed until presented with it. But this is not the mild Jerry Seinfeldesque communality of coffee-drinking and aeroplane etiquette. It concerns the communality of race, about which we are rarely allowed to laugh. To say that the two men become, in that moment, 'more black' is to concede, in one sense, to a racial stereotype – and yet if there is not such a thing as 'blackness', upon what does 'being black' hinge? (To fondly identify a community, you have to think of its members collectively; you need to think the same way to hate them. The only thing a rabbi and an anti-Semite may share is their belief in the collective identity 'Jewishness'.) 'You never want to be the whitest-sounding black guy in a room,' Peele concludes. (In response to which Key muses, 'You put five white-talking black guys in the same room . . . You come back in an hour? It's gonna be like Ladysmith Black Mambazo up in here!')

A few months after this sketch aired, Obama – surely the whitest-sounding black man in most rooms he enters – went on *Jimmy Fallon*, and gave an unexpected shout-out to *Key and Peele*. He was responding to the 'Obama Loses His Shit' sketch, in which Peele, as Obama, sits in a wingback chair for his weekly presidential address and calmly outlines the concerns of early 2012 – Iraq, North Korea, Tea Party pushback, his own legitimacy – while Key, as his Anger Translator, Luther, paces up and down the room, saying the unsayable ('I have a birth certificate! I have a hot-diggity-doggity-mamase-mamasa-mamakusa birth certificate, you dumb-ass crackers!'). The sketch seemed to articulate an unspoken longing among many Obama supporters, and perhaps within the black community as a whole. I certainly hadn't realized how much I wanted Luther until I saw him. Later that year, Obama asked to meet with Key and Peele, and wryly acknowledged the same desire. 'I need Luther,' he told them. 'We'll have to wait till second term.'

The sketch employs a comic reversal (Key: 'I think reversals end up being the real bread and butter of the show'), but the emotional recognition gets the belly laugh. It has a famous antecedent in a 1986 sketch from *SNL*, in which Phil Hartman, playing Ronald Reagan, bumbles around the Oval Office – photo-ops with Girl Scouts, speaking inanities to journalists – but as soon as the press corps leaves, he's all business: conversing in Arabic, understanding the Contras, quoting Montesquieu. 'And that's informed a handful of scenes of ours,' Peele explained. 'It's a version of that.' When they're writing, they're looking for the emotional root of the humour. 'What's the mythology that is funny just because people know it's not true?' he continued. You need to be able to guess what many people really feel about something, even if they won't ever dare say it. It's this skill that is, in the end, every comic's bread and butter. How does one develop it? Key, who has given a lot of thought to the matter, feels that both his empathic and his imitative skills are essentially a form of hyperresponsiveness. 'The theory is: There's no one in the world – there may be people as good as I am at this, but no one's better than me at adapting to a situation.' If comic skill is a form of adaptation, Key and Peele had completed the necessary apprenticeship while still in short pants.

Peele, reared in a one-bedroom walkup by a white 'bookish' mother (a fact one might have been able to glean solely from his middle name: Haworth), barely knew his black father. (He was mostly absent and died in 1999.) A sketch from the second season, written by Peele's old room-mate Rebecca Drysdale, has Peele, playing himself, visiting a trailer park in search of his long-lost father (played by Key), who treats Peele with contempt until Peele lets slip that he has his own TV show. It's a brutally funny scene, painful to watch once you're aware of the personal history behind it. 'I was in this ABC special called *Kids Ask President Clinton Questions*,' Peele recalled. 'It was the last question of the day. I ask him, "What would you do: is there any way for you to help kids who aren't getting child support?" ' Yet Peele has, in common with Key, a tendency to interpret past pain as productive: 'I was a kid that got to go to the White House and talk to the president. I was really in seventh heaven!' As well as appearing on television, Peele watched an epic amount of it – 'Everything I do now, part of it is the fact that I had television as my second parent. Hours and hours' – and, for him, after the age of six, the most consistent black father figure in the home was on TV, refracted through the fun-house mirror of American pop culture. Many of the sketches on *Key and Peele* seem to play off black shows of the period, or reruns (*Roots*, *Good Times*, *Family Matters*), in scenes both loving and accusatory. In one, Steve Urkel turns up as a homicidal maniac.

But if Peele wasn't lonely, exactly – 'There was a precedent for biracial latchkey kids' – and always, he says, felt loved, other people's reactions complicated things. 'I went to school, and the first kid goes, "Your mom's *white*?" ' he said. He had to quickly adapt to 'what other people were used to and what other people were taught, and we were asked to identify what I was or whose side I was on: was I one or the other?' Key and Peele's somewhat unusual insistence on their biracialism is motivated in part by a refusal to obscure white mothers to whom they were very close. For Peele's mother, Lucinda Williams, who still lives in that walkup on the Upper West Side, the situation was made easier by living in Manhattan. 'Having parents with different ethnic identities was not a particularly unusual situation here, nor was being raised by a single parent,' she told me. Peele, Williams says, was 'obviously my joy', but she had her share of dealing with other people's incredulity, especially as a pale, blue-eyed blonde. Strangers, she said, tended to 'assume he was adopted or I was watching someone else's child. When he was still in a stroller, I would see people's faces freeze and then look away upon leaning in to admire the baby. You could almost see a "Does Not Compute" sign light up in their eyes.'

As Peele grew, his increasing interest in performing surprised his mother. He had always seemed shy, 'the quiet kid who likes to draw', who loved movies about aliens, monsters and robots – all of whom tend to have no race at all. There were many literary books on the shelves, but Peele gravitated toward fantasy. ('*Labyrinth*. That's my world,' Peele confirmed. '*NeverEnding Story. Willow.*') Twenty years later, *Key and Peele* features many zombies and vampires, and annually delights in its Halloween episode. But Peele was part of that generation of nerds who, as Key pointed out, have conquered the earth – at least, the part that makes most popular entertainment. Wendell, whom Peele plays on the show – a three-hundred-pound recluse, fond of cheesy crusts and action figures, overly anxious to convince people that he's 'seeing someone, sexually' – is only a kind of obscene, comic extrapolation of Peele-the-fantasy-fan. 'I think that "nerd" is kind of an elusive term,' Peele said. 'I guess technically it means someone who is obsessed with pop culture, and possibly without having the social graces themselves to deal with things. But the term "nerd" that I relate to is more of the first part, where it's just to be an unabashed fan of something.' Fandom remains the easiest way to draw Peele out. He is cautious on intimate subjects, happier discussing the classic nerd topics of his peers: Kubrick movies, nineties hip-hop, the inadvertent comic genius that is Kanye West.

Key, who thinks of himself as being from a slightly different era, has no interest in hip-hop ('I'm a sixties R&B man') and speaks of his personal life and history more readily, in a great flowing rush, though perhaps this is simply to save time, as the story comprises an unusual number of separate compartments. Born in Detroit, he is the child of an affair between a white woman and her married black co-worker, and was adopted at birth by another mixed-raced couple, two social workers, Patricia Walsh, who is white, and Michael Key, who hailed from Salt Lake City, 'with the other twelve black people'. The couple raised Key but divorced while he was an adolescent. Key's father then married his stepmother, Margaret McQuillan-Key, a white woman from Northern Ireland. Key's familial situation was often in flux: after his own adoption came a sibling; then his parents' divorce and his father's remarriage.

As a boy, he had ambitions in veterinary science, movie stardom and football, but when childhood epilepsy ruled out football his interest in performing surged ahead of everything else, a passion in which he was encouraged by his mother. Later, his stepmother suggested that he go abroad to study drama, and when he was eighteen she and his father sent him on a reconnaissance trip: 'That was my end-of-high-school gift: to go to England. My stepmother said, "If you're going to do theatre for a living, you've got to do it right" ' – here Key took a stab at a Belfast brogue – '*They don't fookin' do it right here.*' Key is, like Peele, a man of many voices. (His wife, Cynthia Blaise, is a dialect coach, though Key claims that her role is more supportive than instructive: 'She doesn't usually help me. She's very sweet to say things like "No, I think you've got that, honey." ') He picked up a few voices during his stay in London, where he had to adapt to yet another culture and another concept of 'blackness'. While visiting family in Northern Ireland, he watched some TV coverage of Brixton and had a minor racial epiphany: 'Holy shit, those are black people!' He loved the Olympic sprinter Linford Christie, amazed to hear such an unfamiliar voice emerging from so familiar a face. 'My brain started to make that adjustment almost immediately, at eighteen years of age. My brain said, "Oh, I get it. It's all cultural. None of it's about melanin." ' Seven years later, he had a profoundly affecting reunion with his biological mother, Carrie Herr, which brought with it more siblings ('I literally went to bed one day with one sibling and woke up the next morning with seven'), and a sudden acceptance of Jesus Christ as his personal saviour, an event that he has described as 'pretty unexpected'. But adapting to unexpected emotional contingencies is what Key does best. 'I'm not the smartest person in the world,' he offered. 'But my EQ, my "emotional quotient" – off the charts.'

On set, this serves him well. Key acknowledges that his flitting between personas can seem a spooky art to those of us who are stuck with our singular selves: 'Very often, humans latch on to the first thing they can get hold of and go, "This is working. I'm gonna do this," ' he told me. 'And what Jordan and I have latched on to is: "*All* of this is working." ' To Key, 'the varied thing is the normative thing'. This brought to mind Alice Miller, author of *The Drama of the Gifted Child*, who argued that the empathic skills one often finds in gifted children represent a symptom as much as a gift, a child's reactive response to the inconsistencies and unexpectedness around him. Key has read the Miller – he calls it 'an amazing book' – but considers himself removed now from the traumas that may have shaped his skills: 'It was a tool you were using to survive when you were younger and now you can use for other ends.' The way he rattles off his complex past, as if it had all happened to another man, seems related to this; able to see himself from a distance, he speaks like a writer describing a character. He notes, too, that he seldom feels 'strongly about things', and when observing other people he has an almost anthropological reaction: what would it be like to feel so deeply attached to one point of view?

While race can appear abstract to Key and Peele, especially when seen through the lens of their own unconventional backgrounds, for many of their viewers race is neither an especially fluid nor a changeable category; it is the determining fact of their lives. Within the rigid categories of media representation, for example, Key and Peele are two black men who star in a TV show that has unusual crossover appeal, and matters that might seem neutral on other shows – like the casting of 'love interests' – must be more carefully considered. Key, whose wife is white (Peele's partner, the stand-up and comic actress Chelsea Peretti, is also white), pronounced himself 'hyperaware' of the issue: 'It's one thing that you can control.' For a recent sketch, in which Key finds a woman collapsed on the ground, and during his subsequent 911 call falls in love with her, the script required that the woman be 'staggeringly gorgeous'. When casting her, Key said, 'It was very important to me not to have a light-skinned woman.' In telling this story, he assumed, for the moment, the voice of a disgruntled viewer: '*These two niggas ain't got nothing but white women on this show!*'

Once, backstage on a *Key and Peele* college tour, taking pictures with the student volunteers, hugging and chatting with them, Key mentioned to Peele that he sometimes had a bad feeling about the way he conducted these interactions. 'And then Jordan said, "Why?" ' he recalled. 'And I said, "Because when I'm around the black girls I hug them and give them more attention." Because ain't *nobody* been shit on more than black women. They just deserved more because of the fucking shit. It's one thing to get whipped. It's another thing to get whipped *and* raped. Do you know what I mean? It's just horrible. And not that white women don't have problems.' The painful history of black women in America, Key stressed, 'won't leave me. I think of my grandmother and my aunts. It reverberates. And so it's, like, a woman with dark-chocolate skin should be an image of beauty for anybody just as much as a woman with milk-white skin.' Although, he added, 'none of it actually should matter'. But it does, of course. A scene in which Key and Peele play two husbands mortally afraid of their wives could be read as a satire on middle-class marital mores, regardless of race, but when Key appeared on *Conan* and claimed, in reference to the sketch, that 'there is nothing more dangerous on planet Earth than a black wife', he resurrected a familiar insult, too often directed at black women, some of whom pointed out, online, that Key has no personal experience on which to draw his conclusion. They felt hurt precisely *because* they were black women, speaking from a singular place and with a singular experience.

Peele, when asked about how race is dealt with on the show, said, 'Really, there's no actual strategy, and there's no perspective that would be easy to . . . to state. Much like race in this country. It's so nuanced. It's so complicated. It's so deep-seated, and, at the same time, it's evolving, and then it feels like it devolves. And it's this nebulous thing.' I thought of that William Gibson quote: 'The future is already here – it's just not evenly distributed yet.' It can't be easy making race comedy in such a mixed reality: a black president on the one hand, black boys dying in the streets on the other. It's a difficult omelette, and you're going to break some eggs trying to make it. But getting it right means penetrating to the heart of a long and painful national conversation.

In one sketch, Peele appears as a young black man walking through a white suburb. A mother shoos her children indoors; a man mowing his lawn gives Peele a warning glare; a cop slowly tracks him in his squad car, his eyes filled with pre-emptory violence. Then Peele puts up his hoodie: the face of a young white man is painted in profile on the side, obscuring Peele's. The cop smiles and waves. A minute long and wordless, it's a wonderfully pure comic provocation. 'We just kind of put ourselves in the centre of it, moment to moment,' Peele said, referring to America's race issue. Ultimately, he hoped that their show will be 'a mirror. I think there's even an element of the Rorschach test.' He meant a mirror held up to the audience, but it is, of course, also a mirror of Key and Peele's own attitudes, which, like everybody's, aren't always completely within their control.

On my last day on set, I sat behind the cameras, next to Joel Zadak. We had some dead time on our hands; Key and Peele's stand-ins, Shomari (tall, light brown) and Brian (shorter, dark brown), were texting while the crew tested the lights against their complexions. Zadak is a youthful forty-three, with a sharp quiff and an unlined face, and was a comedy nerd before he became a comedy manager: hanging around the Second City Chicago, moving to LA to study screenwriting, hoping to be an improv guy himself. Now, as one of the executive producers on the show, he is content to be behind the scenes, and has the aura of a laid-back dude, despite his typical LA TV schedule. ('You know, I wake up in the morning at five o'clock. I read for an hour. I go to the gym for an hour. I take one of the kids to school, come to work . . .') Describing the pair, he reached for a Beatles analogy 'where Keegan is Paul, and Jordan is John. Where Keegan can write and perform a hit song all day long, and people will love him, and Jordan can do the same, but I think people look a little bit more deeper into what Jordan's doing. He's a little bit more of a deep thinker.' (The previous day, Atencio had made the same analogy.) What most impresses Zadak about his clients, though, is their openness. They never 'dismiss anything out of hand. They listen to everything.'

Beyond the introvert-extrovert paradigm, it is perhaps this openness that strikes people as Beatles-like, for, to keep moving forward, as the Beatles did, you have to be constantly listening, second-guessing reactions, pre-empting tastes, adapting. If this is hard enough to do in music, it is even more difficult in comedy. The world is full of calcified comedians who stop – sometimes very suddenly – being funny, too attached to a joke's familiar neural pathway, perhaps, or too dogmatic, unable to change. How do you stay funny? It's a question that 'haunts' Peele: 'My biggest fear is someday reaching that point at which I see a lot of artists and comedians, where they stop growing. They had that success at a certain point, and it worked. And they cash in and they forget to continue to evolve.'

The stand-ins left; Key and Peele arrived, having been transformed into basketball commentators who seem to have taken a truth serum ('Welcome back to another few hours and several million dollars spent on watching adult men play a simple child's game, all while being paid more than the president!'). On form, as funny as I'd ever seen them, their faces were barely dusted with a few whitish wrinkles, yet they appeared as unmistakably Caucasian as Mitt Romney. Every now and then, Jay Martel, one of the show's executive producers – and an occasional writer for the *New Yorker* – walked over to their desk to discuss some verbal tweaking. Tall, thin, tonsured, he looked like a mild-mannered Quaker, and turned out to be a descendant of ministers and missionaries. ('I'm deciding whether a donkey dick is funnier than a dog dick. My ancestors would have been horrified.') At one point, Martel went

97

over to discuss a line Key didn't like: 'The alleged rapist passes the big orange ball to the sweaty legal giant; the sweaty legal giant passes it to the pituitary case.' The term 'pituitary case', Key argued, had 'too much math in it', which meant, Martel explained, that too many mental steps were required to get to the laugh. On set and in the writing room, a series of terms is deployed as useful shorthand. 'A clam': an old joke. 'Lateral': an absence of escalation. 'Map over': to take the beats of a genre piece and 'map' a joke over them, as in the Poitier sketch. 'Dookie': a joke that isn't yet fully formed. In place of 'pituitary case', Martel offered 'huge child-man'. Dookie completed. Key and Peele moved on to trying to amuse each other with improvised catchphrases:

'Shploifus!'

'Hamhocks!'

'Biscuit time!'

'Gudeek!'

'Ebola!'

The last was Peele's, and Key looked at him despondently: 'But they'll probably have Ebola all figured out by 2015.' (When the scene will air.) 'Cut to: urban wasteland,' Peele said, and Key picked up the joke: 'Resident Evil: Whole of the Western World.' Even their off-the-cuff commentary on their genre sketches is framed as genre sketch.

So far, Key and Peele have evolved together within their happy comedy marriage, but it is still subject to all the normal pressures of a marriage (pulling in different directions, wanting different things), and many people close to them, including Zadak, have suggested that it is nearing its natural end. They have other projects under way, some together (including an as yet unnamed Judd Apatow feature) but several apart, though here the Paul-and-John analogy falls short. If and when Key and Peele separate, it will surely be more conscious uncoupling than brutal divorce. Still, there were moments on set when it felt as if they wanted something new thrown at them. Sitting behind a desk at the end of a long day, they tried to nail a short skit with the following mapped-over premise: What if public-school teachers were traded – and paid – like football players? ('Apparently, PS 431 made Ruby an offer she couldn't refuse: 80 million dollars guaranteed over six years, with another 40 million dollars in incentives based on test scores. This salary puts her right up there with Rockridge Elementary's Katie Hope.') There wasn't much maths to do, and hardly any physical business, and they seemed a little bored, making a few uncharacteristic errors. Key, waiting for the cameras to reset, turned to Peele and noted the cushy situation of sports announcers: 'Some people do this shit for a living, *and that's all they do*. This shit is *easy*. Why don't we do this shit?' Peele agreed, but then started laughing, replying in his sports-announcer voice, 'Haven't done it right so far – but still!' The cameras ready, they tried again, messed up again. I got the sense that the problem was that there weren't enough problems.

Some people are simply best suited to a challenge, as Jay Martel reminded me when he emailed, a few days later, with a favourite anecdote from the show: 'In our sketch about competing actors playing Malcolm X and Martin Luther King, we stacked up heightening physical bits, without really stopping to consider if they were physically possible – including asking Keegan (playing Malcolm X) to do the Worm across the stage. When we shot it, Keegan executed a perfect Worm. After the take, he stood up and said, "Apparently, I can do the Worm." He'd never even attempted it before.'

Some Notes on Attunement

The first time I heard her I didn't hear her at all. My parents did not prepare me. (The natural thing in these situations is to blame the parents.) She was nowhere to be found on their four-foot-tall wood-veneer hi-fi. Given the variety of voices you got to hear on that contraption, her absence was a little strange. Burning Spear and the Beatles; Marley, naturally, and Chaka Khan; Bix Beiderbecke, Louis Armstrong, Duke Ellington and James Taylor; Luther Vandross, Anita Baker, Alexander O'Neal. And Dylan, always Dylan. Yet nothing of the Canadian with the open-tuned guitar. I don't see how she could have been unknown to them – it was her peculiar curse never really to be unknown. Though maybe they had heard her and simply misunderstood.

My parents loved music, as I love music, but you couldn't call any of us whatever the plural of 'muso' is. The Smiths owned no rare tracks, no fascinating B-sides (and no records by the Smiths). We wanted songs that made us dance, laugh or cry. The only thing that was in any way unusual about the collection was the manner in which it combined, in one crate, the taste of a young black woman and an old white man. It had at least that much eclecticism to it. However, we did not tend to listen to white women singing very often. Those particular voices were surplus to requirements, somehow, having no natural demographic within the household. A singer like Elkie Brooks (really Elaine Bookbinder – a Jewish girl, from Salford) was the closest we got, though Elkie had that telltale rasp in her throat, linking her, in the Smith mind, to Tina Turner or Della Reese. We had no Kate Bush records, or even the slightest hint of Stevie Nicks, raspy though she may be. The first time I was aware of Debbie Harry's existence, I was in college. We had Joan Armatrading and Aretha and Billie and Ella. What did we need with white women?

It was the kind of college gathering where I kept sneaking Blackstreet and Aaliyah albums into the CD drawer, and friends kept replacing them with other things. And then there she was, suddenly: a piercing sound, a sort of wailing – a white woman, wailing, picking out notes in a non-sequence. Out of tune – or out of anything I understood at the time as 'tune'. I picked up the CD cover and frowned at it: a skinny blonde with a heavy fringe, covered in blue. My good friend Tamara – a real singer, serious about music – looked over at me, confused. *You don't like Joni?* I turned the CD over disdainfully, squinted at the track list. *Oh, was that Joni?* And very likely went on to say something facetious about white-girl music, the kind of comment I had heard, inverted, when I found myself called upon to defend black men swearing into a microphone. Another friend, Jessica, pressed me again: *You don't like Joni?* She closed her eyes and sang a few lines of what I now know to be 'California'. That is, she sang pleasing, not uninteresting words, but in a strange, strangulated falsetto – a kind of Kafkaesque 'piping' – which I considered odd, coming out of Jess, whom I knew to have, ordinarily, a beautiful, black voice. A soul voice. You don't like Joni? *I do not like green eggs and ham. I do not like them, Sam-I-am.*

Perhaps this is only a story about philistinism. A quality always easier to note in other people than to detect in yourself. Aged twenty,

I listened to Joni Mitchell – a singer whom millions enjoy, who does not, after all, make an especially unusual or esoteric sound – and found her incomprehensible. Could not even really recognize her piping as 'singing'. It was just noise. And, without troubling over it much, I placed her piping alongside all the interesting noises we hear in the world but choose, through habit or policy, to separate from music. What can you call that but philistinism? *You don't like Joni?* My friends had pity in their eyes. The same look the faithful tend to give you as you hand them back their 'literature' and close the door in their faces.

In the passenger seat of a car, on the way to a wedding. I no longer had the excuse of youth: I was now the same age as Christ when he died. I was being driven west, toward Wales. Passing through woods and copses, a wild green landscape, heading for the steep and lofty cliffs . . . It is a very long drive to Wales. The driver, being a poet, planned a pit stop at Tintern Abbey. His passenger, more interested in finding a motorway service station, spoke frequently of her desire for a sausage roll. The mood in the car was not the brightest. And something else had been bothering me for several miles without my being quite conscious of its source, some persistent noise . . . But now I focused in on it and realized it was that bloody piping again, ranging over octaves, ignoring the natural divisions between musical bars and generally annoying the hell out of me, like a bee caught in a wing mirror. I made a plea for change to the driver, who gave me a look related to the one my friends had given me all those years earlier, though this was a stronger varietal, the driver and I being bonded to each other for life by legal contract.

'It's *Joni Mitchell*. What is *wrong* with you? Listen to it – it's beautiful! Can't you hear that?'

I started stabbing at the dashboard, trying to find the button that makes things stop.

'No, I can't hear it. It's horrible. And that bit's just "Jingle Bells".'

I hadn't expected to get anywhere with this line, and was surprised to see my husband smile, and pause for a moment to listen intently: 'Actually, that bit *is* "Jingle Bells" – I never noticed that before. It's a song about winter . . . makes sense.'

'Switch it off – I'm begging you.'

'Tintern Abbey, next exit,' he said, closed his jaw tightly, and veered to the left.

We parked; I opened a car door on to the vast silence of a valley. I may not have had ears, but I had eyes. I wandered inside, which is outside, which is inside. I stood at the east window, feet on the green grass, eyes to the green hills, not contained by a non-building that has lost all its carved defences. Reduced to a Gothic skeleton, the abbey is penetrated by beauty from above and below, open to precisely those elements it had once hoped to frame for pious young men, as an object for their patient contemplation. But that form of holy concentration has now been gone longer than it was ever here. It was already an ancient memory two hundred years ago, when Wordsworth came by. Thistles sprout between the stones. The rain comes in. Roofless, floorless, glassless, 'green to the very door' – now Tintern is forced to accept the holiness that is everywhere in everything.

And then what? As I remember it, sun flooded the area; my husband quoted a line from one of the Lucy poems; I began humming a strange piece of music. Something had happened to me. In all the mess of memories we make each day and lose, I knew that this one would not be lost. I had Wordsworth's sensation exactly: 'That in this moment there is life and food/For future years.' Or thought I had it. Digging up the poem now, I see that I am, in some ways, telling the opposite story. What struck the author of 'Lines

Written a Few Miles above Tintern Abbey' (1798) was a memory of ecstasy: 'That time is past,/And all its aching joys are now no more,/And all its dizzy raptures.' The Wye had made a deep impression on him when he'd visited five years earlier. Returning, he finds that he still loves the area, but the poem attests to his development, for now he loves it with a mellowed maturity. Gone is the wild adoration: 'For nature then/(The coarser pleasures of my boyish days,/And their glad animal movements all gone by)/To me was all in all. – I cannot paint/What then I was.' To be back in Wales was to meet an earlier version of himself; he went there to listen to 'the language of my former heart'. And though it's true that the young man he recalls is in some senses a stranger, the claim that he 'cannot paint' him is really a humble brag, because, of course, the poem does exactly that. It's striking to me that this past self should at all times be loved and appreciated by Wordsworth. He understands that the callow youth was the basis of the greater man he would become. A natural progression: between the boy Wordsworth and the man, between then and now. His mind is not so much changed as deepened.

But when I think of that Joni Mitchell-hating pilgrim, standing at the east window, idly wondering whether she could persuade her beloved to stop for some kind of microwaved service-station snack somewhere between here and the church (British weddings being notorious in their late delivery of lunch), I truly cannot understand the language of my former heart. Who *was* that person? Petulant, hardly aware that she was humming Joni, not yet conscious of the transformation she had already undergone. How is it possible to hate something so completely and then suddenly love it so unreasonably? How does such a change occur?

This is the effect that listening to Joni Mitchell has on me these days: uncontrollable tears. An emotional overcoming, disconcertingly distant from happiness, more like joy – if joy is the recognition of an almost intolerable beauty. It's not a very civilized emotion. I can't listen to Joni Mitchell in a room with other people, or on an iPod, walking the streets. Too risky. I can never guarantee that I'm going to be able to get through the song without being made transparent – to anybody and everything, to the whole world. A mortifying sense of porousness. Although it's comforting to learn that the feeling I have listening to these songs is the same feeling the artist had while creating them: 'At that period of my life, I had no personal defences. I felt like a cellophane wrapper on a pack of cigarettes.' That's Mitchell, speaking of the fruitful years between Ginsberg at the abbey and 1971, when her classic album *Blue* was released.

I should confess at this point that when I'm thinking of Joni Mitchell it's *Blue* I'm thinking of, really. I can't even claim to be writing about that superior type of muso epiphany which would at least have the good taste to settle upon one of the 'minor' albums that Joni herself seems to prefer: *Hejira* or *The Hissing of Summer Lawns*. No, I'm thinking of the album pretty much every fool owns, no matter how far from music his life has taken him. And it's not even really the content of the music that interests me here. It's the transformation of the listening. I don't want to confuse this phenomenon with a progressive change in taste. The sensation of progressive change is different in kind: it usually follows a conscious act of will. Like most people, I experience these progressive changes fairly regularly. By forcing myself to reread *Crime and Punishment*, for example, I now admire and appreciate Dostoevsky, a writer who, well into my late twenties, I was certain I disliked. During an exploratory season of science fiction, I checked Aldous Huxley out of the library, despite his hideous racial theories. And even a writer as alien to my natural sensibility as Anaïs Nin wormed her way into my sympathies last summer, during a concerted effort to read writers who've made sex their primary concern.

I don't think it's a coincidence that most of my progressive changes in taste tend to have occurred in my sole area of expertise: reading novels. In this one, extremely narrow arena I can call myself more or less a 'connoisseur'. Meaning that I can stoop to consider even the supposed lowliest examples of the form while simultaneously rising to admire the obscure and the esoteric – and all without feeling any great change in myself. Novels are what I know, and the novel door in my personality is always wide open. But I didn't come to love Joni Mitchell by knowing anything more about her, or understanding what an open-tuned guitar is, or even by sitting down and forcing myself to listen and re-listen to her songs. I hated Joni Mitchell – and then I loved her. Her voice did nothing for me – until the day it undid me completely. And I wonder whether it is because I am such a perfect fool about music that the paradigm shift in my ability to listen to Joni Mitchell became possible. Maybe a certain kind of ignorance was the condition. Into the pure nothingness of my non-knowledge something sublime (an event?) beyond (beneath?) consciousness was able to occur.

I just called myself a connoisseur of novels, which stretches the definition a little: 'an expert judge in matters of taste'. I have a deep interest in my two inches of ivory, but it's a rare connoisseur who does not seek to be an expert judge of more than one form. By their good taste are they known, and connoisseurs tend to like a wide area in which to exercise it. I have known many true connoisseurs, with excellent tastes that range across the humanities and the culinary arts – and they never fail to have a fatal effect on my self-esteem. When I find myself sitting at dinner next to someone who knows just as much about novels as I do but has somehow also found the mental space to adore and be knowledgeable about opera, have strong opinions about the relative rankings of Renaissance painters, an encyclopaedic knowledge of the English Civil War, of French wines – I feel an anxiety that nudges beyond the envious into the existential. *How did she find the time?*

On the Shortness of Life, a screed by Seneca, is smart about this tension between taste and time (although Seneca sympathizes with my dinner companion, not with me). The essay takes the form of a letter of advice to his friend Paulinus, who must have made the mistake of complaining, within earshot of Seneca, about the briefness of his days. In this lengthy riposte, the philosopher informs Paulinus that 'learning how to live takes a whole life', and the sense most of us have that our lives are cruelly brief is a specious one: 'It is not that we have a short time to live, but that we waste a lot of it.' Heedless luxury, socializing, worldly advancement, fighting, whoring, drinking, and so on. If you want a life that feels long, he advises, fill it with philosophy. That way, not only do you 'keep a good watch' over your own lifetime but you 'annex every age' to your own: 'By the toil of others we are let into the presence of things which have been brought from darkness into light.' So make friends with the 'high priests of liberal studies', no matter how distant they are from you. Zeno, Pythagoras, Democritus, Aristotle, Theophrastus: 'None of these will be too busy to see you, none of these will not send his visitor away happier and more devoted to himself, none of these will allow anyone to depart empty-handed. They are at home to all mortals by night and by day.'

Well, sure – but you have also to be open to them. Because you needn't have had even a whiff of whoring in your life to legitimately find yourself too busy to visit Aristotle. Busy changing nappies.

Busy cleaning the sink or going to work. And since, in the contemporary world, we have to place in 'liberal studies' not only a handful of canonical philosophers but also two thousand years of culture – plus a bunch of new forms not dreamed of in Seneca's philosophy (Polish cinema, hip-hop, conceptual art) – you can understand why many people feel rather pushed for time. It's tempting to give up on our liberal studies before even making the attempt, the better to continue on our merry way, fighting, drinking, and all the rest. At least then, we have the satisfaction of a little short-term pleasure instead of a lifetime of feeling inadequate. Still, I admire Seneca's idealism, and believe in his central argument, even if I have applied it haphazardly in my own life: 'We are in the habit of saying that it was not in our power to choose the parents who were allotted to us, that they were given to us by chance. But we can choose whose children we would like to be.' Early on, for better or worse, I chose whose child I wanted to be: the child of the novel. Almost everything else was subjugated to this ruling passion, reading stories. As a consequence, I can barely add a column of double digits, I have not the slightest idea of how a plane flies, I can't draw any better than a five-year-old. One of the motivations for writing novels myself is the small window of opportunity it affords for a bit of extracurricular study. I learned a little about genetics writing my first novel, and went quite far with Rembrandt during my third. But these are only little pockets of knowledge, here and there. I think Seneca is right: life feels longer the more you engage with it. (Look how short life felt to the poet Larkin. Look how little he did with it.) I should be loving sculpture! But I have not gone deeply into sculpture. Instead, having been utterly insensitive to sculpture, I fill the time that might have been usefully devoted to sculpture with things like drinking and staring into space.

Nowhere do I have this sensation of loss as acutely as with music. I had it recently while being guided round an underground record shop, in Vancouver, by a young man from my Canadian publishers who wanted to show me this fine example of the local cultural scene (and also to buy tickets for a heavy-metal concert he planned to attend with his wife). I wandered through that shop, as I always do in record shops, depressed by my ignorance and drawn toward the familiar. After fifteen shiftless minutes, I picked up a hip-hop magazine and considered a Billie Holiday album that could not possibly contain any track I did not already own. I was preparing to leave when I spotted an album with a wonderful title: *More Songs about Buildings and Food.* You will probably already know who it was by – I didn't. Talking Heads. As I stopped to admire it, I was gripped by melancholy, similar perhaps to the feeling a certain kind of man gets while sitting with his wife on a train platform as a beautiful girl – different in all aspects from his wife – walks by. *There goes my other life.* Is it too late to get into Talking Heads? Do I have the time? What kind of person would I be if I knew this album at all, or well? If I'd been shaped not by Al Green and Stevie Wonder but by David Byrne and Kraftwerk? What if I'd been the type of person who had somehow found the time to love and know everything about Al Green, Stevie Wonder, David Byrne *and* Kraftwerk? What a delight it would be to have so many 'parents'! How long and fruitful life would seem!

I will admit that in the past, when I have met connoisseurs, I've found it a bit hard to believe in them entirely. Philistinism often comes with a side order of distrust. How can this person possibly love as many things as she appears to love? Sometimes, in a sour spirit, I am tempted to feel that my connoisseur friends have the time for all this liberal study because they have no children. But that is the easy way out. True connoisseurs were like that back when we were all twenty years old; I was always narrower and more resistant. For some people, the door is wide open, and pretty much everything – on the condition that it's *good* – gets a hearing. And I am indebted to my friends of this kind who have, after all, managed to effect some difficult and arduous changes in my taste. I'm grateful for the re-education, while still fearing that my life will never be long enough to give serious consideration to all the different kinds of wine that can be squeezed out of different kinds of grapes.

With Joni, it was all so easy. In a sense, it took no time. Instantaneous. Involving no progressive change but, instead, a leap of faith. A sudden, unexpected attunement. Or a retuning from nothing, or from a negative, into something soaring and positive and sublime. It will perhaps insult sincerely religious people that I should compare something rare and precious, the 'leap of faith', to something as banal as realizing that *Blue*, by Joni Mitchell, is a great album, but to a person like me, who has never known God (who has only read and written a lot of words about other people who have known God), the structure of the sensation, if not the content, seems to be unavoidably related. I am thinking particularly of Kierkegaard's *Fear and Trembling*, and, even more particularly, of the 'Exordium' ('Attunement') that opens that strange book, and which many people (including me) usually skip, in confusion, to get to the meat of the 'Problemata'. The 'Exordium' is like a weird little novel. In it, Kierkegaard summons up a character: a simple, faithful man, 'not a thinker . . . not an exegetical scholar', who is obsessed with the biblical tale of Abraham and Isaac but finds that he cannot understand it. So he tells it to himself four times, in different versions, as if it were an oral fairy tale that mutates slightly with each retelling.

The basic details stay the same. (In all versions, the ram, and not

Isaac, gets killed.) The variation exists in the reactions of Abraham and Isaac. In the first iteration, Abraham, in order to preserve his son's faith in God, pretends that he, Abraham, hates Isaac and wants him killed. In the second, everything goes according to plan except that Abraham can't forgive or forget what God just asked him to do, and so all joy leaks from his life. In the third, Abraham can't believe how he can possibly be forgiven for something that was so clearly a sin. In the final version, it's Isaac who loses his faith: how could his father have considered the terrible crime, even for a moment? Following each of these retellings, there is a small paragraph of analogy to a quite different situation, that of a mother weaning her child:

> When the child is to be weaned, the mother blackens her breast. It would be hard to have the breast look inviting when the child must not have it. So the child believes that the breast has changed, but the mother – she is still the same, her gaze is tender and loving as ever. How fortunate the one who did not need more terrible means to wean the child!

That's the version following the first story, the one in which Abraham tries to take the rap for the Lord. In these peculiar breast-feeding anecdotes it is not always obvious where the analogy lies. Professional philosophers spend much time arguing over the precise symbolic links. Is God the mother? Is Isaac the baby? Or is Abraham the mother, Isaac the baby, and God the breast? I really haven't the slightest idea. But in each version a form of defence is surely offered, some kind of explanation, a means of comprehending. *It's not that my mother is refusing me milk; it's that I don't want it any more, because her breast is black. It's not that God is asking something inexplicable;*

it's that my father wants me dead. All the versions the simple man tells himself are horrible in some way, but they are at least comprehensible, which is more than you can say for the paradoxical truth: God told me I would be fruitful through my son, and yet God is telling me to kill my son. (Or: my mother loves me and wants to give me milk, yet my mother is refusing to give me milk.) And after rehearsing these various rationalizations the simple man still finds himself confounded by the original biblical story: 'He sank down wearily, folded his hands, and said, "No one was as great as Abraham. Who is able to understand him?" '

When I read the 'Exordium', I feel that Kierkegaard is trying to get me into a state of readiness for a consideration of the actual biblical story of Abraham and Isaac, which is essentially inexplicable. The 'Exordium' is a rehearsal: it lays out a series of rational explanations the better to demonstrate their poverty as explanations. For nothing can prepare us for Abraham and no one can understand him – at least, not rationally. Faith involves an acceptance of absurdity. To get us to that point, Kierkegaard hopes to 'attune' us, systematically discarding all the usual defences we put up in the face of the absurd.

Of course, loving Joni Mitchell does not require an acceptance of absurdity. I'm speaking of the minor category of the aesthetic, not the monument of the religious. But if you want to effect a breach in that stolid edifice the human personality, I think it helps to cultivate this Kierkegaardian sense of defencelessness. Kierkegaard's simple man makes a simple mistake: he wants to translate the mystery of the biblical story into terms that he can comprehend. His failure has something to teach us. Sometimes it is when we stop trying to understand or interrogate apparently 'absurd' phenomena – like the category of the 'new' in art – that we become more open to them.

Put simply: you need to lower your defences. (I don't think it is a coincidence that my Joni epiphany came through the back door, while my critical mind lay undefended, focused on a quite other form of beauty.) Shaped by the songs of my childhood, I find it hard to accept the musical 'new', or even the 'new-to-me'. If the same problem does not arise with literature, that's because I do not try to defend myself against novels. They can be written backwards or without any 'e's or in one long column of text – novels are always welcome. What created this easy transit in the first place is a mystery; I feel I listened to as many songs in childhood as I read stories, but in music I seem to have formed rigid ideas and created defences around them, whereas when it came to words I never did. This is probably what is meant by that mysterious word 'sensibility', the existence of which so often feels innate. I feel sure that had I, in 1907, popped in on Joyce in his garret I would have picked up his notes for *Ulysses* and been excited by what he was cooking up. Yet if, in the same year, I had paid a call on Picasso in his studio, I would have looked at the canvas of *Les Demoiselles d'Avignon* and been nonplussed, maybe even a little scandalized. If, in my real life of 2012, I stand before this painting in the Museum of Modern Art, in New York, it seems obviously beautiful to me. All the difficult work of attunement and acceptance has already been done by others. Smart critics, other painters, appreciative amateurs. They kicked the door open almost a century ago – all I need do is walk through it.

Who could have understood Abraham? He is discontinuous with himself. The girl who hated Joni and the woman who loves her seem to me similarly divorced from each other, two people who happen to have shared the same body. It's the feeling we get sometimes when we find a diary we wrote, as teenagers, or sit at dinner listening to an old friend tell some story about us of which we have no memory. It's an everyday sensation for most of us, yet it proves a tricky sort of problem for those people who hope to make art. For though we know and recognize discontinuity in our own lives, when it comes to art we are deeply committed to the idea of continuity. I find myself to be radically discontinuous with myself – but how does one re-create this principle in fiction? What is a character if not a continuous, consistent personality? If you put Abraham in a novel, a lot of people would throw that novel across the room. What's his motivation? How can he love his son and yet be prepared to kill him? Abraham is offensive to us. It is by reading and watching consistent people on the page, stage and screen that we are reassured of our own consistency.

This instinct in audiences can sometimes extend to whole artistic careers. I'd like to believe that I wouldn't have been one of those infamous British people who tried to boo Dylan offstage when he went electric, but on the evidence of past form I very much fear I would have. We want our artists to remain as they were when we first loved them. But our artists want to move. Sometimes the battle becomes so violent that a perversion in the artist can occur: these days, Joni Mitchell thinks of herself more as a painter than a singer. She is so allergic to the expectations of her audience that she would rather be a perfectly nice painter than a singer touched by the sublime. That kind of anxiety about audience is often read as contempt, but Mitchell's restlessness is only the natural side effect of her art-making, as it is with Dylan, as it was with Joyce and Picasso. Joni Mitchell doesn't want to live in my dream, stuck as it is in an eternal 1971 – her life has its own time. There is simply not enough time in her life for her to be the Joni of my memory for ever. The worst possible thing for an artist is to exist as a feature of somebody else's epiphany.

Finally, those songs, those exquisite songs! When I listen to them, I know I am in the debt of beauty, and when that happens I feel an obligation to repay that debt. With Joni, an obvious route reveals itself. Turns out that while she has been leading me away from my musical home she has been going on her own journey, deep into the place where I'm from:

> For twenty-five years, the public voice, in particular the white press, lamented the lack of four-on-the-floor and major/minor harmony as my work got more progressive and absorbed more black culture, which is inevitable because I love black music: Duke Ellington, Miles Davis. Not that I set out to be a jazzer or that I am a jazzer. Most of my friends are in the jazz camp. I know more people in that community, and I know the lyrics to forties and fifties standards, whereas I don't really know sixties and seventies pop music. So I'm drawing from a resource of American music that's very black-influenced with this little pocket of Irish and English ballads, which I learned as I was learning to play the guitar. Basically, it was like trainer wheels for me, that music. But people want to keep me in my trainer wheels, whereas my passion lies in Duke Ellington, more so than Gershwin, the originators, Charlie Parker. I like Patsy Cline. The originals in every camp were always given a hard time.

I wonder what it will be like to hear the music of my childhood processed through Joni Mitchell's sensibility? I didn't know anything about her 'black period' until I started to write this piece and read some of her interviews online, among them a long discussion she had with a Texas DJ in 1998. Now I mean to seek out this later music and spend some time with it. Make the effort. I don't imagine it *will* be such an effort these days, not now that I feel this deep current running between us. I think it must have always been there. All Joni and I needed was a little attunement. Those wandering notes and bar crossings, the key changes that she now finds dull and I still hear as miraculous. Her music, her life, has always been about discontinuity. The inconsistency of identity, of personality. I should have had faith. We were always going to find each other:

I'm contracted for an autobiography. But you can't get my life to go into one book. So I want to start, actually, kind of in the middle – the *Don Juan's Reckless Daughter* period, which is a very mystical period of my life and colorful. Not mystical on bended knee. If I was a novelist, I would like that to be my first novel. And it begins with the line 'I was the only black man at the party.' (Laughs) So I've got my opening line.

Windows on the Will: Anomalisa

On a wintry afternoon, alone with the kids, I visited the Central Park Zoo. It's not a very big place, just zoo-sized, and after seeing the animals, we found ourselves lining up to enter the little movie theatre to watch something called *The Polar Express 4-D Experience*. A Christmas-themed spin-off from the 2004 movie, it employs the same 'performance capture' animation technique, familiar from video games, in which an actor's movements are turned into computer-generated images. Hero Boy – the original protagonist – is still only about ten years old. We find him in his room, enduring his own voiceover, as spoken by his avuncular adult self, Tom Hanks:

> On Christmas Eve, many years ago, I lay quietly in my bed. I did not rustle the sheets, I breathed slowly and silently. I was listening for a sound I was afraid I'd never hear: the ringing bells of Santa's sleigh.

Hero Boy looks like a human, his flesh is fleshy, his yellow pyjamas flap and wrinkle, and his hair has the hair-like quality of hair. But those eyes! They belong to a puppet, a waxwork, an automaton. Realistic eyes prove a step too far for 3-D imaging. The effect – as many noted the first time around – is creepy. Uncanny valley. But kids don't care. My children loved Hero Boy and his dead zombie eyes, and the snow that fell on their heads from the ceiling of the theatre and the breeze blowing out of their seats on to the backs of their tiny necks. And because I was alone with them, I had nobody to talk with about my own 4-D experience, no one with whom to express that vague dread adults tend to feel in the face of an attempt at absolute verisimilitude. I had no one to bore with a Schopenhauer reference:

> The true work of art leads us from that which exists only once and never again, i.e. the individual, to that which exists perpetually and time and time again in innumerable manifestations, the pure form or Idea; but the waxwork figure appears to present the individual itself, that is to say that which exists only once and never again, but without that which lends value to such a fleeting existence, without life. That is why the waxwork evokes a feeling of horror: it produces the effect of a rigid corpse.

For the children the great interest of the movie – aside from its reality effect – was the manner in which it probed the ontological status of Santa. Is Santa real? For Hero Boy is having a crisis of faith and, sneaking from bed, pulls out a volume of an encyclopaedia and looks up the entry on the North Pole. 'Stark and barren,' he reads. Also: 'Devoid of life.' My thoughts exactly.

The rest is easily summarized: the *Polar Express* arrives, Hero Boy and some other dead-eyed zombie children get on board, and we, the audience, get snowed on, blown on and shaken – as if on a real train – until we reach the real Santa, who exists, and drops a little silver bell from his sleigh, which the boy later finds. The thing about this bell is that only those who 'believe' can hear it ring. While other children grow up and cease being able to hear the ringing of the bell,

Hero Boy always hears it, for the rest of his life, even when he's late-middle-aged Tom Hanks. He believes.

It has no denomination, this belief of the boy's: it belongs to a generalized American faith that long ago detached itself from any particular monotheism, achieving autonomy in and of itself. Believing in belief is what makes Luke a Jedi and Cinderella a princess and Pinocchio a real boy, and my children have been believers of this kind from the earliest age – ever since they could say 'Netflix'. This is the lesson: *If you believe – it will be real!* The movie ended, more snow came down. I wiped the foam from my delighted children and we went back out into the light.

By aesthetic coincidence, that evening I had a date to see Charlie Kaufman's new movie *Anomalisa* with my friend Tamsin, a professional philosopher, a Nietzsche scholar by trade, but not averse to the odd Schopenhauer reference, should a layman – or woman – try to force one upon her. During that long week of solo parenting I'd been carrying around my little pocket Schopenhauer, *On the Suffering of the World*, and it had become, for better or worse, the filter through which I saw everything, from the wants of insatiable children, to the global bad news in *The Times*, to the snow falling from the sky. As we walked to the cinema we considered the idea that all Kaufman's movies have been somewhat Schopenhauerean, in the sense that they concern suffering in one way or another: the experience of suffering, the inevitability of it, and the possibility of momentary, illusory relief from it. This relief tends to arrive, for Kaufman, in the form of a woman (although these women are almost always the cause of much suffering, too). I thought of Catherine Keener, as Maxine, in the film *Being John Malkovich* all those years ago, ravishing in her white shirt and pencil

skirt, offering a schlumpy depressive – a classic Kaufman protagonist – fifteen minutes' relief from his suffering:

Erroll: Can I be anyone I want?
Maxine: You can be John Malkovich.
Erroll: Well that's perfect. My second choice. Ah, this is won-
    derful . . . Malkovich! King of New York! Man about town!
    Most eligible bachelor! Bon vivant! The Schopenhauer of the
    twentieth century!

Now, that last line was cut from the film, but I can take a hint. 'It
had puppets in it,' Tamsin noted, as we took our seats. 'And this
one's all puppets?'
  'All puppets.'
For the second time that day, then, I waited in the dark for
something not quite human – and all too human – to begin. A model
aeroplane flew into view through modelled clouds. Everything to be
seen on screen was modelled, either by hand or digital 3-D printer,
and is the work of the stop-motion-animation specialists Starburns
Industries. In order to suggest the animate quality that surges
through all living things – that makes plants reach for the sun or a
woman fall to the ground or a man scream, turn, and run – these
puppeteers move each model minutely, by hand, photograph it in
that position, and then move it once again. The sixty seconds the
model plane took to fly through those clouds therefore represented
one week's labour for God knows how many people. And on that
little plane, in the year 2005, sits Michael, a British customer-sales
expert, living in LA, but on his way to Cincinnati for a conference,
who is now reading an old letter from an angry ex-girlfriend, Bella.
As he reads she appears before him in ghostly puppet form:

November 12th, 1995. Dear Michael. Fuck you. Just fuck you. You
just walk away?
After all you said to me? After all we did? After all those fucking
promises? After all that *fucking* fucking?

Many viewers, as soon as they hear Bella's voiceover, must at once
understand the central conceit of the movie, but I don't think I was
the only one initially misdirected by wonder. I was too busy
marvelling at the puppets, at the mixture of artifice and realism they
represent, with their peach-fuzz skins of silicone, and their hair-like
hair, and not-quite fluid and yet entirely recognizable human gestures.
Although not physically proportional – they are slightly shorter and
squatter than us – they seem to buy their clothes from the same big-
box stores, and pop the same pills, and use the same neck rests. They
fly the same bland planes and land in the same anonymous airports.
But across their eyes and around their hairline they sport a visible
seam, indicating where the separate plates of their puppet faces fit
together. Usually these seams are obscured in post-production;
Kaufman and his co-director Duke Johnson decided to leave them in,
feeling they 'related to the themes that were in the story'.

The effect is uncanny, but not of the *Polar Express* kind. The seams
feel Brechtian: reminding us that Michael is not real, but representation.
Running contrary to this, though, are his eyes, which really appear to
see as we see. Images pass over their surface, light filters through
them. 'The eyes were a big thing,' Caroline Kastelic, the head pup-
peteer on the film, told the *Hollywood Reporter*. 'They had to have
realistic eyes that reflected the light properly.' A special enamel was
found – one that wouldn't bubble – and hand-painting them took
weeks. The digital eyes of Hero Boy cannot compare. And yet I would
not say that Michael's eyes look real, exactly: they look like a puppet's

eyes. He belongs to a strange new category: a puppet who can see, who feels pain – who suffers! Not an analogy for us, in the Brechtian sense, but rather an *example* of us, in the Schopenhauerean sense, for Schopenhauer thought puppets are essentially what we are:

> The human race . . . presents itself as puppets that are set in motion by an internal clockwork . . . I have said that those puppets are not pulled from outside, but that each of them bears in itself the clockwork from which its movements result. This is the *will-to-live* manifesting itself as an untiring mechanism, as an irrational impulse, which does not have its sufficient ground or reason in the external world.

Yes, to look in Michael's eyes is to know he's suffering. The question is: why? You find yourself diagnosing him by his symptoms. The kind of man who pursues a woman, falls deeply in love, only to then leave – the moment the love is returned – without any explanation, not even one he can give himself. The type who suffers intensely from the boredom and banality of everyday life, who sits in the cab from the airport, wincing in pain as his driver offers unsolicited tips for the overnight visitor:

> The zoo is great. World class, they say . . . Ya, you should check it out. And you gotta try some Cincinnati chili. It's chili like you never had . . . You don't need more than a day for the zoo. It's just zoo-sized . . .

More than anything, Michael suffers from acute loneliness, which can strike you particularly strongly if an overly friendly bellboy called Dennis happens to lead you into the perfect brown-beige sterility of an upscale hotel bedroom (king-size, smoking) and leaves you there.

But it was only at this point, as Dennis shut the door behind him, that I realized the bellboy had the same voice as the cab driver, as Bella, as everyone on the plane – as everyone in the world. That all these people look alike – despite their various heights, weights, genders and hairstyles – is a little more difficult to discern, but also true. Everybody is one person (with the voice of Tom Noonan) except Michael (with the voice of the British actor David Thewlis). When Michael calls room service, it's Noonan who answers. When he phones his wife and son, they're both Noonan. Rewind a little and you notice the name of the hotel Michael has just checked himself into: the Fregoli, a reference to the Fregoli delusion, a rare psychiatric disorder in which a person believes that many different people are in fact a single person. But a narrowly neurological interpretation of *Anomalisa* (i.e., the trouble with Michael is he has a brain lesion) can't account, I don't think, for the profound identification the viewer feels with Michael's experience, or the strong part desire plays in the scheme of his suffering.

The ex-girlfriend Bella sounded like no one else when Michael wanted her and then like everybody else when he didn't. One obvious diagnosis, then, might be that Michael is suffering from a bad case of misogyny. It's a misogynist, after all, who puts a woman on a pedestal only to knock her off, who believes she is speaking to him only, with a voice unique among her kind, until, all of a sudden – and usually after he's detected some minor alteration in her person – she sounds like all the rest of 'em. ('Did you change?' asks Michael of Bella, during an ill-fated reunion in the Fregoli's bar. 'Did anything change? Did a change occur?') But if it were only misogyny, it's unclear why the sameness of Michael's experience should affect everyone he comes across equally, from the bellboy up to and including his own son. Narcissism, then? Certainly Michael has his moments ('They're all one person,' he cries out, during a vivid dream. 'And they love me!') although far more frequently we see him straining toward compassion.

Michael wants to know and understand the people he's hurt, and never exhibits any self-love. But if not narrowly narcissistic Michael is surely solipsistic in the obvious, wider sense that we all are, limited, as he is, by his own subjectivity, his only possible window on the world. Our eyes – popularly 'windows on the soul' – work precisely the other way around, bringing the world to us, in the form of a representation of reality, and it happens that through Michael's own hand-painted enamel everybody appears as one person, or (which amounts to the same thing) as nobody in particular. (In the final scene – the only one Michael is not in, and therefore separate from his subjectivity – we see characters restored to their unique faces and voices, no longer phenomena presented to Michael's consciousness but precisely people in particular.)

Yes, only when Michael desires someone does she become fully real to him. At all other times he is struck by an all-encompassing *Weltschmerz*, into which misogyny, narcissism, solipsism – and a brain tumour! – might all easily be folded. Weariness pervades everything he says and does, the simplest human interactions elicit sighs and groans, and yet this weariness of the world includes his own part within it; or, to put it another way, whatever is driving all the phenomena of the world surges up through Michael, too, taking the form, in him, of a kind of blind striving, a relentless desire for something, which, the moment it is achieved, is already exhausted. *After you get what you want*, runs the old song, *you don't want it. When you get what you want, you don't want what you get.* This is, essentially, the charge Bella lays before Michael. Schopenhauer saw it as a general malaise:

Desiring lasts a long time, demands and requests go on to infinity; fulfilment is short and is meted out sparingly. But even the final satisfaction itself is only apparent; the wish fulfilled at once makes way for a new one.

Once Dennis has left the room, Michael picks up his hotel phone. He is hungry, thirsty. His needs are not complex. But when he tries to order the Bibb lettuce salad and the salmon, this happens:

Room service: Yes, sir. Would you like anything to drink tonight?
Michael: No. I'll find something in the mini-bar.
Room service: Very good. Dessert? We have a lovely —
Michael: No, no, no, no thanks.
Room service: Very good, sir. So that's a Bibb lettuce, Gorgonzola, prosciutto and walnut salad . . .
Michael: Yes.
Room service: . . . with honey raspberry vinaigrette dressing . . .
Michael: Yes.
Room service: . . . and the wild-caught Copper River Alaskan salmon almandine . . .
Michael: Yes.
Room service: . . . with baby asparagus and black truffle broth.
Michael: Yes.
Room service: Very good. And that's for room 1007?
Michael: Yes.
Room service: Very good. It's . . . 9.13 now. It should be there within thirty-five minutes, which will make it . . . 9.48.
Michael: Thank you.
Room service: Thank y—

One way of dealing with the boredom of our own needs might be to complicate them unnecessarily, so as always to have something new to desire. Human needs, Schopenhauer thought, are not in their essence complex. On the contrary, their 'basis is very narrow: it consists of health, food, protection from heat and cold, and sexual gratification; or the lack of these things'. Yet on this narrow strip we build the extraordinary edifice of pleasure and pain, of hope and disappointment! Not just salmon, but wild-caught Copper River Alaskan salmon almandine! And all to achieve exactly the same result in the end; health, food, covering, and so on:

> [Man] deliberately intensifies his needs, which are ordinarily scarcely harder to satisfy than those of the animal, so as to intensify his pleasure: hence luxury, confectionery, tobacco, opium, alcoholic drinks, finery and all that pertains to them.

When Michael hangs up on room service his puppet face is struck through with boredom, an emotion unknown to wild animals, whereas, for us, boredom 'has become a veritable scourge. Want and boredom are indeed the twin poles of human life.'*

Michael's hotel room is, in literal miniature, the concrete expression of the problem. In such a room you can, in theory, get whatever you want, and many things you didn't even realize you wanted. (*Try the chili!* insists the cover of the glossy yet depressingly parochial magazine on Michael's side table. *It's ɀoo-siɀed!* screams the billboard outside his window.) Hotel rooms exist to satisfy. The water in your shower may at first be too hot and then too cold ('Fuck

---

* Schopenhauer argued that a mild form of boredom could be detected in some domesticated dogs and cats.

you! Fuck you!' screams Michael, naked under the shower head) but you can be sure the perfect temperature is achievable, and that when you adjourn to your king-size bed you'll find a chocolate on your pillow. Yet if hotel rooms exist to anticipate desire, to meet and fulfil all our needs, why do we so often feel despair in them? Is the fulfilment of the desire itself the despair?

From his upscale hotel room Michael calls Bella; it's been eleven years since they last spoke. The conversation is awkward. She compliments him on his lodgings. ('It's boring,' he groans in response. 'Everything's boring.') Somehow he manages to convince her to meet him in the hotel bar for a vodka Martini. It goes badly: he can't explain why he so suddenly stopped wanting her, and when he asks her up to his room to discuss it further she walks out. He finds himself out on the street, drunk, still pursued by a ghostly vision of Bella ('And the next minute you're out the door with barely a goodbye!') and seeking a store in which to buy a present for his insatiable son, Henry. In the only kind of 'toy' store that's open at night, Michael finds an antique mechanical Japanese sex doll. She consists of a mechanized torso, half covered in porcelain, with the face of a geisha and her mouth permanently open. She stares out at Michael with her dead zombie eyes. He stares back with the glazed, happy look of the momentarily satisfied customer.

'Thus the subject of willing,' Schopenhauer writes, 'is constantly lying on the revolving wheel of Ixion, is always drawing water in the sieve of the Danaids, and is the eternally thirsting Tantalus.' But what, if anything, lies on the other side of all this endless wanting, getting and wanting again? Back in his room, Michael takes that shower and begins singing Delibes's 'flower duet' from *Lakmé*, in which two voices so beautifully merge they can seem to be one. We heard it in the airport, too, playing on Michael's iPod, and again when Michael tried to hum it to himself in the back of the cab. (Driver: 'That's British Airways!')

Approaching the mirror, he wipes away the steam, stares at himself. He seems on the brink of a realization. We realize his face is moving without him consciously willing it, just like a puppet's face: his eyebrows jerk up and down, his mouth makes odd, unnatural shapes, and dozens of distinct expressions dart over his features. Out of his mouth come strange, unindividuated noises: the indistinct chattering of many people, then the clatter of mechanical gears – or perhaps it's the striking of typewriter keys – and finally a rushing, whooshing kind of emptiness. (Ah, that's what the world would sound like, I found myself thinking, illogically, if there was no one present to hear it.) Michael reaches for the separate plates of his face: he's about to peel them back. Is there a way out of wanting? Perhaps if he were not Michael at all? With his unique face, voice, desires? If he were, in reality, someone, or something, else? Something both less and more than Michael, something . . .

Michael: *Jesus! Someone else!*

Just then, Michael hears a voice in the corridor, a unique voice, unlike all the others! Whatever he was about to realize he instantly forgets: he lets go of his face plates and they click back together. He rushes around the room, seeking his trousers. It is the sound he was afraid he'd never hear again! The voice of someone else! And when this voice speaks, Michael, just like Hero Boy, hears something nobody else hears, something that makes him believe. Madly he runs down the corridor, half dressed, deaf to the warnings of Schopenhauer, as if he's got no idea at all what's going on here, as if he thinks this whole bloody film is about him, Michael, when in reality of course it's all about Schopenhauer:

The striving of matter can always be impeded only, never fulfilled or satisfied. But this is precisely the case with the striving of all the will's phenomena. Every attained end is at the same time the beginning of a new course, and so on *ad infinitum.*

Her name is Lisa. She's staying a few doors down and she's a lovely, homely girl, perfectly average. She has a scar on her face that she tries to cover with hair: people usually prefer her friend Emily. She likes grande mocha frappuccinos, and Cyndi Lauper and Sarah Brightman, she works in a call centre in Akron, drinks mojitos made with apple schnapps, and is generally the very definition of what we might call, if we were being uncompassionate, a basic bitch. To Michael, though, she is the only other person on earth. She has 'a miraculous voice' (which belongs, in reality, to Jennifer Jason Leigh). And to Lisa, too, Michael is magic, an especially individuated individual, because he's famous, he wrote the book *How May I Help You Help Them?*, a customer-service guide that raised productivity, Lisa informs him, by '90 per cent' in her department. When he walks her to his hotel room for a nightcap, she's so anxious she falls flat on her face, succumbing to the will of the world, in the form of gravity. 'It happens all the time,' she assures him.*

The following extended love scene is of such a delicacy and beauty that it reduced the audience to nervous giggles, as if embarrassed to be intruding upon such intimacy between puppets. But before anybody takes off their clothes, Michael, besotted by

---

* We learn that Bella, too, struggles with gravity – 'I have a fake tooth in the front because I fell and hit a cement bench with my mouth' – and perhaps this is where comedy and Schopenhauer meet, somewhere in the tragi-comic inevitability of the pratfall.

Lisa's voice, asks her to sing one of her beloved Cyndi Lauper songs, and Lisa, fearful she is being ridiculed, closes her eyes and cautiously begins. This song should rightly, thematically, be 'True Colors' and so there is something unexpectedly amusing about Lisa opening her miraculous mouth and singing 'Girls Just Wanna Have Fun'.

We get the whole song, in all its lyrical banality,* and it acts as a prelude to sex that proves equally pared down, simple, human, and from which all the usual cinematic fantasy has been stripped. The two sit on the edge of the bed, undressing to reveal our own lumpy bodies. When he gives her head, she is a little shy, as we can be, and he, in his turn, silent and workman-like, as often happens. When they shuffle up to the headboard, they move as we move – laboriously, without elegance – and then lie with each other as we all have, moving back and forth slightly, and finishing about a minute later. What strikes us above all is the gentle compassion these two bodies show each other. Elsewhere in this film, in many chilling glimpses, we see people treating each other without any compassion at all, or with brutality, pushing past one another, yelling at strangers, or standing by the icemaker in the hotel hallway repeatedly telling each other to fuck off. Everywhere you look, the world is pain:

> The life of the individual is a constant struggle, and not merely a metaphorical one against want or boredom, but an actual struggle against other people. He discovers adversaries everywhere, lives in continual conflict and dies with sword in hand.

---

* In accounting for the impact of Lisa's simple rendition we might turn to Schopenhauer explaining the power of folk songs: 'Everything superfluous is prejudicial.'

Still, amid Schopenhauer's pessimism there is this shred of light: compassion. Even if the idea that we have separate bodies at all *is* a form of illusion (enabled only by the supporting illusions of space, time and causality), these bodies of ours still feel pain, still suffer when they are subjugated, oppressed, exploited or simply laughed at. For Michael (and Kaufman) certain women are both a vital source of this compassion and the unique recipients of it.* Lisa, for Michael, is an anomaly. An *Anomalisa*. And this compassion, this choosing of each other, is objectified in their miraculous voices: David Thewlis's Northern English mix of reticence, pragmatism and despair, and Leigh's cloud-free all-American innocence.

Noonan, Leigh and Thewlis were in the original cast of *Anomalisa*, in its previous incarnation as a radio play, and their sublime performances lend the film a rare aural self-sufficiency: you could close your eyes and still enjoy it. And yet, in the 2016 Oscars, this witty and profound script has received no nods, nor is the film nominated for its acting or direction.† A reminder that alongside its noted myopia toward distinct genres, races and subcultures, the Academy has also proved reliably blind to a more general category: genius. (Which category, so problematic for us, is, for Schopenhauer, easily defined: 'The *gift of genius* is nothing but . . . the ability . . . to discard entirely our own personality for a time, in order to remain *pure knowing subject*, the clear eye of the world.')

That same night of the compassionate hook-up, Michael – self-confessed 'sloppy sleeper' – thrashes in his bed. He's having a

---

* Schopenhauer – though he wrote so poisonously of women, hated his own mother and famously pushed his landlady down the stairs – also argued that women tend toward compassion more consistently than men.

† It's up for Best Animated Feature, with *Shaun the Sheep* and *Inside Out*.

nightmare, though as it's happening we think it is real. In this dream, the central problem of the film is restated – everybody is one person – but with an added, paranoid twist: they're out to destroy Lisa-and-Michael! For one of the features of the compassion Michael now feels for Lisa is that he is able to make, in Schopenhauer's words, 'less of a distinction than do the rest' between him and another person; he recognizes, in some sense, that Michael and Lisa are one – and now it's them against the world. As he runs from that world, down the hotel corridor, one of his face plates falls off entirely – we see the grey, gaping cavity beneath – and when Michael wakes up he finds he has hit his new love in the face with an elbow. But what if this nightmare (that Michael, too, is nobody) is not dream at all but a glimpse of a deeper truth?

> Life can be regarded as a dream and death as the awakening from it: but it must be remembered that the personality, the individual, belongs to the dreaming and not to the awakened consciousness, which is why death appears to the individual as annihilation.

That we believe ourselves to be separate from each other, and separate from the apparent objects of our desire, was, for Schopenhauer, the root of our suffering. A better consciousness was possible, one that recognized our essence as 'will' (expressed in us as will-to-live, and objectified, with varying degrees of consciousness, in our urges, desires and actions), and that this essence was not individual but rather shared with all people (not just Lisa), all animals, all plants, all the phenomena of the world. What we can know intimately through our bodies has, for Schopenhauer, its equivalent in the keenness of the iron to fly to the magnet, in the determination of water to flow downwards, in the force of gravity itself, and though such knowledge is not a synonym for 'force' or 'energy', it contains both those terms. The will lies behind all, contains all, is the 'thing-in-itself . . . the innermost essence, the kernel, of every particular thing and also of the whole', a somewhat loopy metaphysics that real academic philosophers, like my friend Tamsin, must take with a large pinch of salt, though it has captivated artists for generations. Is it possible that the problem in *Anomalisa* is not that Michael thinks everybody is the same but that Michael thinks he is Michael?

> Your individuality is not your essential and ultimate being, only a manifestation of it . . . Your being in itself . . . knows neither time nor beginning nor end . . . It exists in everyone everywhere.

The erroneous belief that one is an individual at all – what Schopenhauer called the *principium individuationis* – may be the deeper truth hiding behind Michael's face plates. (It would also help explain his fondness for *Lakmé*, an opera set among the transcendental Brahmin, for whom ultimate reality is likewise 'All-One' and individual existence merely an emanation, made possible by the illusory veil of Maya.)* In the dream we are separate beings. In reality we are one. If only there were a way to reach out to the hinges of your individual face plate and tear away all that stops you from knowing that! But Michael never reaches this awakened consciousness: like so many of us he remains stuck between those twin poles of want and boredom.

---

* The lyrics of the 'flower duet' can be read as a transcendental merging of the many into the one: 'Thick dome of jasmine/Under the dense canopy where the white jasmine/Blends with the rose . . ./Come, let us drift down together.'

With Lisa the change comes far sooner than with Bella. That same morning over breakfast, Michael begins to realize that Lisa's unique voice is disappearing and Tom Noonan's already starting to overlay it. 'Who would've thunk it?' asks Lisa, and Tom Noonan. 'It's just so beautiful. Life can be. Things can work out. That's the lesson.' But the next time she speaks there will be no Lisa, there will be only Noonan. Michael hangs his head in pre-emptive despair. 'Sometimes there's no lesson,' he replies. 'That's a lesson in itself.'

When Michael finally gives his speech on customer service, at the conference podium, it starts pretty well ('And always remember, the customer is an individual. Just like you . . . Each person you speak to has had a childhood. Each has a body. Each body has aches') but soon turns strangely philosophical ('What is it to be human? What is it to ache? What is it to be alive? I don't know. What is it to ache? I don't know . . . Our time here is limited. We forget that. Death comes, that's it. Soon it's as if we never existed. So remember to smile . . .') until it veers off its track altogether and becomes a pessimistic Schopenhauerean rant ('This is not working. The world is falling apart. The president is a war criminal. America is going down the tubes and you're talking about goddamn intelligent design!').

The horrors of the will are historical as much as personal and seem to have no end in view. 'History shows us the life of nations,' writes Schopenhauer, 'and finds nothing to narrate but wars and tumults; the peaceful years appear only as occasional brief pauses and interludes.' What we might find bleakly funny in all this is that Schopenhauer's proposed and partial remedy to this situation – compassion – sounds not very different from Michael's customer-service bromides:

So remember to smile. Remember there is someone out there for everyone. Someone to love. Remember every person you speak to needs love. Remember to –

Conference over, Lisa abandoned, Michael returns home to find his wife Donna throwing him a surprise party. The surprise is he knows nobody and they're all the same person. His son grabs his present, the Japanese sex toy. It starts singing. A liquid oozes from it. Donna asks Michael if it's semen. But Michael does not find that an important line of enquiry. Instead he turns to his wife: 'Who are you, Donna? Who are you *really?*' ('If only,' whispered Tamsin-the-Nietzschean in my ear, 'there was a way to stop asking that question!') Our final vision of Michael is of a man stuck in the middle of a party of nobodies – all with the same face – who is choosing to focus on a singing doll leaking semen, in which substance Schopenhauer saw a clear manifestation of the will, seeking only its own replication and continuance, without regard for what we, as individuals, may 'want'.

What Donna 'really' is, in Schopenhauer's view, is the same thing semen is, really: will. Reality is the will, expressed in everything that we do and are and see, independent of belief; we are both the prisoners and perpetrators of the will, it never lets us go, not even in late middle age, although, every now and then, there will come along an object or experience of sufficient beauty – an aria, say, or an antique Japanese sex doll, or a really good film – that offers itself up to us as an object of aesthetic contemplation, by means of which we might be able, for a moment, to will-lessly contemplate the will. Oh, and also? Be kinder to Donna. Compassion helps. You might not sleep the deep, unruffled sleep of Hero Boy, but in Kaufman's reality (and Schopenhauer's) that's about as good as it's going to get.

Dance Lessons for Writers

The connection between writing and dancing has been much on my mind recently: it's a channel I want to keep open. It feels a little neglected – compared to, say, the relationship between music and prose – maybe because there is something counter-intuitive about it. But for me the two forms are close to each other: I feel dance has something to tell me about what I do. One of the most solid pieces of writing advice I know is in fact intended for dancers – you can find it in the choreographer Martha Graham's memoir. But it relaxes me in front of my laptop the same way I imagine it might induce a young dancer to breathe deeply and wiggle their fingers and toes. Graham writes:

> There is a vitality, a life force, an energy, a quickening that is translated through you into action, and because there is only one of you in all of time, this expression is unique. And if you block it, it will never exist through any other medium and it will be lost. The world will not have it. It is not your business to determine how good it is nor how valuable nor how it compares with other expressions. It is your business to keep it yours clearly and directly, to keep the channel open.

What can an art of words take from the art that needs none? Yet I often think I've learned as much from watching dancers as I have from reading. Dance lessons for writers: lessons of position, attitude, rhythm and style, some of them obvious, some indirect. What follows are a few notes toward that idea.

Fred Astaire/Gene Kelly

'Fred Astaire represents the aristocracy when he dances,' claimed Gene Kelly, in old age, 'and I represent the proletariat.' The distinction is immediately satisfying, though it's a little harder to say why. Tall, thin and elegant, versus muscular and athletic – is that it? There's the obvious matter of top hat and tails versus T-shirt and slacks. But Fred sometimes wore T-shirts and slacks, and was not actually that tall, he only stood as if he were, and when moving always appeared elevated, to be skimming across whichever surface: the floor, the ceiling, an ice-rink, a bandstand. Gene's centre of gravity was far lower: he bends his knees, he hunkers down. Kelly is grounded, firmly planted, where Astaire is untethered, free-floating. Likewise, the aristocrat and the proletariat have different relations to the ground beneath their feet, the first moving fluidly across the surface of the world, the second specifically tethered to a certain spot: a city block, a village, a factory, a stretch of fields. Cyd Charisse claimed her husband always knew which of these dancers she'd been working with by looking at her body at the end of the day: bruised everywhere if it was Kelly, not a blemish if it was Astaire. Not only aloof when it came to the ground, Astaire was aloof around other people's bodies. Through fifteen years and ten movies it's hard to detect one moment of real sexual tension between Fred and his Ginger. They have great harmony but little heat. Now think of Kelly with Cyd Charisse in the fantasy sequence of *Singin' in the Rain*! And maybe this is one of the advantages of earthiness – sex.

When I write I feel there's usually a choice to be made between the grounded and the floating. The ground I am thinking of in this case is language as we meet it in its 'commonsense' mode. The language of the television, of the supermarket, of the advert, the newspaper, the government, the daily 'public' conversation. Some writers like to walk this ground, re-create it, break bits of it off and use it to their advantage, whereas others barely recognize its existence. Nabokov – a literal aristocrat as well as an aesthetic one – barely ever put a toe upon it. His language is 'literary', far from what we think of as our shared linguistic home. One argument in defence of such literary language might be the way it admits its own artificiality. Commonsense language meanwhile claims to be plain and natural, 'conversational', but is often as constructed as asphalt, dreamed up in ad agencies or in the heart of government – sometimes both at the same time. Simultaneously sentimental and coercive ('the People's Princess', 'the Big Society', 'Make America Great Again), commonsense language claims to take its lead from the way people naturally speak, but any writer who truly attends to the way people speak will soon find himself categorized as a distinctive stylist or satirist or experimentalist. Beckett was like this, and the American writer George Saunders is a good contemporary example. (In dance, the example that comes to my mind is Bill 'Bojangles' Robinson, whose thing was tapping up and down the stairs. What could be more normal, more folksy, more grounded and everyday than tapping up and down some stairs? But his signature stage routine involved a staircase pressed right up against another staircase – a stairway to itself – and so up and down he would tap, up and down, down and up, entirely surreal, like an Escher print come to life.) Astaire is clearly not an experimental dancer like Tharp or Bausch but he is surreal in the sense of surpassing the real. He is transcendent. When he dances a question proposes itself: what if a body moved like *this* through the world? But it is only a rhetorical, fantastical question, for no bodies move like Astaire, no, we only move like him in our dreams. By contrast, I have seen French boys run up the steps of the High Line in New York to take a photo of the view, their backsides working just like Gene Kelly's in *On the Town*, and I have seen black kids on the A train swing round the pole on their way out of the sliding doors – Kelly again, hanging from that eternal lamp post. Kelly quoted the commonplace when he danced, and he reminds us in turn of the grace we do sometimes possess ourselves. He is the incarnation of our bodies in their youth, at their most fluid and powerful, or whenever our natural talents combine ideally with our hard-earned skills. He is a demonstration of how the prosaic can turn poetic, if we work hard enough. But Astaire, when he dances, has nothing to do with hard work (although we know, from biographies, that he worked very hard, behind the scenes). He is 'poetry in motion'. His movements are so removed from ours that he sets a limit on our own ambitions. Nobody hopes or expects to dance like Astaire, just as nobody really expects to write like Nabokov.

Harold Nicholas/Fayard Nicholas

Writing, like dancing, is one of the arts available to people who have nothing. 'For ten and sixpence,' advises Virginia Woolf, 'one can buy paper enough to write all the plays of Shakespeare.' The only absolutely necessary equipment in dance is your own body. Some of the greatest dancers have come from the lowliest backgrounds. With many black dancers this has come with the complication of 'representing your race'. You are on a stage, in front of your people and other people. What face will you show them? Will you be your self? Your 'best self'? A representation? A symbol? The Nicholas Brothers were not street kids – they were the children of college-educated musicians – but they were never formally trained in dance. They learned by watching their parents and their parents' colleagues performing on the 'Chitlin' circuit, as black vaudeville was then called. Later, when they entered the movies, their performances were usually filmed in such a way as to be non-essential to the story, so that when these films played in the south their spectacular sequences could be snipped out without doing any harm to the integrity of the plot. Genius contained, genius ring-fenced. But also genius undeniable. 'My talent was the weapon,' argued Sammy Davis Jr, 'the power, the way for me to fight. It was the one way I might hope to affect a man's thinking.' Davis was another Chitlin hoofer, originally, and from straitened circumstances. His logic here is very familiar: it is something of an article of faith within the kind of families who have few other assets. A mother tells her children to be 'twice as good', she tells them to be 'undeniable'. My mother used to say something like it to me. And when I watch the Nicholas Brothers I think of that stressful instruction: be twice as good. The Nicholas Brothers were many, many magnitudes better than anybody else. They were better than anyone has a right or need to be. Fred Astaire called their routine in *Stormy Weather* the greatest example of cinematic dance he ever saw. They are progressing down a giant staircase doing the splits as if the splits is the commonsense way to get somewhere. They are impeccably dressed. They are more than representing – they are excelling. But I always think I spot a little difference between Harold and Fayard, and it interests me, I take it as a kind of lesson. Fayard seems to me more concerned with this responsibility of representation when he dances: he looks the part, he *is* the part, his propriety unassailable. He is formal, contained, technically undeniable: a credit to the race. But Harold gives himself over to joy. His hair is his tell: as he dances it loosens itself from the slather of Brylcreem he always put on it, the irrepressible Afro curl springs out, he doesn't even try to brush it back. Between propriety and joy choose joy.

Michael Jackson/Prince

On YouTube you will find them, locked in many dance-offs, and so you are presented with a stark choice. But it's not a question of degrees of ability, of who was the greater dancer. The choice is between two completely opposite values: legibility on the one hand, temporality on the other. Between a monument (Jackson) and a kind of mirage (Prince). But both men were excellent dancers. Putting aside the difference in height, physically they had many similarities. Terribly slight, long-necked, thin-legged, powered from the torso rather than the backside, which in both cases was improbably small. And in terms of influence they were of course equally indebted to James Brown. The splits, the rise from the splits, the spin, the glide, the knee bend, the jerk of the head – all stolen from the same source. Yet Prince and Jackson are nothing alike when they dance, and it's very hard to bring to mind Prince dancing whereas it is practically impossible to forget Jackson. It sounds irrational, but try it for yourself. Prince's moves, no matter how many times you may have observed them, have no firm inscription in memory, they never seem quite fixed or preserved. If someone asks you to dance like Prince, what will you do? Spin, possibly, and do the splits, if you're able. But there won't appear to be anything especially Prince-like about that. It's mysterious. How can you dance and dance, in front of millions of people, for years, and still seem like a secret only I know? (And isn't it the case that to be a Prince fan is to feel that Prince was your secret alone?)

I never went to see Michael Jackson but I saw Prince half a dozen times. I saw him in stadiums with thousands of people, so have a rational understanding that he was in no sense my secret, that he was in fact a superstar. But I still say his shows were illegible, private, like the performance of a man in the middle of a room at a house party. It was the greatest thing you ever saw and yet its greatness was confined to the moment in which it was happening. Jackson was exactly the opposite. Every move he made was absolutely legible, public, endlessly copied and copiable, like a meme before the word existed. He thought in images, and across time. He deliberately outlined and then marked once more the edges around each move, like a cop drawing a chalk line around a body. Stuck his neck forward if he was moving backwards. Cut his trousers short so you could read his ankles. Grabbed his groin so you could better understand its gyrations. Gloved one hand so you might attend to its rhythmic genius, the way it punctuated everything, like an exclamation mark. Toward the end, his curious stage-wear became increasingly tasked with this job of outline and distinction. It looked like a form of armour, the purpose of which was to define each element of his body so no movement of it would pass unnoted. His arms and legs multiply strapped – literal visualization of his flexible joints – and a metallic sash running left to right across his breastplate, accentuating the shift of his shoulders along this diagonal. A heavyweight's belt accentuated slender hips and divided the torso from the legs, so you noticed when the top and bottom half of the body pulled in opposite directions. Finally a silver thong, rendering his eloquent groin as clear as if it were in ALL CAPS. It wasn't subtle, there was no subtext, but it was clearly legible. People will be dancing like Michael Jackson until the end of time. But Prince, precious, illusive Prince, well, there lies one whose name was writ in water. And from Prince a writer might take the lesson that illusiveness can possess a deeper beauty than the legible. In the world of words, we have Keats to remind us of this, and to demonstrate what a long afterlife an illusive artist can have, even when placed beside as clearly drawn a figure as Lord Byron . . . Prince represents the inspiration of the moment, like an ode composed to capture a passing sensation. And when the mood changes, he changes with it: another good lesson. There's no freedom in being a monument. Better to be the guy still jamming in the wee hours of the house party, and though everybody films it on their phones no one proves quite able to capture the essence of it. And now he's gone, having escaped us one more time. I don't claim Prince's image won't last as long as Jackson's. I only say that in our minds it will never be as distinct.

Janet Jackson/Madonna/Beyoncé

These three don't just invite copies – they demand them. They go further than legibility into proscription. They lead armies, and we join them. We are like those uniformed dancers moving in military formation behind them, an anonymous corps whose job it is to copy precisely the gestures of their General. This was made literal on Beyoncé's 'Lemonade' tour recently when the General raised her right arm like a shotgun, pulled the trigger with her left and the sound of gunshot rang out. There is nothing intimate about this kind of dancing: like the military, it operates as a form of franchise, whereby a ruling idea – 'America', 'Beyoncé' – presides over many cells that span the world. Maybe it is for this reason that much of the crowd I saw at Wembley could be found, for long periods, not facing in the direction of the stage at all, instead turning to their friends and partners. They didn't need to watch Beyoncé any more than soldiers need to look fixedly at the flag to perform their duties. Our queen was up there somewhere dancing – but the idea of her had already been internalized. Friends from the gym stood in circles and pumped their fists, girlfriends from hen nights turned inwards and did 'Beyoncé' to each other, and boys from the Beyhive screamed every word into each other's faces. They could have done the same at home, but this was a public display of allegiance. Janet Jackson kicked off this curious phenomenon, Madonna continued it, Beyoncé is its apex. Here dancing is intended as a demonstration of the female will, a concrete articulation of its reach and possibilities. The lesson is quite clear. *My body obeys me. My dancers obey me. Now you will obey me.* And then everybody in the crowd imagines being obeyed like Bey – a delightful imagining. Lady writers who inspire similar devotion (in far smaller audiences): Muriel Spark, Joan Didion, Jane Austen. Such writers offer the same essential qualities (or illusions): total control (over their form) and no freedom (for the reader.) Compare and contrast to, say, Jean Rhys or Octavia Butler, lady writers much loved but rarely copied. There's too much freedom in them. Meanwhile every sentence of Didion's says: Obey me! Who runs the world? Girls!

David Byrne/David Bowie

The art of not dancing – a vital lesson. Sometimes it is very important to be awkward, inelegant, jerking, to be neither poetic nor prosaic, to be positively bad. To express other possibilities for bodies, alternative values, to stop making sense. It's interesting to me that both these artists did their 'worst' dancing to their blackest cuts. 'Take me to the river,' sings Byrne, in square trousers twenty times too large, looking down at his jerking hips as if they belong to someone else. *This music is not mine*, his trousers say, and his movements go further: *Maybe this body isn't mine, either.* At the end of this seam of logic lies a liberating thought: maybe nobody truly owns anything.

People can be too precious about their 'heritage', about their 'tradition' – writers especially. Preservation and protection have their place but they shouldn't block either freedom or theft. All possible aesthetic expressions are available to all peoples – under the sign of love. Bowie and Byrne's evident love for what was 'not theirs' brings out new angles in familiar sounds. It hadn't occurred to me before seeing these men dance that a person might choose, for example, to meet the curve of a drum beat with anything but the matching curving movement of their body, that is, with harmony and heat. But it turns out you can also resist: throw up a curious angle and suddenly spasm, like Bowie, or wonder if that's truly your own arm, like Byrne. I think of young Luther Vandross, singing back-up a few feet behind Bowie, during 'Young Americans', watching Bowie flail and thrash. I wonder what his take on all that was. Did he ever think: Now, what in the world is he *doing*? But a few performances in, it was clear to everybody. Here was something different. Something old, and yet new.

Rudolf Nureyev/Mikhail Baryshnikov

When you face an audience, which way will you turn? Inwards or outwards? Or some combination of the two? Nureyev, so fierce and neurotic, so vulnerable, so *beautiful* – like a deer suddenly caught in our headlamps – is faced resolutely inwards. You 'can't take your eyes off him', as people like to say, but at the same time he is almost excruciating to watch, because he is unprotected from our gaze. We feel we might break him, that he might crumble – or explode. He never does, but still whenever he leaps you sense the possibility of total disaster, as you do with certain high-strung athletes no matter how many times they run or jump or dive. With Nureyev you are an onlooker, you are a person who has been *granted the great honour of being present while Nureyev dances*. I don't mean this sarcastically: it *is* an honour to watch Nureyev, even in those grainy old videos on YouTube. He's a kind of miracle, and is fully cognizant of this when he dances: And what did *you* do today to warrant an audience with a miracle? (See also Dostoevsky.) With Baryshnikov, I have no fears of disaster. He is an outward-facing artist, he is trying to please me and he succeeds completely. His face dances as much as his arms and legs. (Nureyev's face meanwhile is permanently lost in transcendent feeling.) Sometimes Baryshnikov wants to please me so much he'll even try tap-dancing with Liza Minnelli, risking the scorn of the purists. (I am not a purist. I am delighted!) He is a charmer, an entertainer, he is comic, dramatic, cerebral, a clown – whatever you need him to be. Baryshnikov is both loving and loved. He has high and low modes, tough and soft poses, but he's always facing outwards, to us, his audience. (See also Tolstoy.) Once, I met Baryshnikov over a New York dinner table: I was so star-struck I could hardly speak. Finally I asked him: 'Did you ever meet Fred Astaire?' He smiled. He said: 'Yes, once, at a dinner. I was very star-struck, I hardly spoke. But I watched his hands all the time, they were like a lesson in themselves – so elegant!'

IN THE GALLERY

Killing Orson Welles at Midnight

It's two in the afternoon. No one is groaning; no one turns over in bed or hits an alarm clock – it's much too late for that. 'Love set you going like a fat gold watch' . . . But by two o'clock the morning song is just a memory. We are no longer speculating as to what set us going, we just know we are going. We are less sentimental in the afternoon. We watch the minute hand go round: 2.01 becoming 2.02 becoming 2.03. It's relentless, when you think about it. Mostly we don't think about it. We're very busy, what with everything that's going on. The foreign schoolchildren have already left for the day, a burly gentleman is having his tea in a glass, Billy Liar is being asked, 'What time d'yer call this?' (seventeen minutes past two), and Charlotte Rampling is all by herself eating chocolate éclairs and smoking, in a garden somewhere, in France, probably.

There's no slowing it down and no turning back: the day is too far along to be denied. Though some will try, some always do. At two o'clock precisely a man screams at a grandfather clock ('That'll be enough of that!') and smashes it to pieces. But the day continues. It always does. The Japanese – a pragmatic people, a realistic people – deal with the situation by having a meeting at a long white conference table. Faced with the same reality, we in the West tend to opt for a stiff drink instead. But people will insist upon shooting us sideways glances and saying things like, 'It's two o'clock in the afternoon!' and so we put down our glasses and sigh. The afternoon – free from the blur of hangover or the fug of sleep – is when our shared predicament on this planet becomes clear.

Coincidentally, the afternoon is also the time when many people will first go to see Christian Marclay's *The Clock*. Not too early, just after lunch. After all, it may be good, it may be bad – you don't want to lose a whole morning over it. But very soon, sooner than you could have imagined – in fact at exactly 2.06, as Adam Sandler patronizes a Spanish girl – you realize that *The Clock* is neither bad nor good, but sublime, maybe the greatest film you have ever seen, and you will need to come back in the morning, in the evening, and late at night, abandoning everything else, packing a sleeping bag, and decamping to the Paula Cooper Gallery until sunrise. Except: Christ, is that the time? Oh well. Come back tomorrow.

The things you notice on a second visit are quite small but feel necessary for orientation, like drawing an x and y axis before attempting to plot a great mass of information on a graph. In my notebook I tried to state the obvious, to get it clear in my own mind. *The Clock* is a twenty-four-hour movie that tells the time. This is achieved by editing together clips of movies in which clocks appear. But *The Clock* is so monumental in intention and design that even the simplest things you can say about it need qualification. There isn't, for example, a clock visible in every scene. Sometimes people will only mention the time, or even just speak of time as a general concept. Mary Poppins does less than that; she glances at her wristwatch, the face of which we cannot see, then opens her umbrella and flies, to be replaced, a moment later, by a man, also flying with an umbrella, who soon floats past a clock tower, thus revealing the time. There are many moments like this, and when you first notice them their synchronicity and beauty are a little unnerving. They reveal a creative constraint even larger and more demanding than the one you had assumed. If *The Clock* cares to match a flying umbrella with a flying umbrella, it must have aesthetic currents passing beneath its main flow, moving in a variety of directions, not simply clockwise.

You sit in the dark, trying to figure out *la règle du jeu*. Clearly there are two types of time, real and staged. There are a few ways to say that. Accidental clocks versus deliberate clocks. Time that has been caught on film versus time that has been manipulated for film. It turns out that accidental clocks are more poignant than deliberate clocks. The actors in the street valiantly approximate reality, but the clock tower behind them has captured reality, a genuine moment in time, now passed for ever, unrecoverable, yet reanimated by film. It really was 3.22. 3.22 would have happened, whether it was filmed or not, and consequently this moment feels unvarnished, unmanipulated, true. By contrast, staged time obeys certain conventions. Afternoon sex is the sexiest, probably because it often involves prostitutes. Between four and five o'clock transport is significant: trains, cars and aeroplanes. If the phone rings after one in the morning, do not expect good news. Cuckoo clocks, no matter when they chime, are almost always ominous. When Orson Welles says what time it is, it lends the hour an epic sound. At two a.m. everyone's lonely.

A few clips are anticipated and people applaud when they arrive. Christopher Walken in *Pulp Fiction* with Butch's father's watch up his ass. Big Ben exploding. These are meta-clips, because their clocks are already notorious. Embedded in *The Clock*, all kinds of run-of-the-mill cinematic moments become profound or comic or both. A comment as innocuous as 'I just don't have the time' reduces the audience to giggles. Very unlikely people become philosophers. Owen Wilson, speaking to himself: 'You're about to die. You're on the minute hand of a clock.' Marisa Tomei, in a rowing boat: 'Time is a relative thing . . . an emotional thing!'

Other tendencies are more obscure and may be your own solitary delusion. Watching *The Clock* is a trancelike experience, almost hallucinogenic: you're liable to see things that aren't there. For instance, isn't it the case that the charm of certain actors is so overwhelming they seem to step out of the concept of time? To operate outside it? When Paul Newman lifts his foot on to the bed and ties his shoe and smiles, you find you are no longer waiting for the next clock. You settle in to watch a Paul Newman movie. And when the inevitable cut comes, a sigh passes through the gallery. Is that what people mean when they speak of 'star quality'? The ability to exist outside of time? (This side effect happened rarely, and didn't seem connected to relative fame. Nobody sighed when Tom Cruise came and went.) Repetitions occur, and appear to be meaningful. If we see a lot of James Bond and Columbo it is because time – *staged time* – is their natural milieu. Fake clocks drive their narrative worlds: countdowns and alibis, crime scenes. This may also account for the frequency of Denzel Washington.

The Clock makes you realize how finely attuned you are to the rhythms of commercial (usually American) film. Each foreign clip is spotted at once, long before the actor opens his mouth. And it's not the film stock or even the moustaches that give the game away, it's the variant manipulation of time, primarily its slowness, although of course this 'slowness' is only the pace of real time. In commercial film, decades pass in a minute, or a day lasts two and a half hours. We flash back, we flash forward. There's always a certain pep. 'Making lunch' is a shot of an open fridge, then a chopping board, then food cooked on the stove. A plane ride is check-in, a cocktail, then customs. Principles dear to Denzel – tension, climax, resolution – are immanent in all the American clips, while their absence is obvious in the merest snatch of French art house. A parsing of the common enough phrase 'I don't like foreign movies' might be 'I don't want to sit in a cinema and feel time pass.'

Given that nobody has given you the rules – given that you have imagined the rules – how can you be indignant when these rules of yours are 'broken'? But somehow you are. If Christian Marclay returns to the same film several times – a long 'countdown' scene, say, from some bad thriller – it feels like cheating. And because you have decided that the sharp 'cut' is the ruling principle of the piece, you're at first unsure about music bleeding from one scene into another. But stay a few hours and these supposed deviations become the main event. You start to find that two separated clips from the same scene behave like semicolons, bracketing the visual sentence in between, bringing shape and style to what we imagined would have to be (given the ordering principle of the work) necessarily random. Marclay manages to deliver connections at once so lovely and so unlikely that you can't really see how they were managed: you have to chalk it up to blessed serendipity. Guns in one film meet guns in another, and kisses, kisses; drivers in colour wave through drivers in black and white so they might overtake them.

And still *The Clock* keeps perfect time. And speaks of time. By mixing the sound so artfully across visual boundaries (Marclay's previous work is primarily in sound), *The Clock* endows each clip with something like perdurance, extending it in time, like a four-dimensional object. As far as the philosophy of time goes, Marclay's with Heraclitus rather than Parmenides: the present reaches into the future, the past decays in the present. It's all about the sound. The more frequently you visit *The Clock* the more tempted you are to watch it with your eyes closed. Is that the Sex Pistols leaking into the can-can? Nostalgia is continually aroused and teased; you miss clips the moment they're gone, and cling to the aural afterglow of what has passed even as you focus on what is coming, what keeps coming.

So far *The Clock* has had few opportunities to play to audiences for its full twenty-four hours, but whenever it has the queues have been almost as long as the film itself. Naturally everyone wants to see midnight. 'Why does it always happen at midnight?' asks a young man by a fireplace, underneath a carriage clock. 'Because it does!' replies his friend. In the run-up, only Juliette Binoche in France is able to remain calm: quietly, foxily, ironing a bag of laundry, while wearing a bra-less T-shirt. In America everyone's going crazy. Both Bette Davis and Joan Crawford start building to climaxes of divadom early, at around a quarter to the hour. Jaws going, eyeballs rolling. At ten to midnight Farley Granger looks utterly haunted, though I suppose he always looked that way. At three minutes to midnight people start demanding stays of execution: 'I want to speak to the governor!' And the violins start, those rising violins, slashing at their strings, playing on our midnight angst. This works up into a joke: Marclay can cut seamlessly through dozens of films for the last two minutes without manipulating the sound at all: they all have the same screeching violins, the only difference is the key. At midnight a zombie woman pops out of a grandfather clock and gets a big laugh, but I preferred the clip that came a moment later, when a twelve-foot clockwork soldier, swinging out of a bell tower to mark the hour, impales Orson Welles on his giant sword. It reminded me of Owen Wilson's memento mori: 'You're about to die. You're on the minute hand of a clock.'

Thirst, Taxi Driver, The X-Files, a lot of Kurosawa, *Fatal Attraction, The Prime of Miss Jean Brodie*, some Woody Allen, a little

Bergman – Marclay's sources will be very familiar to his New York and London audiences. Maybe if *The Clock* had been drawn from a more alien culture it would have a different emphasis, but as it is, it's our film and looks at time our way: tragically. 'Do not squander time. That is the stuff that life is made of' – so reads the engraving on an old sundial. We recognize its provenance (Ashley Wilkes's estate, *Gone with the Wind*) and accept it as the gospel of our culture. Time is not on our side. Every minute more of it means one minute less of us. Witness Jeff Bridges in *The Vanishing* (and also some other guy, in the original Dutch version), taking his own pulse and writing it out neatly next to the time. We are tied to the wagon and it's going in only one direction, whether we like it or not.

Film constantly re-enacts and dramatizes this struggle with time: except in film, time loses. We are victorious. Narrative is victorious. We bend time to our will. We tie a man to the floor, put a gag in his mouth and set the clock ticking – but we will decide how fast or slow that clock moves. ESTABLISH TIME: a note written in a thriller. And this is film's whole challenge and illusion. Without it there is no story, no film. If we believe Marclay, no shot in the history of cinema is as common as the desperate close-up of a clock face. ESTABLISH TIME! But the time thus established has, until now, always been a fantasy, a fiction. *The Clock* is the first film in which time is real.

A lot of people speak of a crisis in the purpose and value of the fictional realm. *The Clock* feels to me like a part of that conversation: a factual response to the fantasies of film. It has a very poor predecessor in the TV show *24*, which also promised an end to 'narrative time' but instead bent to commercial concerns, factoring in ad breaks, and was, anyway, with its endorsement of torture, ideologically vile. With its real-time synchronization *The Clock* has upped the ante exponentially. Honestly I can't see how you could up it much more. It's the art object Sontag was hoping for almost half a century ago in *Against Interpretation*, which reminds me that this supposed crisis of the Noughties has in fact been going on a long time: '*Transparence* is the highest, most liberating value in art – and in criticism – today. Transparence means experiencing the luminousness of the thing in itself, of things being what they are.' A very long time. Plato would recognize it.

But what I love about *The Clock* is that while appearing to pass 'beyond' fiction it also honours and celebrates it. Fiction is Marclay's material; after all, he recycles it. What else is *The Clock* if not thousands of fictional interpretations of time *repurposed to express time precisely*. That's why you don't feel that you are *watching* a film, you feel you are *existing alongside* a film. People even leave the gallery following the conventions of time: on the hour, or a quarter past. No one can seem to stand to leave at, say, 6.07. Most wonderful is listening to people on their way out. 'How did he do it, though? You can't google for clocks. How did he do it then? Did he have hundreds of people or what?'

The awe is palpable, and thrilling because it has become so unusual. A lot of the time, when standing in a gallery, I am aware of two feelings, one permitted, and one verboten. The first is boredom: usually the artist's subject is boredom (the boredom of twenty-first-century life, etc.) and my reaction is meant to be one of boredom, or, at the most, outraged boredom. The second is 'wonder at craft'. I am not meant to have this feeling. Asking how something was made, or having any concern at all with its physical making, or being concerned with how hard the thing might have been to make – asking any of these questions will mark me out as a simpleton. The question is childish, reactionary, nostalgic.

But *The Clock* is not reactionary, and manages to reintroduce these questions, without being nostalgic or childish. Marclay has made, in essence, a sort of home-made Web engine that collates and cross-references an extraordinary amount of different kinds of information: scenes that have clocks, scenes with clocks in classrooms, with clocks in bars, Johnny Depp films with clocks, women with clocks, children with clocks, clocks on planes, and so on, and so on, and so on. You're never bored – you haven't time to be.

Really an essay is not the right form in which to speak of it. A visual representation of some kind would be better; a cloud consensus, or a spectacular graph. It's hard to convey in words what Marclay does with data, how luminous he makes it. And if this data were all lined up on a graph, what conclusions would we draw? That life is epic, varied and never boring, but also short, relentless and terminal. *The Clock* is a joyful art experience but a harsh life experience because it doesn't disguise what time is doing to you. At 2.45 p.m., when Harold Lloyd hung off the face of that clock, I couldn't access the delight I have felt in the past watching that fabulous piece of fiction, because if Harold was up on that screen it meant I had somehow managed to come at the same time again, the early afternoon, despite all my efforts to find a different moment, between childcare and work. I looked around the walls of the gallery where all the young people sat, hipsters, childless, with a sandwich in their bags and the will to stay till three in the morning. I envied them; hated them, even. They looked like they had all the time in the world.

Flaming June

I'm trying to think of the first bits of art I ever saw.* They were all in my mum's flat. I don't know why I say 'were' – it's all still there, unchanged. Two small African heads, refined of profile, sit on a bookshelf facing each other. There are many framed posters of elongated Kenyans – or maybe they're Masai – carrying baskets on their heads or walking past the huge orange lozenge of the sun. There's a lot of Africana generally, and as a child I never really loved it or loathed it – it was just there, the wallpaper of our lives. The metaphoric wallpaper. The real wallpaper was/is a very heavy geometric Laura Ashley print, against which all the tribal sculpture, masks and prints are set. The remaining unpapered walls are ox-blood red, as is the sofa, as are the various rugs. It looks like someone has spliced Miss Marple's bedroom with Marcus Garvey's lounge. Visually there's a lot going on.

In the relative relief of the bathroom hangs a black-and-white photograph of black and white kids playing in the East End, in the forties or fifties. I've always liked that. There is also a pencil sketch of my mother in her cain-rows – an idealized portrait of an already beautiful woman – drawn by the only real artist we knew when I was growing up: a bohemian Australian guy married to an Israeli ballet

---

* *Sotheby's Magazine* asked me to write on the first piece of art I ever owned. I wanted to lie but ended up telling the (shameful) truth.

dancer. This thrilling couple lived in bohemian Hampstead, back when that sentence was still economically possible. I admired his sketch, but it unnerved me: there seemed a lot of undisguised desire in it, and I was always worrying (back when my parents were still married) that my father might finally notice. This same Australian was responsible for the sole oil in the place: a small, heavily framed but delicately painted still life of daisies in a blue-and-white jug. In the context of my family aesthetic it has a quite uncharacteristic minimalism. It was the first 'real' painting I ever saw or for which I had any feeling, and even now, if the flat were burning – and all humans accounted for – I think it's the daisies I'd rescue.

But those daisies represent my mother's good taste – or perhaps my father's – and I think the first picture you truly connect with must be the one you choose yourself. And so I wish I had chosen better. It was the first week of college and everyone seemed to be in the same poster shop on Trumpington Street, looking for the print that would best express their personality/attract sexual partners. Ten quid for the poster, fourteen if you took it with a frame. I'm afraid most people chose Klimt, *The Kiss*. Second favourite: something by Schiele in black stockings. Closely followed by Matisse's *Blue Nude*. Slightly more interesting people went for Frida Kahlo. The utterly hopeless simply arrived with their mother's print of Monet's bloody waterlilies and hung it crooked above the bed. A hotbed of radical art theory Cambridge was not. But my choice – *Flaming June* by Frederic Lord Leighton – was no better. Really it was considerably worse, and apart from accurately reflecting a lifelong preoccupation with redheads, when I look at it now I struggle to think myself back into the person who connected with it – who went as far as spending fourteen quid on it! It was an outlier, even at the time. Your Klimts, your Schieles, your Matisses, they were all at least in tune with the nineties aesthetic, their protagonists vaguely resembling that angular young girl of the moment – Kate something-or-other – who was suddenly everywhere, appearing knock-kneed and lank-haired on the front of *i-D* magazine and *The Face*. No one wanted anything to do with a big, fleshy, healthy-looking girl with orange hair happily snoozing among a lot of silk and flowers. Looking at it now the decadence of it makes me laugh – also the incongruence. What's a black girl from Willesden doing with a painting like that? As an attempt to fit in – for I suspect that's what it was – it was wildly off base anyway. While I was trying to demonstrate my appreciation of British aesthetics, it was de rigueur among my fellow students to have, alongside your modernist poster, a piece of 'ethnic' art from your year off: an Asian buddha here, an African mask there. I didn't have a year off. I had done no good works in Africa or anywhere else. Instead, the summer before arriving, I had, in preparation, read a lot of Oscar Wilde and G. E. Moore, and the poetry of the Barrett Brownings, and Christina Rossetti and – well, you get the idea. It was 1994 but my vision of the institution to which I was heading was basically stuck in the 1890s. Art for art's sake! This was the carrot I hung in front of myself as I ground through my A-levels. And if, by some miracle, I got the grades, and if Brent Council covered my rent, well, then – I promised myself – then I will become a totally non-utilitarian person. I am going to spend three years on a sofa thinking about truth and beauty in a long skirt and big floppy hat, my long nose in a book, like a sort of black Ottoline Morrell. I will not count pennies and worry like my father, nor go on marches and take up political commitments like my mother. I am going to live for art.

The miracle came to pass. Blessed Brent Council covered my rent. My uncle gave me £250, an act of such staggering generosity that it is, to this day, still legend among my clan. But unbeknownst to my kind Uncle Howard the first thing I did with his money was buy a red silk chemise from Marks and Sparks. The second: a pair of box-fresh Nike Air. The third: *Flaming June*. A-levels were over. Struggle was over. Willesden was sixty miles hence. From now on I was going to live for love, and art, and food, and silk and nipples and redheads and sleep – lots of sleep. *Flaming June* is not a very good picture, but it was a perfect reflection of my ridiculous mood, at the time.

'Crazy They Call Me': On Looking at Jerry Dantzic's Photos of Billie Holiday*

Well, you certainly don't go out any place less than dressed, not these days. Can't let anybody mistake you for that broken, misused little girl: 'Eleanora Fagan'. No. Let there be no confusion. Not in the audience, or in your old man, in the maître d', or the floor manager, the cops, or the goddamn agents of the goddamn IRS. You always have your fur, present and correct, hanging off your shoulders just so. 'Take back your mink, take back your pearls.' But you don't sing that song, it's not in your key. Let some other girl sing it. The type who gets a smile from a cop even if she's crossing Broadway in her oldest Terylene housedress. You don't have that luxury. Besides: you love that mink! Makes the state of things clear. In fact – though many aren't hip to this yet – not only is there no more Eleanora, there isn't any Billie either. There is only Lady Day. Alligator bag, three rows of diamonds nice and thick on your wrist – never mind that it's three o'clock in the afternoon. You boil an egg in twinset and pearls. They

---

* I was asked to write an introductory essay for a book of Billie Holiday photos. I did try to write an essay about Billie, but every angle seemed too formal or cold. In the end, I opted for some form of ventriloquy instead.

164

got you holed up in Newark for the length of this engagement and one day the wife of the Super says to you: 'So you can't play New York no more, huh? Who cares? To me, you always look like lady.' Nobody can deny. She's Italian. She gets it. No judgement. She says: 'I look after you. I be your mother.' God bless her, but your daughter days are done. And if a few sweet, clueless bobby-soxers, happy as Sunday, stop you on 110th to tell you how much they loved you at Carnegie Hall, how much they loved you on *The Tonight Show*, try your best not to look too bored, take out your pearl-encrusted cigarette box and hand them a smoke. Girl, you must give away twenty smokes a day. You give it all away, it streams from you, like rivers rolling to the sea: love, music, money, smokes. What you got, everybody wants – and most days you let 'em have it. Sometimes it's as much as you can do to keep a hold of your mink.

It's not that you don't like other women, exactly, it's only that you're wary. And they're wary of you right back. No surprise, really. Most of these girls live in a completely different world. You've visited that world on occasion but it's not home. You're soon back on the road. Meanwhile they look at you and see that you're unattached – even when you're hitched – they see you're floating, that no one tells you when to leave the club, and there's nobody crying in a cot waiting for you to pick them up and sing a lullaby. No, nobody tells you who to see and where to go, or if they do you don't have to listen, even when you get a sock to the jaw. Now, the women you tend to meet? They don't know what to do with that. They don't know what to do with the God-blessed child, with the girl that's got her own, who can stay up drinking with the clarinet player till the newspaper boys hit the corners. And maybe one of these broads is *married* to that clarinet player. And maybe the two of them have a baby and a picket fence and all that jazz. So naturally she's wary. You can understand that. Sure. And you've always been – well, what's the right term for it? A man's lady? Men are drawn to you, all kinds of men, and not just for the obvious. Even your best girlfriends are men, if you see what I mean, yes, you've got your little gang of dear boys who aren't so very different from you, despite appearances: they got nobody steady to go home to either. So if some lover man breaks your heart, or your face, you can trust in your little gang to be there for you, more often than not, trust them to come round to wherever you're at, with cigarettes and alcohol, and quote Miss Crawford, and quote Miss Stanwyck, and make highballs, and tell you that you really oughtta get a dog. Honey, you should get a *dog*. They never doubt you're Lady Day – matter of fact they knew you were She before you did.

You get a dog.

Women are wary, lover men come and go and mostly leave you waiting, and truth be told even those dear boys who make the highballs have their own thing going on, more often than not. But you're not afraid to look for love in all kinds of places. Once upon a time there was that wild girl Tallulah, plus a few other ladies, back in the day, but there was no way to be in the world like that, not back then – or no way you could see – and anyhow most of those ladies were crazier than a box of frogs. Nobody's perfect. Which is another way of saying there's no escape from this world. And so sometimes, on a Friday night, after the singing is over and the clapping dies down, there's simply no one and nothing to be done. You fall back on yourself. Backstage empties out, but they're still serving. You're not in the mood for conversation. Later you'll open your vanity case and take a trip on the light fantastic – but right at this moment you're grateful for your little dog. You did have a huge great dog, a while back, but she was always knocking glasses off the side tables and then she went and died on you, so now you got this tiny little angel. Pepi. A dog don't cheat, a dog don't lie. Dogs remind you of you: they give everything they've got, they're wide open to the world. It's a big risk! There are people out there who'll kick a little half-pint dog like Pepi, just for something to do. And you know how that feels. This little dog and you? Soul mates. Where you been all my life? He's like those dogs you read about, that sit on their master's grave for years and years and years. Recently you had a preview of this. You were up in the stratosphere, with no body at all, floating, almost right there with God, you were hanging off the pearly gates, and nobody and nothing could make you come back – some fool slapped you, some other fool sprayed seltzer in your face – nothing. Then this little angel of a dog licked you right in your eye socket and you came straight back to earth just to feel it and three hours after that you were back on a stage, getting paid. Dogs are too good for this world.

Maybe a lot of people wouldn't guess it but you can be the most wonderful aunt, godmother, nursemaid, when the mood takes you. You can spot a baby across a room and make it smile. That's a skill! Most people don't even try to develop it! People always telling these put-upon babies what to do, what to think, what to say, what to eat. But you don't ask anything at all from them – and that's your secret. You're one of the few who just likes to make a baby smile. And they love you for it, make no mistake, they adore you, and all things being equal you'd stay longer if you could, you'd stay and play, but you've got bills to pay. Matter of fact, downstairs right this moment there's five or six of these business-minded fellows, some of them you know pretty well, some you don't, some you never saw before in your life, but they're all involved in your bills one way or another and they say if you don't mind too much they'd like to escort you to the club. It's only ten blocks but they'd like to walk you there. I guess somebody thinks you're not going to get there at all without all these – now, what would you call them? *Chaperones.* Guess somebody's worried. But with or without your chaperones, you'll get there, you always get there, and you're always on time, except during those exceptions when exceptional things seem to happen which simply can't be helped. Anyway, once you open your mouth all is forgiven. You even forgive yourself. Because you are exceptional and so exceptions must be made. And isn't the point that whenever a lady turns up onstage she's always right on time?

Hair takes a while, face takes longer. It's all work, it's all a kind of armour. You got skinny a while back and some guys don't like it, one even told you that you got a face like an Egyptian death mask now. Well, good! You wear it, it's yours. Big red lips and now this new high ponytail bouncing around – the gardenias are done, the gardenias belonged to Billie – and if somebody asks you where exactly this new long twist of hair comes from you'll cut your eyes at whoever's doing the asking and say: 'Well, I wear it so I guess it's mine.' It's my hair on my goddamn head. It's arranged just so around my beautiful mask – take a good look! Because you know they're all looking right at it as you sing, you place it deliberately in the spotlight, your death mask, because you know they can't help but seek your soul in the face, it's their instinct to look for it there. You paint the face as protection. You draw the eyebrows, define the lips. It's the border between them and you. Otherwise everybody in the place would think they had permission to leap right down your throat and eat your heart out.

~

People ask: what's it like standing up there? It's like eating your own heart out. It's like there's nobody out there in the dark at all. All the downtown collectors and the white ladies in their own fancy furs love to talk about your phrasing, that's the fashion to talk about your phrasing, but what sounds like a revolution to others is simple common sense to you. All respect to Ella, all respect to Sarah, but when those gals open their mouths to sing, well, to you it's like someone just opened a brand-new Frigidaire. A chill comes over you. And you just can't do it like that. Won't. It's obvious to you that a voice has the same work to do, musically speaking, as the sax or the trumpet or the piano. A voice has got to feel its way in. Who the hell doesn't know that? Yet somehow these people don't act like they know it, they always seem surprised. They sit in the dark, drinking Martinis, in their mink, in their tux. People are idiots. You wear pearls and you throw them before swine, more or less. Depends what pearls, though, and what swine. Not everybody, for example, is gonna get 'Strange Fruit'. Not every night. They've got to be deserving – a word that means a different thing depending on the night. You told somebody once: 'I only do it for people who might understand and appreciate it. This is not a June-Moon-Croon-Tune. This song tells a story about pain and heartache.' Three hundred years of heartache! You got to turn each room you play into a kind of church in order to accommodate that much pain. Yet people shout their request from their tables like you're a goddamn jukebox. People are idiots. You never sing anything after 'Strange Fruit', either. That's the last song no matter what and sometimes if you're high and the front row look rich and stupid and dull that's liable to be your only song. And they'll be thankful for it! Even though it's not easy for them to listen to and not easy for you to sing. When you sing it you have been described as punishing, you have been described as relentless. Well, you're not done with that song till you're done with it. You will never be done with it. It'll be done with you first.

In the end, people don't want to hear about dogs and babies and feeling your way into a phrase, or eating your heart out – people want to hear about you as you appear in these songs. But they never want to know about the surprise you feel in yourself, the sense of being directed by God, when something in the modulation of your throat leaps up, like a kid reaching for a rising balloon, except most kids miss while you catch it – yes, you catch it almost without expecting to – landing on an incidental note, a perfect addition, one you never put in that phrase before, and never heard anyone else do, and yet you can hear at once that it is perfection. Perfection! It has the sound of something totally inevitable – it's better than Porter, it's better than Gershwin – in a moment you have written over their original versions finally and completely . . . No, they never ask you about that. They want the cold, hard facts. They ask dull questions about the songs, about which man goes with which song in your mind, and if they're a little more serious they might ask about Armstrong or Basie or Lester. If they're sneaky with no manners they'll want to know if chasing the drink or the dragon made singing those songs harder or sweeter. They'll want to know about your run-ins with the federal government of these United States. They'll want to know if you hated or loved the people in your audience, the people who paid your wages, stole your wages, arrested you once for fraternizing with a white man, jailed you for hooking, jailed you for being, and raided your hospital room, right at the end, as you lay conversing with God. They are always very interested to hear that you don't read music. Once you almost said – to a sneaky fellow from the *Daily News*, who was inquiring – you almost turned to him and said, *Motherfucker, I* am *music*. But a lady does not speak like that, however, and so you did not.

Alte Frau *by Balthasar Denner*

Strange to be writing on painting the day after John Berger died. In fact I was asked to do this a long time ago, I am far past my deadline, but it is only now, the day after Berger died, that I find myself sitting down to write it. Berger was ninety. I would say Balthasar Denner's *Alte Frau* is ninety, too, or thereabouts. I never met Berger. This summer I considered a trip, with a mutual friend, to his home in Antony, in the southern suburbs of Paris, but I was staying in the sixth, the city was boiling, the children were with me, and in an example of the kind of wishful thinking that characterizes middle age, I decided there would be another opportunity, another summer. Honestly, I was a little nervous to meet him. What could I say to such a man? What could I offer that wouldn't fall short? I felt something of what I feel now, before the *Alte Frau*, or rather before a small postcard reproduction of it. *Who am I to speak of this painting?* I have her propped up on a little book-chair of violent vermilion. But now, mindful of Berger, I take her off and place her on the dark brown walnut of my kitchen table, and then try her once more against the black card of a document folder. The effect is different each time: she is at her angriest framed by red; resigned and historical against the grain of the wood; an acute memento mori backed by black. But her real context, her true backdrop, is me, the viewer. I chose her after all, from a pile of postcards depicting masterpieces

from the Kunsthistoriches Museum, a stack at least six inches high. I passed through many horses and gods and pietàs and angels and landscapes and crucifixions to get to her. I decided in her favour, over greater paintings and more striking ones, only stopping at her, because – as the layman has it – she spoke to me. I am a laywoman: that is part of the worry. A casual appreciator of painting, a dilettante novelist, a non-expert – not to mention a woman of lower birth than the personage here depicted. I have always had this uneasiness before paintings. And though I am certainly more confident now then when I was young, I am still the type of person who will tend, if I am in a public gallery, to whisper as I stand in front of the art, the type to frantically consult the catalogue before daring to look up. I don't trust myself in front of a painting as I do when I open a book. *What do I need to know in order to look at this object?*

Many years ago, on a trip to the Uffizi with my father, this baleful tendency was thrown into relief by my father's own more relaxed attitude. He was a great fan of Berger, or rather, he was a great fan of Berger's 1972 TV show *Ways of Seeing*, which he referenced throughout my childhood whenever art came up in any context: school permission slips for a gallery visit, a poster advertising the latest Monet blockbuster, a conservative art critic's column in the *Evening Standard*: 'Well, of course, Berger showed them! He told them what's what! He turned over the establishment, the Kenneth Clarks and so on. Art's for everybody – not just the privileged few!' Long before I came across Berger myself I had a childish fondness for him, as the source of my father's apparent late-life confidence in front of a painting. My father had a way of seeing that was not mine, and our ways clashed as we stood there in the Uffizi, in front of the *Venus of Urbino*. I was reading about the duke who had commissioned it. My father meanwhile was remarking on how beautiful she was.

Not the painting – Venus herself. What an attractive body she had, lithe, with good breasts and nice legs, and so on. I was nineteen, easily excruciated. It seemed to me he was almost *aroused* by the painting, and I wished, like the little housemaid in the back of that famous picture, for a nearby linen chest to bury my head in. What a bluestocking I was – and how wrong-headed. Surely many learned things can be said about the *Venus of Urbino* but if you don't open your eyes and recognize her first and foremost as an erotic object how can you claim that you've seen her at all?

I'm not going to make that mistake with the *Alte Frau*. I am writing about her first and foremost because she is an old woman and therefore a destination point on a journey that lies before me. For I have finished being a young woman. Now I embark upon the process of becoming an old one, a long process, to be sure – I don't pretend I am very far along in it – but it would be another kind of delusion to imagine I haven't begun. I choose to bring this reproduction of the *Alte Frau* into my visual field in the hope that she will speak to me of age through the medium of paint. Paintings, Berger believed, speak to us as elements of a language, a modern language, made possible by their reproduction. We don't go to them any longer as pilgrims went to icons to see them in their particular sacred context – instead they come to us. And for a generation of non-experts, working-class aesthetes, generalists, TV viewers, anxious gallery-wanderers, Berger offered a long-overdue process of demystification. He urged us to throw aside the school-taught sensations of high-culture anxiety and holy awe. They were to be replaced with a fresh and invigorating mix of scepticism and pleasure. Scepticism toward the false aura of the masterwork (which largely consisted, in his view, of a toxic mix of capital value and sham religiosity). Pleasure at the meaningful channel that can open up – if we are attentive – between the decontextualized painting and our own sensibilities.

What interests me most about the channel between the *Alte Frau* and myself is how utterly indifferent *she* is to it. As far as eighteenth-century portraits of women are concerned this is unusual. In *Ways of Seeing*, Berger argues that portraits of women in the European tradition are constructed around the concept of availability. The *Venus of Urbino*, for example, offers eternal sexual receptiveness – to the viewer. Everything about her body is arranged in response to our erotic attention. You don't need to be an art theorist to know this. Any woman looking at it can tell you that no woman has ever lain on a bed like *that* without being conscious of a gaze: actual, projected or internalized. 'Men look at women,' wrote Berger. 'Women watch themselves being looked at.' So it is with the *Venus of Urbino*. She exists to be observed, and what consciousness she has is restricted to consciousness of this. *I see you looking at me.*

The *Alte Frau*, on the other hand, seems to me some way past such considerations. For one, she looks resolutely away. No matter how I angle her or move myself in relation to her, I will never catch her eye. Whether I look at her or not appears to be a matter of complete irrelevance, to her. Berger, on Woman: 'From earliest childhood, she is told to survey herself continually. Behind every glance is a judgement . . . Those who are judged not beautiful are not beautiful – those who are, are given the prize. The prize is to be owned – that is to say: available.' But the *Alte Frau* is unavailable. Age has put her outside the bounds of the contest. And perhaps (this painting suggests, to me) it is not so awful to be, once and for all, placed outside of that contest. It is fascinating to learn that when Balthasar Denner showed the *Alte Frau* to a pair of respected Dutch painters and art critics – Adriaen van der Werff and Karel van Mander – they were so stunned by it they could compare it only to the enigma of the *Mona Lisa*. Is it possible that what men consider enigmatic in women is actually *agency?* As in: *If she does not want me, what the hell* does *she want?* In room after room at the Louvre we will find painted women receptive to our gaze, applying for it, offering themselves up for judgement, whether it is the judgement of Paris or Cupid or Brian who just this minute got off the Eurostar. But the most famous portrait in the place, *the exceptional portrait,* is the one of the woman who doesn't appear to want our gaze or need it or even to know we're there. The woman who is in her own world, occupied with her own unknowable thoughts, though she is every hour surrounded by iPhone-wielding tourists. The woman who has ceased to be – or never was – concerned with whether or not you are looking at her. The woman with other things on her mind. Who has, precisely, *mind*! And like that famous enigma, the *Alte Frau,* too, has mind. Her thoughts are inaccessible, and not to do with us, but you can see they exist. Whatever concerns *I* may bring to her – *I'm forty-one! I'm scared of aging!* – it's clear she's heard it all before. Lived it, had the children, lost the children, won and lost the men, the women, the world. Nothing new under the sun.

Of course I am reading the *Alte Frau* through a certain channel of my own creation. I look at her spotted fur and rich silk and see the stubborn commitment to luxury that so many rich women maintain once their flesh has betrayed them, choosing to replace the crumpled, disloyal skin with a new and more glorious surface – fur, silk – which the ruthless logic of capital tells them cannot be devalued as they themselves have been. And I see the great unsexing. The disappearance of gender, over time. To look, in the end, like neither man nor woman. To look only: old. A state that is here neither mourned nor celebrated, only firmly stated, an undeniable destination to which the viewer, too, will travel, *if* they survive, *if* they are as firm and resolute as the *Alte Frau*. I see age without illusion. Wishful thinking, perhaps.

It happens that Denner showed his *Alte Frau* to prospective clients as proof of the quality of his work. It was his calling card. When he took it to London, it caused such a sensation that it had a steady stream of rich and influential visitors, including the ambassador of Austria, who persuaded the artist to sell his famous old lady to Charles VI, Holy Roman Emperor, a deal for which Denner received 5,875 guilders. A simple question occurs: Why? Why was she so popular? It's a question that does not occur in the case of the *Venus of Urbino*, nor with the countless other portraits of beauty, grace, sex and feminine vitality that define the European tradition of female portraiture during this period. Easy to imagine how pleasant it must have been for the Duke of Urbino to stand each morning before his Venus and find her still making eyes at him, ever young and available, even as the wife he commissioned it for aged and wrinkled as wives will tend to do . . . But what did the Holy Roman Emperor – or anyone else – want with a shrivelled old woman? It is not like other portraits in its genre. It is not a comforting portrait of a grandmotherly type. Nor is it a heartening symbolic depiction of wisdom, or at least, if she *is* indeed one of the less deceived, it is not a form of knowledge that appears to have brought with it much peace or satisfaction, as we hope wisdom will. She does not have a peaceful or contented look. That pursed-up little mouth! She is not looking with patient optimism – as with so many portraits of old women – just past the viewer, toward Christ, who awaits her on the other side of the veil that separates life from death. Nor is she a comic grotesque, a warning. No. She simply *is*. To paint her, it is believed, Denner used a magnifying glass, and it is through this process that he caught every patch of facial fuzz, those wrinkles deep and fine, each spidery broken vein and wisp of white hair. The painting was a boast – of technical expertise, of mastery, and by extension of the superior taste of its owner. *My court painter is better than yours.* The *Alte Frau* is the latest thing in portraiture: the King wants it. The human subject may be unappealing but as aesthetic object the painting makes an impressive claim to a new way of seeing: microscopically, scientifically, hyperrealistically, non-symbolically. Just as the old woman has reached a point in her life where she simply *is* – without explanation, defence, application for pity or even understanding – so the paint itself seems to claim an ultimate *thusness*. Marvelling at the technical achievement, proud of scooping such a masterpiece from under the nose of so many deep-pocketed Englishmen, I imagine Charles VI well pleased with his acquisition. Up until the moment he hangs her. Then he finds himself somewhat unnerved. Who *is* this old woman on his wall? Who cost him so many guilders and yet makes no attempt to please? Every time he passes she annoys him a little more. Why does she insist on looking past him, and so severely? She who has no interest in or need of him. Unimpressed, unreceptive. Oh, he still talks her up for curious visitors: here is technical mastery, here is a dear old soul prepared to shuffle off her mortal coil and meet her maker, here is a good woman awaiting her heavenly reward. His guests smile and nod but they're not convinced. Unsettled, they pass on to the next picture. The *Alte Frau* couldn't care less. It matters not what any soul who looks at her thinks of her now – you, me, or the Holy Roman Emperor. She is beyond it all. Beyond!

Mark Bradford's Niagara

There is walking and then there is dancing. Between the two I like to think of a curving line, with plain utility at one end and the scandalously unnecessary at the other. As everyone knows, Marilyn Monroe was pretty far along that curve, as close as one can come to dancing while still walking. In her classic 1953 movie *Niagara* she takes a legendary walk away from the camera, hips swinging – *roiling* – in a mode long since memorialized by catwalk models, drag queens, prima donnas, freaks and queers, street punks of all persuasions. Anyone looking to make their daily stroll down the street something more than the usual slog from A to B.

We have on hand a popular shorthand for this way of moving through the world: 'camp'. But it's a word too often stupidly and narrowly used, or else brutally defined. There is the familiar camp of excess – the extra flourish, the elaborate vibrato, the gold taps on the gold sink – but this is only one corner of camp's vast kingdom. A hip-hop swagger is as camp as Marilyn's mosey. Ditto the young recruit's goose-step march across the parade ground. Camp: *doing more than is necessary with less than you need*. The less-than-you-need part is important. Camp begins in lack, in absence. It is the nuclear option of the disenfranchised. When you take everything from the slave, for example – family, clothes, paper, ink, and finally even his drum – you then leave only the body, yes, only that. And one of the

things the disenfranchised slave did with his body was the shim-sham, that fabulous dance of a walk, as camp as any movement on earth. Camp is our flagrant and delicious survival *in the face of* and *despite the fact*. Camp makes lemonade without lemons – or sugar. It can make cocktails – as Frank O'Hara once had it – 'out of ice and water.' And now I watch Mark Bradford's neighbour walking away from me just as Marilyn did, albeit in a baggy pair of yellow shorts, battered boots, a half-ruined vest, and pristine white tube socks. Here is sex appeal and swagger and a fierce aesthetic, all managed on the tiniest of budgets. An outdoor public performance for whoever happens to be watching. *All eyes on me.* What does the unseen passer-by make of him? We can't know, but we certainly understand that not all such walks are received equally. Here is Marilyn, for example, in her very last interview, recalling one of her own earliest walks:

> The whole world was always closed to me . . . you know? I just felt like I was on the outside of the world and suddenly when I was eleven – everything opened up! Kids in school . . . well, it's true mostly they were boys but even the girls paid a little attention to you just because they thought: *hmm, she's to be dealt with!* For instance I had this long walk to school . . . It was a two-and-a-half-miles to school and a two-and-a-half-miles back and it was just sheer pleasure! Every fellow honked his horn and I'd wave back and I thought: gee, what happened?! The world became friendly, you know? It opened up to me.

For Marilyn, a large part of this was technique, a response to her puberty but not a necessary one: she chose the path. It was an affect she learned to 'turn on'. But some of us may find we have less choice about it: we never *could* simply walk from A to B, it doesn't come naturally. Indeed it would be a great and effortful performance in itself to walk 'straight'. This can be dangerous: our place on the curve is too visible to everybody at all times. We are at the mercy of others – gawkers, school bullies, stand-up comics, guffawing audiences – who are all too eager to humiliate and demean. There used to be a category in the New York drag balls – 'Realness' – precisely to defend against such humiliation. Realness was about walking in a convincing straight line. Could you get from A to B in the dullest way possible, as if dancing to B never occurred to you? Can you play it straight, look utterly real? Pass when passing is required? A cloak of temporary invisibility. Marilyn, by contrast, chose to make herself permanently sexually visible, but she did it in the knowledge that when a hot blonde dances down the street – in America at least – the world opens up to her. (Although that's not the whole story, as Marilyn well knew: all the approval couldn't heal the wound within her, and for this reason she remains an idol to street punks, drag queens, prima donnas, freaks and queers, and all the lost and wounded. But still: at the level of performance, for Marilyn, the world 'opened up'.)

In Bradford's *Niagara* there's no way of knowing if the world is open for his neighbour's performance or filled with daily threat and fear. As with Marilyn's walk, possible viewers are not contained in the frame – the walk itself takes up the visual landscape. The image is defiant in its very hermeticism, it is fabulously insulated and self-sufficient. It is a performance *in the face of* and *despite the fact*. Way ahead of him we can see the traffic light showing its red hand – symbol of a closed world – but he pays it no mind and strides into the future no differently when this light eventually turns and stays green. Camp does not ask permission. It marches to the beat of its own drum. You are king – or queen – of this particular stretch of sidewalk, simply because you woke up this morning and decided that it should be so. In such walks we spy resistance, defiance, joy. It is a miraculous matter that some people should be able to telegraph all these things simply by walking. It is as if, having realized that invisibility is not a viable option, they choose to do something practical with their constant audience. *You looking at me? Well now, let me give you something to see!* In this frame of mind, a pothole in the sidewalk is easily overcome by way of a joyful and balletic leap.

I want to linger on the word 'frame'. What turns a walk into a strut is precisely a frame, even if the frame is only a certain intention. Just as it is in a gallery, something has been isolated and therefore illuminated. I had never seen endpapers, for example, not really – though I had used them often enough in my hair – until Bradford framed them for me. Turning utility into pleasure is a deep, rich seam in his work. Those now famous endpapers, once employed – by the artist himself – in the treatment of hair, he transformed into a wavelike visual grammar. He gave the people of New Orleans an ark that does not literally rescue yet still uplifts. He has appropriated and revealed merchant posters, demonstrating the dynamic and visual artistry that exists in street-level local economies all over America. *Doing more than is necessary with less than you need.* This has been the cultural legacy of so many oppressed and minority groups in America. 'We shall overcome' is the phrase that historically has encapsulated their struggle: the approved, authentic, mainstream and acceptable face of struggle. It is a noble slogan. But underneath it and all around us is the unruly daily application, which has as much to do with leaping defiantly over cracks in the sidewalk as with sit-ins and marches, speeches and elections. 'As a culture,' Bradford claimed, in a 2009 interview, 'the black community is in flux.

Nobody knows who's in charge, and everybody's screaming that it's them, but ain't nobody really at the helm right now.' In 2016 the Black Lives Matter movement has consolidated this sense of a leaderless movement with foot soldiers in every corner of the land. Some of them are indeed sitting in and marching and campaigning, but it's my sense that many more have taken the message and applied it in disparate ways to their daily practice. I see black hair, in its natural state – free of endpapers – springing out of all the scalps of my friends and students and myself. I see kids expanding the old strictures of the hip-hop aesthetic into Afro-punk and Afro-weird and black-girl-magic and every kind of hyphenated existence. And I see the walk. I see folks making a lot of a little.

To swagger and to slay. To take it to church – or to the bridge. Killing it, shaking it, remaking it. All eyes on *me*. Camp is a dunk shot in a ballgown. It's knowing that sometimes the most brutal words you'll ever have thrown at you in the street will come from the people who look just like you. Given that this is true, there can be defiance in the smallest, campiest of actions. In being seen in all your glory, and within the terms of your own self-conception. If you can slay in a pair of baggy old yellow shorts and a tattered vest! Bradford reminds us of the performance art of everyday life, the political urgency of street-level grace.

A Bird of Few Words: Narrative Mysteries in the Paintings of Lynette Yiadom-Boakye

The exhibition space on the fourth floor of the New Museum, in New York, is a long room with a high ceiling. You might expect towering video screens in here, or something bulky and three-dimensional, requiring circling – entering, even. But on a recent day the room was filled with oils. The show has a melancholy, literary title, 'Undersong for a Cipher', and consists of seventeen paintings hung low, depicting a set of striking individuals, all slightly larger than human scale, though not imposingly so. Most are on herringbone linen; one is on canvas. It's impossible to avoid noticing that they are all – every man and each woman – physically beautiful. Mostly they are alone. They sit, stretch, lounge, stand, and are often lost in contemplation, their eyes averted. If they are with others, the company is never mixed, as if too much heat might be generated by introducing that half-naked man over there to this sharp-eyed dancing girl.

In the oeuvre of the British-Ghanaian painter Lynette Yiadom-Boakye, there are quite a few dancers, lithe in their leotards, but all her people look as though they might well belong to that profession. They are uniformly elegant. One young man puts his hands on his knees and laughs, with his legs apart and his feet turned out; he is dressed simply, like the rest, in blocks of swiftly laid paint, creating here a black vest, there some white trousers. No shoes. The artist dislikes attaching her figures to a particular historical moment, and there's no way around the historicity of shoes. Sometimes the men hold animals like familiars – an owl, a songbird, a cat. The colours are generally muted: greens and greys and blacks and an extraordinary variety of browns. Amid this sober coloration splashes of yellow and pink abound, and vivid blues and emerald greens, all tempered by the many snowdrop gaps of unpainted canvas, like floral accents in an English garden.

The surrounding walls are painted a dark heritage red, bringing to mind national galleries and private libraries, but also, for this viewer, the books you might find in such places, specifically the calico covers of nineteenth-century novels. This red has the effect of bringing a diverse selection of souls together, framing and containing them, much like a novel contains its people, which is to say, only partially. For Yiadom-Boakye's people push themselves forward, into the imagination – as literary characters do – surely, in part, because these are not really portraits. They have no models, no sitters. They are character studies of people who don't exist.

In many of Yiadom-Boakye's interviews, she is asked about the source of her images, and she tends to answer as a novelist would, citing a potent mix of found images, memory, sheer imagination and spontaneous painterly improvisation (most of her canvases are, famously, completed in a single day). From a novelist's point of view, both the speed and the clarity are humbling. Subtleties of human personality it might take thousands of words to establish are here articulated by way of a few confident brushstrokes. But the deeper beguilement is how she manages to create the effect of wholly realized figures while simultaneously confounding so many of our assumptions about the figurative. The type of questions prompted by, say, Holbein

(What kind of a man was Sir Thomas More?) or Gainsborough (What was the social status of Mr and Mrs Andrews?), or when considering a Lucian Freud (What is the relation between painter and model?), are all short-circuited here, replaced by an existential query not much heard in contemporary art: Who *is* this? The answer is both literal and liberating: No one. Nor will the titles of these paintings identify them. A dancing girl in the midst of an arabesque bears the caption 'Light of the Lit Wick'. A gentleman in an orange turtleneck with a cat on his shoulder: 'In Lieu of Keen Virtue'. That antic fellow with his hands on his knees: 'A Cage for the Love'. We have become used to titles that ironize or undercut what we are looking at, providing conceptual scaffolding for feeble visual ideas, or weak punchlines to duller jokes. For Yiadom-Boakye, titles are allusive; they should be considered, she has said, simply as 'an extra mark in the paintings'. For an artist, she is unusual in describing herself as a writer as much as a painter – her short stories and prosy poems frequently appear in her catalogues. In a recent interview in *Time Out*, she reflected on the relation between these twin roles. 'I don't paint about the writing or write about the painting,' she said. 'It's just the opposite, in fact: I write about the things I can't paint and paint the things I can't write about.' Her titles run parallel to the images, and – like the human figures they have chosen not to describe or explain – radiate an uncanny self-containment and serenity. The canvas is the text.

Given the self-confidence of this work, it's strange to note the anxiety that Yiadom-Boakye provokes in some critics. In the catalogue that accompanies the New Museum show, there is an essay by the academic art critic Robert Storr in which he deems it necessary to defend the work against the perceived retrogression of figurative painting: 'If you accept Greenbergian premises and methodologies, representation was definitively eclipsed by abstraction sometime in the early fifties' – a line of argument that might lead you to believe Clement Greenberg is still busy over at *Commentary* instead of being dead for more than two decades. The mid-century debate over the figurative and the abstract – which Greenberg's coining of the term 'post-painterly abstraction' did much to further – aligned the figurative with illusion: the illusion of depth in a canvas, and the pretence of three-dimensional human life on what was, in truth, an inert, two-dimensional surface. The figurative was fundamentally nostalgic; its subject matter was kitsch; it was too easily manipulated for the purposes of propaganda, both political and commercial. Sentimental scenes of human life were, after all, what the Nazis and the Stalinists had championed. They were what the admen of Madison Avenue utilized every day. Meanwhile, the abstract sought to continue, in the realm of the visual, the modernist critique of the self. But, even when a critic allows for the somewhat antique formulation of these arguments (as Storr goes on to do), there is still something about the vicarious emotion provoked by the figurative that must be explained away or excused.

And so, in the same essay, Yiadom-Boakye is cautiously framed as the kind of artist who depicts an extreme otherness: 'The impact of her pictures is of encountering people "we" – the general North American art audience – have never met, coming from a world with which "we" are unfamiliar. One that we have no basis for generalizing about or projecting our fantasies onto.' Yet the subjects of these paintings are not members of a recently discovered indigenous tribe in Papua New Guinea but, rather, many handsome black men and women in unremarkable domestic settings.

There is a respectful caution in this kind of critique which, though undoubtedly well intended in theory, in practice throws a patronizing chill over such work. Yiadom-Boakye is doing more than exploring the supposedly uncharted territory of black selfhood, or making – in that hackneyed phrase – the invisible visible. (Black selfhood has always existed and is not invisible to black people.) Nor are these paintings solely concerned with inserting the black figure into an overwhelmingly white canon. Such pat truisms have a limited utility, especially when we find them applied without alteration to artists as diverse as Chris Ofili, Kerry James Marshall and Kehinde Wiley. Ofili, in a delicate written response to Yiadom-Boakye's work, passes over the familiar rusty argument of figuration versus abstraction and attends instead to the intimate visual details: 'The tightness of her bun. The size of his ear. She knew so much about so little of him. She said so little he heard so much.' Exactly. Here are some paintings of he and she, him and her. They say little, explicitly, but you hear much.

There are a few moments when the paintings also seem to respond more or less directly to a generalized notion of the 'white canon'. An overly literal triptych, *Vigil for a Horseman*, features a handsome man laid out – in three different art-historical poses – on a candy-striped divan, calling to mind a riot of similar loungers: the Rokeby Venus, the picnickers of *Le Déjeuner sur l'herbe*, Adam meeting the finger of God, a Modigliani nude. But these are the weaker moments in the show. The strongest paintings pursue an entirely different relation: not the narrow point-for-point argument between artist and art history but the essential, living communication between art work and viewer, a relationship that Yiadom-Boakye reminds us is indeed vicarious, voyeuristic, ambivalent and fundamentally uncontrollable.

For even if you are intimately familiar with the various shades of brown on offer here – even if you've always known these particular broad noses, the specific kink of Afro hair, the blue and orange tints that rise up through very dark skin – you are still, as a viewer, entirely engaged in the practice of fantastical projection. The figures themselves are the basis for your fantasy, with their teasing, ambiguous titles, women dancing to unheard music, or peering through binoculars at objects unseen. They seem to have souls – that ultimate retrogressive term! – though by 'soul' we need imply nothing more metaphysical here than the sum total of one person's affect in the mind of another. Having this experience of other people (or of fictional simulacra of people) is an annoyingly persistent habit of actual humans, no matter how many convincing theoretical arguments attempt to bracket and contain the impulse, to carefully unhook it from transcendental ideas, or simply to curse it by one of its many names: realism, humanism, naturalism, figuration. People will continue to look at people – to listen to them, read about them, or reach out and touch them – and on such flimsy sensory foundations spin their private fantasias. Art has many more complex pleasures and problems, to be sure, but still this consideration of 'souls' should be counted among them.

And when I asked myself, inevitably, who these souls in the gallery were, I thought of a group of intensely creative people in a small community, living simply in poky garrets, watchful and sensitive, determined and focused. Sometimes when they were flush – having sold a painting or a story – they'd do something purely for aesthetic pleasure, like buy a candy-striped divan or an owl or travel to Cádiz. Early New York beatniks, maybe, or some forgotten, south London chapter of the Bloomsbury Group. Poets, writers, painters, dancers, dreamers, philosophers – and lovers of same.

This fantasy was certainly my own projection, but I could find its narrative roots in the muted, modernist colour palette and the 'timeless' clothes, which turn out to be not so timeless: during the early decades of the twentieth century, Vanessa Bell wore these simple shifts (and no shoes) and Duncan Grant painted both his daughter and his Jamaican lover, Patrick Nelson, in similar swift blocks of colour, where shirt or blouse meets trousers or skirt in a single mussed line, without recourse to belts or buttons. Yiadom-Boakye often cites the unfashionable British painter Walter Sickert as an influence, and it is perhaps here that the congruence occurs: Virginia Woolf was also an admirer of Sickert, and published a monograph about him; Vanessa, her sister, illustrated the cover.

Born in 1860, and a member of the Camden Town Group, Sickert, like Yiadom-Boakye, was gifted at painting wet-on-wet (completing canvases quickly, to avoid having to break the 'skin' of paint that had dried overnight), disliked painting from nature and specialized in ambivalently posed figures in domestic settings, about whom one longs to tell stories. Certainly from Sickert (and Degas before him) Yiadom-Boakye has inherited a narrative compulsion, which has less to do with capturing the real than with provoking, in her audience, a desire to impose a story upon an image. Central to this novelistic practice is learning how to leave sufficient space, so as to give your audience room to elaborate. (Sickert, with his spooky and suggestive tableaux of Camden prostitutes, was so successful in doing this that he unwittingly planted the seeds of an outrageous fiction – that he was Jack the Ripper, a theory still alive today.)

Yet the keenness to ascribe to black artists some generalized aim – such as the insertion of the black figure into the white canon – renders banal their struggles with a particular canvas, and with the unique problem each art work poses. (For Yiadom-Boakye, the problem of a painting, she has said, begins with 'a colour, a composition, a gesture, a particular direction of the light. My starting points are usually formal ones.') It also risks flattening out individual conversations with tradition. Kerry James Marshall, for his recent show 'Mastry', at the Metropolitan Museum of Art, included a marvellously eclectic and unexpected selection of pieces from the

Met's permanent collection, a supplementary 'show within a show', which had the effect of positioning Marshall's own 'mastry' as both a confrontation with and a continuation of the familiar Western European mastery of such figures as Holbein and Ingres. But Marshall also took us on a journey down side roads more obscure and intimate, deep into the thickets of an artist's individual passions. Why, out of all the masterpieces in the Met, does a man pick out a certain Japanese woodblock print, or a bull-shaped boli from West Africa? These are the mysteries of personal sensibility, often obscure to critics but never less than essential to artists themselves.

Sometimes the process of making art is a conversation not so much with tradition as with the present moment. Born in 1977, Yiadom-Boakye was nineteen when an exhibition of works from the collection of Charles Saatchi, 'Sensation', opened in London, at the Royal Academy. The show presented, among other excitements, Damien Hirst's shark, the Chapman brothers' polymorphously perverse child mannequins, and Sarah Lucas's mordant mattress with its cucumber penis. 'Sensation' and its Young British Artists dominated the art conversation, enraptured the tabloids and relegated British portraiture to the debased realm of one-note arguments and conceptual gimmicks. (The most famous portrait in 'Sensation' – Marcus Harvey's *Myra*, a re-creation of a notorious photo of the British child-murderer Myra Hindley, rendered in a child's handprints – sparked so much controversy that the show was almost shut down.) Even the good work was ill served by the central conceit of the show, which encouraged visitors to look 'past' the paint to the supposed sensation of the manifest content (Chris Ofili's madonna with elephant dung, Jenny Saville's 'fat' female nudes). At the time, Yiadom-Boakye had just finished a dispiriting one-year foundation course at Central Saint Martins, a prestigious art school in London, where she'd discovered, as she explained in a 2013 interview with Naomi Beckwith, a curator at the Museum of Contemporary Art in Chicago, that the conversations about her chosen form revolved around 'what painters should or shouldn't be doing, linked to what the art world was or wasn't doing/saying'. Some relief came when she left London, to pursue a BA at Falmouth College of Arts, in Cornwall, where the discussion was broader, though no less stringent: 'If you were going to paint, you had to have a bloody good reason to do it. There was shame involved.'

By the time Yiadom-Boakye returned to London, to do an MFA at the Royal Academy, she had endured many lectures on the death and/or the irrelevance of painting, and her own practice came to reflect some of these debates. Some of her earlier work, by her own admission, uses narrative literally, with both image and title supporting each other tautologically. From the Beckwith interview: 'Four black girls standing with headphones on plugged into the floor, basically taking instructions from the devil, and its title was: 'The Devil Made Me Do It' . . . I hadn't really defined a style yet. Because I hadn't got to grips with painting yet, I ignored the actual power that painting could have; I didn't trust that paint could do anything.'

In the early noughts, her work began to feature rather cartoonish figures, which perhaps owe something to George Condo's grotesques and carry with them the strong sense of a young artist giving herself a deliberate handicap, or, to put it another way, a series of exploratory formal constraints. In these works, blackness seems to be depicted from the outside and therefore appears – as blackness is often seen, by others – under the sign of monstrosity. (A parallel example is Kerry James Marshall's *A Portrait of the Artist as a Shadow of His Former Self* (1980), in which the artist appears as a grinning, minstrelesque mask.) Asked, in an email, about this earlier style,

Yiadom-Boakye replied, 'It must have been a reaction to a lot of what was said to me. Humour and horror made sense because that was how I felt. Oftentimes it really worked, other times it was hugely dissatisfying. I think that's why I got rid of so much of it as I went along. Over time I realized I needed to think less about the subject and more about the painting. So I began to think very seriously about colour, light and composition. The more I worked, the more I came to realize that the power was in the painting itself. My "colour politics" took on a whole new meaning.'

One of the most persistent misapprehensions that exists between artists and viewers – and writers and readers – concerns the relative weight of content and form. Just as, in the mind of a writer, individual novels will tend, privately, to be considered 'not the one in which John kills Jane' or 'the one in which Kwame gets married' but, rather, 'the one with the semicolons' or 'the one in which I realized the possibility of commas' so that which looks like figuration to a layman like me ('Isn't that a beautiful fellow with his owl?') is, for the artist, as much about paint itself – its various possibilities, moods and effects, limits and freedoms. In non-figurative work, these technical preoccupations are perhaps easier to spot, but whether a human figure can be discerned in the work or no, the same battles with colour, light, composition and tone apply. One way to track intellectual movements in the arts is to follow the rise and fall of content versus form (as Susan Sontag, in her essay 'On Style', pointed out not long after Greenberg effected his great separation of the abstract from the figurative). Falsely separating the two – and then insisting on the elevation of one over the other – happens periodically, and often has the useful side effect of revitalizing the art practice of the time, repressing what has become overly familiar or championing the new or the previously ignored.

'Sensation' marked Britain's parochial, delayed response to thirty years of complex aesthetic theory (mostly French and American) that had privileged content (in the form of 'the concept') over form, but it also fatally and impurely mixed these ideas with the careerism of the YBAs themselves, who contributed their own professional anxieties, dressed up in contempt. Portraiture came to be considered 'content', and therefore a subject that could be exhausted, despite (or maybe because of) its long, exalted history. And, once it was deemed to be exhausted, the consensus was that only the most hubristic (or nostalgic) young British artist would dare attempt it. *What is she trying to prove? Who does she think she is — an Old Master?* If you were a student in art school at the time, these debates could sound as much personal as theoretical. Over the years, Yiadom-Boakye has responded in paint, but also in writing, though always obliquely, as she seems to respond to everything. Some of her stories and poems involve people, and many more involve animals, but all of them have the sly, wise tone of fable. In a typically Kafkaesque short prose poem, 'Plans of the Night', she gives to an owl and a 'Deeply Sceptical Pigeon' the role of artist and antagonist:

> *It was possible to perform the feats for which he was famed*
> *During the Day.*
> *But for the Owl there was something Infinitely Preferable*
> *About the Night.*
> *The Owl had difficulty explaining this to other birds.*

The same difficulty, I imagine, that a young, talented painter at Saint Martins in the late nineties might have had explaining her preference for portraiture:

The Pigeon argued that the Owl's insistence on a Nocturnal Routine
Had more to do with Self-Mythologizing and
By extension, Self-Aggrandisement
Than any Practical Need.

But in fact the Owl has 'his mind on other things'. He is an owl obsessed with practice itself, which, in his case, involves the hunting of a mouse in the grass. But the Sceptical Pigeon won't let it go:

This Mystery, it's not real you know.
You're as dull and predictable as the Rest of Us.

The Owl, silent, focuses on his prey. Meanwhile, the Pigeon continues to upbraid him for his unseemly ambition:

How appropriate! Always sat a Bough or two higher than the Rest of Us,
looking down on everyone as usual.
. . .
You think you're Special, that you have some Authority over the Night.

The Owl, no longer listening, readies himself to swoop and catch that mouse, but, when he finally does so, his wing smacks the Pigeon in his head, breaking his neck and killing him. Cold comfort – the mouse, who has witnessed it all, escapes:

The Owl, a Bird of Few Words, cursed the Pigeon for depriving him of a
meal
. . .
The Owl decided to go in search of something substantial
Like a rabbit or a mole or a skunk.

'Under-song for a Cipher' is substantial. There is an owl-like virtuosity to it, silent, unassuming – but deadly. Not yet forty, Yiadom-Boakye is a long way down the path to 'mastry', and you do not doubt she will reach her destination. But the past two decades of art criticism have not been kind to formal mastery: it has been considered something inherently suspicious, a message sometimes too swiftly absorbed by artists themselves. From an essay on Yiadom-Boakye, 'The Meaning of Restraint', by the French cultural critic Donatien Grau: 'We can sense virtuosity in every inch of the artist's paintings, but it is always rather subdued, and never blatantly exposed. She makes the decision to not abandon herself in representational extravagance, to rather be discreet in the demonstration of her painterly capacity.'

Those days are done: here is blatant virtuosity, hiding in plain sight, and the restraint has shifted to the narrative itself, which now offers us only as much as we might need to prompt our own creative projections – no more, no less. Many critics have noted that this return to 'painterly capacity' is particularly notable in black artists, and, strange indeed, that they should be the gateway – the permission needed – to return to the figurative, to the possibility of virtuosity! Why this might be the case is a fraught question, and Yiadom-Boakye, in her interview with Beckwith, proves herself slyly aware of its implications: 'How many times have I heard from someone saying, "You're lucky. You were born with a subject." Well, isn't everyone?'

It's a familiar, backhanded compliment. *Blackness is in fashion – lucky you!* Implicit is the querulous ressentiment of the Sceptical Pigeon, who would be the type to come right out and say it: if these paintings were all of white people, would they have garnered the same attention, the same success? (In 2013, Yiadom-Boakye was shortlisted for the Turner Prize, and in the past few years her paintings have begun to sell at auction for prices approaching seven hundred thousand dollars.) Well, the new has an aesthetic value, of this there is no doubt, and it's one that any smart artist is wise to exploit. But what Yiadom-Boakye does with brown paint and brown people is indivisible. Everyone is born with a subject, but it is fully expressed only through a commitment to form, and Yiadom-Boakye is as committed to her kaleidoscope of browns as Lucian Freud was to the veiny blues and the bruised, sickly yellows that it was his life's work to reveal, lurking under all that pink flesh. In his case, no one thought to separate form from content, and Yiadom-Boakye's work is, among other things, an attempt to insist on the same aesthetic unities that white artists take for granted.

'Under-song for a Cipher'. If it were a novel's title, we would submit it to textual analysis. *Undersong*: 1. A subordinate or subdued song or strain, esp. one serving as an accompaniment or burden to another. 2. An underlying meaning; an undertone. *Cipher*: 1. A person who fills a place, but is of no importance or worth, a nonentity, a 'mere nothing'. 2. A secret or disguised manner of writing, whether by characters arbitrarily invented, or by an arbitrary use of letters or characters in other than their ordinary sense. To these definitions, taken from the *Oxford English Dictionary*, I'd add the significance of 'cipher' in hip-hop: a circle of rappers taking turns to freestyle over a beat. Then, with this knowledge in hand, I might turn to one Yiadom-Boakye painting in particular, *Mercy over Matter*, in which a man holds a bird on his finger. The undersong here is underplumage: those jewel-like greens and purples and reds you can spot beneath the oil-slick surface of certain black-feathered birds. The man's jacket magically displays this same underplumage; so does his skin; so does his bird. He is a black man. He is often thought of as a nothing, a cipher. But he has layers upon layers upon layers.

The Tattered Ruins of the Map:
On Sarah Sze's Centrifuge

In writing about *Centrifuge* I'm at a disadvantage. Like so much of Sarah Sze's work, *Centrifuge* is a complex constellation of elements, in which all constituents present themselves simultaneously. But to write and to read is to move necessarily from left to right in a linear fashion: I plot a course from A to B, you follow it, we are both equally constrained in the same direction. This is frustrating. The temptation is to respond to *Centrifuge* in kind, with a linguistic constellation, perhaps a scattered display.

But I am an analog person, born in 1975, and can still be overwhelmed by simultaneity. In fact, walking into Sze's studio with a gaggle of children provided a telling contrast: they found nothing peculiar in this centrifuge constructed from thin bamboo sticks, upon which hang slices of reality – *cinema* – recorded, repurposed and projected on to little scraps of dangling paper, themselves held in place with bulldog-clips and tape, like a home-made image search engine. My sense was that if it was a centrifuge it appeared to be broken: the circular structure only three-quarters closed, like a half-ruined amphitheatre, damaged in some seismic event. But to them, it was almost familiar, simply a sort of exploded iPhone, with all the technology deconstructed and the liberated images floating free in the world. (In this, their instincts happened to be correct: most of the snatches of film were shot on Sze's iPhone.) The eldest daughter of

Representation   Elemental separations

               Image culture

                              Simulacra   Shadows

          Caves

Spielberg

                                        TV static

               The coliseum

          Baudrillard

The map and the territory   Home-made image search engine

                    Borges

                                        Plato

Materiality

                                   Immateriality

               iPhones

               Google Earth   Nostalgic toddlers

Recorded time

          Real time

                         The Unabomber

Hauntings

                    Seams

          Mirrors   Screens in boxes

               Screens in hands

Liberated screens

                         Ponds

                              Forces and states

          Projections and projectors

the artist found it somewhat 'creepy' that a certain piece of film should be of herself, a year earlier, sleeping. But no child present thought twice about the Pyramids of Giza hanging next to a clay pot (eternally being painted orange) next to a hummingbird taking off, a building coming down, moons, skies, flowers opening and closing, a milk drop in slow motion, a stop-motion butterfly emerging from its chrysalis, popcorn popping, volcanoes and rain storms, woods and waterfalls, bullets and burning pyres, and so much more and so much else. This landscape of concomitant images, this procession of disconnected visual simulacra, was as natural as mother's milk to them. On one flimsy screen a tiny, tracking arrow shifted across the surface of the earth, impatiently pulling itself over countries and oceans – as if it had an autonomous desire to get somewhere in particular – but to those raised to traverse a planet just like this – in a moment, using Google Earth – there was nothing too remarkable in this, either. Only the several scraps of screen that displayed analog TV static – or 'snow' – gave them pause: as children of the digital age it was completely unknown to them.

For me – and I must presume for the artist (born 1969) – things are different. For us, the image-map that has been made of the world is not exactly the same as the territory itself, or rather, we can still remember – if only very vaguely – a moment in time when the seams were still partially visible. A time just before the time we ceased thinking of images as the representation of any particular external reality and started to live within images themselves. *Centrifuge* – simultaneously nostalgic and apocalyptic – takes us back and forward to the moment before (or after?) image entirely overlaid phenomena and screen ate world. And when we are confronted with Sze's centrifugal swirl of rapidly revolving ideas, I say it is hard to know which element to separate from the rest. Yet if you are to write about something you *must* choose, and so I choose the next-door room in the studio, in which a companion piece, as yet unnamed, partially repeats *Centrifuge* and reflects upon it. Here the bamboo scaffold continues, and the same flickering scraps of screens hang from it, but the main amphitheatre is now presented in the form of a desk – the artist's own – one of these semicircular working areas that create a private cocoon for whoever places their Aeron chair into the snug, enclosing gap. Sitting behind such desks, consulting perhaps two or three screens at once (desktop, laptop, phone), we are the masters of our domains, daily fabricating our own visual maps of the territory. Sze takes the types of images we store in our personal hardware and projects them outwards, remaking them as apparently independent objects in the world, and refitting them with a sense – however partial – of actuality and authenticity. (On the surrounding walls, for example, projections of animals run, each at their own speed, but Sze has mapped their *relative* speeds so that the difference between the bird and the big cat as they race round the room is as it would be in reality. Aligning recorded images to present time is one way of tethering the symbolic order more firmly to the real. A similar effect is achieved by Christian Marclay.) This is a sense rarely available to the millions of us who now spend the larger part of our lives in the consideration and curation of digital simulacra, roving round the world without so much as leaving our chairs. Every kind of image is available to us: random, chosen, local, global, microscopic, immeasurable, personal, political, sacred, pornographic, iconic, anonymous. And, after the workday is over, the process seamlessly continues, thanks to the miniature computer/camera in our pockets. In this life, the material world becomes peripheral, although it continues to exist, dragging itself slowly behind us like uncoiled viscera, often unpleasant and inconvenient yet apparently still necessary. How tiresome it is to eat and drink and dress and move one's body and take a shit! But all these things must be done, and around Sze's desk the abject evidence of bodily existence lingers, the remnants and effluvia of the non-virtual world. Toilet paper, milk cartons, many empty food boxes. Pot-plants, packaging from Amazon, a tower of tatty books. On top of which pile there sits the *Collected Fictions* of Jorge Luis Borges. And inside *that* you will find Borges' famous one-paragraph tale, 'On Exactitude in Science', which tells of 'a map of the Empire whose size was that of the Empire, and which coincided point for point with it'.* In this fable, the ingenious map eventually falls out of favour, as it happens that following generations are 'not so fond of the Study of Cartography'. They neglect the map, considering it useless, and so it is left to rot, although by some desperate folk it is repurposed: 'In the deserts of the West still today, there are tattered Ruins of that Map, inhabited by Animals and Beggars.' It was this Borgesian sketch that was famously repurposed by the philosopher Jean Baudrillard, in his *Simulacres et simulation*, a book that transforms allegory into theory, while reversing the moral of the tale. In Baudrillard's vision of post-modernity, it is reality that has become a kind of tattered ruin, a desert. It is the map itself upon which we all now, seamlessly, live.

How can this simulation we live within be made truly visible to us? Perhaps only a total rupture could affect it. In the ruins of a catastrophic event we can imagine an inspired, practically minded artisan undertaking the construction of something like *Centrifuge*. She would be someone who recalls the simulation and believes she can re-create it piece by piece, with the materials available – with whatever is to hand. But how could you reboot, using only what was

---

* 'On Exactitude in Science', Jorge Luis Borges, translated by Andrew Hurley.

left? Unwieldy, ugly, heavy, noisy, white projectors might do the trick, casting their various simulations on to those barely there screens, and further abroad, to the containing space, although this stream of images is sometimes interrupted with the message *Now Loading* – the digital equivalent of TV snow – which zips round Sze's studio walls like a shadow, like a ghost. Now loading the world and everything in it. Or might it not be the work of a figure like the Unabomber, who turns from technology in favour of the 'natural', of the 'real', but is simultaneously forced to re-create, out in the woods, at least some of its systems (bomb-making, computer viruses) precisely to communicate his rejection? *Centrifuge* comes back to us from the future, with a memory of how we once lived. Consider the Colosseum, in whose image *Centrifuge* is built. It is a model of the repurposed image factory – and an object lesson in the desertification of the real. Once, the Colosseum was a place of performance, in which faithful copies of the world – sea battles and dramatic re-enactments and combats between man and beast – were performed. Now it is the distant and somewhat unconvincing original source of an infinite series of postcards, tea-cosies, snow-globes, and so on, a place where Romanian migrants dressed as centurions charge tourists for selfies in front of a crumbling edifice they know only from the movie *Gladiator*. And, just like all those little colosseums you can buy within the Colosseum, *Centrifuge* contains a little version of itself in its left-hand corner, a colosseum within a colosseum. In its broken bamboo centrifuge flickers an identical selection of images, but all of it miniaturized. A map to the territory, at a scale of about an inch to a yard.

After the rupture, after the apocalypse, amid the ruin of cables and wires, someone might ask: what was the purpose of all of those images within and through which we lived? (Just as Romans, in the Middle Ages, wondered about the great stone arc of antiquity that lay at the end of the Via dei Fori Imperiali, but, mostly uninterested in the answer, instead stripped it for parts.) What was the Internet? What was it for? How did it feel? In the rubble somewhere, patching together this and that, *Centrifuge* would be one form of an answer, for it not only recalls the recent image factories of our iPhones but the infinitely longer history of our image-making practices, period. The pre-histories of symbol, image and simulacra are continually evoked, from Plato's shadows in the cave – which those projectors cast all around the room – to our earliest sources of image replication: mirrors, water. You can place your hand in front of one of the projectors and see an image factory laid out on your palm, but you can also lean over one of the many shards of glass and see your palm repeated there, as pure reflection, and then again there are pieces of film that project a reflecting pool or puddle over a secondary image – of the sky or a black wall – so that the light that dances on water is consumed by the landscape behind it and reflects nothing at all. Paint – once the great medium of image replication – is also present, though it is put in its place. It is only another 'material'. Little scraps of it are daubed here and there, or spilt, or left to harden in thin wafer scraps that hang from the structure like plastic bags caught in the branches of trees. Gone but not forgotten.

To the great mass of images to which we are every day subjected – and to which we ourselves industriously contribute – Sze applies a centrifugal force, separating base elements from each other. If most of these images are from her iPhone it is to be noted that they are never social images. There are no relationships recorded, no conversations, or even people passing time together. She has chosen instead only those pieces of film that demonstrate forces and states. To go fast, to go slow. To be open/closed or whole/broken. To fall and to rise. To be wet, to be dry. Heat and cold, forward and back, light and dark. To be orange. To explode, to wither. A few shards feature Sze's daughters but what is captured in those moving images is not human personality but rather human states: child sleeping, child running, child submerged in water. This is not to say the work is impersonal or cold: exactitude in science involves looking as closely and intimately at your subject as any poet. But different qualities are picked out. *Centrifuge* speaks of one of our oldest technological instincts: to record what we have seen. In rock, in pencil, in print, in paint, in film – and now in pixels. Images have always been a form of haunting, but when film arrived it became possible to see the dead walking and talking, something previously only conceivable in the realms of witchcraft and myth, and though film has never lost its trace of the occult we have always attempted to tame, control or disguise it. Once upon a time, cinema screens were flanked by reassuring velvet curtains, as if to convince us that what we were watching was simply a more vivid version of theatre. Our televisions used to nestle in great wooden containers, disguised as perfectly ordinary pieces of bourgeois furniture. But sometimes, when you came downstairs in your pyjamas, to get a glass of water at 2 a.m, and the TV was still on – emitting that strange fizzing 'snow' – didn't you feel the presence of something . . . else? During my childhood (and Sze's) Steven Spielberg was the great popular interpreter of these strange screen emissions; he saw that our technology was trying to tell us something through all that mesmerizing static. But what was the message? Sometimes, as in *Poltergeist*, historical demons haunted it (note to self: never build a house on an Indian burial ground) but elsewhere, in *ET* and *Close Encounters*, disturbances in electromagnetic waves signalled an attempt at communication, to which we were to respond with our own technology. This technology tended to be basic, home-made, cobbled together. Spielberg – an incorrigible technological optimist – always shunned the spectre of apocalypse, but like Sze he was deeply attracted to home-made tech, and so to create the necessary conditions usually placed his stories in the hands of technological incompetents – children, or 'everymen' – who were then forced to use 'whatever was to hand'. This is perhaps why – of all the images in *Centrifuge* – it strikes me, as a child of the eighties, that it is only Sze's Spielbergian static that represents a break or rupture in the image factory, a seam that allows for the possibility that images not only communicate with each other but can attempt a communication with *us*. For TV static is what happens when your television tries to turn junk signals from elsewhere into images. These signals can come from other appliances, from distant cables, from stray radio waves. But they can also be the unimaginably distant echoes of the Big Bang, arriving from a distance of many billions of years, travelling down our old analog TV antennas and interpreted as that flickering black-and-white dance of fizzing atoms. Only there, in the static, can I make out the seam between the real and the image. Only there do I experience a transmission that is not merely a replication, but rather a genuine transformation and communication of an event, authentic in itself. I look again at that scrap of screen, upon which a child runs past the Pyramids of Giza. That is not the child nor is it Giza, they are only representations – copies. But when I look at analog snow, I am truly in the presence of the audiovisual remnants of the Big Bang, I can see the past haunting the present, speaking to me – shimmering.

In our digital age it is tempting to say that we are no longer haunted by external phenomena as we once were. The seam is gone.

The source cut off. The image, freed from hardware – and disturbances from the universe – can haunt whatever space, unimpeded. It doesn't speak of the beginnings of the world any more, or have any hint of alien life about it. Instead we seem to be the ghosts in our own machines. Sze's eldest daughter looked at her sleeping image with something like wistfulness, and I myself have known many a nostalgic toddler who bends like Narcissus over his mother's phone to gaze at images of himself drinking milk from the breast or sleeping in his cot. He sighs blissfully – he wonders where the time has gone. We are being constructed out of images of ourselves, haunted by our own past, by last year, last week, by #throwbackthursday. We have become so used to summoning up dead images of ourselves that we barely notice we live among ghosts, and it is left to our artists to truly spook us, to make us see anew what has become second nature.

Centrifuge plays this role wonderfully – the role of the art-spectre – not least because it was originally commissioned to haunt the Middle Hall of the Haus der Kunst in Munich. That survivor of neoclassical Nazi architecture is itself an infamous simulacrum – a monument to a glorious Greco-German past that never existed – and it was within its galleries that Hitler hoped to effect a centrifugal separation of pure from 'degenerate' art. What better place for Sze's haunted image factory, which records the twenty-first century's deep-dive into the supremacy of the image, but never forgets the persistent abjection of real human bodies, which, unlike images, must at some point meet their end.

Getting In and Out

You are white —
yet a part of me, as I am a part of you.
That's American.
Sometimes perhaps you don't want to be a part of me.
Nor do I often want to be a part of you.
But we are, that's true!
As I learn from you,
I guess you learn from me —
although you're older — and white —
and somewhat more free.

— Langston Hughes, from 'Theme for English B'

Early on, as the opening credits roll, a woodland scene. We're upstate, viewing the forest from the perspective of a fast-moving car. Trees upon trees, lovely, dark and deep. There are no people to be seen in this wood — but you get the feeling somebody's in there somewhere. Now we switch to a different world. Still photographs, taken in the shadow of public housing: on the basketball court, the abandoned lot, the street corner. Here black folk hang out on sun-warmed concrete, laughing, crying, living, surviving. Both the shots of the woods and the city have their natural audience, people for whom such images are familiar and benign. There are those who think of Frostian woods as the pastoral, as America the Beautiful, and others who see summer in the city as, likewise, beautiful and American. One of the marvellous tricks of Jordan Peele's debut feature, *Get Out*, is to reverse these constituencies, revealing two separate planets of American fear – separate but not equal. One side can claim a long, distinguished cinema history: *Why should I fear the black man in the city?* The second, though not entirely unknown (*Deliverance*, *The Wicker Man*), is certainly more obscure: *Why should I fear the white man in the woods?*

A few years ago I interviewed Peele as he came to the end of a long run on the celebrated sketch show *Key and Peele*. On that occasion he spoke about comic reversals ('I think reversals end up being the real bread and butter of the show') and of finding the emotional root of a joke in order to intensify it: 'What's the mythology that is funny just because people know it's not true?' *Get Out* is structured around such inversions and reversals, although here funny has been replaced, more often than not, with scary, and a further question has been posed: which mythology? Or, more precisely: whose? Instead of the familiar, terrified white man, robbed at gunpoint by a black man on an urban street, we meet a black man walking in the leafy white suburbs, stalked by a white man in a slow-moving vehicle, from whose stereo issues perhaps the whitest song in the world: 'Run, rabbit, run, rabbit, run run run . . .'

Get Out flips the script, offering a compendium of black fears about white folk. White women who date black men. WASPy families. WASPy family garden parties. Banjos. Crazy younger brothers. Crazy younger brothers who play banjos. Sexual psychopaths, hunting guns, cannibalism, mind-control, well-meaning conversations about Obama. The police. Well-meaning conversations about basketball. Spontaneous arm-wrestling, spontaneous touching of one's biceps or hair. Lifestyle cults, actual cults. Houses with no other houses anywhere near them. Fondness for woods. The game Bingo! Servile household staff, sexual enslavement, nostalgia for slavery – slavery itself. Every one of these racial reversals 'lands' – just like a good joke – simultaneously describing and interpreting the situation at hand, and I think this must account for the homogeneity of reactions to *Get Out*: it is a film that contains its own commentary. For black viewers there is the pleasure of vindication. It's not often they have both their real and irrational fears so thoroughly indulged. For white liberals – whom the movie purports to have in its satirical sights – there is the cringe of recognition, that queer but illuminating feeling of being suddenly 'othered'. (Oh, that's how *we* look to *them*?) And I suppose the satisfaction of being 'in' on the joke. For example, there is the moment when the white girl, Rose (Alison Williams), and her new black boyfriend, Chris (Daniel Kaluuya), hit a deer on the way to her parents' country house. She's driving yet when the police stop them he's the one asked for his licence. Rose is sufficiently 'woke' to step in front of her man and give the cop a self-righteous earful – but oblivious to the fact that only a white girl would assume she could do so with impunity. The audience – on both sides of the divide – groans with recognition. Chris himself – surely mindful of what happened to Sandra Bland, and Walter Scott, and Terence Crutcher, and Samuel DeBose – smiles wryly but remains polite and deferential throughout. He is a photographer, it was his photographs of black city life we saw behind the credits, and the very different lens through which white and black Americans view the same situations is something he already understands.

This same point is made again, more fiercely, in one of the final scenes. Chris is standing in that dark wood again, covered in blood; on the ground before him lies a far more badly wounded Rose. A police car is approaching. Chris eyes it with something like resigned dread. As it happens, he is the victim in this gruesome tableau, but neither Chris nor anyone else in the cinema expects that to count for a goddamn thing. ('You're really in for it now, you poor motherfucker,' said someone behind me. These days, a cop is apparently a more frightening prospect than a lobotomy-performing cult.) But then the car door opens and something unexpected happens: it is not the dreaded white cop after all but a concerned friend, Rod Williams (Lil Rel Howery), the charming and paranoid brother who warned Chris, at the very start, not to go stay with a load of white folks in a wood. Rod – who happens to work for the TSA – surveys the bloody scene and does not immediately assume that Chris is the perp. A collective gasp of delight bursts over the cinema, but in this final reversal the joke's on us. How, in 2017, are we still in a world where the idea of presuming a black man innocent before he is proved guilty is the material of comic fantasy?

These are the type of self-contained, ironic, politically charged sketches at which Peele has long excelled. But there's a deeper seam in *Get Out* that's mined through visual symbol rather than situational comedy. I will not easily forget those lengthy close-ups of suffering black faces; suffering, but trapped behind masks, like so many cinematic analogues of the arguments of Frantz Fanon. Chris himself, and the white family's maid, and the white family's handyman, and that young, lobotomized beau of an old white lady – all frozen in attitudes of trauma, shock, bland servility, or wearing a chillingly fixed grin. In each case, the eyes register an internal desperation. *Get me out!* The oppressed. The cannibalized. The living dead. When a single tear or a dribble of blood ran down these masks, we were to understand that this was a sign that there was still somebody in there. Somebody human. Someone who had the potential to be whole.

As the movie progresses we learn what's going on: black people aren't being murdered or destroyed up here in the woods, they're being used. A white grandmother's brain is now in her black maid's body. An old blind white gallerist hopes to place his brain in Chris's cranium and thus see with the young black photographer's eyes, be in his young black skin. Remnants of the black 'host' remain in these operations – but not enough to make a person. Peele has found a concrete metaphor for the ultimate unspoken fear: that to be oppressed is not so much to be hated as obscenely loved. Disgust and passion are intertwined. Our antipathies are simultaneously a record of our desires, our sublimated wishes, our deepest envies. The capacity to give birth; the capacity to make food from one's body; perceived intellectual, physical or sexual superiority; perceived intimacy with the natural world, animals and plants; perceived self-sufficiency in a faith, or in a community. There are few qualities in others we cannot transform into a form of fear and loathing in ourselves. In the documentary *I Am Not Your Negro*, which came out in late 2016, James Baldwin gets to the heart of it:

> What white people have to do is try to find out in their hearts why it was necessary for them to have a nigger in the first place. Because I am not a nigger. I'm a man. If I'm not the nigger here, and if you invented him, you the white people invented him, then you have to find out why. And the future of the country depends on that.

But there is an important difference between the invented nigger of 1962, and the invented African-American of 2017: the disgust has mostly fallen away. We were declared beautiful back in 1962 but it has only recently been discovered that we are so. In the liberal circles depicted in *Get Out* everything that was once reviled – our eyes, our skin, our backsides, our noses, our arms, our legs, our breasts, and of course our hair – is now openly envied and celebrated and aestheticized and deployed in secondary images to sell stuff. As Chris himself notes, black is cool now. To be clear, the life of the black citizen in America is no more envied or desired today than it was back in 1962. Her schools are still avoided and her housing is still sub-standard and her neighbourhood still feared and her personal and professional outcomes remain disproportionally linked to her postcode. But her physical self is no longer reviled. If she is a child and comes up for adoption, many a white family will be delighted to have her, and if she happens to be in your social class and social circle, she is very welcome to come to the party; in fact, it's not really a party unless she does come. No one will call her the N-word on national television, least of all a black intellectual. (The Baldwin quote is from a television interview.) For liberals the word is interdicted and unsayable. But in place of the old disgust comes a new kind of cannibalism. The white people in *Get Out* want to get inside the black experience: they want to wear it like a skin and walk around in it. The modern word for this is 'appropriation'. There is an argument that there are many things that are 'ours' that must not be touched or even looked at sideways, including (but not limited to) our voices, our personal style, our hair, our cultural products, our history, and perhaps more than anything else, our pain and sorrows. A people from whom much has been stolen is understandably protective of its possessions, especially the ineffable kind. In these debates my mind always turns to a line of Nabokov, a writer for whom arrival in America meant the loss of pretty much everything, including a language: 'Why not leave their private sorrows to people? Is sorrow not, one asks, the only thing in the world people really possess?'

Two weeks after watching *Get Out*, I stand with my children in front of *Open Casket*, Dana Schutz's painting of Emmett Till, the black teenager who in 1955 was beaten and lynched after being accused of flirting with a white woman. They do not know what they are looking at and are too young for me to explain. Before I came, I had read the widely circulated letter to the curators of the Whitney Biennial objecting to their inclusion of this painting in the show: 'I am writing to ask you to remove Dana Schutz's painting *Open Casket* and with the urgent recommendation that the painting be destroyed and not entered into any market or museum . . . because it is not acceptable for a white person to transmute Black suffering into profit and fun, though the practice has been normalized for a long time.' I knew, from reading about this debate, that in fact the painting has never been for sale, so I focused instead on the other prong of the argument – an artist's right to a particular subject: 'The subject matter is not Schutz's; white free speech and white creative freedom have been founded on the constraint of others, and are not natural rights.'

I want to follow the letter very precisely, along its own logic, in which natural rights are replaced with racial ones. I will apply it personally. If *I* was an artist, and if I could paint – could the subject matter be mine? I am biracial. I have Afro-hair, my skin is brown, I am identified, by others and by myself, as a black woman. And so, by the logic of the letter – if I understood it correctly – this question of subject matter, in my case, would not come up, as it would not come up for the author of the letter, Hannah Black, who also happens to be, like me, biracial, and brown. Neither of us is American, but the author appears to speak confidently in defence of the

African-American experience, so I, like her, will assume a transnational unity. I will assume that Emmett Till, if I could paint, could be my subject, too.

Now I want to inch a step further. I turn from the painting to my children. Their beloved father is white, I am biracial, so by the old racial logic of America, they are 'quadroons'. Could *they* take black suffering as a subject of their art, should they ever make any? Their grandmother is 'black as the ace of spades', as the British used to say; their mother is what the French still call *café au lait*. They themselves are sort of yellowy. When exactly does black suffering cease to be their concern? Their grandmother – raised on a post-colonial island, in extreme poverty, and descended from slaves – knew black suffering intimately. But her grandchildren look white. Are they? If they are, shouldn't white people like my children concern themselves with the suffering of Emmett Till? Is making art a form of concern? Does it matter which form the concern takes? Could they be painters of occasional black subjects (Dana Schutz paints many different subjects)? Or must their concern take a different form: civil-rights law, state-school teaching. If they ignore the warnings of the letter and take black suffering as their subject in a work of art, what should be the consequence? If their work of art turns out to be a not especially distinguished expression or engagement with their supposed concern – must their painting be removed from wherever it hangs? Must it be destroyed? To what purpose?

Often I look at my children and remember that 'quadroons' – green-eyed, yellow-haired people, like my children – must have been standing on those auction blocks with their *café au lait* mothers and dark-skinned grandmothers. And I think, too, of how they would have had many opportunities to 'pass', to sneak out and be lost in the white majority, not visibly connected to black suffering and so able to walk through town, marry white, lighten up the race again. To be biracial in America at that time was almost always to have been the issue of rape. It was in a literal sense to live with the enemy within, and have your physical being exist as an expression of the oppression of your people. Perhaps this trace of shame and inner conflict has never entirely left the biracial experience.

To be biracial at any time is complex. Speaking for myself, I know that racially charged historical moments, like this one, can increase the ever-present torsion within my experience until it feels like something's got to give. You start to yearn for absolute clarity: personal, genetic, political. I stood in front of the Dana Schutz and thought how cathartic it would be if this picture filled me with rage. But the painting never got that deep into me, neither as representation nor appropriation. I think of it as a questionably successful example of both, but the letter condemning it will not contend with its relative success or failure, the letter lives in a binary world in which the painting is either facilely celebrated as proof of the autonomy of art, or condemned to the philistine art-bonfire. The first option, as the letter rightly argues, is more often than not hoary old white privilege dressed up as aesthetic theory, but the second is – let's face it – the province of Nazis and censorious evangelicals. Art is a traffic in symbols and images, it has never been politically or historically neutral, and I do not find discussions on appropriation and representation to be in any way trivial. Each individual example has to be *thought through*, and we have every right to include such considerations in our evaluations of art (and also to point out the often dubious neutrality of supposedly pure aesthetic criteria). But when arguments of appropriation are linked to a racial essentialism no more sophisticated than the antebellum miscegenation laws, well, then we head quickly into absurdity. Is Hannah Black black enough to write this letter? Are my children too white to engage with black suffering? How black is black enough? Does an 'octoroon' still count?

When I look at *Open Casket* the truth is I don't feel very much. I tried to transfer to this painting – or even to Dana Schutz – some of that same cold fury that is sparked by looking at the historical photograph of Emmett Till, whose mother insisted he have an open casket at his funeral, or when considering the crimes of Carolyn Bryant, the white woman who falsely accused him of flirting with her, but nothing I saw in that canvas could provoke such an emotion. It's an abstraction without much intensity, and there's a clear caution in the brushstrokes around the eyes: she's gone in only so far. Yet the anxious aporia in the upper face is countered by the area around the mouth, where the canvas roils, coming toward us three-dimensionally, like a swelling – the flesh garroted, twisted, striped – as if something is pushing from behind the death mask, trying to get out. That *did* move me. What's harder to see is why this picture was singled out. In the very next gallery there hangs a painting by a white artist, Eric Fischl, *A Visit to/A Visit from/ the Island*, in which rich white holidaymakers on a beach are juxtaposed with desperate black Haitian boat people washed up on the sand, some dead, some half naked, writhing, suffering. Painted in 1983, by an artist now in his late sixties, it is presumably for sale, yet remains unmentioned in a letter whose main effect has been to divert attention from everything else in the show. Henry Taylor, Deana Lawson, Lyle Ashton Harris and Cauleen Smith are just a few of the artists of colour presently lighting up the Whitney in a thrilling biennial that goes deep into black experience, illuminating its joys and suffering both. Looking at their work, I realized I resent the implication that black pain is so raw and so unprocessed – and black art practice so vulnerable and invisible – that a single painting by a white woman can radically influence it one way or another. Nor do I need to convince myself of my own blackness by drawing a line between somebody else's supposed fraudulence and the fears I have concerning my own (thus evincing an unfortunate tendency toward overcompensation that it must be admitted is not unknown among us biracial folks). No. The viewer is not a fraud. Neither is the painter. The truth is that this painting and I are simply not in profound communication. This is always a risk in art. The solution remains as it has always been. Get out (of the gallery) or deeper in (to the argument). Write a screed against it. Critique the hell out of it. Tear it to shreds in your review or paint another painting in response. But 'remove' it? 'Destroy' it? I think instead I will turn from this painting, not offended, not especially shocked or moved, nor even terribly engaged by it, and walk with my children to another part of the gallery. We have been warned not to get under each other's skin, to keep our distance. But Jordan Peele's horror-fantasy – in which we are inside each other's skins and intimately involved in each other's suffering – is neither a horror nor a fantasy. It is a fact of our experience. The real fantasy is that we can get out of each other's way, mark a clean cut between black and white, a final cathartic separation between us and them. For the many of us in loving, mixed families this is the true impossibility. There are people online who seem astounded that *Get Out* is written and directed by a man with a white wife and a white mother, a man who will soon have – depending on how the unpredictable phenotype lottery goes – a white-appearing child. But this is the history of race in America. Families can become black then white then black again within a few generations. And when they are not genetically mixed they live in a mixed reality at the national level if no other. There is no getting out of our intertwined history.

But in this moment of resurgent black consciousness, God knows it feels good – therapeutic! – to mark a clear separation from white America, the better to speak in the collective voice. We will not be moved. We can't breathe. We will not be executed for traffic violations or for wearing hooded tops. We will no longer tolerate sub-standard schools, housing and health care. *Get Out* – as evidenced by its huge box-office ratings – is the right film for this moment. It is the opposite of post-black, or post-racial. It reveals race as the fundamental American lens through which everything is seen. That part, to my mind, is right on the money. But the 'us' and 'them'? That's a cheaper gag. Whether they like it or not, Americans are one people. (And the binary of black and white is only one part of this nation's infinitely variegated racial composition.) Lobotomies are the cleanest cut; real life is messier. I can't wait for Peele – with his abundant gifts, black-nerd smarts, comprehensive cinematic fandom and complex personal experience – to go deeper in, and out the other side.

ON THE BOOKSHELF

Crash *by J. G. Ballard*

I met J. G. Ballard once – it was a car crash. We were sailing down the Thames in the middle of the night, I don't remember why. A British Council thing, maybe? The boat was full of young British writers, many of them drunk, and a few had begun hurling a stack of cheap conference chairs over the hull into the water. I was twenty-three, had only been a young British writer for a couple of months, and can recall being very anxious about those chairs: I was not the type to rock the boat. I was too amazed to be *on* the boat. (Though it was no pleasure barge, more like a Travelodge afloat, with an interior that put you in mind of a Shepperton semi-detached. A Ballardian boat. Everything brown and grey with accents of Tube-seat orange.) I slunk away from the chair-hurlers and walked straight into Ballard. That moon of a face, the shiny tonsure, the lank side-curtains of hair – ghost of a defrocked priest. An agonizing ten-minute conversation followed in which we two seemed put on earth to vivify that colloquial English phrase 'cross purposes'. Every book I championed he hated. Every film he admired I'd never seen. (We didn't dare move on to the visual arts.) The only thing we seemed to have in common was King's College, but as I cheerily bored him with an account of all the lovely books I'd read for my finals, I could see that moon face curdling with disgust. In the end, he stopped speaking to me altogether, leaned against a hollow Doric column and simply stared.

I was being dull – but the trouble went deeper than that. James Graham Ballard was a man born on the inside, to the colonial class, that is, to the very marrow of British life; but he broke out of that restrictive mould and went on to establish – uniquely among his literary generation – an autonomous hinterland, not attached to the mainland in any obvious way. I, meanwhile, born on the outside of it all, was hell-bent on breaking *in*. And so my Ballard encounter – like my encounters, up to that point, with his work – was essentially a missed encounter: ships passing in the night. I liked the Ballard of *Empire of the Sun* well enough, and enjoyed the few science-fiction stories I'd read, but I did not understand the novels and *Crash* in particular had always disturbed me, first as a teenager living in the flight path of Heathrow Airport, and then as a young college feminist, warring against 'phallocentricism', not at all in the mood for penises entering the leg wounds of disabled lady drivers.

What was I so afraid of? Well, firstly that west London psychogeography. I spent much of my adolescence walking through west London, climbing brute concrete stairs – over four-lane roads – to reach the houses of friends, whose windows were often black with the grime of the A41. But this all seemed perfectly natural to me, rational – even beautiful – and to read Ballard's description of 'flyovers overlay[ing] one another like copulating giants, immense legs straddling each other's legs' was to find the sentimental architecture of my childhood revealed as monstrosity: 'The entire zone which defined the landscape of my life was now bounded by a continuous artificial horizon, formed by the raised parapets and embankments of the motorways and their access roads and interchanges. These encircled the vehicles below like the walls of a crater several miles in diameter.'

Those lines are a perfectly accurate description of, say, Neasden along the North Circular, but it can be shocking to be forced to look at the fond and familiar with this degree of clinical precision. ('Novelists should be like scientists,' Ballard once said, 'dissecting the cadaver.') And Ballard was in the business of taking what seems 'natural' – what seems normal, familiar and rational – and revealing its psychopathology. As has been noted many times, not least by the author himself, his gift for defamiliarization was, in part, a product of his own unusual biography: 'One of the things I took from my wartime experiences was that reality was a stage set . . . the comfortable day-to-day life, school, the home where one lives and all the rest of it . . . could be dismantled overnight.' At age fifteen, Ballard left decimated Shanghai, where he'd spent the war, for England, to study medicine at Cambridge, and found it understandably difficult to take England seriously. This set him apart from his peers, whose habit it was to take England very seriously indeed. But if his scepticism were the only thing different about Ballard he would not be such an extraordinary writer. Think of that famous shot in David Lynch's *Blue Velvet*, when the camera burrows below the manicured suburban lawn to reveal the swarming, dystopian scene underneath. Ballard's intention is similar, but more challenging. In Ballard the dystopia is not hidden *under* anything. Nor is it (as with so many fictional dystopias) a vision of the future. It is not the subtext. It *is* the text. 'After this sort of thing,' asks the car-crash survivor Dr Helen Remington, 'how do people manage to look at a car, let alone drive one?' But drive she does, as we all do, slowing down on motorways to ogle an accident. Like the characters in *Crash* we are willing participants in what Ballard called 'a pandemic cataclysm that kills hundreds of thousands of people each year and injures millions'. The death-drive, Thanatos, is not what drivers secretly feel, it's what driving explicitly *is*.

'We live in a world ruled by fictions of every kind . . . We live inside an enormous novel . . . The fiction is already there. The writer's task is to invent reality.' The world as text: Ballard was one of the first British novelists to apply that French theory to his own literary practice. His novels subvert in particular the world that advertising presents, with its irrational convergences sold to us as if they were not only rational but natural. In the case of the automobile, we have long been encouraged to believe there is a natural convergence between such irrational pairs as speed and self-esteem, or leather interiors and family happiness. Ballard insists upon an alternative set of convergences, of the kind we would rather suppress and ignore.

It is these perverse convergences that drive the cars in *Crash*, with Ballard's most notorious creation, Dr Robert Vaughan, at the wheel, whose 'strange vision of the automobile and its real role in our lives' converges with Ballard's own. And once we are made aware of the existence of these convergences it becomes very hard to un-see them, however much we might want to.

There is a convergence, for example, between our own soft bodies and the hardware of the dashboard: 'The aggressive stylization of this mass-produced cockpit, the exaggerated mouldings of the instrument binnacles emphasized my growing sense of a new junction between my own body and the automobile.' There is a convergence between our horror of death and our love of spectacle: 'On the roofs of the police cars the warning lights revolved, beckoning more and more passers-by to the accident site.' And there is an acute convergence, we now know, between the concept of celebrity and the car crash: 'She sat in the damaged car like a deity occupying a shrine readied for her in the blood of a minor member of her congregation . . . the unique contours of her body and personality seemed to transform the crushed vehicle. Her left leg rested on the ground, the door pillar realigning both itself and the dashboard mounting to avoid her knee, almost as if the entire car had deformed itself around her figure in a gesture of homage.'

This vision of a fictional Elizabeth Taylor – written twenty-five years before the death of Princess Diana – is as prescient as anything in Ballard's science fiction. How did he get it so right? How did he know that the price we would demand, in return for our worship of the famous and beautiful (with their unique bodies and personalities) would be nothing less than the bloody sacrifice of the worshipped themselves? Oh, there were clues, of course: the myth of decapitated Jayne Mansfield, Jimmy Dean with his prophetic licence plate ('Too fast to live, too young to die'), Grace Kelly's car penetrated by a tree. But only Ballard saw how they were all related, only he drew the line of convergence clearly. Once you see you cannot un-see. What are all the DUIs of Lindsay Lohan if not a form of macabre foreplay?

Still, it's easy to be shocked the first time you read Ballard. I was for some reason scandalized by this convergence of sex and wheels, even though it is enshrined in various commonplaces (not to mention the phrase 'sex on wheels'). What else do we imply when we say that the purchase of a motorbike represents a 'mid-life crisis', or that a large car is compensation for a lack of endowment? But, of course, in the fictional version of our sexual relationship with cars, it is we, the humans, who are in control; we determine what we do in cars. In Ballard's reality it is the other way round: 'What I noticed about

231

these affairs, which she described in an unembarrassed voice, was the presence in each one of the automobile. All had taken place within a motor-car, either in the multi-storey car-park at the airport, in the lubrication bay of her local garage at night, or in the lay-bys near the northern circular motorway, as if the presence of the car mediated an element which alone made sense of the sexual act.'

In 1973, horrified readers condemned such passages as fantastical pornography. Thirty years later, in England, a very similar scene burst on to the front pages and even received an official term: dogging. (And at the centre of that scandal was one of the biggest television stars in the country, *natch*.) The real shock of *Crash* is not that people have sex in or near cars, but that technology has entered into even our most intimate human relations. Not man-as-technology-forming but technology-as-man-forming. We had hints of this, too, a long time ago, in Marinetti's Futurist Manifesto of 1909, which makes explicit the modernist desire to replace our ancient gods and myths with the sleek lines and violent lessons of the automobile. It also features an orgasmic car crash: 'When I came up – torn, filthy, and stinking – from under the capsized car, I felt the white-hot iron of joy deliciously pass through my heart!'

But Marinetti's prose is overwrought, deliberately absurd ('We went up to the three snorting beasts, to lay amorous hands on their torrid breasts. I stretched out on my car like a corpse on its bier, but revived at once under the steering wheel, a guillotine blade that threatened my stomach') where Ballard is calm and collected. That medic's eye, dispassionate, ruthless: 'Braced on his left elbow, he continued to work himself against the girl's hand, as if taking part in a dance of severely stylized postures that celebrated the design and electronics, speed and direction of an advanced kind of automobile.'

Marinetti's hot-headed poets and artists wrestled with the icon of the motorcar. Ballard's ciphers coolly appraise it. The iciness of Ballard's style is partly a consequence of inverting the power balance between people and technology, which in turn deprives his characters of things like interiority and individual agency. They seem mass-produced, just like the things they make and buy. Certainly his narrators and narrators manqués are not concerned with the personalities of human beings: 'Vaughan's interest in myself was clearly minimal; what concerned him was not the behaviour of a 40-year-old producer of television commercials but the interaction between an anonymous individual and his car, the transits of his body across the polished cellulose panels and vinyl seating, his face silhouetted against the instrument dials.'

It's almost as if the stalker-sadist Vaughan looks at humans as walking-talking examples of that Wittgensteinian proposal: 'Don't ask for the meaning; ask for the use.' When Ballard called *Crash* the first 'pornographic novel about technology', he referred not only to a certain kind of content but to pornography as an organizing principle, perhaps the purest example of humans 'asking for the use'. In *Crash*, though, the distinction between humans and things has become too small to be meaningful. In effect things are using things. (And a crazed stalker like Vaughan becomes the model for a new kind of narrative perspective.)

Now, I don't think it can be seriously denied that some of the deadening narrative traits of pornography can be found here: flatness, repetition, circularity. 'Blood, semen and engine coolant' converge on several pages, and the sexual episodes repeat like trauma. But surely this flatness is deliberate; it is with the banality of our psychopathology that Ballard is concerned: 'The same calm but curious gaze, as if she were still undecided how to make use of me, was fixed on my face shortly afterwards as I stopped the car on a deserted service road among the reservoirs to the west of the airport.'

That seems to me a quintessential Ballardian sentence, depicting a denatured landscape in which people don't so much communicate as exchange mass-produced gestures. (Reservoirs are to Ballard what clouds were to Wordsworth.) Of course, it was not this lack of human interiority that created the furious moral panic around this book (and later David Cronenberg's film). That was more about the whole idea of penetrating the wound of a disabled lady. I was in college when the *Daily Mail* went to war with the movie, and found myself unpleasantly aligned with the censors, my own faux-feminism existing in a Venn diagram with their righteous indignation. We were both wrong: *Crash* is not about humiliating the disabled or debasing women, and in fact the *Mail*'s campaign is a chilling lesson in how a superficial manipulation of liberal identity politics can be used to silence a genuinely protesting voice, one that is trying to speak for us all. No one doubts that the abled use the disabled, or that men use women. But *Crash* is an existential book about how *everybody uses everything.* How everything uses everybody. And yet it is not a hopeless vision:

> The silence continued. Here and there a driver shifted behind his steering wheel, trapped uncomfortably in the hot sunlight, and I had the sudden impression that the world had stopped. The wounds on my knees and chest were beacons tuned to a series of beckoning transmitters, carrying the signals, unknown to myself, which would unlock this immense stasis and free these drivers for the real destinations set for their vehicles, the paradises of the electric highway.

In Ballard's work there is always this mix of futuristic dread and excitement, a sweet spot where dystopia and utopia converge. For we cannot say we haven't got precisely what we dreamed of, what we always wanted, so badly. The dreams have arrived, all of them: instantaneous, global communication, virtual immersion, bio-technology. These were the dreams. And calm and curious, pointing out every new convergence, Ballard reminds us that dreams are often perverse.

The Buddha of Suburbia *by Hanif Kureishi*

Many kinds of contraband got passed around our school: cigarettes, drugs, porn mags, video nasties, every now and then some poor fool's diary – but books were not considered hot property. *The Buddha of Suburbia* changed all that. It was moving surreptitiously around our history class, it had one page folded, so that anyone who cared to could read the following line:

'Now, Karim, I want you to put some ice up my cunt. Would you mind going to the fridge?'

To see this expletive inside a book – instead of on a wall – was, in and of itself, very good value. But there was also something truly striking in seeing a name like *Karim*, familiar to us – though rarely seen in typeface – sitting there calmly only nine words away from the word 'cunt'. Kureishi was another familiar name, we had a Kureishi in our class (spelled with a Q), and felt we recognized the world of this novel, at least as it was depicted on the front of that first edition: the cream living room with the bad curtains, the lady in the sari, some mysterious old white people of probable renown, a lone Tory boy, a few pretty, posh English roses and a psychedelic-looking Indian with a red headband. Word got round that there was a useful, masturbatory section depicting an orgy, somewhere around page 205 (you can go look it up now if you like; I'll wait), and I confess I hurried down to our local W. H. Smith primarily for that reason. I meant to skim-read the thing, the way you skim-read *Lady Chatterley's Lover*, leaping over paragraphs in search of genitals. But it was not possible to skip over those opening lines:

> My name is Karim Amir, and I am an Englishman born and bred, almost. I am often considered to be a funny kind of Englishman, a new breed as it were, having emerged from two old histories. But I don't care – Englishman I am (though not proud of it), from the South London suburbs and going somewhere.

This was thrilling. I had no idea you could start a book like that. In school we were reading – per the syllabus – Austen, Milton, Shakespeare, Keats, Iris Murdoch. Consequently I thought an English sentence was a kind of cat-o'-nine-tails, to be used, primarily, as a tool for whipping children into submission. I didn't know you could speak to a reader like this, as if they were your equal – as if they were a friend. I'd had a hint of it with Holden Caulfield, but at some fundamental level Holden always remained exotic: an American prep-school kid suffering from ennui. There were Dickens's various waifs and strays, often closer in postcode, but distant in time. Karim was different, I knew him; I recognized the way class worked in his family, the complex mix of working- and lower-middle-class realities, and all the strange gradations that can exist between these two states. And of course he was one of the 'new breed', like me, like so many kids in our school, although the only other mentions of us I'd ever come across before were all of the 'tragic mulatto' variety. But the kids I knew were not tragic. They were like Karim: pushy, wild, charismatic, street-smart, impudent, often hilarious. Despite their relatively lowly position in the British class system they suspected they were cool, and knew they had talent and brains. They felt special, even if the rest of the world thought they were marginal. 'Although I hated inequality,' explains Karim, 'it didn't mean I wanted to be treated like everyone else.' Yes, exactly that. But how did he know so much about us, this Kureishi person, born in south London, twenty years earlier? Yet he knew:

> Past turdy parks, past the Victorian school with outside toilets, past the numerous bomb sites which were our true playgrounds and sexual schools, and past the neat gardens and scores of front rooms containing familiar strangers and televisions shining like dying lights.

He seemed to be walking through the neighbourhood. He knew the school ('One day the woodwork teacher had a heart attack right in front of our eyes as one of the lads put another kid's prick in a vice and started to turn the handle.' In our school, it was the kid's head.)* He had certainly visited the high street: 'They were fanatical shoppers [. . .] Shopping was to them what the rumba and singing is to Brazilians.' And he was in my house. I cringed through Eva's pseudo Buddhist evenings; they reminded me, unfairly, of my own mother's recent forays into sophisticated culture, especially the (perfectly innocent, I see now) attempt to gather some friends for dinner to offer them what she believed, at the time, to be sushi. Pretentious young Charlie with Keats in his pocket ('The book was extracted and opened [. . .] Charlie imbibed a beakerful of the warm south') reminded me of, well, pretentious young me with Keats in my pocket. As much as I laughed, at times it was painful to read, and

* And I later put this detail in a novel.

some of the most painful details were, paradoxically, the ones that seemed invested with the most love. I owe a lot, both personally and professionally, to Kureishi's account of the strange relationship that can exist between first-generation immigrants and their children. Back in 1990 many self-serious think-pieces were being written on the subject, but none of them was more psychologically acute, or more intimate, than his fictional version. 'I like having you with me, boy,' explains Karim's father, 'I love you very much. We're growing up together, we are.' The child is trying to find his way through adolescence; the father is trying to find his way through a country. These two events are happening simultaneously. You're growing up together. What a beautiful, painful way to put it. 'The cruellest thing you can do to Kerouac,' Eva informs Karim one evening, 'is reread him at thirty-eight.' Rereading Kureishi now, at exactly that age, I find the opposite. I get the same thrill, the same perverse pleasure, all of it made a little stronger by nostalgia. Perversity is the central sensibility of *The Buddha of Suburbia*: it's a book that refuses to toe the party line. In his role as narrator, Karim is rude where you might expect piety, fractious where you were counting on peace, and queer where it would have been far easier, at the time, to play it straight. Even the most innocuous sentences never quite end as you might expect: 'One day Anwar made a serious mistake in the betting shop and won a lot of money.' Or: 'I was in my usual state; I had no money. Things were so desperate it had become necessary for me to work.' The immigrants here are not always good and hard-working, and Karim is neither consistently right-on nor especially grateful. There is an equal-opportunity policy here when it comes to bad behaviour; everyone is shown to be capable of it. Received ideas – particularly about race and class – are gleefully upended in such a way as to annoy both sides of the usual debates:

Ted and Jean never called Dad by his Indian name, Haroon Amir. He was always 'Harry' to them, and they spoke of him as Harry to other people. It was bad enough his being an Indian in the first place, without having an awkward name too.

It's a funny idea, and familiar, now, as a comic trope – but Kureishi was the first to note it. He saw that the highest compliment a white Englishman can give himself is the assertion that he is 'colour-blind', by which he means he has been able to overlook the fact of your colour – to look past it – to the 'you' beneath. Not content with colonizing your country, he now colonizes your self. So, anyway, ran the new dogma, in 1990, but rereading the novel you remember that Karim questions the blanket application of this liberal piety, too. Here he is considering his cousin Jamila's relationship with a teacher at her school:

> Jamila thought Miss Cutmore really wanted to eradicate everything that was foreign in her. 'She spoke to my parents as if they were peasants,' Jamila said. She drove me mad by saying Miss Cutmore had colonized her, but Jamila was the strongest-willed person I'd met: no one could turn her into a colony. Anyway, I hated ungrateful people. Without Miss Cutmore, Jamila wouldn't have even heard the word 'colony'. 'Miss Cutmore started you off,' I told her.

For Karim, what passes between black and white people is never quite black and white. In the case of Miss Cutmore and Jamila, it turns out colonization and genuine education may indeed have some overlap; in the case of his white uncle and Indian father, the essentially racist concept of 'colour-blindness' and real human affection are able to coexist, too. Readers who prefer their ideologies delivered straight – and straight-faced – will find *Buddha* a frustrating read. To Kureishi the world is weird and various, comic and tragic. If this mixed reality can't always be fully admitted while standing on soapboxes, sitting in parliament, or marching down Whitehall, it should at least be allowed an existence in novels. There's a sharp section of *Buddha* where the old argument between politics and art – the problem of 'responsibility' – is dramatized. Karim is an actor in a radical drama group, and has chosen, as his subject, to play a version of his own uncle, Anwar, who is on hunger-strike, for the purpose of forcing his daughter, Jamila, into an arranged marriage. Tracey, a black female actress in the group, objects to the portrayal:

'Two things, Karim,' she said to me. 'Anwar's hunger-strike worries me. What you want to say hurts me. It really pains me! And I'm not sure that we should show it!'

'Really?'

'Yes.' She spoke to me as if all I required was a little sense. 'I'm afraid it shows black people –'

'Indian people –'

'Black and Asian people –'

'One old Indian man –'

'As being irrational, ridiculous, as being hysterical. And as being fanatical.'

'Fanatical? [. . .] It's not a fanatical hunger-strike. It's calmly intended blackmail.'

Such light, comic work is made here of several well-meaning debates of the eighties, battlegrounds of racial categorization and alliance, language, political responsibility. I don't think Tracey is exactly wrong, she is trying to be responsible – but Karim is on the side of irresponsibility, and needs to be, in order to tell his story. Tracey's arguments belong to another sphere. She may win the argument but fiction can't be written to comply with winning arguments. Tracey continues: 'Your picture is what white people already think of us. Why do you hate yourself and all black people so much, Karim?' It's a familiar, crushing double admonition, and so many aspiring 'minority' artists have crumbled before it. The first part means, basically: *Don't wash 'our' dirty laundry in public.* The second: *'For beware, if you do, you are then a Self-hating _____'* (fill in the blank). Bellow was told the same thing; Roth, too. And Zora Neale Hurston. Once upon a time they even said it to Joyce, back when the Irish were thought of as a 'minority' rather than as a poetic stand-in for all humanity. Writers with a sense of humour seem to get these warnings more than most, perhaps because irresponsibility is an essential element of comic writing. Some, like Karim, try a high-minded argument against responsibility ('Truth has a higher value') and find it knocked down easily, as Tracey rightly knocks it down here, critiquing its abstract tone and specious subjectivity ('Pah. Truth. Who defines it? What truth? It's white truth you're defending here'). But there is another truth, particular to writers, that in order to work with any effectiveness you will have to abandon, at least for a time, these familiar battles. If you want to create that 'one old Indian man', you will have to take liberties, you will have to feel free to write as you like, even if Tracey is right, even if it is irresponsible. All the great energy of *Buddha* comes from watching the liberty of creative freedom being taken, over and over again – as if it were a right – without too much concern for what that (perhaps entirely imagined) unified group called 'white people' will think about it.

The Buddha of Suburbia *by Hanif Kureishi*

In the memory *Buddha* is a lot about race. In the rereading it's actually far more concerned with what Karim's director, Pyke, calls 'the only subject there is in England' – class. Again right and left get an equal satirical poke. To his fellow actor – and committed Marxist – Terry, Karim has this to say: 'I wanted to tell him that the proletariat of the suburbs did have a strong class feeling. It was virulent and hate-filled and directed entirely at the people beneath them.' On a posh girl called Eleanor, also from the group: 'She always did whatever occurred to her, which was, admittedly, not difficult for someone in her position, coming from a background where the risk of failure was minimal; in fact, you had to work hard to fail in her world.' My favourite example is when Boyd, another white actor in the group, who has watched Karim's rise through the ranks, falls into a well of self-pity and spite: 'If I weren't white and middle class I'd have been in Pyke's show now. Obviously mere talent gets you nowhere these days. Only the disadvantaged are going to succeed in seventies England.' When I first read this, in 1990, it seemed to be absurdist parody. Twenty-five years later we can read similar sentiments all day long on the Internet, as armies of Boyds gather under any article online concerning brown-skinned artists and their works. Here – as in so many matters of English life – Kureishi has proved a kind of seer. And hugely influential for a generation of writers, me included, of course. What he gave us most of all was a sense of irresponsibility, of freedom, in the smallest things as well as the biggest:

Auntie Jean really knew how to give you frightening looks, so much so that I found myself struggling to suppress a fart that needed to be free [. . .] But it was no use. The naughty fart bubbled gaily out of me.

This is a naughty, bubbly book. It says things frankly and with delight. Nothing is agonizing to Karim, really – not race, class or sex – it's all interesting, it's all worth talking about, without shame, and without making heavy weather of it either:

> It was unusual, I knew, the way I wanted to sleep with boys as well as girls. I liked strong bodies and the backs of boys' necks. I liked being handled by men, their fists pulling me; and I liked objects – the end of brushes, pens, fingers – up my arse. But I liked cunts and breasts, all of women's softness, long smooth legs and the way women dressed. I felt it would be heart-breaking to have to choose one or the other, like having to decide between The Beatles and The Rolling Stones.

It's all a little naughty – but is it nice? The novel itself is preoccupied with the question. 'I thought about the difference between the interesting people and the nice people,' writes Karim, 'and how they can't always be identical.' When it comes to writing and acting Karim is concerned not only with the political risk (which might, as Jamila puts it, 'expose our culture as being ridiculous and our people as old-fashioned, extreme and narrow-minded') but of the personal risk, which – as every novelist knows – involves hurting the people you love. *The Buddha of Suburbia* is, among other things, a first novel and a *Bildungsroman*, and that form usually plays fast and loose with authorial experience. Real uncles and aunts are combined into one paper person, siblings change sex, living parents die, and so on. For his part, Karim stridently defends his right to base a dramatic character on his brother-in-law, Changez, but he also – perhaps not entirely consciously – reveals the deep psychological peculiarity that compels him to do so:

There were few jobs I relished as much as the invention of Changez/ Tariq [. . .] I uncovered notions, connections, initiatives I didn't even know were present in my mind. I became more energetic and alive as I brushed in new colours and shades. I worked regularly and kept a journal; I saw that creation was an accretive process which couldn't be hurried, and which involved patience and, primarily, love. *I felt more solid myself, and not as if my mind were just a kind of cinema for myriad impressions and emotions to flicker through.* [my italics]

It's what I believe actors and writers have in common: this personal sense of immateriality that becomes, perversely, more solid when they pretend to be someone else. Karim notices this tendency himself early on, long before he is an actor, in his sexual passion for his stepbrother, Charlie:

My love for him was unusual as love goes: it was not generous. I admired him more than anyone but I didn't wish him well. It was that I preferred him to me and wanted to be him. I coveted his talents, face, style. I wanted to wake up with them all transferred to me.

It's not nice. But it is interesting. And funny. In *Buddha* cruelty, humour and affection work hand in hand to make character, and even the smallest walk-on part is brought to sharp, momentary life by means of this potent mixture. I love Karim's poor uncle Ted, DIY genius and clinical depressive, and the way Kureishi makes us both care for and laugh at him, in the space of a paragraph:

'He can talk and work at the same time, can't he?' said Dad as Ted, sometimes in tears, inserted rawl-plugs into brick as he made a shelf for Dad's Oriental books, or sanded a door, or tiled the bathroom in exchange for Dad listening to him from an aluminium garden chair. 'Don't commit suicide until you've finished that floor, Ted,' he'd say.

At the time Kureishi's first novel was celebrated for possessing the same punk spirit that the novel itself documents, but there are many quieter moments, too, of elegant and beautiful prose, which rereading reveals. Here is Karim on his mother, whose one outlet from domestic drudgery is her sketching: 'Her mind had turned to glass, and all life slid from its sheer aspect. I asked her to draw me.' That could be Woolf. And this could be Forster: 'So this was London at last, and nothing gave me more pleasure than strolling around my new possession all day. London seemed like a house with five thousand rooms, all different; the kick was to work out how they connected, and eventually walk through all of them.' Karim is making the new out of the old. Keats and Shelley and Donne are nestled in these pages, and the shadow of Kipling, and the even longer shadow of Dickens. Karim's own new angle is that he's, well, Karim: he's got a different walk, a different talk, a fresh sensibility. He knows perfectly well he's the kind of kid never before seen between the covers of an English novel, and like any smart-arse kid from the suburbs he's going to use that and everything else. When he finds himself cast as Mowgli in his first big role, he knows it's ludicrous – but it's still a break. 'I've found my little Mowgli at last,' says the director:

'An unknown actor, just right and ready to break through [. . .] Isn't he terrific?' The two women examined me. I was just perfect. I'd done it. I'd got the job.

The job, of course, is the job of the exotic. But like Bellow, Roth, Hurston and Joyce before him, Kureishi sees, in this role, more comedy – and opportunity – than tragedy. Karim is nobody's victim. And though it is certainly often tiring and usually offensive when people mistake you for such cultural types as the 'Comical Urban Jew' or the 'Soulful Black Woman' or the 'Mystic Indian', Kureishi's point in *Buddha* is that it can also be very amusing. From the point of view of our twenty-first-century world where the only possible reaction to anything seems to be outraged offence, I find it a relief to go back to that more innocent, hardier time, when we were not all such delicate flowers that every man's casual idiocy had the awesome power to offend us to our very cores. 'To be truly free,' argues Karim, 'we had to free ourselves of all bitterness and resentment, too. How was this possible when bitterness and resentment were generated afresh every day?' In *Buddha* this remains an open and unanswered question, for Karim is both free and not free at the same time. For him England is, in so many ways, impossible – but it is also his playground. Both versions of his experience are true. That is the great discomfort and irresponsible charm of this lovely, funny, honest novel.

Notes on NW

What's this novel about?* My books don't seem to me to be *about* anything other than the people in them and the sentences used to construct them. Which makes *NW* sound like an 'exercise in style', a phrase you generally hear people using as an insult of one kind or another. But to me, an 'exercise in style' is not a superficial matter – our lives are also an exercise in style. The hidden content of people's lives proves a very hard thing to discern: all we really have to go on are these outward, manifest signs, the way people speak, move, dress, treat each other. And that's what I try to concern myself with in fiction: the way of things in reality, as far as I am able to see and interpret them, which may not be especially far.

When I was writing this novel what I really wanted to do was create people in language. To do that you must try to do justice simultaneously to the unruly, subjective qualities of language, and to what I want to call the concrete 'thingyness' of people. Which was Virginia Woolf's way of being a modernist – she loved language and people simultaneously – and her model is important to me. I admire

* I feel I must mention that I'm not in the habit of sitting around wondering about my novels after I've written them. The question was put by the *Guardian*, and this piece part of a series in which writers reflect on the roots and inspirations behind a particular work.

Beckett and respect Joyce. I love Woolf. Whenever the going gets tough I reread her journals and it helps me through.

What inspired this novel? Two seeds seem important, one involving thingyness and the other, language. Sometime in 2004 a girl in distress came to my door, a stranger, and asked me for help. Said she needed money – so I gave it to her. Later I found out that it was probably a scam of some sort. A lot of questions followed from this in my mind. Was the girl really desperate? Was I a fool to give her the money? But wouldn't you have to be really desperate to come up with such a scam? The episode, tiny as it was, stayed with me. It became a fruitful sort of problem – connecting with ideas I'd had for a long time about class and desperation and ethics – and eight years later a whole novel sprung from it.

The other inspiration was textual, and subconscious: Shakespeare's *Measure for Measure*. I've always loved the 'problem play' as a form, which I think of as a situation in which not everyone ends up happy and married, nor everyone bleeding or dead. Problem plays seem closest to the mixed reality of our lives. 'Some rise by sin, and some by virtue fall' – that line is embedded deep in *NW*. I'd almost finished the book before I realized it. And with this realization came the submerged memory that years ago, as a teenager, I was taken by my school to see an unusual performance of *Measure for Measure* in which the actor playing Claudio was a young black man and the woman playing his sister, Isabella, the nun, was white. And when Isabella tried to convince Claudio that he should let himself be executed rather than ask her to give up her precious virginity, I was more struck by that scene than anything I've seen onstage either before or since. I've never forgotten it, neither the words, nor its staging. There was poor Claudio alone, at the back of the stage, in prison for much of the play, while the rest of the characters were busy downstage, seeking their happy endings. I can remember thinking: Yes, that's right. The happy ending is never universal. Someone is always left behind. And in the London I grew up in – as it is today – that someone is more often than not a young black man.

One last thing: writing this novel reminded me that a writer should not undervalue any tool of her trade just because she finds it easier to use than the others. As you get older you learn not to look a gift horse in the mouth. If I have any gift at all it's for dialogue – that trick of breathing what-looks-like-life into a collection of written sentences. Voices that come from nowhere and live on in our consciousness, independent of real people . . . It's this magic, first learned in the playroom, that we can never quite shake off, and which any true lover of fiction carries within him or her somewhere. Isn't it better to die than to live in shame? asks the voice called Isabella of the voice called Claudio. And the voice called Claudio replies: 'Ay, but to die, and go we know not where;/To lie in cold obstruction and to rot . . .' Over four hundred years after these words were written they are still my first thought whenever I hear of anyone dying or when I consider the inevitable event for myself. It really is a sort of magic. I like writing that makes you hear voices. In this case, for this author, the very different voices of Leah, Felix, Natalie and Nathan.

The Harper's *Columns**

On Harlem, Hatred and Javier

A new book considers 'Harlem'. Hopes that we'll come to know this
place with a degree of certainty are raised by the Flannery O'Connor
epigraph ('The writer operates at a peculiar crossroads where time
and place and eternity somehow meet. His problem is to find that
location') and promptly crushed by the title: *Harlem is Nowhere: A*
Journey to the Mecca of Black America. For the book's author, Sharifa
Rhodes-Pitts, Harlem is a notional place, an idea threatened by a
reality, existing most concretely in the minds of those who have
loved and defended it. Rhodes-Pitts is one such, and her account of
this stretch of land that may or may not begin at 110th Street and end
at 168th is fittingly idiosyncratic, as much meditation as history. We
open with a personal anecdote: 'I had already put the key into the
door of my building on Lenox Avenue when the question came at
my back. In one movement I withdrew my key and turned to face
my inquisitor. He stood waiting for my reply and then asked again:

---

* I was in Northern Ireland at my in-laws watching television when my phone
rang. It was New York, a girl from *Harper's* magazine, Gemma Sieff. She asked if
I had any interest in reviewing books. I had a four-month-old baby and a misplaced idea of maternal bravado. I said yes. I lasted six months.

Do you think you'll ever go home?' It's a local man who wants to know: the author is an interloper, a Texan, sole black student in her high-school class. She comes to Harlem seeking a place familiar to her imagination, admired from a distance. First stop: *The Columbia-Lippincott Gazetteer of the World*. Its entry on Harlem is, I think, full of interesting facts, but to the author they are sterile, useless: 'At first it seems to give an all-encompassing view – complete with official borders, colonial heroics, and important urban planning highlights. Yet it manages to say nothing at all.' We move instead to scenes from novels Rhodes-Pitts read as a teenager, when she 'plotted an itinerary through my library's shelves, searching for the El Dorado of black literature'. Characters arrive in Harlem, hopeful, disappointed, angry, eager, created by Wallace Thurman, Zora Neale Hurston, Claude McKay and Nella Larsen. We realize how much the *idea* of Harlem has meant to Rhodes-Pitts, and what a romantic vision of a writer's business she has: a magpie with a notebook, who collects everything, and always shows her workings – leading to many scenes set in the library. Although this technique of authorial transparency grows long in the tooth – a classic of the genre is *A Room of One's Own* – it still has its intimate pleasures. Like Woolf, Rhodes-Pitts is bookish and devoted, interested in everyday matters: how people walk and talk, dress, go about their day. But where Woolf staged such 'incidents' artfully, and fashioned from them forceful arguments, Rhodes-Pitts finds literary artifice lame: 'As early as my high school lessons on Langston Hughes, I had absorbed the platitude that the task of the writer was to glean universal lessons from specific and personal experiences.' She detects (and disapproves of) James Baldwin's habit of speaking to Harlem folk, having experiences, and deriving from these encounters 'a metaphor about all of black existence', as Woolf took from a single Cambridge dinner a metaphor for all of women's. (She is so struck by this rhetorical move that she gives it a name, 'The Jimmy', where others might simply have called it 'writing'.) She prefers to record random street conversations, information printed on flyers, messages chalked on pavements by a local eccentric. She is not at all – as Baldwin could be – a polemical writer. Here individual experience is honoured, and judgement reserved. Occasionally this generosity misses the wood for the trees. Certain key historical facts, surely useful to the general reader, become afterthoughts (page 245 of 262: 'It is something of an accepted idea among some historians that Harlem began with a parade'). But once you abandon wanting to know anything very precise about historical Harlem, this is a lovely book about the romance – and dangers – of bibliophily. The author is, by her own account, afflicted by 'single-girl-doing-research fantasies', and the inclusion of that word 'single' is strange, being so unnecessary. It suggests a narrator in pursuit of a love object. This object turns out not to be Harlem itself as much as the library within it: the Schomburg Center for Research in Black Culture. Harlem may be nowhere, but the Schomburg is definitely on the corner of 136th and Lenox, and within it Rhodes-Pitts pursues Black madonnas, Haiti, Liberia, Black Communism, the African Nationalist Pioneers, and much more besides. Upon finding the same individual mentioned in two entirely unrelated portions of her research, she reflects upon the classic researcher's dilemma: 'One book held the key to another, though it solved a riddle I had not been trying to answer, and provided information I did not know how to use. What other mysteries might be unravelled the more often I came and the longer I stayed?' Regularly she emerges from this beachcombing to display a substantial haul: the beautiful pebbles need no polish to shine. Take James Van Der Zee, famous for his portraits of Harlem dandies, here rediscovered as a photographer of the bereaved and the deceased, *in the same frame*: a mourning couple, formally posed, with their dead child in their arms. Or the impresario Raven Chanticleer (1928–2002), inventor and creator of the African American Wax and History Museum (first statue: himself), and son of 'a Haitian-born school principal and a Barbados-born concert pianist' – at least it seemed that way until, in death, he was revealed to have invented his parentage, too (mother, sharecropper; father, sharecropper). And here, most memorably, is Alexander Gumby, who dedicated his life to making 'Negroana' scrapbooks – photographs, playbills, news clippings. In 1934, a cellar flood ruined much of this great collection. What remains Rhodes-Pitts uncovers and describes, with obvious fellow feeling. In a sense, her book, too, is a scrapbook, and a beguiling one. I am so glad to have met Van Der Zee, Chanticleer, Gumby, and the many other curious figures featured: a more tightly organized approach might have passed over them entirely as flotsam. As it stands, her dreamlike style takes its sweet time reaching its central argument, that Harlem is 'nowhere' in a practical, non-metaphorical sense: 'It all comes down to a point that is as simple as it is terrible: . . . this is our land that we don't own.' But this tragedy – of high rents and absentee landlords, of the construction of luxury high-rise condominiums – only ever pulsates in the background, as if the author felt too strongly her own pangs of illegitimacy. ('There is that man who asked me how long one had to live in Harlem before being allowed to write a book about it – implying, of course, that I had not lived in Harlem long enough to write a book about it.') It's a misplaced fear: no geographic or racial qualification guarantees a writer her subject. Baldwin's Harlem pedigree didn't gift him 'The Jimmy'. Only interest, knowledge and love will do that – all of which this book displays in abundance.

Some writers fear opinions; others are famous for 'em. In *My Prizes* Thomas Bernhard opines himself into absurdity. This short work of memoir surveys the many Austrian literary prizes Bernhard hated yet accepted, using the money to buy things he wanted, while complaining of the indignities of the ceremonies. All of that is very funny. Those who love him for his misanthropy will find their cup runneth over. Example: when Bernhard is awarded the (despised) Anton Wildgans Prize, the ceremony is cancelled because a minister declines to share the stage with him (see previous ceremonies for reasons). Yet they send Bernhard the money anyway. Still he is enraged(?), and demands that his friend Gerhard Fritsch resign from the jury. But Gerhard has children and alimony and asks Bernhard 'to show him consideration in a tone that was repellent. The poor man, the malleable, pitiable, wretched man. Not long after this conversation Fritsch hanged himself from the hook on his apartment door, his life, which he'd bungled with no help from anybody, had closed over his head and extinguished him.'

Americans think of this aspect of Bernhard as the art of exaggeration. Europeans, who know him better, think of it as being an incredible bastard. The gap between what actually happened and how Bernhard writes of it can be interpreted variously as postmodern playfulness or deceitful paranoia. (Video footage reveals he was not deprived of a seat at the Grillparzer Prize but led to the front; Austrians of a certain age will tell you his work was not ignored by the state but taught regularly in schools. Nor did he ignore the state, at one point attempting to become head of the Austrian Burgtheater, the most heavily funded in the world!) It's the same difference: we all enjoy an intemperate paragraph of syntactically inspired bile. My quibble with Bernhard's reputation is the idea that it rests on his *philosophical* contribution. Take that line so beloved of Bernhardians: 'It is all absurd, when one thinks about *death*.' In *My Prizes* we can read the speech from which it came. It continues:

> We go through life impressed, unimpressed, we cross the scene, everything is interchangeable, we have been schooled more or less effectively in a state where everything is mere props: but it is all an error! We understand: a clueless people, a beautiful country – there are dead fathers or fathers conscientiously without conscience, straightforwardly despicable in the raw basics of their needs . . . it all makes for a past history that is philosophically significant and unendurable.

Hmmm. 'Everything is interchangeable' is about right.

All the acceptance speeches read the same: sonorous, apocalyptic, pop-philosophical bullshit. This has a retrospective effect on the Bernhard we have loved. Maybe the vital line is interchangeable, too? Couldn't it just as easily be: 'In the face of death, nothing is absurd'? Doesn't he confuse permanence with value? If we lived for ever would life be meaningful? This hollowness is amusing in the novels. (The Austrian writer Daniel Kehlmann tells of a PhD candidate who dutifully tracked all Bernhard's mentions of Goethe, Kant, Wittgenstein, et al. before coming to the conclusion that nothing – beyond their names – is ever said of them.) In the speeches, it begins to look endemic: 'We say we have a right to what's right and just, but we only have a right to what's not right and what's unjust'; 'The question is: to go on, heedless of the consequences, to go on, or to stop, to call it a day . . . it is the question of doubt, of mistrust and impatience. I thank the Academy, and I thank you for your attention.' Though maybe *My Prizes* is totally ironic? Does that help? Is it ironic to rail against state prizes and then spend two decades *collecting more state money than any other Austrian writer?* 'I hated the prize-givers but I took their money. Today I can no longer do it. Until you're forty, I think, but after that?' Like an Internet troll, never in the wrong, constantly changing the parameters to suit his own sense of virtue. Depressing. And not in the usual, good, way. For the best (worst?) of Bernhard, look in the usual places (*Woodcutters, Concrete, The Loser*).

Mix a boyhood of Conan Doyle, Dumas and Stevenson with a fabulist heritage of Borges and García Márquez and an early career spent translating Nabokov, Updike, Faulkner, James and Shakespeare. Result: the stories of Javier Marías. In *While the Women are Sleeping* (New Directions, $22), doppelgängers meet, ghosts hand in resignation letters, a poet-tramp is king of Redonda, and a boy writes a story from the point of view of a dead man. That last is both fiction and reality: the boy author was Marías himself. It tells you something about the childlike pleasures of his style that 'The Life and Death of Marcelino Iturriaga', composed when the author *was fourteen*, is the equal of anything else in the book. Child*like*, but not child*ish*. In 'A Kind of Nostalgia Perhaps', a maid, who happens to be reading aloud to the ghost of Emiliano Zapata, chooses Sherlock Holmes, 'for she put more faith in Conan Doyle's narrative skills than in any other scientific or literary bait'. Marías, too. He plays Borgesian games without the obscurity. Sometimes the Anglophile echoes are overpowering, producing penny-dreadful imitations ('Lawson could stand it no longer'; 'She would stare at the empty armchair and curse the silence . . . hurl reproaches into the invisible air'). And perhaps the doppelgänger theme belongs to Nabokov. But Marías has the loveliest inversions ('It is quite possible that the main aim of ghosts, if they still exist, is to thwart the desires of mortal tenants, appearing if their presence is unwelcome and hiding away if it is expected or demanded'), the most startling domestic insights ('There's nothing worse than being someone's sole source of distraction'). You don't get that in Conan Doyle.

Marías's literalism is especially striking. Characters tell their tall tales awkwardly, stating the obvious, describing the same detail multiple times. The implicit becomes explicit. A butler who practises black magic on the boss's wife describes her fetish for precision a little too precisely: 'She likes me to wear my silk gloves all the time, in the belief that a butler should be constantly running his finger over every surface, over the furniture and along the banisters, to check for dust, because if there is any dust, the gloves will pick it up immediately.' Why not put a full stop after that first 'dust'? Elsewhere – in a story about a man obsessively filming the perfect wife he means to kill – this technique is obliquely revealed, mere 'looking' contrasted with 'the capacity to *see*, which is what we almost never do because it is so at odds with the purely temporal. For it is then that one sees everything, the figures and the background, the light, the composition and the shadows, the three-dimensional and the flat, the pigment and the line, as well as each brushstroke.' The fantastic is made credible by its banal clarity, its lack of shade.

Of Death and Duchesses

John Gray's *The Immortalization Commission: Science and the Strange Quest to Cheat Death* offers two portraits of human hubris. The first depicts a circle of 'psychical researchers' in nineteenth-century England; the second, a ragbag of Bolshevik 'God-builders' intent on remodelling life on earth. What unites these movements, in Gray's view, is the attempt to 'conquer death'. It was science, in the form of Darwinism, that had revealed to the British and the Russians the intolerable truth of human extinction, yet in the absence of credible religious belief, both 'turned to science for escape from the world that science had revealed'. It's Gray's subtle idea that when science is used against itself in this way it becomes 'a channel for magic'. Sometimes this magic is benign, prompting otherwise sensible Victorians and Edwardians to believe they are receiving messages from the dead; at other times it is the kind of lethal black magic capable of 'vanishing' all of Moscow's Boy Scouts on a single day in 1919. As you'll gather from the previous sentence, Gray's case studies are so different in nature it is difficult to fit them together in summary – actually it's difficult, full stop. Despite a bit of bullying parallelism in the introduction ('The Russian God-builders believed death could be defeated using the power of science. The English psychical researchers believed science could show death was a passage into another life. In both cases the boundaries between science, religion and magic were blurred or non-existent'), this begins as a book of two halves, and remains so. The attempted synthesis is bold – it is also essentially metaphorical. Readers may find metaphor insufficient to establish a profound connection between the paranormal practice of 'automatic writing' and the murderous rampages of the Cheka. It's certainly a difficult tonal exercise, moving from bleak comedy to purest tragedy in two hundred pages.

The British section opens at a seance in 1874 in the London house of Erasmus Darwin. Among the invited guests are brother Charles and George Eliot. Seance of the season, surely. It didn't go very well:

Charles found it 'hot and tiring' and left early; Eliot had only her scepticism confirmed. But one man present that night was a believer, and an influential one: Frederic Myers, inventor of the word 'telepathy' and future president of the Society for Psychical Research (SPR). In this role, he was in surprisingly good company: William James was another president, as were the philosophers Henry Sidgwick and Henri Bergson. Members included John Ruskin, Prime Minister Gladstone and Prime Minister Balfour. If in life Myers was a key player in this world, in death he became its main object of study, having instructed surviving friends to be on the alert for his posthumous communications. James tried hard to receive a message but came up empty; more successful were the wives and widows of various SPR members, who became 'automatists', transcribing beyond-the-grave messages from Myers, Sidgwick and others for more than thirty years. 'The people involved in the cross-correspondences,' Gray explains, 'belonged in the topmost stratum of Edwardian society. Many of those involved had suffered agonizing bereavements; some had long-hidden personal relationships. The scripts became a vehicle for unresolved personal loss, and for secret love.' Incredible what the British won't do (talk frankly about their feelings). Incredible what they *will* do (transpose painful feelings into mediated communications from the dead). It's a really crazy scene Gray exhumes: half a dozen genteel ladies channelling a stream-of-consciousness, cross-referenced, fantastical fiction network, peppered with 'stories and phrases from ancient Greece and Rome, the King James Bible and Shakespeare . . . Wordsworth, Browning and Tennyson'. But Gray, a philosopher, is less interested in the literary and subconscious motivations than in the overt rationale, expressed by Sidgwick: 'Unless human personality survived bodily death [. . .] morality is pointless.' That is, if humans have no special destiny, if their existence is not eternal but contingent, then the belief in morality as a system of duties is unsustainable. The same dilemma presented itself to Kant and Nietzsche, whose respective responses to the problem (defence, abandonment) mark the poles of ethical debate through the twentieth century. Sidgwick was in the defence camp, in a style typical of his time: he meant to fight contingency with science. Darwinian science being the revelation of extreme contingency, Sidgwick could continue thinking of himself as a man of science only by wilfully misinterpreting Darwin's message. Death was just a stage of the evolutionary process: 'Rather than the end of life, death was a phase in cosmic progress.' The idea that evolution necessarily describes the progress from lower to higher forms of life was – is – a misapprehension as common as the idea that 'survival of the fittest' means the 'strongest' animal wins. Darwin himself was conflicted on the issue, sometimes arguing there is no more design in natural selection 'than in the course in which the wind blows'; sometimes speaking of the tendency 'toward perfection'. Gray is not conflicted: 'There is nothing in the theory of natural selection to support [the latter] notion.' But the notion has always had its own momentum, morphing easily into eugenics. A famous adherent, H. G. Wells, serves as a bridge here between London and Moscow. An early enthusiast of the Soviet project, in *Anticipations* (1901) he wrote passionately, prophetically, about an oligarchy led by the genetically 'evolved': 'And for the rest, those swarms of black and brown, and dirty-white, and yellow people, who do not come into the new needs of efficiency? Well, the world is a world, not a charitable institution, and I take it they will have to go . . . It is their portion to die out and disappear.' Wells's 1920 trip to Moscow frames Gray's interpretation of Bolshevism as a 'materialist version of gnosticism' in which salvation is 'collective and physical' and the idea is to deliver man from nature: 'Aiming to create a new type of human no longer subject to mortality, the Soviet state propagated death on a vast scale. Unnumbered humans had to die, so that a new humanity could be free of death.' Bye-bye, Boy Scouts.

At this point you can't help but feel, flicking through pages of Stalinist mass murder, that we seem to have drifted some distance from our original subject, immortality – unless you accept Gray's proposal that all this murder of *individual* men is committed for the future benefit of *eternal* man. Matters grow Grayer still when a final metaphorical link is made between occultism and espionage, which seems, again, too loose to hold: 'They attract those who look for a concealed pattern in events.' What is the purpose of this strange book? The answer comes in a brief but devastating final section. It's entitled 'Sweet Mortality'. Here we learn that 'this confusion of science with magic is not an ailment of a kind that has a remedy'. You find it today in scientists who think they can solve global warming ('They cannot stop the climate shift they have set in motion'); in the Dawkins crowd, who believe science can magically subvert belief in God ('No form of human behaviour is more religious than the attempt to convert the world to unbelief, and none is more irrational, for belief has no particular importance in either science or religion'). This is the first time Dawkins is mentioned, but it's possible to read the whole book as a subtle anti-Dawkins enterprise, an attempt to shift the argument away from the familiar Punch and Judy fight – science versus religion – and toward a fuller comprehension of the shared delusions of both. Gray wants scientists to admit (as philosophers long ago conceded) that their theories are only so many tools 'we use to tinker with the world', which always sounds *conceptually* good to literary types like your reviewer, though I wonder what a real scientist would make of Gray's assertion that there are no 'Laws of Nature', only 'regularities'. Even to me it seems sophistical: I can't know with absolute certainty that an apple will fall every time I drop it, but it is my very strong expectation that it will, and it is on such contingent forms of certainty – drawn from abundant experiential evidence of natural 'regularities' – that science, surely, performs its business (and wouldn't most scientists freely admit this mild form of contingency?). Still, if you object to Dawkins's elevation of science at the expense of religion, as many do, you will find appealing Gray's sober view of its limits ('Reality is exhausted by what is and what happens. Beyond this there is nothing'), even while you raise an eyebrow as Gray himself overreaches: 'The resurrection of the dead at the end of time is not as incredible as the idea that humanity, equipped with growing knowledge, is marching toward a better world.'

Personally, I get a contact thrill from this kind of rhetoric, without ever being able to quite dismiss my inner Dawkins, who sits, persistent, in a corner of my brain comparing the Law of Gravity with the Second Coming, asking me baldly which I'd stake my life upon. Then again, Gray's target isn't really the reality status of religion. Unlike Dawkins, he does not waste energy confronting readers of Genesis with the palaeontological record ('The heart of all religions is practice – ritual and meditation. Practice comes with myths, but myths are not theories in need of rational development'). Gray's target is science itself. For Gray, scientific naturalism and religious fundamentalism both refuse to accept that 'there is no hidden order in things', that the world is 'riddled with chaos' and human will in the face of it 'finally powerless'. Darwinism always has been a uniquely bitter pill, not much easier for men of science than for men of God – even Darwin gagged on it. Gray ends on a Kafka note: 'All things may be possible, but not for us.'

~

Speaking of attempts at immortality, did you know the Duchess of Devonshire is ninety-one this month?* In the past decade she seems to have performed a little voodoo of her own: magically extending her life by continually writing about it. This one is called *Wait for Me!* and should feel overfamiliar, but like Chatsworth itself (the four-hundred-year-old seat where she was chatelaine), the Duchess's life is so voluminous she is forever finding enough material for another memoir in some nook or cranny of it, like the time she found a Van Dyck sketchbook at the back of an old cupboard. No matter how many memoirs she writes she will never meet demand: no amount of Mitford will satisfy admirers of that eccentric clan. You can read all Nancy's novels, the letters and biographies, and you will still want to hear more about these seven siblings and their irresistible, monstrous, Communist, Nazi, absurdly posh ways. The Duchess ('Debo', to Mitfordiacs) understands this, and sprinkles Mitford manna on the fans with her opening 'Note on Family Names', three whole pages long, from which I can quote only a representative paragraph:

> Muv and Farve called Nancy *Koko* . . . Pam and Diana called her *Nuance* and to me she was the *Ancient Dame of France*, the *French Lady Writer*, or just *Lady*. Pam was *Woman* to us all, with variations thereof. Tom was *Tuddemy* to Unity and Jessica ('Tom' in Boudledidge, their private language) and this was taken up by the rest of us. Diana was *Dayna* to Muv and Farve, *Deerling* to Nancy, and *Honks* to me . . . Unity was *Bobo*, but *Birdie* or *Bird* to me. Jessica called her *Boud* ('Bobo' in Boudledidge). Jessica was *Little D* to Muv, *Stea-ake* to Pam and *Hen* or *Henderson* to me, but she was *Decca* universally – and remains so in this book.

---

* The Duchess unfortunately left us on 24 September 2014.

For your reviewer this book was a great and guilty pleasure, my own relationship with the Mitfords being somewhat agonized. In a manner that the Duchess makes clear she finds banal and bourgeois, I am repelled by various individual Mitfords' anti-Semitism, unlimited sense of entitlement, affection for Oswald Mosley, Hitler and Stalin, and calm certainty that 'a man who [has] spent all his life in politics or public affairs was more likely to have a son capable of following in his footsteps than a man who has never paid attention to either'. I don't believe that, nor do I believe that decolonization, like the nationalization of coal, was a lot of pointless show, nor that the next best person to clean one's house is the son or daughter of the person who has been cleaning it for forty years. My own grandmother was in service in a great house: thank God the war broke this natural law of inheritance. But! I can't resist the Mitford comedy. Love that Farv read only one book in his life – *White Fang* – and considered it so good he didn't want to spoil matters by reading another. Love older sister Nancy torturing Debo at bedtime: 'As soon as you've gone I shall do the joy dance.' Love Nancy disguising herself as a tramp and accosting her terrified sisters in public places, leering 'Give us a kiss.'

You tend to think of Nancy as the engine of comedy in the Mitford house because she transcribed it so well, but reading Debo's account your respect shifts to Farv, whose comic capacity was as enormous as it was unintended. Upon finding a lot of Nancy's smart Oxford friends at the breakfast table he enquires of Muv (very loudly): 'Have these people no homes of their own?' Here he is answering the phone to Peter Watson, a beau of Nancy: 'Nancy, that hog Watson wants to speak to you.' When Muv tries to remedy Farv's illiteracy by reading *Tess of the d'Urbervilles* aloud, she is surprised to find him moved by Tess's fate: 'Oh, darling, don't cry,

It's only a story.' Farv: 'WHAT. Do you mean to say the damn feller made it up?'

As for class consciousness, you can't hope for that from the Mitfords. They felt themselves to be the natural ruling class the same way they knew buttercups appeared in spring. Churchill was 'Cousin Winston' to them, and Macmillan 'Uncle Harold'; Jack Kennedy was a cute boy who turned up at a few balls the year Debo came out. They had nicknames for the royal family, for Christ's sake (Prince Charles was 'Friend', the Queen Mother 'Cake'). Educational achievement of any kind was considered irredeemably vulgar and the English seasons marked not by meteorological change but mass alighting from different train stations: Ascot, Glyndebourne, Henley. I have a fairly high tolerance for this sort of thing, but also a limit. When an American friend (Bunny Mellon) decides to send Debo's mother-in-law, who runs an East End women's charity, a consignment of clothes, Debo and the girls are shocked to find the boxes, when they arrive, full of Balenciaga. They intercept the gowns, and send the women instead 'decent, unworn clothes of our own that satisfied my mother-in-law's purposes'. Meanwhile the Mitfords step out in their new couture. Debo: 'No-one could have appreciated them more.' Where to begin?

Class is a cocoon – it takes genius to think your way out of it. Debo is no genius, as she'd be the first to admit. But she is a funny, honest and unpretentious writer, with a winning mix of naivety and wisdom. Her social experiences may have been narrow (aren't all our social experiences, whether on the top or the bottom, narrow?), but her domestic experience was broad and often sad, and serves as a reminder that there exist human troubles from which no amount of money or class will protect you. Debo had six pregnancies: three babies who died at birth, three survivors. This dark period – and her husband's lifelong alcoholism – she dispatches in only a few pages, demonstrating those once-general British qualities, discretion and stoicism, whose disappearance she elsewhere laments, along with elbow-length gloves and that bit in Harrods where a fellow could leave his country hounds while he went to his club.

Édouard Levé and Peter Stamm

On 15 October 2007, ten days after handing in the manuscript for a novel called *Suicide*, the Parisian writer and photographer Édouard Levé killed himself, aged forty-two. Levé's suicide is the de-centred centre of *Suicide*, as he must have known it would be. A conceptual artist, Levé was fond of the 'deferred' term, which exists outside a structure and yet informs every part of it – a strategy once considered Derridean until ubiquity rendered it simply French. In *Oeuvres* (2002), Levé described 533 of his own works that did not, at that point, exist. His photographic project *Homonymes* is a series of portraits of 'ordinary' people who share names with the famous. He used a variation on the same concept in *Amérique* (2006), a visual record of 'three months in the United States travelling only to cities that share a name with a city in another country'. Many of these photographs are a bit run-of-the-mill: slovenly Americans, tract housing, desolate highways. The irony is straight out of Urban Outfitters. I don't say that just to be smart – the adolescent aesthetic is at the core of Levé's art, for good and for bad. *Pêcheur de Bagdad et sa fille*, a sneering portrait of an obese father and (in fact) his son fishing in Bagdad, Florida, is a neat example of the impenetrable superiority that makes teenagers (and Parisians) so frequently annoying. Elsewhere, specifically in a shot called *Jeune femme de*

Paris, Levé finds exactly the right teenage girl in the right white jeans: her sullen beauty would not look out of place on the Champs-Élysées. Levé's prose is like this, too, veering between the banal and the sublime. Take the opening lines of *Autoportrait*, his penultimate, paragraph-free novel, consisting solely of authorial assertions:

> As an adolescent I believed that [Perec's] *Life A User's Manual* would help me to live, and that [Claude Guillon and Yves le Bonniec's] *Suicide A User's Manual* would help me to die. I don't really listen to what people tell me. I forget things I don't like. I look down dead-end streets. The end of a trip leaves me with a sad aftertaste the same as the end of a novel. I am not afraid of what comes at the end of life. I am slow to realize when someone mistreats me, it is always so surprising: evil is somehow unreal.

That mixture of thoughtfulness and self-regard, honest interrogation and mere posing – if I were fifteen, *Autoportrait* would be my bible. As an adult, I still find Levé hard to resist, perhaps because his adolescent aesthetic reminds us of the kind of writing that got us reading in the first place. Tales like 'A Perfect Day for Bananafish', another suicide narrative and one of the most adolescent, and beautiful, stories in American literature. As adults we know the dilemma Salinger sets up for Seymour is heavily freighted, unfair. (Basically: If you can't live with the authenticity of a child, why live at all?) But to read 'Bananafish' is to be taken back to a time when simply overhearing a phoney conversation could make you want to kill yourself. I think we dutifully admire the Shakespearean writer, able to capture the seven ages of man from mewling infant to second childishness, but we reserve our special adoration for writers who get – how to put it? – *stuck* at this intense,

imbalanced and unforgiving age. ('Art that unfolds over time,' writes
Levé, 'gives me less pleasure than art that stops it.') It's no
coincidence that writers who stop time in this way tend to remember
their own adolescence as the time of their lives:

> The best conversations I had date from adolescence, with a friend at
> whose place we drank cocktails that were made by mixing up his
> mother's liquor at random, we would talk until sunrise . . . in the
> course of those nights, I delivered speeches on love, politics, God,
> and death of which I retain not one word, even though I came up
> with some of them doubled over in laughter; years later, this friend
> told his wife that he had forgotten something in the house just as
> they were going out to play tennis, he went down to the basement
> and put a bullet in his head with the gun he had left there
> beforehand.

And that shocking little addendum, tucked nonchalantly (just as
a teenager would!) into *Autoportrait*, leads directly to the opening
lines of *Suicide*:

> One Saturday in the month of August, you leave your home wearing
> your tennis gear, accompanied by your wife. In the middle of the
> garden you point out to her that you've forgotten your racket in the
> house . . . you head down into the basement. Your wife doesn't
> notice this . . . A few moments later she hears a gunshot.

From the narcissistic claustrophobia of *Autoportrait* to the
narrative power of *Suicide* it's only a little leap – from *je* to *tu* – but
it's the difference that makes all the *différence*. It is a book balanced
thrillingly between monologue and biography. But what kind of a

guy is this *tu*? Well, he's you. You're too pure for this world. Also too brilliant. You're like Seymour Glass and Young Werther. You find social experience inauthentic: 'One evening you were invited to dine at a friend's house with other guests . . . you couldn't make yourself lie in response to the simple question, "How are you doing?" ' You are very pure. You are like Wittgenstein, or Christ: '[Y]ou were told that you had been accepted. Your speech about death had received one of the highest grades. You refused to enter the school.' You are alienated from yourself: 'You approached the mirror; you recognized your physiognomy, but it seemed to belong to someone else.' You are very easy to read about (I couldn't put you down!), even if Levé's ideas about you are not always wildly original. That Levé is able to think of you with such affection – in his own moment of extremity – lends great emotional heft to this simple list of facts about you. What else? Sometimes your story is interrupted by theoretical proselytizing:

> A dictionary resembles the world more than a novel does, because the world is not a coherent sequence of actions but a constellation of things perceived . . . If events follow each other, they are believed to be a story. But in a dictionary, time doesn't exist: ABC is neither more nor less chronological than BCA. To portray your life in order would be absurd: I remember you at random. My brain resurrects you through stochastic details, like picking marbles out of a bag.

There was some of this in *Autoportrait*, too ('I prefer a ruin to a monument'; 'I write fragments'). Parisian writers seem convinced that the rest of the world thinks life is like a chronological novel. But your character survives the argument that character cannot be made: 'Far from your home, you used to taste the pleasure of being mad without being alienated, of being an imbecile without renouncing your intelligence, of being an impostor without culpability.' And beyond these abstractions of your personality, there is the un-philosophical revelation that antidepressants can rob you of your selfhood entirely: 'Suddenly, you no longer had a brain. Or rather, it was another person's brain. You sat like this for two hours, asking yourself if you were yourself.' 'Was a little bit of fake happiness worth losing your free will?'

Now, is all of this about you – or Levé? Does the difference matter? It is as if Levé has found an existential way to depict a friendship: two souls intermingled in a pronoun. The sadness of this book is overwhelming. Yet at the same time it's a cause for happiness, because it's the final record of a writer who found, in the end, the correct vessel for his talents. In *Suicide* Levé's fragments become wonderfully sharp, conjuring tragedy in a few sentences: 'You kept a tape of the messages left on your answering machine by mistake. One of them went: "We've arrived fine. We've arrived fine. We've arrived fine." Uttered slowly by an old lady in despair.'

Seven Years is the fourth novel by Peter Stamm, a forty-eight-year-old Swiss. It has a bewitching cover: a photograph of an antique bedstead with stylish contemporary sheets, set against a tasteful grey wall. I took one look at it and thought: God, I wish I lived like that. This bourgeois response proved thematically important, as we shall see. It gets under your skin, this novel. It welcomes you into a clean, modern space as appealing as that room – and then it really fucks with you, if you'll excuse my Swiss-German. It's about 'lifestyle' – in the broadest sense – and it's a devastating read. It begins like this: 'Sonia stood in the middle of the brightly lit space; she liked to be at the center of things.' Sonia is a brilliant, beautiful young woman studying to be an architect in early-eighties Munich. The narrator is Alex, another trainee architect, who begins as an admiring acquaintance ('She was more gifted than me, and had more application') and ends up being her husband. How this comes about is interesting. Sonia is dating one of Alex's more gregarious friends; they seem a 'dream couple', but when that boyfriend inexplicably leaves her ('That I don't understand, I said, how anyone could leave a woman like you'), Alex begins to consider a potential knock-through, from his life into Sonia's: 'Sometimes I entertained the idea of falling in love with Sonia myself, but however plausible it was as an idea, it didn't seem at all appropriate . . . I couldn't picture her as my girlfriend, not in bed, not even naked . . . She was like one of those dolls whose clothes are sewn on to their bodies.' Sonia is oppressively perfect, with a will to power that Alex lacks. She believes 'the world could be transformed by architecture'. She adores Le Corbusier; Alex prefers deconstructivism.

Still, they begin circling each other, because Sonia, too, thinks Alex 'has potential'. They take a trip to Marseille to see Le Corbusier's Cité Radieuse. En route they have an instructive argument: 'She said, Anyway, what could be bad about a building that improved the people who lived in it? I said, People have a history that you have to respect.' Their trip is, to Alex, like 'a scene from a French movie of the fifties or sixties, our whole life was a film put together from distance shots, wide angles under white light, with little people moving through it, all very esthetic and intellectual and cool'. The potential couple stay in the apartment of Sonia's friend Antje, a German artist in her forties, who is, like Alex, curious about human perversity, as he gathers from her wall murals: 'I saw the strange beings in the paintings, a man with a fish head and an enormous cock he was holding in both hands, a bull mounting a cow, both with human heads, two dogs with human privates, licking each other.' Even to Antje, Alex and Sonia look irresistibly good on paper. When night comes, she pushes Alex into Sonia's room as she sleeps. 'There was a small dark sweat stain in [Sonia's] armpit, the one flaw in an otherwise perfect picture. I stroked it with my finger, I didn't dare any other touch.' The relationship begins. They move into an apartment together and have a strange moment in front of a mirror, more chilling to me than Levé's:

> We stood next to each other in the bathroom and looked at ourselves in the mirror. Two beautiful people in a beautiful apartment, said Sonia, and laughed. I turned and kissed her, and thought of the beautiful couple in the mirror kissing as well, and that excited me more than the actual kiss itself. I reached into Sonia's short hair with my hand and rubbed her shaved neck. You look like a boy. She laughed and asked if I'd gone off her? I stepped behind her and placed my hands over her breasts, and said, Luckily there were still a few points of difference.

This is the stealthy way Stamm operates; the anxious misogyny of our narrator is not hidden (Alex wants a brilliant modern woman, but her new haircut makes him nervous; he still wants a woman in whom the 'points of difference' have not been obscured). But Sonia also has a depressingly familiar way of pursuing her life as if it were an advert for itself. Christmas presents are exchanged, future plans are made: 'It was a cardboard model of a single-family house, very carefully done. In front of the house stood two little human figures, a man and a woman. Someday, said Sonia. I wanted to kiss her on the mouth, but she turned her head away, and I kissed her on the cheek.' They get married, despite the apparent sexual coolness between them. They start a firm together, building housing projects, Sonia enthusiastically, Alex ambivalently:

> [W]hen I visited one of these projects years later, when I saw how
> the buildings had been taken over – laundry hanging out to dry on
> balconies, bicycles dumped higgledy-piggledy outside the doors,
> little flowerbeds arranged in defiance of any understanding of
> landscaping – then . . . I didn't feel annoyance so much as fear and
> a kind of fascination with life swarming and seething and escaping
> our plans.

The business grows. They move into larger premises. To celebrate, Alex frames Sonia's favourite Corbusier quote: 'Everything is different. Everything is new. Everything is beautiful. She hung it over her desk and said, Everything is the way it's supposed to be.' God, I wish I lived like that . . .

You might feel Stamm is stacking the deck against Sonia somewhat, and you'd be right. A furious feminist reading is legitimate. So, we became your liberated partners, and now you *hate* us for it? I felt this but at the same time couldn't deny the power of Stamm's wider critique, which implicates men and women both. First you sell your lifestyle to your family and friends (the centrepiece of which is your relationship). Then you spend the rest of your life selling it to each other. In a tedious catch-up lunch with Sonia's ex-boyfriend, now a successful businessman, Alex gets to hear all about it:

> He talked about spontaneous networks and people who had a sort of
> entrepreneurial approach to their lives, and kept asking themselves,
> Okay, what are my strengths, my preferences, my assumptions?

What am I making of them all? Where am I going, and how will I get there? That's where the future is, E G O plc. And what if E G O plc goes bust? I asked.

But that possibility is never allowed, it can't even be thought:

[Sonia] had once likened our relationship to a house we were building together, something that wasn't an expression of either one of us, but that came about through our joint wills. There were many rooms in this house, she said, a dining room and a bedroom, a children's room, and a pantry for our common memories. And what about a cellar, I said, but at that she had merely laughed.

Yes, what *about* that cellar? In this perfect picture, something is missing, or some*one*: Ivona. Ivona is the cellar of this book, the id to Sonia's ego. Alex meets her just as his relationship with Sonia begins. A random encounter in a beer garden. She is a Polish immigrant, a devout Catholic, heavyset and poorly dressed, like a peasant ('She wore beige knickerbockers and a sort of folksy embroidered blouse'). She has no ambition. She works in a Christian bookshop. She is almost monosyllabic. They sleep together the first day they meet. 'Without anything happening, I had the feeling she was giving herself to me.' She is perhaps insane, for the first full sentence she says to him is: 'I love you. 'And his attraction to her is utterly inexplicable to him: 'Ivona bored me, we had nothing to say to each other. It was only in bed that I liked being with her, when she lay there heavy and soft in her ugly clothes, and I felt completely free and uninhibited.' In this upside-down world, kitsch interiors become pornographic ('At the head of the bed was a small plastic crucifix, the walls were covered with postcards and framed Bible sayings. On the bed were any number of soft toys in garish colors, the kind you can buy at railway station kiosks'), and clutter and filth irresistible: 'The pokiness, the untidiness, and the absence of any esthetic value only seemed to intensify my desire.' Good sex is beside the point: 'when I touched her she barely reacted, or faked a reaction. The thing that kept me fascinated with her was her utter devotion.' We seem to be witnessing the return of an ancient character to contemporary fiction: the simple, devoted girl. There's another example in Jonathan Franzen's *Freedom*. Turns out the house of human sexuality has (a) basement, no matter how much we try to focus our attention on the fitted kitchen.

Alex does his best to forget this strange episode. But even after his marriage to Sonia, the memory of Ivona keeps returning. Then comes the seven-year itch. What happens next is shocking; I won't ruin it for you. It is all anyway confessed – in a neat framing device – to Antje twenty years later. She is the judge of the situation, and also the social engineer who nudged Sonia and Alex together in the first place. No accident, I imagine, that she is twenty years older, and the right age to be a first-wave feminist. Unimpressed by Alex's confession, she is a stand-in for the angry reader:

> But I had no choice, I couldn't help myself. Antje said I was making things a bit too easy for myself. She believed in free will. Has it never happened to you, I said, that you did something, even though you knew it was wrong? That's a part of free will too.

Seven Years feels to me like a Catholic novel, an intriguing addition to a tradition that includes *The Power and the Glory*, *The Prime of Miss Jean Brodie* and the lesser-known *An Experiment in Love* by Hilary Mantel (which is also about the failures of first-wave feminism, and features a proto-Ivona, heavyset and Eastern European, in the character of Karina). What links novels in this tradition, I think, is a tendency to confront perversity without trying to obscure or resolve it. Stamm's prose (beautifully translated by Michael Hofmann) is plain but not so simple: missing quotation marks allow thought and speech to mingle and culpability to be confused, and the only things separating Alex's benign words from his poisonous actions are a few commas, grammatical equivalents of the 'thin veneer' he detects between civilization and ugly chaos while watching a *Jerry Springer*-style show on TV. A subtle but deadly style. You're warned early, in the epigraph, which is (for once!) not surplus to requirements but actually essential: 'Light and shadow reveal form – Le Corbusier.' I found Stamm's light and shadow so absorbing I'd almost finished the novel before I realized he had made an argument I would have violently rejected had it been presented to me *in any other form than this novel*. On the last page, Alex is in an airport watching the departures and spots a man with two children: '[The father] turned to [them] and said, She's gone now, and one of the children, a boy of ten or so, asked, Where did she go? I don't see her. There, said the father, pointing into the air, that's where she is. But there was nothing to be seen where he was pointing except the overcast sky.' *You've come a long way, baby*, I wrote in the margin – *too far?* And couldn't believe what I'd written. *Seven Years* is a novel to make you doubt your own dogma. What more can a novel do than that?

Paula Fox and Geoff Dyer

Now that any decent American bookshop shelves Paula Fox between Ford and Gaitskill, it's easy to forget how long she spent in the wilderness. The story of her rediscovery has been told many times: along with the restoration of Richard Yates, it's one of the happier New York publishing stories of the nineties. Both revivals were a response to present need. A fresh crop of writers sought a way of writing 'around-the-house-and-in-the-yard' fiction, as Don DeLillo once called it – without incurring the scorn of writers like DeLillo. A new domestic realism: unsentimental yet vivid, self-accusatory without being morose, symbolic of a nation but not diagrammatic. Sometimes the books you're dreaming of have already been written. Fox's *Desperate Characters* turned up in Jonathan Franzen's 'Perchance to Dream', his *Harper's* essay in defence of the novel, and in David Foster Wallace's classroom; writers recommended it to readers and to one another. And though it was Yates who became the supernova, Fox remains the writer's writer. Her adult oeuvre is smaller than Yates's and more emotionally composed (without his penchant for self-pity), though she had plenty of reasons – both personal and professional – to feel sorry for herself. The unwanted child of two pretty desperate characters, she was abandoned often, sometimes for years, and like Yates suffered especially at the hands of a 'creative' parent, who put art before child and drink before both. Like Yates, she watched her work fall out of print while mediocre peers were celebrated. Both writers were sceptics when it came to the exceptionalism so many artists claim as their right (and the commercial reception of their books must have compounded this feeling). Neither had much affection for the conventional middle-class life that awaited them on the other side of childhood chaos. Their mutual lack of bombast was part of what endeared them to readers of the nineties, wearied by the irrepressible personae and prose of writers like Wolfe and Mailer. It was time again for a writer with Hemingway's self-described 'built-in shock-proof shit detector'. Fox certainly has one; in some ways it's superior to those of Hemingway and Yates, both of whom drank themselves into caricature. Fox knew the type well. Her father, the novelist and screenwriter Paul Hervey Fox, she flatly describes as 'a writer and a drunk'. In *News from the World: Stories and Essays* she refines that caricature into indelible portrait:

> On the few occasions I saw my father during my childhood and ado-
> lescence, he was drunk most of the time. As a young man he had been
> handsome. His voice, poetic and slurred, was given over to intermin-
> able, stumbling descriptions of the ways in which he and fellow
> writers tried to elude domesticity and women. All writers, he asserted,
> were defeated romantics, trying to escape domesticity and females to
> aspire upwards to the mountain heights, only to be dragged down to
> the lowlands by the female urgencies of breeding and nesting.

Fox has spent forty-five years cultivating two qualities her father lacked, self-control and empathy: 'a living interest in all living creatures'. In the new collection this interest is widely displayed, across fiction, memoir, lecture and essays, with no formal distinction made between genres. This feels true to Fox's self-conception:

> Interviewer: But what, then, is the difference, for you, between
>   autobiography and fiction?
> Fox: Well, for me there isn't much difference.

Certainly the fine texture of her fiction, its visual acuity, folds seamlessly into non-fiction. In the *Paris Review* interview, defending herself against the identity 'intellectual', she explains her gift thus: 'I can *see.*' She really can. In an essay detailing her move to Brooklyn: 'But you saw the sky in a way you rarely saw it in Manhattan. As I looked up at it I realized . . . that it was limitless, not a roof for a city, not a part of a stage décor, but the heavens.' Being shown round her future home: 'I saw a bathroom, its door open, looking like plain white underwear, slightly soiled.' Reaching forty years back for a memory, she reanimates an acquaintance with masterful adjectival amalgams: 'I shared a vast room with a woman who had been a member of an acting troupe in her youth. I saw her sober in-frequently. She slept mostly, and when she was awake, showed me an elaborate blurred courtesy.' Occasionally all this fine attention is lavished on obscure subjects. Like many a New York writer, she assumes our intimate familiarity with behind-the-scenes machinations at famous local literary journals, in this case *Commentary*, where the Greenbergs (Fox's husband's family) apparently played out their dramas. More interesting for the general reader is her encounter with D. H. Lawrence's widow, Frieda, in Taos, New Mexico, where she comes across Lawrence's paintings: 'I found them repellent. The subjects were naked women crawling on a stone floor, their breasts and buttocks enormous, their faces angry or as blank as balloons. The work was done in raw, brutal colors, full of energy and hysteria.' The precise opposite of Fox's MO: controlled anxiety. Holding back the savagery that lies at the edge of civilization – the classic Foxian situation. 'Is this what thousands of years of human life is to come to?' she finds herself crying at two fighting children she is attempting to separate. 'Is this all we are – snarling, murderous things?'

Whether Fox believes human savagery to be innate or the product of circumstance is a troubling ambiguity in her work. A persistent racial tension runs through it (white liberals representing civilization, poor blacks and Latinos symbolizing chaos), a theme made more uncomfortable by her refusal to place her cards face up on the table. Severe judgements tend to be placed in the mouths of other people:

'[I] mentioned neighborhood crime, attributing it to poverty and hopelessness. But then she took me by surprise. "Human beings," she said, "have an inborn capacity for wickedness." I think she means to track misery, from whichever direction it comes, as it encroaches on happiness, wherever it may be. *Et in Arcadia ego.* And that's a large enough battlefield to stage a lot of messy American contests: between classes, races, beliefs. It ain't always pretty. In 'The Tender Night', a moving account of her friendship with a gay neighbour, AIDS is the beast in the garden, and Fox brings her crisp yet tender view to the poor man's bedside: 'his fingers felt like a handful of pencils'. But some of her conclusions will sound a little off to contemporary readers:

> What I had sensed, fleetingly, as a child with four uncles, three of whom were homosexual, had become plain as I grew older. There is as much diversity among homosexual people – in some instances, more – as there is among other people.

An uncivilized part of me wants to call that a 'senior moment', sweet in its superfluity. Then you remember it's a supernatural writer who is able to travel as far in age from her readers as Fox (she was born in 1923) and not fall out of step with their orthodoxies. Generational gaps show up now and again. Fox spends perhaps more time than is necessary bemoaning latter-day linguistic infelicities (misuse of 'like' and 'role model', of 'impact' as a verb, and so on). This line of attack invades the recent stories, appearing in the dialogue of disgruntled types as they shout at the TV. For Fox, the degeneration of language represents another phalanx of the encroaching chaos, but in combating it she sometimes loses her sense of proportion, as people who make their living out of words are liable to do. She mourns the replacement of radio by TV, and sees in modern childhood a kitsch myth of innocence. She quotes E. M. Forster ('She gave up trying to understand herself, and joined the vast armies of the benighted, who follow neither the heart nor the brain, and march to their destiny by catch-words'), but if you're warning against platitudinous thought, you must also strive to avoid the oldest and deepest: *Things were better back then.*

I prefer Fox the fiction writer, who has such an ear she once wrote several 'black' stories (two are included here) and submitted them to *The Negro Digest*, where they were accepted. The editor at the time, Hoyt Fuller, 'wrote to find out if I was black. He did it very subtly, but I could see that was the question behind the letter.' Not only can Fox *see*, she can *hear*, she can *feel* – and in these vital areas there has been no weakening in her powers. One story, 'Grace', dated 2003, absolutely floored me. It is about a bachelor with a sick dog. Against his will he has to leave it at the vet for an operation. At a loss, he wanders into a bar to eat, and drink:

> The steak, when it came, was leathery, and it reminded him of the gloves he wore when he played with Grace. At this very moment she was in a cage in the dark, bewildered but stoical. Long-suffering was more like it, poor thing, carried along on the current of existence. No wonder she suddenly got up and went to another room to lie down. It wasn't thought that roused her, only a need for a small movement of freedom inside of fate. Why, after all, had he stopped in this awful, shadowy bar?

Now *that* is empathy. When the dog dies, the man feels the need to phone an ex-girlfriend:

> 'And what do you want?' She was breathing rapidly.
> 'I'd like to see you.'

'What for?'

'Jean. I know how bad it was, the way I spoke to you.'

'You were so – contemptuous!'

'I know. I had no right –'

She broke in. 'No one has.'

Not blacks, not whites, not the rich, not the poor, not parents, not children. No one.

'Would it be immodest,' asks Geoff Dyer, in the introduction to *Otherwise Known as the Human Condition: Selected Essays and Reviews*, 'to claim that this book gives a glimpse of a not unrepresentative way of being a late-twentieth-early-twenty-first-century man of letters?' Yes, Geoff, it would. Then again, it wouldn't be inaccurate. And if it didn't happen to be you saying it, you could go ahead and replace 'not unrepresentative' with 'exemplary'. Many reviewers who are not Geoff Dyer have noted the extraordinary variety of this book, moving as it does from photography, to literature, to music, to travel, to sport, to war to peace, to love to sex to family – to sex *with* your family, of which more later. But the eclecticism is less important to me than the unity of approach. Considering a 1943 Robert Capa photograph in which an Italian soldier and his girl walk along a country lane, Dyer writes: 'Works of art urge us to respond *in kind* and so, looking at this photograph, my reaction expresses itself as a vow: I will never love another photograph more.' Every essay here is an attempt to respond *in kind*, to be equal to the art work, in some way to meld with it, like a love object. The act of critical appreciation is, for Dyer, very close to longing ('I want to *be* that soldier'). Discussing a snapshot (by Jacques Henri Lartigue) of an attractive woman on a sunlounger, it is Dyer himself who leans over her and murmurs, '*Excusez-moi, mademoiselle. J'espère que je ne vous dérange . . .*' He wants to be *in* these photographs, but he also wants to *be* these photographers. His critical apparatus is essentially novelistic: voyeurism. What if I weren't me? What if I could be someone else, *do* something else? What is it like, being a photographer? Or a musician? Or a sculptor? The title of an essay on Susan Sontag, 'Regarding the Achievement of Others', in fact applies throughout. While quoting the photographer (and obsessive quote-transcriber) William Gedney, Dyer finds a line that illuminates his own interest in role reversal: 'I go to encounter for the millionth time the reality of experience,' wrote Joyce. Gedney marked that with an asterisk and inverted the terms – 'the experience of reality' – to distinguish the photographer's quest from the novelist's.

Dyer seems always to be questing to comprehend somebody else's quest. A 'literary and scholarly gate-crasher', who turns up 'uninvited at an area of expertise', he quotes approvingly Sontag's exacting dictum ('My idea of a writer: someone interested in "everything" ') but his own way of being a writer is a little less pompous than Sontag's, and a lot more comic – I'm tempted to say, more British. For Dyer the line between being not at all interested in something and being very interested in it is remarkably thin: concentration, even obsession, is born of distraction and boredom. His experience with photography is typical. Quite suddenly he went from not being interested in photography, to being very interested in it, to – and this is the step 99 per cent of normal people don't take – getting *so* interested in it he wrote a whole book about it. Yet in all that time, as he explains, he never bought a camera. When asked by a librarian at the Institute of Jazz Studies what his credentials were for writing a book about jazz, he replies, 'I like listening to it.' And once he's successfully established himself in a subject, 'making myself at home, having a high old time for a year or two', he then abruptly abandons it, 'moving on elsewhere'.

There's a restless current to these essays, as if a net were being thrown ever wider in search of fresh versions of that original burst of aesthetic delight, literature, which managed to turn a working-class grammar-school boy from Cheltenham into an international 'man of letters'. It will not surprise long-time Dyer readers to learn that D. H. Lawrence was central to that transformation. Coincidentally, Lawrence was essential to Paula Fox, too; both writers read the same book, *Sons and Lovers*, at the same age, fifteen. For Fox the book was an 'awakening'; for Dyer 'it dramatized a process of which reading this novel was an exemplary part', the process being that peculiarly English problem of 'growing up in – and moving away from – the working class'. But Lawrence is much more to Dyer than a class role model (forgive me, Paula). Lawrence means frank discussion of sex, he means escape from the academy, he means 'not belong[ing] to any class' and instead feeling 'everywhere . . . at home', he means childlessness and adventure, he means 'never let[ting] the fact that [you are] technically ill qualified to write about something deter [you] from doing so'. In the claustrophobic world of British letters, Lawrence means freedom. It is a spiritual connection that exists between the two writers: stylistically they have almost nothing in common. What Dyer admires in Lawrence is his fundamental openness to the world, 'his bond with everything in creation', as Frieda had it. But the purple prose for which Lawrence is, in my opinion, rightly notorious is nowhere in Dyer.

At a certain point in that Gedney essay, Dyer transcribes a line of the photographer's that feels self-reflexive: 'It is not easy to be unpretentious, simple, direct, honest and yet intelligent.' For British writers it can feel almost impossible, for reasons that are profoundly bound to class, as Dyer, in a very brilliant essay on Richard Ford, recognizes:

> Lucky American writers for whom the dominant narrative voice of literature is so close to the lives of the people *within* the narra- tive! . . . Think of the hoops James Kelman has to wedge himself through to close the gap between narrative and dialogue; then think of Ford and that all-accommodating, middle-of-the-road voice that is equally at home on either side of quotation marks.

And this is what I find most remarkable about Dyer: his tone. Its simplicity, its *classlessness*, its accessibility and yet its erudition – the combination is a trick few British writers ever pull off. It allows him to say things like this: 'Not only is ours a time when anyone – from presidents of the United States to nameless peasants – might die on film; this has been the time when, to a degree, people die *only* on film. I have seen hundreds of bodies on film and never one in real life.' As a mode you might call it 'the conversational sublime'. It's very close to the tone of John Berger – another of Dyer's heroes – but Dyer isn't tied to Berger's political stringencies, and so can indulge the personal in ways Berger cannot. It's very difficult to imagine Berger writing about anal sex, or sex in hotels, or explaining that one of the pleasures of fiction writing is the way you get to invent people, precisely, a sister, more precisely 'the *perfect* sister – one you were sexually attracted to'.

Dyer knows, like Martin Amis – from whom a lot of the Dyer humour comes – that writers' lives are 'mostly anxiety and ambition'. In the literary essays this gives him an acute psychological edge.

Discussing the romance between American writing and boxing, he begins with Hemingway's brag ('I started off very quietly and I had Mr. Turgenev . . . I fought two draws with Mr. Stendhal, and I think I had an edge in the last one') before wittily tracking a masculine contest, among Papa's descendants, to produce the most muscular, brutal, 'broken' sentences, at the end of which zero-sum game lies 'the quandary of a contemporary American literary ideal: if only it were possible to not be able to write at all – *and still be able to write*'.

Which is all to say Geoff Dyer has a very refined shit detector indeed. But every shit detector has a flaw. Dyer's may be unnecessary self-defence. 'To what extent,' he asks of Sontag, 'is it possible to be a great prose writer without being a great writer of fiction?' The answer is comically obvious ('As for *In America*, I respected myself so much for finishing it that I felt I deserved a prize myself'), but he doesn't seem to believe we believe it. On Rebecca West: 'If she is not regarded as a writer quite of the first rank, that is largely because so much of the work on which her reputation should rest is tacitly considered secondary to the forms in which greatness is expected to manifest itself, namely, the novel.' On Ryszard Kapuściński: 'he is the victim of a received cultural prejudice that assumes fiction to be the loftiest preserve of literary and imaginative distinction'. Maybe fifty years ago. It is the only subject in four hundred pages on which Dyer is (slightly) dull. In the end he is rescued from the accusation of self-seriousness by his humour. It's what separates him from Berger and Lawrence and Sontag: it's what makes these essays not just an education but a joy. His piece on the blue-chip gallery photographer Edward Burtynsky opens like this:

Whether these are seen on the walls of the Corcoran Gallery in Washington or in the accompanying book published by Steidl, the photographs in *Oil* bring the viewer face to face with huge and troubling questions. How can we go on producing on this scale? How can we go on consuming like this? Aren't we at the point where we say, okay, enough is enough? Is it sustainable, the level of luxury and lavishness to which we have become accustomed? In short, how many more of these high-concept, high-value Edward Burtynsky productions can we take? I am being only slightly facetious.

Facetious inversions are a speciality. One of the funniest things on the Internet is Dyer pulling the same trick while introducing an unsmiling J. M. Coetzee at a literary festival.

In the memoir section, the familiar archness gives way to something softer. Here the tantalizingly cool life of the independent writer is rooted in the longueurs of life as an only child, and an excess of empty time was not, *is* not, always the paradise it may seem to those looking on: 'whereas many people my age are starting to feel worn down by the burden of obligations, responsibilities, and commitments, it's the *freedom* that's getting to me'. Dyer is an excellent chronicler of his own ennui, and is perhaps most moving when he reveals that the young man who created himself from books now finds it hard to even finish reading one: 'But how could it have happened? How did I go from being interested in *everything* to not being that bothered about *anything*?'

I once compared Dyer with Kingsley Amis, a comparison I suspect he wouldn't thank me for, given that Amis's interests were, in the end, so narrowly parochial and British, and Dyer's are so stunningly wide. But it's a connection I've always felt without being able to give a very rational reason for it. I was glad, then, to find in his essay on Rebecca West's *Black Lamb and Grey Falcon* a funny moment where the two men seem to coalesce. Dyer is discussing

West's 'affirmation of the agreeable' over the disagreeable. This is Dyer's preference, too, and in his resourceful way, he finds an Auden quote (from 'In Time of War') to echo the sentiment: 'It's better to be sane than mad, or liked than dreaded;/It's better to sit down to nice meals than to nasty;/It's better to sleep two than single; it's better to be happy.' And it's *this* poem that Kingsley bastardized to come up with his much-repeated credo: *Nice things are nicer than nasty ones.* That's where Kingsley and Dyer meet: in a commitment to the moral integrity of pleasure. It also explains why, in all these many pages of Dyer, there is not one conventionally 'bad' review. A man who can't be bothered to do yoga is unlikely to rouse himself to write a thousand words about something he hates. What gives Dyer the edge over Amis Sr – and over so much of what he calls 'the tucked-up, hospital corners school of British fiction' – is his ability to hold both the beauty and horror of existence in his mind simultaneously, as he demonstrates in Algeria, while shadowing another of his literary idols, Camus: 'I am seized by two contradictory feelings: there is so much beauty in the world it is incredible that we are ever miserable for a moment; there is so much shit in the world that it is incredible we are ever happy for a moment.'

Two Legs Bad, Six Legs Good – Sontag Worse!

Am I a redundant human being? A question asked by many a novel – many a novelist – but rarely so explicitly, and not usually on the front cover. But that's the title of Mela Hartwig's novella, written in 1931 and now reissued by Dalkey Press, and it works like a life buoy, alerting us to a writer drowning in obscurity. Born in Vienna in 1893, Hartwig was an actress before becoming a writer; she married

Dr Robert Spira, an art historian and critic, and when the Anschluss came, the couple escaped to London, where they befriended Virginia Woolf. That much the publisher tells you; it's difficult to find more. There was another early novel with an equally provocative title, *Das Weib ist ein Nichts* (*The Woman is a Nothing*), which became a scandal (and almost a Greta Garbo movie). And I was pleased to unearth an issue of the Association of Jewish Refugees newsletter reporting Mela's seventieth birthday, a short paragraph sprinkled with poignant information ('When she came to this country in 1938 she encountered insurmountable difficulties in carrying on her activities as a writer. This frustration caused her to find another outlet for her artistic inclinations, which was independent of her German mother tongue: painting'). The next reference in the same organ is her 1967 obituary. In the English-speaking universe she seems to exist mainly in the blinding contrails of Woolf, who used her influence to help release Dr Spira from a brief internment on the Isle of Man, and came again to the couple's aid when some paintings Robert had brought from Vienna were judged to be fakes (Woolf promised to get Sir Kenneth Clark, Surveyor of the King's Pictures, to take a look at them). We have a footnote: a cache of letters between Woolf and Vita Sackville-West was recently discovered in a hidden drawer in Sissinghurst, one of which was found to mention Mela in passing, a stray ball lobbed between two pros, long lost in the high grass. Was Mela grateful to be the object of Virginia's well-connected generosity? Or did she feel patronized, pained by the status gap between them? Friend or frenemy? You'd expect a little volatility from the woman who opened a novel this way:

I'm a secretary. I have nearly twelve years of experience. My short-hand is first rate and I'm an excellent typist. I don't mention it to brag. I just want to show that I amount to something . . . This is the story that I want to write. Though, it's so laughably mundane, so incontestably banal, that it's really no story at all.

The story, such as it is, is an oppressive, monologic rant, not dissimilar to those of Hartwig's compatriot Thomas Bernhard: the sort of writing that seems dictated from a Viennese chaise longue, though without any hope of therapeutic closure. Never mind Anna O.; meet Aloisia Schmidt: self-hater, compulsive masturbator, narcissistic manic-depressive, all-round good-time gal:

> I'm neither pretty nor ugly. My face is neither pleasant nor unpleasant, neither attractive nor unattractive. It's a face you simply don't see. It goes without saying that I wish I were beautiful. That's hardly a confession worth making. However, I swear that sometimes I want to be ugly too – revoltingly ugly. Of course, I can't explain why I want to be revoltingly ugly. Perhaps it's because people would at least notice me then.

At first the comparison with Bernhard is depressing: why do male writers channel rage into sadism while their female counterparts collapse into masochism? After hearing of Aloisia's unhappy and furious childhood ('I don't mean to make myself sound any more neurotic than I already have – who am I to have neuroses anyway? – but I have to admit that even as a child I suffered when someone didn't pay attention to me'), the reader peeks fearfully through her fingers as Aloisia reaches adulthood and men enter the scene:

> I think, in fact, that this was what impressed me most about Emil K.: the fact that I only understood half of what he was saying, most of

the time . . . I couldn't understand why an intelligent person like him would stoop to associate with someone like me. It wouldn't always be enough for him that I had a pretty face. If he was sticking around, it could only be because he still hadn't found me out.

Aloisia is an accomplished self-saboteur ('I think I have a special talent for seeing the failure I deserve behind every success I might have stumbled into: I had every reason to be content, but wasn't') who even in her retelling of events doubts her ability to do precisely that. The sentence 'I don't know if I'm making myself clear' – usually following a paragraph of perfect clarity – keeps coming back, like a stutter.

In an online review, someone called Kate calls Hartwig a 'Viennese Carrie Bradshaw from Hell'. It's a smart comparison, although I think Kate means to condemn her and I'm more inclined to praise. While struggling along with Aloisia – by turns delighted and infuriated, as I once felt watching Carrie – it occurred to me that people consistently misunderstand the logic of these feminine narratives, wherein what looks like self-abasement is very often an inverse form of self-display and self-assertion. That it should be so often mistaken is not surprising: every effort is made to make the self-abasement as persuasive as possible. Think of medieval mystics offering to rip holes in their chests so that Jesus might enter, or present-day comediennes and columnists tearing strips off themselves – death by a thousand self-deprecations. And yet don't they all, as Orwell put it – describing the 'sheer egoism' of writers – 'live their own lives to the end'? Doesn't Carrie always do, in the end, exactly what she pleases?

So why write it otherwise? Perhaps because there is no clear feminine language for triumph, no 'bragging rights', no external symbols that bespeak luck and power. We can't, as the saying goes, pull it out and slap it on the table. The male narrative ego has never lacked avatars – from the labours of Hercules to the complaints of Portnoy – but female egos, for so long without access to mainstream narrative avenues, seem to have compensated by charting strange and indirect side roads. Heroic tales that don't sound heroic. Self-performance that looks like self-obliteration. But egos we do have. We want, and we get. It's simply a devious sort of wanting, always changing, adapting to circumstance – or, better put – always apparently reacting. For example, sometimes Aloisia tells us she is 'neither pretty nor ugly'; sometimes she claims she is repulsive; at other times she appears to consider herself the very picture of fabulousness. It's never an established fact in her mind. It depends upon whom she's reacting to –

> Of course I knew that being near me excited him. I didn't doubt that he found my face and perhaps my body uncommonly appealing. And I even agreed on this point. I also believed my face and body were worthy of being admired; back then I was convinced (because he was convinced) that I was extremely pretty.

– or does it? Women like Aloisia tend to draw from their more conscious sisters a well-worn critique: these women exist only in relation to men! Who are they, without men? Aren't they redundant human beings? But then you look closer at these 'men', and a slightly different story emerges. Aloisia's men are like Carrie's, they come and go interchangeably and never really shift her from her course; they prove to be paper-thin, ciphers. They are caught in an overheated performance of female self-realization that invents not only itself but also the men to whom it is supposedly reacting.

Whether it's masochism or sadism is less interesting than its overt *egotism*.

Hartwig knows all this:

It's hubris, Luise, to think so little of yourself. Do you really think that people – including me – aren't all sometimes or often or maybe even always dissatisfied with themselves in some way? Do you really think that people – including me – ever really manage to get through life without finding a way to balance their gifts and their pride? That people can ever avoid being humbled by the world and finally accepting themselves as they are? But you're acting as if you've been singled out.

That's Aloisia's first love, Emil K., calling her out on what today we might call 'her bullshit'. He spells it out in a way even Carrie could understand: 'You're obviously only happy when you're unhappy.' And that's what makes this book intriguing, despite its sometimes clumsy phrasing and Freudian posturing: it's not simply an expression of feminine 'hysteria' but an arch critique of it, from the inside. It recasts its much-trumpeted 'redundancy' as a vital kind of agency, for it is Aloisia's self-obsession that powers and determines everything. I don't think this makes her, or Carrie, particularly admirable, but it does explain the pleasure their narrative arcs provide. Power trips are pleasurable. And what power! Not for a moment are we permitted to withdraw from Aloisia; not only is she *not* redundant, but other people can only hope for significance in terms of their relation to her, real or imagined. She invents entire relationships with men who are barely aware of her existence. She breaks the hearts of men who adore her by insisting they don't. From behind a curtain she watches the woman she most admires be rejected by the man she most wants; later the woman shoots herself and the man despairs. And Aloisia herself? Well, despite that title, as the story closes she seems to be the only one left standing:

> I'm still employed at the construction firm. I'm known for my first-rate shorthand and my excellent typing skills . . . One colleague, an accountant, has pursued me quite eagerly, and has even proposed marriage. I don't mention it to brag. I only bring it up to show that there are still people who think better of me than I think of myself. If I were a man, I certainly wouldn't find myself desirable.

Reader, don't you believe it.

Given her difficulties with the opposite sex, I wonder whether Aloisia wouldn't prefer to be a silverfish? You see, the male silverfish leaves a sperm packet hanging from a silk thread attached to a twig, which the female picks up later with her genital opening. After she's drained the packet, she eats it. Zero emotional fallout. This I learned from *Sex on Six Legs: Lessons on Life, Love and Language from the Insect World*, by Marlene Zuk, a book that has given me almost more insect anecdotes than I know what to do with. At dinner, they don't just end the conversation, they end dinner. It is a powerful feeling: I recommend it. Whatever the person sitting opposite thinks he knows about insects, after reading this book I guarantee you will know more. He will say, 'Oh, sure, some wasps inject their cockroach prey with a paralysing poison which allows them to drag the roach back to the wasp nest and keeps it fresh.' You will sigh and look down at the butter dish. You will inform your friend – not without humility – that there exists a jewel wasp who rather than using simple paralysis injects the roach with 'a judicious sting inside [its] head, so that its nervous system, and legs, still function well enough to allow it to walk on its own'. Then the wasp leads the roach to its doom, effectively 'hijack[ing its] free will'. Zombie-cockroach! And PS: if you ever see a silent male cricket failing to attract any females, it's not because he's shy, it's because a fly has, at some earlier point, deposited some tiny larvae on him, and one or more of the resulting maggots have gone into his body, eaten him from the inside, grown as big as the cricket itself, and now live inside him. Zombie-cricket-fly! Game, set, match: you.

But there is much more to this book than the opportunity to lord it over your acquaintances. It's a chance to look at the way genes behave, free from the wishful thinking, cultural assumption and ideological prejudice we sometimes bring to the study of our own species. What gives insects the edge here is the great variety of their genomes – 'A monkey is a lot more like a mouse than a grasshopper is like a flea' – and their profoundly alien ways, which makes it more difficult for us to anthropomorphize them, though we do give it our best shot, as we'll see.

There is a trend, in the arts and social sciences, to affect a sort of disdain for the 'naivety' of purely genetic explanations of behaviour. We are, finally, animals of culture, the argument goes, and the idea that genes can be point-for-point attached to human behavioural characteristics is a category error. In a sense, Zuk comes to a similar conclusion, but for her, the argument that genes can't be 'associated de novo with a single trait and that trait only' is not an anti-science argument; it's a more nuanced reading of the science. For genes associated with one behaviour are also associated with myriad other behaviours, as well as continually differing in expression depending on environmental factors such as nutrition and chemical manipulation. She demonstrates with honeybees. The dogma used to be that honeybees were made, not born, via the consumption of royal jelly. In fact it's not just what you eat, it's also the way you're born – but more importantly, it's the interaction between these two factors: 'In honeybees, different nutrients interact with the genome to switch some developmental pathways on and off.' Having the queen gene makes a larva more likely to become a queen but doesn't guarantee it: honeybees are 'exquisitely sensitive to small changes in their environment'. Pumping CO_2 into a chamber of virgin queens and workers for ten minutes creates immediate differences in gene expression; ovary development is increased in the queens and suppressed in the workers. Even when the genes are the same (queens and workers share at least two thousand genes), they express themselves differently in the brains of the two kinds of individuals. The picture is, Zuk argues, 'both more complex and more genetically determined'. In some ways it's a messy, unsatisfying picture: so much of our genetic material turns out to be redundant, non-functioning, left over from earlier incarnations. We, like the insects, are walking junkyards of our own evolutionary pasts.

But in another sense, the picture is more richly coloured than we ever could have imagined, with our hermeneutic tendency to interpret phenotype evidence in genotype black and white. Take the bees (again). Zuk manages generally to be cheerful about our ignorance of insect biology, but she also has a limit, and that limit is *Bee Movie*, in which Jerry Seinfeld plays a *male* honeybee. 'There are errors and errors,' she complains, 'poetic license versus jarring ineptitude.' It is not much comfort to her that Aristotle made a similar assumption about the gender of bees, and so did Ben Franklin and the nineteenth-century poet Charles Stuart Calverley ('When, his thighs with sweetness laden,/ From the meadow comes the bee'). It's a predictable error: the big bee, served by everyone in the hive, surely had to be the 'king' bee, and the ones lying about doing nothing had to be female, and the ones with the ability to sting, again, must be male. But then why were the males doing all the childcare? That part perplexed Aristotle to such a degree that he 'eventually concluded that bees might have the organs of both sexes in a single individual'. Zuk's point is that by making these assumptions not only do you get a skewed version of the insect world's sex roles, you further distort the roles in your own world. Also, you simply 'miss out on stuff'. In the insect world, fiction has nothing on the truth. How wild that (male) drones are born of unfertilized eggs, thus making sisters more closely related to each other than to their mothers!

Interesting that almost all the anthropomorphic errors Zuk recounts in this book are gender-related. She has fun talking us through 'army ants', also female, whom generations cast as blood-lusting masculine warriors: what's really going on, Zuk counters, is extreme predation, 'and predation is not waging war, it is acquiring food'. Less like marauders on the rampage, more like a crowd of mums tearing through Whole Foods. But there I go, anthropomorphizing. It's hard not to. And isn't the title an invitation to apply insect lessons to human life? Maybe we can explore our connections without smothering our differences: '[B]ecause we shared a common ancestor with insects so long ago, we can use them as a way to explore how we arrive at similar-seeming destinations with such radically different modes of transportation.' I kept this in mind as I read of infanticide among beetles:

> Its documented occurrence in insects somehow didn't seem relevant
> to people, perhaps because we don't automatically see ourselves

mirrored in their behavior . . . [N]ow it is clear that at least some of
the time it is probably adaptive in nature, because rearing young
when life is harsh, or at the expense of the parents' well-being, may
be too big a gamble for it to be continued . . . If the going gets tough,
the tough – and the smart – stop taking care of their children.

Zuk doesn't make this analogy, but my thoughts turned to those
'witch' children of West Africa, murdered by their families. When
you have ten mouths to feed and food for only four, maybe the folk
tale is not the cause but the cover. How else can the human animal
explain to itself its most brutal survival choices?

Given that Zuk's subject is so inherently engaging, it's a shame
about all the lame scientist jokes made in the name, I suppose, of
'popularization'. When, in the 1600s, Jan Swammerdam, a Dutch
microscopist, cuts open a 'king' bee to prove it's female, we get this:
' "Hey, did you hear? Ol' Jan Swammerdam is cutting open a bee
next Tuesday! Who knows what peculiar structures he will reveal!
Let's go watch – I'll buy the mead." Do you suppose he sold tickets?'
There're also a few strange attempts at 'relevance'. When telling us
of the extraordinary ability of bees to 'learn to recognize individual
human faces', Zuk goes off on a flight of 'war on terror' fancy: 'I was
seized by the image of a chamber with a bee at airport security, for
instance, scrutinizing the faces of passengers to look for matches
with photos of known terrorists. Whether this would work better
than some of the current efforts is an interesting question.' Professor,
you had me at 'sperm packet'.

There is such a thing as the flightless blister beetle; it is found in
the sand dunes of the south-western United States. They lay their
eggs on a plant called the milk vetch, which it happens they can't

survive on. Instead they parasitize a single species of bee that also lives in the desert. Now get this: the newly hatched larvae, hundreds of them, gather together on the tip of a plant. Viewed collectively they look like the female version of that bee I just mentioned; they even emit something that smells like her sex pheromone. So the male bee comes along and mistakes this pulsing fake for his mate; before he gets wise, a few opportunistic larvae jump on his back. Later, when he finds his real mate, the larvae transfer on to her, and subsequently to her nest, and grow there, feeding off her stash of pollen and nectar. Why am I telling you this? Because it reminds me of the life cycle in *Sempre Susan: A Memoir of Susan Sontag*, by Sigrid Nunez. Sontag must have had a hell of a lot of nectar; so many people continue to grow fat on it. What is the relationship between blister beetles and bees? Friends? Frenemies? Nunez walks that line in a cruel, stylish belles-lettres style that is only ever vulgar in its sentiments, never in the sentences themselves. You sense she wants you to morally judge what she's done here, and that all her defences are already prepared – but that feels like an exhausting way to approach this book, a sprung trap laid by a needy author. No, what's interesting is how alien a sight we seem to find a female intellectual, poking and prodding her with rumour and curiosity – even after she's died – as if she were a fat king bee of whose gender we're never quite sure. Did she ever cook? Did she never clean? Was she maternal at all? Was she attracted to men and women equally? Did she treat them differently? Did she dye her hair? Did she watch her weight? Was she vain? Did she truly have no sense of humour? Was she really sleeping with her son? (This, the shabbiest of rumours, repeated by Nunez, is an example of the vulgarity of which I spoke.) Poor Susan. We all have our faults, but not everyone gets pinned and mounted like a bug to a board and held up for all to see.

A St Aubyn Summer

We have an idea of a 'summer book'. To be read on the beach, or in a hammock, or amid long grass. It promises pleasure and total immersion: if every few minutes you find yourself laying it flat upon your chest and wondering about lunch then it is probably not a summer book. A real summer book is more real than the summer: you abandon friends and family, retreat to your room, draw the mosquito net round, and get back – in my case – to the doings of Patrick Melrose. *At Last* by Edward 'Teddy' St Aubyn, is the culmination of what we must now call the Patrick Melrose Trilogy (*Some Hope* – itself originally a trilogy of novellas – has been reissued as the first volume; *Mother's Milk* is the second). This series tells the (basically autobiographical) story of the Melroses, a 'good family' in name only. Left unprotected by his alcoholic heiress mother, Eleanor, raped from the age of five by his aristocratic father, David, Patrick grows up to become the kind of English gentleman who (depending on which book you pick up) shoots heroin in the suites of New York hotels, carries 'a copy of *The Myth of Sisyphus* in his overcoat pocket', downs whiskey miniatures while walking Kew Gardens with his children, and in even the direst state of incapacity recalls many stray lines of English poetry.

St Aubyn's speciality is packing all the action of a novel into a single day (with much swooping into the past). Often the day in question is the occasion of some sort of 'social ordeal', best defined as a horrible gathering full of people you wish you didn't know. Holding a vol-au-vent, waiting for a refill, contemplating suicide as some fool across the room gives a speech – the bad-party theme has been a source of pathos for generations of English writers. (The three most depressing words

in the English language, according to Kingsley Amis: 'Red or white?')
In *At Last* we have arrived, finally, at Patrick's mother's funeral (his
father died mercifully early, in *Some Hope*). It is a *mise en scène* far
funnier than it sounds ('Gothic script seemed to warp every letter that
passed through the door of the funeral parlour, as if death were a
German village'). Patrick has reached middle age, been married and
divorced, and recently passed a spell in the Priory, Britain's famous
rehab centre. He fears relapse. But he has high hopes for this funeral:

> Now that he was an orphan everything was perfect. He seemed to
> have been waiting all his life for this sense of completeness. It was
> all very well for the Oliver Twists of this world, who started out in
> the enviable state it had taken him forty-five years to achieve, but the
> relative luxury of being brought up by Bumble and Fagin, rather
> than David and Eleanor Melrose, was bound to have a weakening
> effect on the personality.

Parental death, heroin, childhood rape, emotional frigidity,
suicide, alcoholism – stop me when it sounds summery. Nothing
about the plots can prepare you for the rich, acerbic comedy of St
Aubyn's world or – more surprising – its philosophical density. For
much of his publishing career (until a Booker short-listing for
Mother's Milk in 2006) a wide readership eluded St Aubyn, perhaps
because of this perceived division between style and content. With
the wit of Wilde, the lightness of Wodehouse and the waspishness
of Waugh, he wraps his fancy prose style around the self in extremis
('suffocated, dropped, born of rape as well as born to be raped'),
situations more familiar to readers of Cooper or Burroughs.

Now the Melrose books are suddenly in vogue, and it's tempting
to chalk that up to the tidal wave of poshness presently crashing over

England: a royal wedding, a conservative prime minister, a Bullingdon Club Cabinet, Terence Rattigan revivals at the National, *Downton Abbey* on the telly. But that's a blue herring. St Aubyn comes not to praise the upper classes but to bury them – though never completely, and not without some fondness – employing the same ironic, conversational mode in which this set are expert (' "It's the hardest addiction of all," said Patrick. "Forget heroin. Just try giving up irony" '). With their robust sense of entitlement, St Aubyn's characters can make his job look easy: less like writing than getting out of the way. They don't skulk around waiting to be introduced by some workmanlike plodder of an omniscient narrator. They grab the bloody reins themselves, as if to say: *For Godssakes, give it to me. Obviously you haven't the faintest idea what you're doing.* The first lines:

'Surprised to see me?' said Nicholas Pratt, planting his walking stick on the crematorium carpet and fixing Patrick with a look of slightly aimless defiance, a habit no longer useful but too late to change. 'I've become rather a memorial-creeper. One's bound to at my age. It's no use sitting at home guffawing over the ignorant mistakes of juvenile obituarists, or giving in to the rather monotonous pleasure of counting the daily quota of extinct contemporaries. No! One has to 'celebrate the life': there goes the school tart. They said he had a good war, but I know better! – that sort of thing, put the whole achievement in perspective. Mind you, I'm not saying it isn't all very moving. There's a sort of swelling orchestra effect to these last days. And plenty of horror, of course. Padding about on my daily rounds from hospital bed to memorial pew and back again, I'm reminded of those oil tankers that used to dash themselves on to the rocks every other week and the flocks of birds dying on the beaches with their wings stuck together and their bewildered yellow eyes blinking.'

Blimey. In St Aubyn's case, it's just a bit *dull* to say the man has a 'good ear for dialogue'. Some might protest that there can't possibly be anyone left on this earth who actually speaks like Nicholas Pratt, but walk into the Garrick any day of the week and you'll find half a dozen of them, slumped in their wingback chairs, nursing a postprandial brandy. (NB: Don't try this if you're not a member. Or not a man.) It may be a tiny demographic, but smaller groups have spawned longer novel cycles (Proust!). Nor does Patrick consider himself superior to the superior community from which he hails; on the contrary, he identifies, recognizing in himself a 'man who had tried to talk his way out of everything he had thought and felt'. These novels nail that type and their endless chatter, but what ultimately lingers is a defence of the humble English sentence, its twists and turns, its subtlety and comedy – its *control*, above all. For whereas the tale of Patrick Melrose appears superficially to be one of excess, the books themselves are structured around the idea that linguistic control is a potent force. In St Aubyn's world, whoever controls the retelling controls the event. We might call it, after Lewis Carroll, the Humpty-Dumpty Effect.

Certainly the question of 'which is to be master' preoccupies Patrick, who deals with his terrible family by encapsulating them with devastating verbal diagnoses. As he glances across the aisle at his 'unhappy aunt' Nancy, who is complaining about the sparse and proletarian turnout at her sister's funeral (' "I mean, for example, Mummy only ever had one car accident in her entire life, but even then, when she was hanging upside down in the buckled metal, she had the Infanta of Spain dangling next to her" '), Patrick's inner monologue perfectly reveals the root of her problem as well as St Aubyn's two inches of ivory:

The psychological impact of inherited wealth, the raging desire to get rid of it and the raging desire to hang on to it; the demoralizing effect of already having what almost everyone else was sacrificing their precious lives to acquire; the more or less secret superiority and the more or less secret shame of being rich, generating their characteristic disguises: the philanthropy solution, the alcoholic solution, the mask of eccentricity, the search for salvation in perfect taste; the defeated, the idle, and the frivolous, and their opponents, the standard-bearers, all living in a world that the dense glitter of alternatives make it hard for love and work to penetrate.

Writing reviews, you spend quite a lot of your time typing out the sentences of other people, i.e. quoting. Usually this is dull work; with St Aubyn, it's a joy. Oh, the semicolons, the discipline! Those commas so perfectly placed, so rhythmic, creating sentences loaded and blessed, almost o'erbrimmed, and yet sturdy, never in danger of collapse. It's like fingering a beautiful swatch of brocade. This refusal to submit to the puritan brevity of the American sentence (or, worse, the artificial naivety of an English sentence intended to sound as if it has been translated from the French) – it's almost enough to make you feel patriotic.

These sentences aren't merely decorative. They're important because they enable the comedy: when you create this many compartments in each line, you have space for at least two jokes and one sly dig. And it's humour of the blackest kind, with Patrick's parents feeling the brunt of it, even in death. In this final outing we learn more of Eleanor's 'philanthropy solution' – first described in *Mother's Milk* – which drove her, in life, to give her attention (and fortune) first to children's charities ('He had often been left alone with his father while Eleanor went to a committee meeting of the Save the Children Fund') and then, in her final years, to a commune of new-age phoneys who swiftly relieve her of the house in Saint-Nazaire (setting of Patrick's childhood misery and marital disaster). And all 'without sinking one millimetre into the resistant bedrock of [her] self-knowledge'. Meanwhile, if readers of the earlier books were in any doubt about David Melrose's psychopathy, an anecdote from his safari days casts new and horrible light on his demented personality: 'He walked over to the rabies victim' – a man his hunting party have left writhing in a net normally reserved for pigs – 'and shot him in the head.' Returning to the dumbfounded table, he sat down with a 'feeling of absolute calm' and said, ' "Much the kindest thing to do." Gradually, the word spread around the table: much the kindest thing to do.' In that story, something crystallizes: how telling a tale can be a form of tyranny; how the English – out of politeness, class deference, or just plain fear – too often defend a narrative that is least true and most cruel.

This question of what constitutes the truth – of whose version of events shall rule – starts as a wry query, before building into a debate about the nature of consciousness. To aid this unlikely transition, we're offered Erasmus Price, a celebrated academic, guest at Eleanor's funeral and author of *None the Wiser: Developments in the Philosophy of Consciousness*. Patrick's ex-wife, Mary (also present), once had an affair with Erasmus, a fact that dawned on Patrick only after he spotted her reading Erasmus's tome one night in bed:

'You couldn't be reading that book unless you were having an affair with the author,' he guessed through half-closed eyes.
    'Believe me, it's virtually impossible even then.'

This revelation prompts a relapse: 'an "absolutely maddening" period, when Patrick only emerged from his new blackout bedsit in order to lecture or interrogate [Mary] about consciousness studies':

'Who will rid us of the Explanatory Gap?' he shouted, like Henry II requesting an assassin for his troublesome priest. 'And is that gap just a product of our misconstrued discourse?' He ploughed on, 'Is reality a consensual hallucination? And is a nervous breakdown in fact a *refusal to consent*? Go on, don't be shy, tell me what you think.'

'Why don't you go back to your flat and pass out there? I don't want the children seeing you in this state.'

'What state? A state of philosophical enquiry?'

Are the brain and the mind the same? What is the material of consciousness? Is a 'person' simply the sum of a series of anecdotes consciousness tells about itself? It's no surprise that Patrick longs for what Mary calls 'a convincing and practical theory of consciousness': if you're taking medication for misery, you're putting all your faith in the 'explanatory gap', in the hope that treating the brain will cure the mind.

The trouble is, Patrick doesn't experience things as a unified self with a single mind; instead, life is inchoate, almost formless:

Social life had a tendency to press him up against his basic rejection of the proposition that an individual identity was defined by turning experience into an ever more patterned and coherent story. It was in reflection and not in narrative that he found authenticity. The pressure to render his past in anecdote, or indeed to imagine the future in terms of passionate aspirations, made him feel clumsy and false . . . His authentic self was the attentive witness to a variety of inconstant impressions that could not, in themselves, enhance or detract from his sense of identity.

The Melrose novels articulate this basic rejection. No one character, not even Patrick, is privileged; the trilogy ignores neat borders between central and minor characters, instead invading the minds of everybody all the time. What's revealed is never pretty: a filthy stream of desires, incorrect impressions, strong opinions, self-defence and self-delusion. Structurally, it's ideal comic material, but it's also serious, because the central question of the comic novel – How can I know I'm not ridiculous? – has a deep affinity with the central question of the philosophy of consciousness: How can I know what's real? At the funeral's afterparty, Fleur, a lunatic acquaintance of his mother, whom Patrick recognizes from rehab, is found walking around asking people if they've ever tried the antidepressant she's on. She reaches Erasmus:

'Have you tried Amitriptyline?' she asked.
'I've never heard of him,' said Erasmus. 'What's he written?'
Fleur realized that Erasmus was much more confused than she had originally imagined.

Patrick knows Fleur is mad and we know Fleur is mad, and Erasmus will work it out in a minute – but does Fleur know it? If we saw this funeral through Fleur's consciousness, and only hers, we would, knowing no better, call it 'reality'. Which is preposterous – who in their right mind would rely on the testimony of Fleur? Yet this singular, limited, unreliable access to the real is the fate of everyone on earth.

The most brilliant line in this book is not witty at all, it's just painfully acute: 'He had long regarded [his relationship with his mother] as an effect on his personality rather than a transaction with another person.' Patrick's is an extreme case, but for all of us locked in repetitive and poisonous relationships with our 'loved ones', the questions of *At Last* are no joke. Refusing Mary's invite to come and eat with his children, Patrick hears his son, Thomas, say, 'You should change your mind, because that's what it's for!' But is a changed mind possible? Is it possible to be free? So long directed by forces apparently beyond his control – trauma, personality, brain chemistry – for Patrick, the idea of living a 'voluntary life' is 'extravagant': 'What would it mean to be spontaneous, to have an unconditioned response to things – to anything?'

The young Teddy St Aubyn created novels of dazzling portraiture, not unlike the paintings hanging in the great houses of his ancestors. Perfectly rendered, often cruel, easily admired; but missing some central mystery, that bit of a person that can't be pinned down by acts of spiky mimesis. Everyone exposed and categorized. *At Last* confesses the limits of explanation. 'It's very helpful,' Patrick concedes, 'to see [my mother] from other points of view than the one I've been trapped in.' He is speaking to the new-age guru Annette, during whose speech – 120 pages earlier – he had experienced the following:

Oh, please get on with it, thought Patrick. Charles Bronson was having a panic attack in a collapsing tunnel, Alsatians were barking behind the barbed wire, searchlights were weaving over the breached ground, but soon he would be running through the woods, dressed as a German bank clerk and heading for the railway station with some identity papers forged at the expense of Donald

Pleasence's eyesight. It would all be over soon, he just had to keep staring at his knees for a few moments longer.

The slow encroachment of something like sincerity inevitably means the comic integrity suffers, as the acid pleasures of saying-what-you-don't-mean give way to the therapeutic impulse: saying what you really mean. It's simply not funny to add, after the subtle quip about Save the Children, the explicit line: 'Patrick could not help thinking that this passion for saving all the children of the world was an unconscious admission that she could not save her own child.' And the final sentences of the book would have been improved quite a bit by the removal of the very last ('He picked up the phone and dialled Mary's number. He was going to change his mind. After all, that's what Thomas said it was for'). But here and elsewhere, one senses an emotional imperative that means more to the author than matching Evelyn Waugh barb for barb. (Nicholas: 'Whatever [David's] drawbacks as a parent, you must admit that he never lost his sense of humour.' Patrick: 'He only saw the funny side of things that didn't have one. That's not a sense of humour, just a form of cruelty.') In this sparkling adult book, a little boy's cheesy line shouldn't be dredged up for a closer look. But I can't help soften toward it when I think of St Aubyn – who has credited his children with bringing him, at last, some measure of happiness – placing it there like a seal on a love letter.

Despite the stiff-upper-lip contempt for psychiatry common among Patrick's class (after the funeral, Nicholas keels over dead from a heart attack while delivering a diatribe on the subject: 'Polluting the human imagination with murderous babies and incestuous children . . .'), and in spite of his own ironic armour, Patrick appears to have drawn real strength from therapy and rehab, finding himself repeating – to his own amazement – slogans from the Priory that would have made Nicholas foam at the mouth ('Resentment is drinking the poison and hoping someone else will die'). The Beckett-quoting heroin addict 'drowned in dreams and burning to be gone' is no more. And, like Krapp, the new Patrick Melrose is someone who no longer needs to be someone – who isn't even *trying* to be someone. Words fail him, in a good way. One of the most articulate descriptions of just that kind of inarticulacy is William Empson's six-line masterpiece 'Let It Go'. On the brink of a relapse, in the back of a taxi, Patrick thinks of the poem:

> 'Back to the Priory?' said the driver, no longer quite as sympathetic to his passenger.
>
> He doesn't want to know about those of us who have to go back, thought Patrick. He closed his eyes and stretched out in the back seat. 'Talk would talk and go so far askance . . . something, something . . . You don't want madhouse and the whole thing there.' The whole thing there. The wonderful inarticulacy of it, expanding with threat and contracting with ostensive urgency.

Many writers would do the ellipsis thing there, but it takes St Aubyn to misquote in such a humble, deliberate way. In novels things are always 'coming to mind', but usually with a gloss and polish that belie real consciousness. With St Aubyn, madhouse is never very far away.

On Island Life and Mother Love

All across the Jamaican diaspora you can hear versions of this conversation:

First Jamaican: You go back recent?
Second Jamaican: [*Sighing*] If I go, I don't tell *nobody* I come.
Me cyaan have no holiday dere. Jamaica *change*.

Followed by a misty-eyed reminiscence about Jamaica in the seventies, or fifties, or thirties – depending on the age and political persuasion of the participants – and a few envious words about a neighbouring island ('You been St Lucia? St Lucia *nice*'). Finally, talk turns to one's own 'yard' – be it in London, Manchester or Miami – where your extended Jamaican clan are usually embroiled in some 'vexing' interpersonal drama, which everybody in the family condemns ('Them got no respeck for nutting!') but nobody seems able to resolve.

Ian Thomson's excellent *The Dead Yard: A Story of Modern Jamaica* is a 350-page disquisition on the above. Filled with many sympathetic and surprisingly well-transcribed examples of Jamaican conversation (Thomson is a white Scot), the book was, apparently, prompted by a brutal English one: 'J. G. Ballard suggested that I go "somewhere depressing, like Chechnya – what about Jamaica?" ' This revelation is unlikely to endear the book to Jamaicans, who tend toward guarded, wounded pride. ('What are you doing in Jamaica?' a woman asks Thomson at a meeting of the Jamaican Historical Society. 'Have you come to stare and make fun?') On the other hand, nobody knows better than Jamaicans themselves the despair that stalks their island paradise. Thomson's book goes beyond the oft-recited dysfunctionalities to provide their essential historical context, and his literary sensibility matches the strange beauty of the place: 'I stood transfixed by the window as the palm trees, lit up by lightning, banged their heads on the lawn, then whipped back like dry-fly rods.'

Thomson, the author of an equally fine book about Haiti, *Bonjour*

Blanc, finds the Jamaicans he meets early on to be full of warnings, which they convey Jamaicanly: 'I had been warned not to go downtown. "People are very grudgeful down there," uptowners would tell me.' Being grudgeful, in Jamaica, usually means you're packing heat: 'If you didn't have gun . . . the drug men kill you – if you did have gun, them kill you even worse.' That's Valerie Salmon, a Kingston housekeeper in her fifties, one of the first Jamaicans to try to explain to Thomson the cycle of envy, self-contempt and poverty that has bestowed upon her country one of the highest murder rates in the world: 'All Jamaicans had "prejudice": even the poor in the shack dumps uptown looked down on those in the squatter colonies downtown. "I don't know if it's a master–slave thing or what," Valerie said, "but is so life go." '

Thomson has little doubt on this matter: 'Jamaica's very social order bears the mark of the slaving past. In 1965, when a statue of Paul Bogle [leader of an 1865 rebellion and a champion of the poor] was unveiled in Morant Bay, riots ensued as locals objected to the way the Baptist preacher had been made to look *too black*' (my italics). This obsession with skin colour, with rough justice and clan politics (both political parties in Jamaica have their respective paramilitary or 'gangsta' wings, shooting it out in the slums of Tivoli Gardens) – all find their precise echo in the slave past. Jamaica's 'native' population arrived three hundred years ago, as cargo, the property of 'triangle merchants' who motivated the slave trade between England, Africa and Jamaica. 'A typical "triangle voyage" carried trading goods (such as beads, rifles and gunpowder) from England to Africa, then slaves from Africa to the Caribbean, and finally sugar, coffee, cotton, rice, and rum on the home stretch to England. It was one of the most nearly perfect commercial systems of modern times.'

On the infamous 1782 crossing of the Liverpool slave ship *Zong*, all

470 slaves aboard perished; first the captain threw overboard those who had died of illness, then he began jettisoning the merely sick, still in manacles: 'The entire remainder, according to one eyewitness, "sprang disdainfully from the grasp of their tyrants, and leapt to their death".' If you did make it to Jamaica, you found yourself in tropical hell: 'For the crime of "rebellion" [it was] recommended that slaves be pinioned to the ground and burned with a flaming brand "by degrees from the Feet and Hands . . . gradually up to the Head, whereby their pains are extravagant". For "lesser" crimes . . . "chopping off half of the Foot with an Ax".' 'Rebellions' included stealing rum, insolence, refusing to pump water and the use of improper language.

Colonial Jamaica imposed upon this bloody history a false little England; the trains ran on time (now there is no train) and everyone could recite 'Jerusalem', but Jamaicans' African roots became a thing of shame and were largely ignored. When the British left in the late fifties, the Americans soon replaced them, first covertly when Jamaica became a Cold War pawn, and later economically when its vulnerable consumer market was flooded with cheap exports. Such history does not the foundation of a healthy modern state make, and the stability it took England six hundred years to achieve is unlikely to come to Jamaica in fifty. Jamaica is like an abused child: who can be surprised when the adult behaves so strangely?

During Thomson's 2007 visit, a man and his family are shot dead on the principle of 'disrespect': the man had looked up a woman's skirt on the bus. Two Mandeville youths caught shoplifting food are 'bludgeoned with shovels and pickaxes, as well as bitten by dogs; one of them was unable to walk after spinal injuries'. On this island of 3 million people, five are murdered every day. Carolyn Gomes, director of Jamaicans for Justice, a human rights group, puts it succinctly: 'The business of dissing and respect is homegrown

Jamaican. When your life's so degraded, you *need* people to respect you, you need a gun to stand out.' As Thomson concludes, notions of respect have hatched in the absence of civic values, and encouraged Jamaican men to pursue power and money 'for their own sake'.

Meanwhile, the social cachet of light skin, established on the plantations, continues. Here is Sheila Hamilton, a seventy-three-year-old Justice of the Peace: 'I'm not black. I'm brown. A light brown lady . . . Actually I'm virtually white.' Almost everyone Thomson interviews sooner or later reveals this colour consciousness. Mary Langford, a Jamaican writer and historian of mixed race, is fairly typical. 'She lived in a smart Kingston house jammed with mahogany furniture, silver polo trophies, silver teapots, and, above all, maids. The maids were very black [and this] served to highlight the "whiteness" of their employers . . . She told me, "I'm not afraid *ipso facto* of Africa, or of African culture. But there's too much ganja, too much dancehall, and too much sleeping in the afternoon." ' Many of the Jamaican elites in this book seem to see siesta as the essence of moral lassitude. In fact the *only* sensible thing to *do* in the Jamaican climate in the afternoon is nap. *Soon come* – 'an expression which haunts Jamaican life and, to outsiders, epitomizes the Jamaican soul' – represents a local wisdom, simple common sense when it's 103 degrees outside and there's a hard rain coming. To put it Jamaicanly, we slow till we wan fi go fast.

The pockets of joy in Jamaica (and in this book) are mostly provided by people trying to make – as George Bernard Shaw once recommended in the Kingston daily the *Gleaner* – a 'Jamaica for the Jamaicans'. Thomson finds a bit of hope in the village descendants of the Maroons, runaway slaves who formed their own communities and retained their Gold Coast heritage, and have no desire to enter the ghettos of Kingston, and also in the self-sufficient Rastafari community (although their most famous pleasure proves somewhat self-defeating: 'The more you smoke,' one of them tells Thomson, 'the more Babylon fall'). Meanwhile, Jewish, Indian and Chinese Jamaicans appear to thrive, much to the annoyance of the black majority. With their own languages, schools and religious institutions, these minority communities were not subject to a state perversely determined to turn Jamaican saplings into English oaks:

> A school inspector in rural Jamaica asked a group of children, 'How many feet has a cat got?' The question was put in strenuously clipped Queen's English, any departure from which was considered 'bush-man talk'. A long bewildered silence followed until a Jamaican teacher re-phrased the question in patois: 'How much foot have puss?' A forest of hands went up.

I have made this book sound depressing; it isn't. The vibrancy and resilience of Jamaican culture emerges everywhere: in the verdancy of the soil, the ingenuity of the patois and the music played in the streets. I'm sure various Jamaicans will have various bones to pick with Thomson: it's a little galling to have a *backra* tell you what's what. Is he bemoaning American ascendancy in Jamaica out of nostalgia for British power? (Why spend so much time interviewing what's left of the Princess Margaret/Errol Flynn/Ian Fleming set?) If I have a central objection, it's his conservative take on the music. Thomson is, like a lot of white guys of his generation, a fan of old-style reggae, of jazz and ska and rocksteady, but baulks at hip-hop and dancehall:

> It seems to have lost its moral bearing and declined from street cele-bration to the degraded soundtrack of venality, with scarcely any

ideology left in it . . . [G]iven up the fight entirely and regressed to dull, computerised rhythms. The journey from Horace Andy's 'In the Light' to Sean Paul's 'Shake That Thing' cannot easily be called progress.

Though I'm no Sean Paul fanatic, I think Thomson's missed an opportunity here. By 'Shake That Thing' I assume he refers to 'Get Busy', a radio and video hit of 2003 that prominently features that lyric. The song is a fantasy, certainly, but not of the guns, rims and bitches kind that Thomson dreads. Sure, Sean Paul steps out of a white Escalade, but where does he go? Into a suburban Jamaican-American house. Upstairs he politely salutes the old-timers, husband and wife – who are cooking up salt-fish dumplings and playing domino – before entering the basement for the party, where he begins toasting – emceeing – over his own record. Down here, young Jamaican men and women dance in rival gangs, displaying awesome and equal skill, vying to outdo one another in moves that would make Pina Bausch want to join the girls' side. Their clothes, their hair, the way they move their heads and hands – you'll find it all copied in Monrovia, in New York, in Tokyo. (Thomson knows this: 'Britain's indigenous culture is now so influenced by Jamaica that a Jamaican inflection is hip among white British teenagers. Black Jamaican culture *is* youth culture in London.') And when Sean Paul, who is, in the Jamaican parlance, 'yellow', moves in on the hot girl at the party, the thing to note is that she is black. Not yellow, not *café au lait*, black-black. A little later the father of the house gets sick of the noise, grabs the mic and shuts the party down – his authority is accepted. No one pulls out a piece, reminding us that the great majority of Jamaicans are peaceable people. To me the scene says: what if all this beauty and talent and style and wit and smarts had a

real home, not on the set of a music video but in a functional nation?
I pray it soon come.

Danzy Senna is about the same colour as Sean Paul, and in 1998
wrote a very good and (as it turns out) prophetic essay called
'Mulatto Millennium', which poked fun at the new American fashion
for all things mixed race. She went on to write *Caucasia*, a clever
semi-autobiographical novel about a family constructed like her
own: white mother, black radical father. Something about her own
physical ambiguity (not to herself, but in the eyes of the people who
look at her) has given her an unusually deep insight into identity.
What if, depending on how you wore your hair, people took you to
be an entirely different genre of person? Not that she ever puts it as
bluntly as that: instead there's a subtle shape-shifting always at
work, as characters respond to one another on the basis of superficial
signifiers which, in a culture gone visual, seem to mean everything.
In her new collection of eight stories, *You Are Free*, the misleading
binary of black/white is still there, and to it another has been added:
mother/non-mother. I confess I much prefer Senna on the former
topic. On the matter of race she is never less than acidly playful; on
motherhood she is dogmatic. An exception is the excellent opening
story, which adroitly mixes the two themes. 'Admission' tells a
middle-class fable of an intellectual black couple trying to get their
toddler into a fancy daycare ('I heard Will and Jada got wait-listed').
They apply only as a sort of joke and expect to be rejected, but when
they are accepted the man objects both to the cost and the pretension
('We will have to scale back – seriously – just so the kid can get to
sit in a classroom with future Rich Fucks of America') and lays down
a veto. The woman realizes suddenly how desperately she wants it
('I don't want Cody to rot away in a public school').

The story seems, at this point, a too-close reflection of one of the more reliably tedious moments in a middle-class life – and then it flips. I won't tell you how, because the power of Senna's stories lies in this gift of the flip, which seems to me an aesthetic response to the human experience of being 'flipped' oneself, in the perspective of others. All the stories that deal with race have a steely humour to them (a lovely story about a mongrel dog begins, 'The bitch was a mystery. She didn't look mixed, more like some breed that hadn't yet been discovered. Strangers on the street were forever trying to guess her background'), and even the most obviously constructed premises work, perhaps because Senna sees, and has lived, the elaborate construction that is race. One story, 'Triptych', tells the same short tale of a family at dinner, three times – but in each version the family is of a different race. You learn this not from descriptions of their skin but from tiny cultural markers: the posters on the wall, the name of the dog, what they're eating. It's subtle and unnerving, the baggage you bring to each retelling of the situation. It's 'situation' that's Senna's great strength (the prose itself is quiet, unshowy): 'There, There' has the fine premise of a girl reading on the Internet about a suicide that's taken place at her boyfriend's place of work, but when he comes home he doesn't mention it, and this fissure of non-disclosure widens throughout the evening until it becomes a chasm between them. Senna has Carver's gift of revealing the things we (don't) talk about when we talk about love.

Given all this subtlety and smartness, it's strange to find motherhood treated so baldly, and with a weird hint of triumphalism. In 'The Care of the Self', we are clumsily asked to compare and contrast our heroine, Livy, who has left the single life in New York to have babies and grow schlumpy in New Mexico, with Ramona, a skinny, glamorous friend who used to be married to a man called

Julian: 'Livy always left those dinners with Ramona and Julian more distressed than when she'd arrived, nearly bludgeoned by the happiness of their union. She even wondered some nights if the real reason they invited her over was to remind themselves that it was better to be married than to be alone.' But now the tables have turned and Ramona is single. She comes to visit new mother Livy and take them both to a spa, where Ramona shows off her wonderful body and talks a lot about 'pampering'. Senna's light touch is gone; we are meant to hate Ramona, and we do: 'It was as if Ramona had come to New Mexico to see just how awful married life, mother-life, could be – and she would leave newly reassured of the superiority of her life being single, free, back in the city.' Ramona, who likes Pilates and 'examin[ing] her toned and glowing figure in the mirror', has career aspirations to 'combine life coaching with being a personal trainer'. She doesn't stand a chance.

Meanwhile, Livy, despite her unkemptness and mild marital difficulties, is proud to realize that she is happier than Ramona, and that it's a deeper, more meaningful happiness. She has transcended the vanity of childlessness: 'It was over. She knew . . . that it was over, this romance with herself.' This unsisterly point is made again a little later: 'She felt the daughter-self, young and vain, dying, and the mother-self, huge and sad, rising up in its wake, linking her to nothing less than history.' This idea, popular these days, that motherhood immediately confers upon women the wisdom of the Buddha, fails to explain why we mothers find our own mothers to be such royal pains in the ass. Nor does it explain how some childless women, such as George Eliot, seem likewise able to link themselves with the huge and sad weight of history. If motherhood makes you such a good, unvain person, if it's such an evolved state, how come we feel the need to judge so harshly our sisters who choose not to have children, or who, for reasons beyond their control, end up not having any? (In New York, in the same week, Ramona is both beaten up in the street and finds out her husband is gay.)

Another story, 'What's the Matter with Helga and Dave?' is again devoted to this straw figure of the perfect woman. This time it is Helga, a new mother, but apparently not the right kind: '[The baby] looked only a few months old, but I could not imagine that the mother – with her svelte shape and placid expression – had ever carried a child inside her, much less pushed one out.' Helga also commits the crime of telling the protagonist, another new mother, not to breastfeed after two months ('You should see what it does to your breasts when you're done,' she warns). The more slovenly and tired the protagonist feels, the more perfect Helga seems to be, but by the end of the story perfect Helga is of course revealed, in fact, to be deeply miserable and unsatisfied ('Dave despises me. I really think he wishes I was dead. We haven't touched each other in months'). And the protagonist ends up breastfeeding Helga's baby. Reading this book, I had the same bittersweet sense many women had when they saw a black president arrive before a female one. On race, perhaps, we're finally getting somewhere. But whatever became of sisterhood?

On Wild Girls, Cruel Birds – and Rimbaud!

The two best books I read this month – *The Left Hand of Darkness* and *The Dispossessed* – are far from new, published in 1969 and 1974 respectively. Their author is now eighty-one years old. Trying to describe their majesty, I feel like one of Ursula K. Le Guin's intergalactic interlopers taking her first step on alien soil – I haven't been so taken with an ulterior reality since I closed the wardrobe door on Narnia. It's not often that we finish a novel with the thought 'What *is* gender, anyway?' or 'What does it really mean to own something?' But these feats of anthropological *Verfremdungseffekt* are what Le Guin (herself the daughter of an anthropologist) achieves, with her unclassifiable inhabitants of the planet Winter (who grow genitals only during acts of passion, known as 'kemmering'). Or her anarchist-cooperative Odonians, natives of Anarres, who possess no concept of either ownership or hierarchy. Le Guin's *The Wild Girls* is a slim publication containing one story, an interview, a few short poems, a brief meditation on the virtues of modesty and an angry essay about corporate publishing, 'Staying Awake While We Read', previously published in *Harper's*. The poems are underwhelming ('The Next War': 'It will take place/it will take time, it will take life/and waste them'), while the essays and especially the interview are zingy and pugnacious ('The only means I have to stop ignorant snobs from behaving toward genre fiction with snobbish ignorance is to not reinforce their ignorance and snobbery by lying and saying that when I write SF it isn't SF, but to tell them more or less patiently for forty or fifty years that they are wrong to exclude SF and fantasy from literature, and proving my argument by writing well'). The strongest reason to pick up *The Wild Girls*, however, is its Nebula Award-winning title story, a tale of master–slave culture on a strange planet. Here we find the City, where Crown people live; meanwhile, down in the country, the Dirt people subsist. The Dirt people are an oppressed nomad tribe. Sometimes Crown men go on forays into Dirt country to kidnap wild girl-children and bring them back to the City to be used as slaves or else cultivated as concubines. The City world has inscribed codes of conduct – ways of eating, sleeping, dancing, speaking – the intricacy of which would suffice for a cycle as long as Le Guin's own *Earthsea* series, yet somehow she sums up this complex community in a handful of pages.

'Show, don't tell,' goes the worn-out workshop mantra: Le Guin shows us how. She never recites long lists of terminology or boring (to me) Tolkienesque genealogies. Her worlds are simultaneously factitious and naturalistic – we wander in and find them fully formed, populated by characters deeply embedded in imaginary habitats:

> In the evening they came to the crest of the hills and saw on the plains below them, among watermeadows and winding streams, three circles of the nomads' skin huts, strung out quite far apart . . . The children were spreading out long yellow-brown roots on the grass, the old people cutting up the largest roots and putting them on racks over low fires to hasten the drying.

When these worlds come under attack, we feel the violence personally, not least because Le Guin writes as well as any non-'genre' writer alive:

> One little girl fought so fiercely, biting and scratching, that the soldier dropped her, and she scrabbled away screaming shrilly for help. Bela ten Belen ran after her, took her by the hair, and cut her throat to silence her screaming. His sword was sharp and her neck was soft and thin; her body dropped away from her head, held on only by the bones at the back of the neck. He dropped the head and came running back to his men.

The Wild Girls is, in part, concerned with the old virgin/whore dialectic: back in the City we meet with a Crown culture not entirely alien to our own, in which women are simultaneously venerated as mothers and debased as sexual property. With its feminist and socialist themes, Le Guin's work has a certain radical chic, and her books have been interpreted, over the years, as overt support for agendas as disparate as anarchism, communalism and lesbian separatism. But just as SF can be misread by ignorant snobs, it can be misconstrued by its greatest fans. In interviews she defends herself, a little archly, against the sloppy, all-purpose label 'progressive':

> I am not a progressive. I think the idea of progress an invidious and generally harmful mistake. I am interested in change, which is an entirely different matter. I like stiff, stuffy, earnest, serious, conscientious, responsible people, like Mr. Darcy and the Romans.

Darcy, with his set ideas and slow emotional evolution, seems to have cast a shadow over Dr Shevek, hero of *The Dispossessed*, who travels from his home planet, an anarchist world he considers perfect, to a capitalist planet he finds repulsive. But the lessons learned on this journey between utopias are ambiguous: when Le Guin's characters encounter other worlds – and other consciousnesses – it usually provides an opportunity to reflect critically upon their own most strongly held assumptions. For her readers, the same principle holds. Le Guin – like Austen and (genre leap!) Seneca – envisions and depicts change seriously, conscientiously, responsibly.

Some would say Magnus Mills writes a kind of SF in which the S stands for 'speculative'. Others might link him to that older tradition of storytelling that includes Lewis Carroll, Mervyn Peake and Shakespeare – really anyone with a working and fantastical imagination. There seem to be fewer and fewer of them around these days, which makes Mills's achievement the more striking. He is a tall-tale-teller in an age of milder fiction and careful reportage. His *Three to See the King* was an excellent fable about the vanities of asceticism. It begins like this: 'I live in a house built entirely from tin, with four tin walls, a roof of tin, a chimney and door. Entirely from tin.'

It's never clear to me how self-conscious he is as an allegorist: his stories are neither closed systems nor point-for-point transpositions of philosophical arguments. He is regularly compared with Kafka, but the differences are more telling than the similarities: Kafka left us – in the form of his letters and diaries – plenty of evidence of the esoteric underpinnings of his 'simple' style. Reading Mills in interviews, one can't tell whether he's innocent of the big ideas people tend to extrapolate from his work (Pynchon is a fan), or else an artful dodger (on his writing process: 'I try not to repeat the same word twice on the same page'). Either way, the comparison with Kafka is not inapt: Mills shares Kafka's commitment to the integrity of the stand-alone paragraph or page, excising all commentary, never undermining irony by explaining it. In a million dissertations the bug in *The Metamorphosis* means a million things: in *The Metamorphosis* itself the bug is only a bug, as Mills's man in a house of tin is a man in a tin house.

For both writers, freedom is illusory and the men who seek it are ridiculous. Women, when they turn up (not often), bring with them emotion and, worse yet, the interruption of routine. Chaos!

At first sight I knew it had everything I could need: somewhere to eat and drink and sleep without disturbance, protected from the elements by a layer of corrugated metal and nothing more.

A very modest dwelling I must say, but it looked clean and tidy so I moved in. For a long while I was quite content here, and remained convinced I would find no better place to be. Then one day a woman arrived at my door and said, 'So this is where you've been hiding.'

I find those lines delicious: a reduced *jus* made from a watery sauce. Mills has a way of winnowing narrative tropes to their essence. In his *Explorers of the New Century* men set out into the heart of darkness ('the Agreed Furthest Point from Civilization') but bring their unequal ideas of civilization with them; in *The Scheme for Full Employment* everyone is employed driving 'UniVans' which each carry a consignment of UniVan parts to UniVan warehouses where more UniVans are built. Work not only fails to make you free; it's perfectly circular. In each case the prose opens wide and featureless to admit the allegory in. What arrives when a woman turns up? Worldliness? Sin? Madness? Mills isn't telling. 'You may ask: who was this woman? Well, I hardly knew her really. A friend of a friend I suppose you might say.'

In his new novel *A Cruel Bird Came to the Nest and Looked In* Mills is back in the world of absurd, inefficient men, men without women, and men perverted by power. He is also back in the realm of archetypal narrative, in this case, an absconded king:

> As the clock struck ten, Smew opened the register.
> 'Let us begin,' he said. 'Chancellor of the Exchequer?'
> 'Present,' said Brambling.
> 'Postmaster General?'
> 'Present,' said Garganey.
> 'Astronomer Royal?'

'Here,' said Whimbrel.

'Present,' said Smew.

'Present,' said Whimbrel.

[. . .]

'Surveyor of the Imperial Works?'

'Present,' said Dotterel.

'Pellitory-of-the-Wall?'

'Present,' said Wryneck.

'Principal Composer to the Imperial Court?'

'Present,' I said.

'His Exalted Highness, the Majestic Emperor of the Realms, Dominions, Colonies and Commonwealth of Greater Fallowfields?'

Smew waited but there was no response . . . 'Absent,' he said, putting a cross in the register.

This is a slightly abbreviated version of the first page (the roll-call is longer). The scene is repeated in full at various points in the novel – each time with a small, elegant variation – the better to establish the Beckettian absurdity of the situation: a kingdom where the actual business of state takes a back seat to the administration of the business of state. It is 'customary in the empire to grant positions of high office to people who know little about their subject':

Our Principal Composer narrator knows nothing about composing music, the Astronomer Royal is a stranger to the concept of north.

'Why do I need to know that?' Whimbrel enquired.

'Believe me, it's important,' I said. 'Besides, someone might ask you.'

'Who?'

'Someone who wants to go there.'

'You mean by ship?'

'Yes, possibly, or even overland.'

'Who, though?'

Whimbrel was evidently unimpressed by the whole notion of 'the north'.

'All right,' I said, changing tack. 'What if the emperor asks you where north is? What will you do then?'

'Oh yes,' said Whimbrel, 'I never thought of that.'

But the emperor remains absent, his only communication a note 'expressing his wish for a courtly entertainment to mark the occasion of the twelve-day feast'. To please him, the council decides to stage an unnamed play, in which the ghost of a murdered king appears at dinner; meanwhile, in the 'real' world, someone who might be the emperor in disguise keeps appearing around town with a group of travelling players — and then of course this *is* the twelve-day feast. *Macbeth, Twelfth Night, Measure for Measure, Hamlet* — it's all swirling around in a slightly infuriating confection that won't reveal its purpose, just as that title (Mills has a gift for the naming of novels) seems certain to be lifted from one of *Macbeth*'s many ornithological lines, and yet isn't, quite. This kingdom is lost in an English fairy-tale world, relying on past glories as surely as English literature looks back to Shakespeare as its golden moment — but on the edge of the forest a new imperium is being built, by the unsentimental Scoffers, who work 24-7, have no cultural nostalgia, and dress like train guards.

With Mills the plot *is* the book, but I'm obliged to note that the prose style, after seven novels and three short-story collections in little over a decade, has begun to show signs of fatigue. I have no doubt that Mills can go on writing his unhinged parables until the beasts come home, but a reader also likes to feel a writer's development, and there are few pleasures in *A Cruel Bird* that can't be experienced nearly identically in his other novels. This latest, interestingly, contains more than Mills's usual quota of (lightly) disguised defences of his sparse style:

> Taking Wryneck by the sleeve, Sanderling guided him over to the picture and started explaining it to him. Cleverly, though, he made no attempt to talk about artistic technique: brushstrokes, light, colour, perspective and so forth. This would have led him straight out of his depth. Instead he described how a ship actually sailed, commencing from first principles.

What happens with buildings, tools, mechanisms, tower rooms, and trains inspires Mills's imagination; what happens with people prompts abstraction and cliché: 'I shuddered as my ninety-eight musicians drove onwards, soaring up to greater and greater heights, then plunging down to new depths.' Individually, they are deliberately inarticulate. 'Good grief!' is about all they can manage, and when combined with Mills's love of repetition, this tic of inarticulacy begins to weary rather than amuse.

For the most part, it's a problem of length. What works in the novella space of *Three to See the King* or *The Restraint of Beasts* here strains to go the distance. There are too many passages revealing cheek by jowl Mills's strengths and weaknesses:

> Behind the station loomed tall buildings shrouded in vapour; factory hooters were blaring and smoke was rising from their immense chimneys; sparks flew inside cavernous steel sheds; beneath a gantry an iron girder descended steadily on a hook and chain; cables

unwound from revolving drums; all around me the City of Scoffers
was gathering momentum for the day ahead, while I could do nothing but gaze haplessly into an apparent void.

Along with the absurdity of the world, Kafka could describe the
void inside human beings – he met irony with agony. Mills can only
conjure the word: void. It's still a very funny and bracingly odd
dystopia, but 276 pages is a long time to spend in a toy town. You
start to yearn for wilder climes.

There was no one wilder than Rimbaud. Before he was twenty-one,
the boy-poet had crossed the Alps on foot, worked as a longshoreman
in Leghorn, fallen in love with Verlaine (and been shot in the wrist
by him, and seen the older poet go to jail for two years), enlisted as
a mercenary, slept on the streets, lived in a flophouse drinking
absinthe daily, walked from Charleville to Paris – oh, and written *A
Season in Hell*, in which he predicted his next move: 'My day is done;
I'm leaving Europe. The sea air will burn my lungs; lost climes will
tan my skin.' Next he joined the Dutch Colonial Army and sailed to
Java, where he soon deserted, vanishing into the jungle. He stayed
a few months and no one knows anything at all about what he did
there.

Jamie James, a former art critic for the *New Yorker*, has written a
necessarily short, delightful book about this 'lost Rimbaud'. *Rimbaud
in Java* was intended as a novel, but James, despairing of putting
dialogue in the mouth of the protagonist, veered into non-fiction: a
sensible decision. His alternate route is still a high-wire performance.
It's not an academic book and it's not really a history either; nor is
it – God help us – a 'meditation'. It generally spares its readers the
pointless formulation: *If Rimbaud had been here he most probably*

would have . . . Instead it offers a more honest motivation for writing, stripped of the veneer of 'professionalization': love. As James puts it, this book is 'an act of enthusiasm'.

He is obsessively enthusiastic about Rimbaud, and so, like his fellow devotees, is profoundly, perhaps irrationally, interested in whether or not Rimbaud smoked opium out there in the jungle, or had a lover, or took the Prins van Oranje steamer or a local *phinisi* schooner on his return journey – all of which it's impossible to know. Such speculations fascinate James, and he weaves the possibilities into his understanding of the poetry, and of the man. If it all sounds too whimsical at first (it did to me, reading the blurb), you soon realize that the best reason to stick with *Rimbaud in Java* is not for the facts or the fantasy but for the spectacle of reading someone write beautifully about something he finds, well, beautiful:

> The glamour that has attached itself to Rimbaud's odyssey-in-reverse, the reason some people care so passionately about reconstructing the itinerary of his ceaseless efforts to escape from home, partakes of the magnetic attraction of his poetry. It derives its potency from an essential quality of the enigma: the longer one ponders Rimbaud's life, the more it can seem as if the pattern of riddles thrown in one's way is a deliberate creation, a premodernist adumbration of a witty postmodernist gesture, rather than a life lived at hazard, like any other life.

You can always find a coffee-table-crushing cultural history, but I quite like the idea of learning, in a few hours, a whole lot about Java, orientalism, Rimbaud, Victorian attitudes toward homosexuality, global shipping routes and the Suez Canal. The book shines a torch down the well of the nineteenth century and illuminates a little patch on an inner wall near the bottom. Before, you had to trawl for miles through the stacks to figure out what you sought; now you know sooner, and know sooner what you'll never find. Microhistory? If it's the beginning of a trend I won't complain.

Finally, a word from your reviewer. I have to fess up to my own irrational fantasy – the one where it's possible to write a novel, teach class, bring up a kid and produce a regular column: at the moment a speculative fiction for me. With regret I must say goodbye to New Books – at least for a while – and welcome my brilliant successor, Larry McMurtry.

The I Who Is Not Me*

1. Impossible Identities

Not long ago I finished working on a novel, written in a voice I've never used before: the first person. Oh, I've written essays that say 'I', and many emails, obviously, and birthday cards and notes for my children's teachers, and several lectures like this one — but never fiction. Honestly, I was always a little repelled by the idea. I think because I started writing very young, at an age where I felt that any reader who picked me up would be well within their rights to say: now, who exactly does this girl think she is? My answer to that was: 'no one'. It became important for me to believe my fiction was about other people, rather than myself, I took a strange pride in this idea, as if it proved I was less self-preoccupied or vain than the memoirist or the blogger or the *Bildungsroman*-er. No one could accuse me of hubris if I wasn't there. Looking back, I think this moral queasiness around the first person is very much a British habit. One of the first things we learn in school about our greatest writer, Shakespeare — right after we are informed that he is the greatest — is that he was, in

* This lecture was the Inaugural Philip Roth Lecture, given at the Newark Public Library on 27 October 2016.

essence, nobody. I don't only mean that we know very little about him autobiographically, although of course we don't. I mean that we are consistently encouraged to believe Shakespeare the supreme example of what Keats called 'negative capability', that is, a man who appeared to hold no firm opinions or set beliefs, who lived in doubt and in a hundred personas, whose empathy for others was limitless, who is simultaneously everywhere and nowhere in his famous plays, like a gnomic god. Now, another way to think about this is that Shakespeare's ego was so very insatiable he thought he could speak for *everybody*: a black duke, a transvestite girl, a carefree prince, a mad king. But we tend not to think of it that way, in Britain, instead we consider Shakespeare's breed of impersonality among the highest literary virtues. The first-person voice, in this elevated context, presents itself as a kind of indulgence, a narcissistic weakness, which the French and the Americans go in for, perhaps, but not the British, or not very often. In Britain we are always doing this: mistaking an aesthetic choice for an ethical one.

Anyway, it was this kind of thinking which I think prompted me to write my novel *On Beauty* in the form I chose, a very elevated third person, which sounded almost Victorian. This voice I then applied to a world that was not mine, to a family I never had, a childhood as distant from mine as could be imagined, at least by me. The children in that book grow up on a university campus, their father is a white, male academic. And then, at other moments in the novel, the narrative voice seems to live inside that white, male academic, and sometimes in his black British teenage lover, and sometimes in his African-American middle-aged wife, and sometimes in a seventeen-year-old, white Midwestern girl, who sits in the back of this academic's class, confused and baffled by the lesson. This is the kind of fiction I have always loved to write and read: worming itself into many different bodies, many different lives. Fiction that faces outwards, toward others. But after my book was finished and I had a chance to reflect upon it I could see more clearly how the I who is me ran through it all in a subterranean way. *On Beauty* is not my life, but it's certainly full of my loves, my interests, my ideas. Mozart's *Requiem* was a passion of mine, at the time, as was Haitian painting, and I dig hip-hop and Rembrandt makes me cry and I adore my siblings and love to swim. I had just got married and was thinking a lot about what marriage might mean. The novel is a record of my preoccupations, although they are mapped on to strangers. Meanwhile the strictly autobiographical, if it occurred at all, was deeply buried and almost entirely subconscious. But it was there. Very close to the end, for example, a teenage girl punches another girl in the face because she finds her kissing a boy the first girl has a crush on. That is the only event in the whole novel that is, in the literal sense, true. When I was fifteen I knocked out a girl for kissing a boy I had a crush on. But I did not plan to have this scene in the novel – I do not plan my novels much in general – and I certainly did not know I was going to write that scene until I did. Yet when you read *On Beauty* much of the plot seems to build to precisely this moment, as if the whole thing had been mapped out for this purpose from the start. Is it possible – I wondered, after the book was done – that my subconscious in some sense tricked me into writing this long novel, led me down the garden path, weaving all kinds of themes and narrative turns into its fabric, permitting me, its author, to think my book was about class or colour or American feminism or whatever I, in my innocence, thought it was about, when all the time she, my subconscious, had constructed the whole thing simply to create a convincing stage upon which to work through the traumatic memory of a single left hook from twenty years ago? It's a funny idea and, to me, a slightly unnerving one. I am someone who likes to be in control when I write, who prefers to believe she is making basically impersonal and rational aesthetic choices. And with *On Beauty* I really set out to be a voice from the mount, the kind I remembered fondly from my childhood, the measured voice of Victorian fiction – I felt I needed that authority. I didn't want to sound like some furious fifteen-year-old girl still licking old wounds.

What is the true role of the autobiographical in fiction? For years I thought of it only as a kind of weakness, a failure of imagination, something a little embarrassing. But perhaps there are other, more positive ways to look at it. 'Happy is the novelist,' claims Nabokov, 'who manages to preserve an actual love letter that he received when he was young within a work of fiction, embedded in it like a clean bullet in flabby flesh and quite secure there, among spurious lives.' Maybe all novels have these 'clean bullets' of lived experience buried in them: maybe that's the reason we write them in the first place, whether we realize it at the time or not. Nabokov was certainly very happy to think of his fiction as a place where the delicate butterflies of his personal experience might be preserved, pinned and mounted for eternal appreciation. When you read him you sense his delight at smuggling in a certain well-turned ankle, remembered from St Petersburg, or a dead lover's fox-fur, or the multicoloured windowpane from his childhood estate. I am myself less happy considering my fiction as a vehicle through which I force personal memories upon a wider public, like a Facebook bore who makes you go through all their old photos: I feel that way indulgence lies. Between the clean bullet of my memories and the spurious lives I depict, I feel – I hope – that my fiction is focused primarily on those spurious lives, that is, on the fiction itself. For me fiction is a way of asking: what if things were other than they are? And a central component of that is to ask: what if I was different than I am? I have always found the practice of writing fiction far more an escape from self than an exploration of it. Yet when I read other people's novels I make the same mistakes as most civilian readers: I confuse Portnoy with Roth, and Humbert with Nabokov and Janie with Zora Neale Hurston. Call it 'The Autobiographical Error'. And if a friend and peer writes a novel set in space among a race of monopods called the Dinglebots, I am still liable to think to myself: *Yes, yes, very well, I see what you've done there with those Dinglebots — but isn't this all about your recent divorce?* I notice, too, that I make this mistake most consistently when I read first-person narratives. But rather than expressing contempt for this autobiographical instinct in readers and in myself I want to try to find a place to reconcile the 'I-who-is-not-me' of the writer with the 'I-whom-I-presume-is-you' that the reader feels they can see. Writers always claim it's all fiction and readers always suspect that it isn't. Who's right?

I think to appreciate fiction fully it helps to conceive of a space that allows for the writer's experience and the reader's simultaneously, a world in which Portnoy is at once entirely Philip Roth and not Philip Roth at all. That sounds like an impossible identity, but literature, for me, is precisely the ambivalent space in which impossible identities are made possible, both for authors and their characters. What I find most striking about *Portnoy's Complaint* is that at the time of its composition both Portnoy and his author were each in their own way burdened with an impossible identity. To deal with Portnoy first: in 1969, though it was possible to go to the moon, and possible to imagine nuclear annihilation, *it was not possible to be Portnoy in the world*. At least, it was not possible to be Alexander Portnoy in Newark. No, you simply could not be a foul-mouthed, sex-obsessed, fundamentally unserious and unpious, masturbating, liver-fucking, mother-hating young Jewish boy from Newark. It's easy to forget this fact now that Portnoy finds himself safely tucked up beneath the prestigious covers of the *Library of America*. But look over the old press clippings and you'll be reminded of just how impossible he seemed at the time. Man, he really caused a riot. Yet these days this foul-mouthed son of Newark is considered as American and beloved as apple pie. He is on college courses and top-ten lists. Jewish mothers buy copies of him for their Jewish sons as birthday presents; grandmothers buy the audiobook in fits of nostalgia. Portnoy was not Roth and he was not real, but in him is enshrined a genuine Rothian freedom, created by Roth, once impossible, now fully realized, a freedom which anyone can now easily access. You don't even have to read the book: you are already living in the world that Portnoy touched and changed. By saying 'I' in a certain mode, an ambivalent, fictional mode, Roth made possible through Portnoy a new kind of 'I' in the world, a gift of freedom that was taken up by a generation of writers, millions of readers and eventually a global community. This gift is sometimes confused with the far duller idea of an artist offering his readers some form of personal role model. I do think art can and often does offer models of behaviour, or at least suggests possibilities of behaviour, but I dislike the aspirational tone of 'role model'. Roth's gift with Portnoy was large precisely because it had no aspirational element and no precise directions. Like any good gift, the less strings we find attached to it the better. The offer was not: *You, too, can be like Portnoy*. The offer was: *Portnoy exists! Be as you please.*

A few minutes ago I suggested that Philip Roth as much as Portnoy had an impossible identity, back in 1969. I call it impossible because Roth wanted to be 'A Great American Novelist', which was, at that particular moment, something a Jewish novelist could not yet be. But from *Goodbye, Columbus* on, he set about furiously writing himself out of that impossibility, a further gift of freedom so large and effective that it seems now like a natural bounty, and people are liable to forget he is responsible for it at all. Alongside Saul Bellow, Roth utterly dissolved the impossible identity of the Jewish-hyphen-American-hyphen-novelist, until the idea of a Jewish man being a Great American Novelist seems as natural and obvious to us now as a California redwood rising up out of the soil. Later a new generation rebelled against the freedom thus proffered: they didn't believe in 'Great' or 'American' or even 'Novel'. Some wanted to replace the secular Jewish world Roth depicted with the sacred Jewish world once more. Others wanted to overwrite his vision of male sexuality run amok with a female counter-narrative. This is all to the good. Freedoms calcify and have to be rejected and/or adapted by the young. And soon the young in their turn will seem old and paternalistic to the kids rising up under them, and the whole Oedipal battle will begin again. But none of this can devalue permanently any particular writer's gift of freedom, and Roth's has been larger than most. Through a dazzling array of literary avatars, he complicated, confused, ridiculed, celebrated, built and destroyed so many of our ideas of what a human life is, what's important in it, and what ridiculous, what beautiful and what ugly, what serious and what fundamentally funny. For me the final and greatest lesson of his work is to insist on the fictional status of identity itself. For all Roth's men are essentially 'self-made'. They talk themselves into a particular existence. And they can talk themselves out of it, too. Nothing is sacred, they are beholden to nobody, fearless, as Roth himself as a writer has been fearless. He's written things down that seemed unsayable, impossible, and in taking this freedom for himself, intentionally or not, passed the freedom down.

To speak personally, I know that I stole Portnoy's liberties long ago to address my own project. He is part of the reason, when I write, that I do not try to create positive black role models for my black readers, and more generally have no interest in conjuring ideal humans for my readers to emulate or use as examples for their children. I took from Roth the liberty to create free characters behaving with freedom, independent of obligation, some good, some bad, some admirable, some perverse, some downright evil. I am trying to counter the narrow path with the wide-open road. For what is impossible about any real-life identity is its narrowness. In my case, I understood myself, as a child, to be a third, impossible option in an otherwise binary culture: neither black nor white but both. There are many negative responses a child can have to this feeling of impossibility: anger, sadness, despair, confusion. But there is another more interesting response that I think of as inherently creative, and I believe it is at the root of the reason so many writers will tell you that they felt in some way alienated as children. When you are not at home in your self, as a child, you don't experience your self as 'natural' or 'inevitable' – as so many other people seem to do – and this, though melancholy at the time, can come with certain distinct advantages. Not to take yourself as a natural, unquestionable entity can lead you in turn to become aware of the radical contingency of life in general, its supremely accidental nature. I am Philip, I am Colson, I am Jonathan, I am Rivka, I am Virginia, I am Sylvia, I am Zora, I am Chinua, I am Saul, I am Toni, I am Nathan, I am Vladimir, I am Leo, I am Albert, I am Chimamanda – but how easily I might have been somebody else, with *their* feelings and preoccupations, with their obsessions and flaws and virtues. This to me is the primary novelistic impulse: this leap into the possibility of another life. And from this position comes the ability to see the self you happen to be from a certain, often ironic, distance, the gap for example that Philip Roth established between himself and his Portnoy. There is a freedom in this, primarily for the writer. I'm one of these people who have come to believe writing is a kind of psychological condition, forged in childhood, with a strong element of compulsion to it. But writers who are compelled to pursue this freedom for themselves almost always inadvertently confer it on others. The rigidity with which I considered my own identity in childhood, for example, was the consequence of a failure of imagination, both my own and others'. Practically the only star I had to steer by was that old, worn-out, paper-thin character the 'tragic mulatto', whom I found in bad novels and worse movies. But then I found Hanif Kureishi, whose own impossible identity – Pakistani and British, Straight and Gay – he transformed into his delightful first novel, *The Buddha of Suburbia*, which I in turn read and felt something impossible loosen itself within me. It was a gift of freedom.

It seems to me that people experiencing impossible identities – who find it impossible to imagine being, for example, Muslim and gay, or Jewish and obscene, or black and nerdy, or female and perverse, or Protestant and Irish – can build up a terrible tension within themselves. The beauty of Portnoy is how he resolves this tension in laughter and in prose, but we know that in the real world impossible identities are too often resolved in violence. The rope inside us is pulled so taut, strung between such apparently incompatible places, that we feel we must cut it. Most often this violence is internal: we kill some part of ourselves. We ignore that we are gay, or smart, or masculine, or melancholy, or scared. We cut that bit out and live in a mutilated way. That is an intimate tragedy. But worse are the occasions when this internal violence faces outwards and becomes lethal to other people: when we project the 'other' we are on to another human and hurt or even kill them in proxy. How many of the young men setting bombs on streets around the world turn out to be also living what they perceive to be doubled and impossible identities: as simultaneously gay and straight men, pious believers and raucous street kids, Westerners and Easterners? Of course it's a naive and romantic fool who offers the novel or any art form as the cure-all for this form of internal confusion. And novels written with this explicit intention are guaranteed to be a great bore. I certainly don't write as a public service. But I am aware, at least as a reader, that remarkable acts of art-making – bold, perverse, unbeholden, free – have had the side effect of changing the weather in a country, in a people, at a certain historical moment, and finally in me, conferring freedoms for which I am now very grateful. And perhaps the most autobiographical part of my writing is the barely conscious awareness, deep down, that a part of me is always writing backwards to the confused brown girl I once was, providing the books I wished back then that I could read.

2. *The Reality Effect*

It sounds very silly but through twenty years of using only the third person I almost completely forgot what the first person was *for*. When my students tried to use it I often found myself giving them one of my very British half-aesthetic, half-ethical lectures, about the limitations, as I saw it, of only saying 'I'. What about other characters? What about facing outwards? But the moment I starting writing in the first person myself I realized how wrong I'd been. I saw how this form utilizes something so fundamental, which we experience every day talking to our children and partners and friends and enemies, overhearing the conversations of others, in almost all our human interactions: the latent power of the anecdote, of testimony, of confession, of witness. *Once upon a time there lived* is the most basic example of the third-person set-up, but how much work one has to do to convince your reader of its reality! She will have so many questions. *Once upon a when, exactly? Where? Who were these people? Why are you telling me about them? On what authority do you tell me this story?* Now compare that to: *Something happened to me yesterday.* The reality effect is so strong, immediate. All questions dissolve. Why am I telling you this? Because it happened to me! What a freedom I felt, constructing this entirely false autobiography which still, at every turn, sounded real, because I had allowed myself to write 'I' and in this way falsely insist on its truth. Quite a lot of the time as I wrote this book I felt a little scandalous. In what other medium are you allowed to lie for four hundred pages and present it as bare-faced truth? And at the same time my relationship with my reader had a new frisson. If before, in our long history, she had suspected my novels were merely me disguised, what would she think now? How many times can you say 'I' and still ask a reader to believe that this is still the I-who-is-not-you?

Well, this all felt very fresh and exciting to me, but of course Philip Roth has been teasing out the potential consequences of this fraught dynamic for forty years. In our minds Roth the man and his many ink-and-paper avatars are inextricably entwined: it's common for readers to consider the term 'fiction' here to be not much more than a publishing-world fig-leaf employed to obscure personal revelation. Knowing this, part of the thrill and dread of writing in the first person, for me, was precisely the realization that once it was published I would have to answer to this fictional self, as Roth has had to do for his fictional selves so many times: Did I share her views, her biography, her history, her mother? I could project myself into the future and see exactly how tiresome I would find these questions once the book was published, and yet it didn't stop me, I kept on doing it, I think because the reality effect – which is, in the end, a *literary* effect – is such an incredibly enjoyable tool to employ while you're using it. You have your reader where you want them, in the palm of your hand, and the whole test, the whole battle of fiction – to make them believe – feels more possible than ever. As distressing as it surely must have sometimes been for flesh-and-blood Roth to be confused with Zuckerman or Portnoy or Mickey Sabbath I now see more clearly why he did it. The first person opens up the delicious possibility of telling someone a true lie: *Let me tell you what happened to me.*

It has been said a lot recently in literary circles that readers have tired of *Once upon a time there lived* and can now only read work that speaks directly of reality, that says only: *Let me tell you what happened to me.* (*Once upon a time there lived* feels too hard, too distant, appears to require too much effort, is too difficult to believe.) People living in a twenty-four-hour news culture have enough real stories to occupy them without being bothered with fairy-tale lands and imagined folk. Those who take this view offer as evidence the great success of writers like Karl Ove Knausgård and Elena Ferrante, memoir-novelists like Ben Lerner and Sheila Heti, and straight-up, non-fiction personal-essay sensations like Ta-Nehisi Coates and Lena Dunham. I love all these writers but not because I find them more real. I think the argument itself is somewhat infantile and mistakes the reality effect for actual reality. I have always believed, for example, that writers of memoir are involved in the exact same practice in which I am engaged: the arranging of sentences on a page and the creation of effects. I'm afraid I do not believe that Karl Ove Knausgård miraculously remembers conversations from his childhood when I know I could not precisely reconstruct a conversation I had yesterday with my husband. It's all writing. The reality effect is one among many literary effects and can be employed to various degrees; it utilizes the flesh-and-blood self, mining it for information, stripping it for parts and re-presenting it. But that flesh-and-blood self can never actually appear on the page. That may seem a very obvious thing to say but I think many of us, bamboozled by the reality effect, tend to forget it. All that can ever appear on a page are verbs and adjectives, nouns and adverbs, and that powerful pronoun 'I'. Philip Roth is not and never can be Portnoy because it is not possible to render a real human being even partially in sentences. Echoes, shadows, inversions, fragments – this much writing can do. But the whole enchilada lives on a different plane. Roth's singular achievement was to use his reader's erroneous beliefs about the relationships between characters and their authors *as one of his literary effects.* Where Roth and Zuckerman join and part, how much of young Philip is in young Portnoy, whether that there is Roth's marriage or not, or Roth's lover or not – these questions are unanswerable in prose, but the provoking of them in the reader's head is a powerful hermeneutic experience. Roth's work plays with the reality effect and thus with your interpretive sensibilities. When Mickey Sabbath masturbates over his lover's grave, who are you offended by? Roth? Mickey? Who do you want to defend? His dead wife (who is made of sentences)? Women in general? Men in general? In the real world we often want our judgements and moral decisions to be swift and singular and decisive. Fiction messes with our sense of what it is possible to do with our judgements. It usefully suspends our great and violent desire to be in the right on every question, and creates an unholy and ungovernable mix of the true and the false. It's the place where things are true and not true simultaneously: the ultimate impossibility. I think great novels free us into an understanding that the tension between true/not true might in fact be liveable, might not have to be judged and immediately neutralized in the court of public opinion or in the oppressive conservatism of our social lives. A novel is fundamentally without real-world consequences, or so we think as we read them, and we can be bold in the spaces they create, braver, more able to tolerate our own uncertainties.

When you write a novel in the first person you take on an impossible identity, someone you can't be, because you are already you – and not this 'I' in the book – and you have lived your life, had your adventures, experienced your own highs and lows. My pretend life story in *Swing Time* ends with 'my' mother dying. When I gave it to my very much alive mother I wondered what she would make of it. I knew the reality effect in it was oddly strong: an acquaintance who had read it sent me an email expressing her sadness on my mother's passing. But my mother read it with equanimity. I suppose she has at this point seen so many false and fictitious mothers from her daughter that she has become very used to the I-who-is-not-me and does not bother too much over it any more, though I know it must not be much fun to be mistaken, by others, for Clara in *White Teeth* or Kiki in *On Beauty*, or to have any fictional self proceed you into a room – or indeed to be presumed dead. The Polish poet Czesław Miłosz once famously warned: 'When a writer is born into a family that family is finished.' But so far my family seems to be holding up, and this despite the fact that I have also one comedian brother and one rapper brother – so that's three kids picking over the narrative bones of one clan. But the Smiths still stand. I have no idea how it was for the Roths but I'm guessing it can't always have been easy. The freedom I have been suggesting novels can offer their readers does not easily extend to those real people mistakenly thought to be depicted within their pages. For them, I fear, these fictions are instead a kind of prison. For this and many other reasons I am forever unsure whether novel-writing is worth it. The balance is hard to measure. I think of all the pain writers like Richard Yates and John Cheever caused their families, and then I place it against all the joy these men provoked in me. Writers create their secondary selves, they use them to slip from every bind and definition, but they can also prove callous with the lives of others and in their dash for freedom knock their loved ones out of the way. Half of Karl Ove's family, or so the newspapers tell us, are presently suing him. And yet the freedom that this writer has conveyed, worldwide, is huge and not easily dismissed. I used to think, as a young writer, that it all boiled down to that crusty old Yeatsian warning: 'The intellect of man is forced to choose/Perfection of the life, or of the work . . .' But now that seems to me another impossibly taut identity in need of loosening up. Why must either life or work be perfect? Writers, like everybody else, are stumbling through this world, constantly re-examining the checks and balances of their choices, knowing they are helping here but hurting there. In my life, at least, the flesh-and-blood 'I' and the I-who-is-not-me stumble equally, neither ever coming close to perfection. But I feel extremely fortunate to be engaged in this lifelong project concerning their inter-relation, communication, mutual rejection and argument. If I can keep saying 'I' both ways for even half as long as Mr Roth managed it, I will count myself a very fortunate woman indeed.

FEEL FREE

Life-writing

For a long time I've wanted to keep a diary. I tried throughout adolescence but always gave it up. I dreamed of being very frank, like Joe Orton, whose diaries I admired; I found them in the library when I was about fourteen. I read them half as literary interest and half as pornography, thrilled to follow Joe around the many corners of the city in which I had only walked but he had managed to have illicit sex. I thought: *If you're going to write a diary, it should be like this, it should be utterly free, honest.* But I found I couldn't write about sexual desires (too shy, too dishonest), nor could I describe any sexual activity – I wasn't getting any – and so the diary devolved into a banal account of fake crushes and imagined romance and I was soon disgusted with it and put it aside. A bit later I tried again, this time concentrating only on school, like a Judy Blume character, detailing playground incidents and friendship drama, but I was never able to block from my mind a possible audience, and this ruined it for me: it felt like homework. I was always trying to frame things to my advantage in case so-and-so at school picked it up and showed it to everybody. The dishonesty of diary-writing – this voice you put on for supposedly no one but yourself – I found that idea so depressing. I feel that life has too much artifice in it anyway without making a pretty pattern of your own most intimate thoughts. Or maybe it's the other way round: some people are able to write frankly, simply, of how they feel, whereas I can't stop myself turning it into a pretty pattern.

As a young adult I read a lot of Virginia Woolf's diaries and again thought that I really should keep a diary. I knew enough about myself by then to know that the retelling of personal feelings in a diary was completely intolerable to me, I was too self-conscious, and too lazy for the daily workload. So I tried to copy the form and style of Woolf's single-volume *Writer's Diary* and make entries only on days when something literary had happened to me, either something I wrote or something I read, or encounters with other writers. That diary lasted exactly one day. It covered an afternoon spent with Jeff Eugenides and took up twelve pages and half the night. Forget it! At that rate the writing of the life will take longer than the living of it. I think part of the problem was the necessity to write in the first person, a form I have, until recently, found laborious and stressful. I was not able to use it with any confidence except in short, essayistic bursts. When I was younger even the appearance of 'I' on the page made me feel a bit ill – that self-consciousness again – and I would always try to obscure it with 'we'. I notice that once I got to America this began to change, and then snowball; looking up the page right now I see more cases of 'I' than a stretch of Walt Whitman. But still I have some mental block when it comes to diaries and journals. The same childish questions get to me. Who is it for? What is this voice? Who am I trying to kid – myself?

I realize I don't want any record of my days. I have the kind of brain that erases everything that passes, almost immediately, like that dustpan-and-brush dog in Disney's *Alice in Wonderland* sweeping up the path as he progresses along it. I never know what I was doing on what date, or how old I was when this or that happened – and I like it that way. I feel when I am very old and my brain 'goes' it won't feel so very different from the life I live now, in this miasma of non-memory, which, though it infuriates my nearest and dearest, must suit me somehow, as I can't seem, even by acts of will, to change it. I wonder if it isn't obliquely connected to the way I write my fiction, in which, say, a doormat in an apartment I lived in years ago will reappear, just as it once was, that exact doormat, same warp and weft, and yet I can't say when exactly I lived there, who I was dating or even if my father was alive or dead at the time. Perhaps the first kind of non-memory system – the one that can't retain dates or significant events – allows the other kind of memory system to operate, the absence of the first making space for the second, clearing a path for that whatever-it-is which seems to dart through my mind like a shy nocturnal animal, dragging back strange items like doormats, a single wilted peony, or a beloved strawberry sticker, not seen since 1986, but still shaped like a strawberry and scented like one, too.

When it comes to life-writing, the real, honest, diaristic, warts-and-all kind, the only thing I have to show for myself – before St Peter and whomever else – is my *Yahoo!* email account, opened circa 1996 and still going. In there (though I would rather die than read it all over) is probably the closest thing to an honest account of my life, at least in writing. That's me, for good and for bad, with all the kind deeds and dirty lies and domestic squabbles and bookish friendships and online fashion purchases. Like most people (I should think), a personal nightmare of mine is the idea of anybody wandering around inside that account, reading whatever they please, passing judgement. At the same time, when I am dead, if my children want to know what I was like in the daily sense, not as a writer, not as a more-or-less presentable person, but simply the foolish human being behind it all, they'd be wise to look there.

The Bathroom

When I was eight years old my family moved out of a council estate and into what seemed to me a mansion. From the front it looked like a whole house; inside it felt like one, too. We had the front door to ourselves, and if you looked out of the back windows you saw a big, square, overgrown garden, which also appeared to be entirely ours. Most visitors never noticed it was a maisonette, or that the bottom half of the building was council accommodation, accessible through a side entrance and occupied by an Indian family whose first act of greeting was to show me how to fold a triangle of pastry into a samosa. Not long after we'd moved in, my father set about splitting the shared garden in half, by way of a slightly warped wooden fence. I don't think the division was contentious: it was just a practical matter, relating to differing concepts of what constitutes a garden (coriander, potatoes; flowers, paddling pool). With the fence completed everyone was satisfied. We each had our little fiefdom. And from the back windows you still had this sense of grandeur, of space.

Inside we had four bedrooms. One each for me and my brother (although out of habit I usually snuck out of mine in the middle of the night and joined him in his), one for my father and mother – who was pregnant – and a 'spare' room, on a lower level, into which we periodically lured European teenagers. These teenagers were very glamorous to me, very exotic. They wore Swatches and pristine

Dunlops and primary-coloured Naf Naf sweaters; they watched – and seemed to genuinely enjoy – the Tour de France. They were forever wanting to be taken to Abbey Road and photographed walking on the zebra crossing. And of course they paid good rent. Later, when my youngest brother was born, the spare room became a place for a series of Spanish 'au pairs' who looked after the three of us, in lieu of rent, while my parents worked, my father in a small paper company, my mother as a recently qualified social worker. Clearly we had risen in the world. We had, for the first time, these non-essential spaces. Besides the spare room, we had the bathroom, which had its own toilet and was right next to another little room *that also had a toilet.* These two toilet-containing rooms were my mother's delight,* decorated with care, always scrupulously clean. Both the European teenagers and the later au pairs were expected – required, really – to express their regular admiration for them if they had any hope of living happily among us.

The spare room, the extra toilet – these represented, for my parents, a very British form of achievement. Raised in poverty, they were now officially what the census-takers call 'lower middle class'. I recognize that for people outside the UK these gradations of class are often bemusing, inherently absurd, and difficult to parse in their delicate separations, but let me try. When you were lower middle class, in the eighties, you went to Europe occasionally – though only on

---

* My mother, who still lives in that maisonette – with all our old rooms rented out – is very fond of toilets: not long ago she put a third one into what is essentially a cupboard in her bedroom. As all her children know well, Yvonne never tires of talking toilets; it's a preoccupation that stretches back to her childhood, in Jamaica, where she had to use a hole in the ground. She rarely comes home from a holiday without a photograph of the local facilities: drop toilets in Ghana, sparklingly clean toilets in Port Verde, supersonic toilets in Japan . . .

flights that left at 3 a.m, and on planes in which you freely chose the smoking section – and you drove a Mini Metro, and you bought fresh orange juice. You went to state school of course and had never seen a ski lift but you took the *Guardian** and, if there was a good front-page sex scandal, the *Mirror,* and you had those nice stripy Habitat blinds in the kitchen and china plates hanging on the walls and you absolutely understood that doormats with jokes on them were in bad taste. You told people you 'never watched ITV', although this was actually a lie: you watched ITV all the time. And each summer you packed the car and motored down the M4 to Devon or Cornwall, stopping along the route to take tea – thanks to the National Trust – in the various country mansions of penniless aristocrats. At least, that's how it was for us. Thinking back on it, I remember a lot of happiness. I'm sure every category in the census will stake its own claim – the noble working poor, the striving bour-geoisie, the elegant rich, the serenely high born, the *haute bourgeoisie* intellectual or artist – but the unlovable lower middle class also have their points of pride, although most of their satisfactions are, in my experience, the consequence of a series of counterfactuals. It's not what happens to the lower middle class, exactly, that makes them relatively content, but rather what *doesn't* happen. When each bill hitting the mat no longer represents an existential threat you are freed from an inhibiting and oppressive form of daily fear. Nor are you touched by the self-contempt that tends to stalk the solidly mid-dle and upper middle class, and you are perfectly ignorant of that sense of enervation too often found in the highest born. The lower-middle-class child has, as the football managers like to say, everything to play for. It's not that you don't hope to redeem your

* If you were on the left.

parents' own thwarted ambitions – particularly in the arena of education – you *do*, but you also understand that if you happen to fail
it's no longer the end of the(ir) world. And, as you motor onwards
through your life, whenever you pause to check behind you in
the rear-view mirror you see a vista quite unlike that of the child of
the long-term unemployed or the working poor or the recently
migrated. You see that your parents have established a small but
relatively stable space for themselves in this world, one that does
not – vitally – depend completely on you. And so there is a little
space for your own dreams, too. You don't *have* to become a doctor.
In fact as long as you don't expect your dreams to be financed in
any way whatsoever you are pretty much free to dream your little
head off. My parents' reaction to the news that they had, among
their children, one aspiring writer and two aspiring rappers was,
basically: knock yourself out.

I see now how liberating that was. Nothing was guaranteed and
nothing could be promised, but this also meant nothing was finally
decided or completely shut off. It gave me a great sense of freedom.
And I'm aware, as I raise my own children, that in a peculiar sense
they inherit from me less freedom than I took from my parents. Their
material circumstances are far better, and their parents aren't
permanently at war (four years after they moved into their 'mansion'
my parents bitterly separated). But I cannot present to my children the
utterly blank slate – equal parts exhilarating and frightening – which
my parents placed in front of me. In their case risk has been largely
eliminated, for to be born solidly middle class in England is still one
of the safest bets in the world – though of course not quite as safe as
it once was. (To truly fall out of the British middle class, when I was
a child, you really had to do something pretty spectacular, like become
a heroin addict or join the Hare Krishnas.) But even with rising house

prices and disappearing pensions, a lot of the important chapters of a middle-class child's life story are already written; they are composed at birth. My children are very likely to go to university. They are very unlikely to become teenage parents. And then of course my children are the children of writers. I've met the adult children of writers, their lives continually overlaid and undercut by another person's words. I think I have a sense of what a suffocating space that can be. Honestly, if I were a child of mine, I imagine I'd have a great urge to flunk out of school and become a teenage parent, if only as a way of asserting my own freedom.

One of the strange, not especially pleasant, things about child-rearing is what I want to call the retrospective swirl. A woozy movement, hovering between present and past, so intense, nausea-inducing, and yet, in its painful way, instructive. An example: I invite my oldest mate, Sarah, round my house, and our kids are running about, basically entertaining themselves, while we surreptitiously smoke fags and drink a bottle of white wine and start cussing all our friends and laughing big hawking laughs, and then the kids wander back in and I force them to call this best friend of mine 'Auntie Sarah' and they are profoundly dubious and I ignore their objections – and also all requests to cook dinner – and carry on talking very loudly and laughing a lot and then in the middle of all this I will think: Oh, right, I get it now! This is what Mum and 'Auntie' Ruth were like; and this is why, after about 6 p.m., they stopped telling us what to do, and we got to stay up an hour or two hours later, until finally somebody thought to cook a frozen pizza – oh, I *get* it now. They were best friends, Mum and Ruth, from before we were born, and they both worked hard and had little time, so it was a big deal when they got together. They loved talking to each other. They were human women with many other concerns besides their children. And they were a bit pissed on cheap white wine. Oh, *right*. Parental behaviour that seemed completely mysterious to me thirty years ago now freshly clarifies itself. Recently this has been happening to me more and more. It'll be about 4 p.m. on a Sunday, after forty-eight hours of uninterrupted childcare, and I'll fall into a black hole, an almost suicidal trough, and my children will be confused; in answer to questions they'll get blank stares or mono-syllables, and then, out of nowhere, I will suddenly rise to my feet and start screaming at them about some tiny, insignificant matter – and in the middle of the yelling a part of me is sent back, into that retrospective swirl, and I think: Oh, right – *this* is what she felt, thirty years ago. This is why she'd suddenly go silent and stare at a wall. She just couldn't take *one more second of it*. Not one more second of children shouting about who took what and what's fair and not fair, and the continual demands and unnecessary meltdowns, and the sense that you do not have even a second to yourself, and meanwhile the TV plays the same show it plays every day with that same fucking theme tune . . . Oh, *right*. Now it all falls into place. And my mother had *three*. Plus a very unhappy marriage, and few of the outlets and freedoms I take for granted. *And she was twenty-nine.* The retrospective swirl leads to retrospective lucidity.

As the picture of the past refines I see one room in particular in a new, semi-tragic light: the bathroom in my parents' maisonette. It wasn't big – about twelve feet by ten – but now I understand how much it had to hold. On the one hand, it was a just a little bathroom, done up in a vaguely 'seaside' theme – a shell here, a piece of coral there – the kind of thing British people like in their bathrooms. But it was also a sort of dream space of my parents, mixing memory and desire, precisely in Eliot's sense. My mum's contribution was plants. They were green and tropical-looking and hugely overgrown: tubers poked out of the soil and sometimes stretched to the next pot along where they grew some more, and every time you had a bath you had to contend with these tendrils, and the insects that were attracted to them, especially in summer. I'm not good with the names but there were definitely many spider plants, a few ferns, and something huge with broad, glossy leaves that blocked the light from the single window and made the whole thing feel like a tropical sweat-box.* The usual comment of visitors was: 'Christ, it's like a bloody jungle in there.' Green grew on green grew on green with lush abandon. Cutting it back only speeded up the process. Thirty years later, while attending a literary festival in Jamaica, I stood amid a lot of green growing on green growing on green and was thrown back, in memory, to a corner of a foreign bathroom that was forever . . . Jamaica. Yet it never occurred to me, as a child, that my mother might be homesick. Children are so narcissistic: nothing about other people ever really occurs to them, least of all about their parents. It further didn't occur to me that there was anything interesting about my father's use of this same small space as a dark room. I wasn't at all curious about it. The first time I even noticed what he was doing was when I accidentally disturbed him; I'd walked into the bathroom, intending to go to one of our several loos, and found the room pitch black, except for a strange red glow. My father shouted at me: 'Close that bloody door!' I did, but with me inside. Weird tableau: my father with his sleeves rolled up, and the bath full of liquid, and this red light, turning the clean Habitat lines of our

---

* My brother Ben suggests this was a 'money plant', which is neat, thematically.

modern home into something subterranean and, to me, unnerving. What was this secret room doing in our house? I looked up and saw he'd strung a clothes-line past the plants, stretching between the walls. On this were pegged large contact sheets from which images were slowly emerging. I'd never seen this process before and stared, wondering what was to come. All my childhood I'd hoped to discover my father had some hidden artistic genius – was this it?

But as the images rose to the fore it turned out that all the pictures were of us. Of me, my brother Ben and my brother Luke, over and over. Scattered around the base of the toilet were many little canisters of Ilford film, black and white, twenty-four shots on a roll. And these, too, turned out to be all of us. I was disappointed. I knew, vaguely, that my father had once had dreams of a career in photography; much later I learned that these dreams had, briefly, some reality, although many years before we were born. By the time we moved to the maisonette he was no more a photographer than the dad who plays five-a-side is a professional footballer. All ambition in that direction had been abandoned. Everything was now about us, everything had been submitted to, and re-formed around, family life. Which, as a child, I had nothing but contempt for, even as I benefited from it. That my father was a boring, reliable and sane man, able to infinitely defer his own pleasures and ambitions, is, I think now, at the root of whatever emotional stability I've been able to maintain in my life. But at the time his inability – or unwillingness – to live for himself filled me with horror. *For the sake of the children* was a phrase I especially detested; it seemed a thing people said to get out of the responsibility of actually living out their own desires and ideas or pursuing their God-given abilities. To stay married to someone you basically couldn't stand – for twelve years! – for the sake of the children! What kind of insanity was that?

Yet now, in the retrospective swirl, I look back at my parents' dedication to this principle with fresh appreciation. I still couldn't do it, but I understand now why they did. They had each grown up without fathers – devastating, in both cases. To employ another classically lower-middle-class cliché, they *wanted something better* for me.

There are of course degrees of these things but I do think every family home is an emotionally violent place, full of suppressed rage, struck through with profound individual disappointments. It's in the nature of the beast that no one gets out of a family unit whole or with everything they want. I think of that wonderful Jerry Seinfeld line: 'There's no such thing as fun for all the family.' Somebody's going to have to give up something: it's only a question of how much and to whom. In moments of retrospective swirl I see clearly that my parents gave me much more than I consider it reasonable to give anybody, and far more than I am able to give my own children. For though, superficially, I seem to give my children more of everything: more money, more 'opportunity', certainly more holidays, certainly more space, my parents gave me their lives. Children and domestic life supplanted art-making, for my father. And, for my mother, a new country supplanted the old, whether she wanted it to or not, that's what happened. I haven't had to make anything like these sorts of stark choices. My parents were fully immersed in the contested space in which adults live with children, each trying to realize their own ambitions, each trying to 'live their lives' and 'have time' – tropical plants here, contact sheets there – and no one ever getting all of what they want. I also live in a contested space with children, but the battles this time round are nowhere near as brutal.

When I think of my parents it's often with some guilt: that I did the things they never got to do, and I did them on their watch, using their time, as if they were themselves just that — time-keepers — and not separate people living out the ever-shortening time of their own existence. This is especially true of my father, if only because the time for his own life ran out. My mother got her education as an adult and now, still pretty young, gets to pursue her own whims and interests, relatively secure as she approaches the state pension she worked thirty years to earn. She travels, she lives — she even writes. But my father waited his whole life to see a certain image of himself rise from the contact sheet and it never did. My image rose instead, and my brother Ben's, and my brother Luke's. If my father was some kind of an artist — and my sense is that he was — his art stayed in that bathroom, and then died with him.* Meanwhile my mother is writing a novel about Jamaica even as I type this. And my own children, well, they have to live around and about and within the art-making of their parents; they have to listen to us talk about the books we're writing or reading, of films we've seen or films we want to write, and they have always known, from the start, that they are not the only things being created, cared for

---

* After my father died I found his earlier, commercial work among his things — mainly pictures of catalogue models of the fifties and sixties — as well as a trove of family photographs that turned out to be far more interesting than I had ever given them credit for being, as a child. My favourite is a family scene. It features Harvey himself, his first wife, Blanche, and his eldest daughter, my half-sister, Diana, to whom, by all accounts, he was a far less effective father: emotionally remote, and often simply not there. I reproduce the photo on page 365. I note its many encroaching shadows and the dramatic battle of the light as it tries to escape this creeping darkness. I note the many enclosing frames and awkward angles; the mixture of the natural and the staged; the contrast of the warm and the cold. He never gave the photo a title; it would never have occurred to him to do so. But I have taken the liberty of giving it one.

and raised up in this many-roomed house. Whether it's good or bad for them – or us – I don't know. But it's my sense that no matter how many rooms you have, and however many books and movies and songs declaim the wholesome beauty of family life, the truth is 'the family' is always an event of some violence. It's only years later, in that retrospective swirl, that you work out who was hurt, in what way, and how badly.

Postscript: two years after I finished writing this my brother Ben – a rapper, among many other things – sent me his new album. Though he had not read this essay, I found he had chosen, for the cover art for his album – and among the many pictures my father left behind – the exact same picture I have placed here.

The Family is a Violent Event, Harvey Smith, date unknown

Man versus Corpse

One September night, running home from dinner to meet a babysitter, I took off my heels and hopped barefoot – it was raining – up Crosby Street, and so home. *Hepatitis*, I thought. Hep-a-ti-tis. I reached my building bedraggled, looking like death. The doorman – who'd complimented me on my way out – blushed and looked down at his smartphone. In the lobby, on a side table, sat a forlorn little hardbacked book. *The World's Masterpieces: Italian Painting*. Published in 1939, not quite thirty pages long, with cheap marbled endpapers and a fond inscription in German: *Meinem lieben Schuler* . . . Someone gave this book to someone else in Mount Carmel (the Israeli mountains? the school in the Bronx?) on 2 March 1946.

The handwriting suggested old age. Whoever wrote this inscription was dead now; whoever received the book no longer wanted it. I took the unloved thing to the fifteenth floor, in the hope of learning something of Italian masterpieces. Truthfully I would much rather have been on my iPhone, scrolling through email. That's what I'd been doing most nights since I bought the phone, six months earlier. But now here was this book, like an accusation. Email or Italian masterpieces?

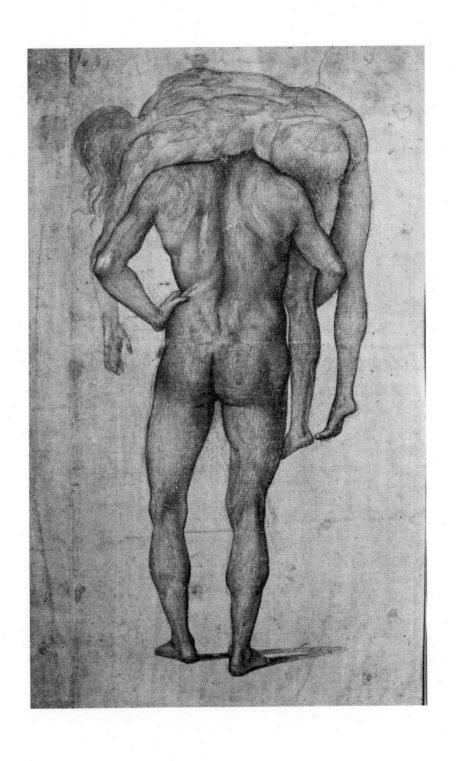

As I squinted through a scrim of vodka, a stately historical process passed me by: Cimabue, Giotto, Fra Angelico, Fra Filippo, Raphael, Michelangelo. Dates of birth and death, poorly reprinted images, dull unimpeachable facts. ('The fifteenth century brought many changes to Italy, and these changes were reflected in the work of her artists.') Each man more 'accurate' with his brush than the last, more inclined to let in 'reality' (ugly peasants, simple landscapes). Madonnas held their nipples out for ravenous babies and Venice was examined from many different angles. Jesus kissed Judas. Spring was allegorized. The conclusion: 'Many changes had taken place in Italian art since the days of the great primitive, Cimabue. The Renaissance had opened the way for realism and, at last, for truth as we find it in nature.'

To any reader of 2013 the works of 1939 may seem innocent. Though how jaded, how 'knowing' we can think ourselves, without knowing much of anything at all. I've worked my way through surveys like this before, and am still no closer to remembering who came first, Fra Angelico or Fra Filippo. My mind does not easily accept stately historical processions. But golden yellows and eggshell blues, silken folds of red and green, bell towers and lines of spruce, the penises and vaginas of infants (which, for the first time in my relationship with Italian masterpieces, I am able to judge on their veracity), the looks that pass between the Madonna and her son – these are the sort of things my mind accepts. And I was making my way through these details pleasantly enough when I was stopped short – snagged – by a drawing in charcoal. The whole stately historical procession dispersed. There was only this: *Nude Man from the Back Carrying a Corpse on His Shoulders* by Luca Signorelli (*c*.1450–1523).

Man is naked, with a hand on his left hip, and an ideal back in which every muscle is delineated. His buttocks are vigorous, monumental, like Michelangelo's *David*. ('Undoubtedly indebted to the works of Luca Signorelli.') He walks forcefully, leading with his left foot, and over his shoulders hangs a corpse – male or female, it's not clear. To secure it Man has hooked one of his own rippling arms around the corpse's stringy leg. He is carrying this corpse off somewhere, away from the viewer; they are about to march clean out of the frame. I stared at this drawing, attempting a thought experiment, failing. Then I picked up a pen and wrote, in the margins of the page, most of what you have read up to this point. A simple experiment – more of a challenge, really. I tried to identify with the corpse.

Imagine being a corpse. Not the experience of being a corpse – clearly being a corpse is the end of all experience. I mean: imagine this drawing represents an absolute certainty about you, namely, that you will one day be a corpse. Perhaps this is very easy. You are a brutal rationalist, harbouring no illusions about the nature of existence. I am, a friend once explained, a 'sentimental humanist'. Not only does my imagination quail at the prospect of imagining myself a corpse, even my eyes cannot be faithful to the corpse for long, drawn back instead to the monumental vigour. To the back and buttocks, the calves, the arms. Across the chasms of gender, colour, history and muscle definition, I am the man and the man is me. Oh, I can very easily imagine carrying a corpse! See myself hulking it some distance, down a highway or through a wasteland, before unloading it, surprised at its ever-increasing stiffness, at the way it remains frozen in an L-shape, as if sitting up to attention. And it's child's play to hear a neck bone crack as I lay the corpse – a little too forcefully – upon the ground.

Imagining *that* reality – in which everybody (except me) becomes a corpse – presents no difficulties whatsoever. Like most people in

New York City, I daily expect to find myself walking the West Side Highway with nothing but a shopping cart stacked with bottled water, a flashlight and a dead loved one on my back, seeking a suitable site for burial. The post-apocalyptic scenario – the future in which everyone's a corpse (except you) – must be, at this point, one of the most thoroughly imagined fictions of the age.

Walking corpses – zombies – follow us everywhere, through novels, television, cinema. Back in the real world, ordinary citizens turn survivalist, ready to scale a mountain of corpses if it means enduring. Either way, death is what happens to everyone else. By contrast, the future in which I am dead is not a future at all. It has no reality. If it did – if I truly believed that being a corpse was not only a possible future but my *only guaranteed future* – I'd do all kinds of things differently. I'd get rid of my iPhone, for starters. Lead a different sort of life.

What is a corpse? It's what they piled up by the hundreds when the Rana Plaza collapsed in Bangladesh this April. It's what lands on the ground each time a human being jumps off the Foxconn building in China's high-tech iPhone-manufacturing complex. (Twenty-one have died since 2010.) They spring flower-like in budded clusters whenever a bomb goes off in the marketplaces of Iraq and Afghanistan. A corpse is what individual angry, armed Americans sometimes make of each other for strangely underwhelming reasons: because they got fired, or a girl didn't love them back, or nobody at their school understands them. Sometimes – horrifyingly – it's what happens to one of 'our own', and usually cancer has done it, or a car, at which moment we rightly commit ourselves to shunning the very concept of the 'corpse', choosing instead to celebrate and insist upon the reality of a once-living person who, though 'dearly departed', is never reduced to matter alone.

It's argued that the gap between this local care and distant indifference is a natural instinct. Natural or not, the indifference grows, until we approach a point at which the conceptual gap between the local and the distant corpse is almost as large as the one that exists between the living and the dead. Raising children alerts you to this most fundamental of 'first principles'. Up/down. Black/white. Rich/poor. Alive/dead. When an Anglo-American child looks at the world she sees many strange divisions. Oddest of all is the unequal distribution of corpses. We seem to come from a land where people, generally speaking, live. But those other people (often brown, often poor) come from a death-dealing place. What a misfortune to have been born in such a place! Why did they choose it? Not an unusual thought for a child. What's bizarre is how many of us harbour something similar, deep inside our naked selves.

A persistent problem for artists: How can I insist upon the reality of death, for others, and for myself? This is not mere existentialist noodling (though it can surely be that, too). It's a part of what art is here to imagine for us and with us. (I'm a sentimental humanist: I believe art is here to help, even if the help is painful – especially then.) Elsewhere, death is rarely seriously imagined or even discussed – unless some young man in Silicon Valley is working on permanently eradicating it. Yet a world in which no one, from policymakers to adolescents, can imagine themselves as abject corpses – a world consisting only of thrusting, vigorous men walking boldly out of frame – will surely prove a demented and difficult place in which to live. A world of illusion.

Historically, the drift from representation toward abstraction has been expressed – by those artists willing to verbalize intent – as the rejection of illusion. From a 1943 mini-manifesto sent by Mark Rothko to *The New York Times*: 'We are for flat forms because they destroy illusion and reveal truth.' But what is 'truth'?

There is no such thing as good painting about nothing. We assert that the subject matter is crucial and that only that subject matter is valid which is tragic and timeless.

Death, for Rothko, was the truth – the tragic and timeless thing – and it's hard not to read his career as an inexorable journey toward it. His 1942 *Omen of the Eagle* (inspired by the *Oresteia* – itself an agonized consideration of three corpses: Agamemnon's, Cassandra's and Clytemnestra's) is the painting that apparently led to the mini-manifesto, and it's clearly transitional, still depicting, within Rothko's famous strata, some recognizable forms: Greek tragic masks, bird heads, many surrealist feet.

By the time of the Rothko Chapel (he killed himself before its unveiling), the strata have emptied out – not only of forms, but of colour, too. With those black-on-black, death-dealing rectangles (he found them a 'torment' to produce), Rothko was explicitly aiming for 'something you don't want to look at'. Which is one way of accounting for their emotional power: like a memento mori, they lead us to an intolerable, yet necessary, place.

Rothko wanted us deeply affected by the thing we don't want to look at. But there exists another solution to our tendency toward illusion: affectlessness. Make the viewer *feel* like a corpse. For when images proliferate among themselves, as if running mechanically with no human involvement, the viewer will find he lacks a natural point of entry. Simulacra seem to run without us, as the world will continue to run without us, once we are gone. Meanwhile, the idea of the artist – and the viewer – as human subjects, capable of deep feeling, of 'torment', grows obscure.

Art that plays with the idea of mechanical reproduction – the obvious example is the work of Andy Warhol – teaches us something of what it would be like to be a thing, an object. Warhol was also, not coincidentally, an enthusiastic proponent of corpse art, his *Death in America* series being strewn with dead bodies, all of which are presented with no whiff of human pity – although neither are they quite cold abstractions. On one level, the level at which they are most often celebrated, Warhol's corpses make you feel nothing. And yet your awareness of your own emptiness is exactly what proves traumatic about them. 'How can I be looking at this terrible thing and feeling nothing?' is the quintessential Warholian sensation and it's had a very long afterlife. *Uncomfortably numb*: that's still the non-emotion that so many young artists, across all media, are gunning for.

Thinking of Warhol and corpses, it's odd (to me) that I met – for the first time – the critic Hal Foster, on that September night, for it was a dinner at his apartment I was coming from. It's almost twenty years ago now that he wrote of the Warhol effect in *The Return of the Real*:

> [T]he famous motto of the Warholian persona: 'I want to be a machine.' Usually this statement is taken to confirm the blankness of artist and art alike, but it may point less to a blank subject than to a shocked one, who takes on the nature of what shocks him as a mimetic defense against this shock: I am a machine too, I make (or consume) serial product-images too, I give as good (or as bad) as I get . . . If you can't beat it, Warhol suggests, join it.

There Foster is defining something called 'traumatic realism', leaning on a Lacanian definition of trauma as 'a missed encounter with the real'. We mechanically repeat the trauma to obscure and control the reality of the trauma, but in doing so reproduce, obliquely, some element of it. The real pokes through anyway, in the process of repetition. One of his examples – Warhol's *White Burning Car III* – has echoes of the Signorelli. Here is a corpse – thrown from a burning car and hanging upon a climbing spike on a utility pole – and here is a live man, strolling by, heading out of the frame. It's an appropriation of a tabloid image, originally published in *Newsweek*.

On the one hand, as with the Signorelli, I am viewing the abject, unthinkable thing (myself as a corpse), and this, for me – and for Andy – is a way of dominating and controlling the trauma (of this idea). The silk screen screens the truth from me. But not entirely. A Warhol image, as Foster brilliantly argues, just keeps coming at you, partly hiding the real from you but also repeating and reproducing it unbearably. The repetition of the image – an unstable tower, three reps stacked beside two – proves key. Somewhere along the line, the sequence begins to morph. *Thank God it wasn't me* starts becoming (perhaps in that final blank space) *Oh Christ it will be me.**

This anxious double consciousness – *it's not me/it will be me* – may be part of the price we pay for living with, and around, machines. Whenever we enter a moving vehicle, for example, or a plane, haven't we always, already, in our minds, crashed and become corpses? Even before receiving our salty pretzels we see ourselves screaming and praying, falling through the sky, incinerated. And if we're in that Warholian moment, everything else is false advertising.

---

* In a crypt in Rome the bones of some four thousand Capuchin monks, buried between 1500 and 1870, have been used to create *mise en scènes*: fully dressed skeletons praying in rooms made of bones, with bone chandeliers and bone chairs and ornamental walls covered in skulls. In the final room a memento mori is spelled out upon the floor: 'What you are now, we once were; what we are now, you shall be.'

That's another ongoing attraction of Warhol: whenever it's strongly implied that we are going to live for ever (almost every ad, TV show, and magazine – in-flight or otherwise – does this) we can think of Andy (who used the commercial language of these mediums) and know, deep in our naked selves, that it isn't true.

Meanwhile the replication of nature at its most beautiful – beloved technique of Italian masterpieces – is the art best suited to sentimental humanism, allowing, as it does, the viewing subject to feel pity and empathy; to weep for all the beautiful people who have become or will become corpses (excluding me). Which is a response I would never entirely forsake, not for a half-dozen burning white cars. To look into the tender, unformed face of Titian's *Ranuccio Farnese* – twelve-year-old scion of the ancient Italian clan – and see a boy whose destiny it was to become a corpse! And this despite his red doublet's intricate embroidery, the adult sword hung about his narrow hips, the heavy weight of inheritance suggested by that cloak his father surely insisted he wear . . . All the signs of indelible individuality are here, yet none proved sufficient to halt the inevitable. (No amount of 'selfies' will do it, either.)

Is my horror of corpses coeval with the discovery that I'm a time-bound 'individual'? Before we were mere bodily envelopes, containing souls for a while, before these souls embarked on their journeys toward the infinite. In a culture that gives credence to eternal consciousness, corpses remain disgusting but aren't, in themselves, 'tragic'. The modern 'trick' of portraiture – the arresting of a 'single' moment in an individual life (made so much more poignant here, on the edge of adulthood) – may be an aesthetic illusion, but at least it helps remind us of what a large 'event' a human life truly is, of how much is lost when corpsification occurs. We may be for ever corpses – but once we were alive! It was the old masters that taught us the emotional power of individual representation. (And five hundred years later, space is still reserved in our newspapers for recent corpses – if they are one of 'ours' – the dead furnished with stories as precise and elaborate as the Farnese embroidery.)

Of course, we learned our attitudes toward human suffering from them, too. Auden's famous words fit Warhol's burning car as snugly as they do Bruegel's *Landscape with the Fall of Icarus* or Piero's *Flagellation of Christ*:

> [. . .] *how well they understood*
> *Its human position; how it takes place*
> *While someone else is eating or opening a window*
> *or just walking dully along;*

But do all old masters do this equally well? The sheer technical skill, the perfected illusion, can sometimes be a block between (this) viewer and the useful emotion she is seeking. There are many beguiling Italian masterpieces. There are also moments when you have to remind yourself that the stable relationship they tend to configure, between me the subject and the painting object (which I am contemplating as if it spoke of a truth that did not include me) is, in the final analysis, a gorgeous illusion.

The Signorelli, by contrast, stops you in your tracks. It has the gift of implication. It creates a triangular and unstable relationship – between you, the corpse and the 'someone else'. Looking at it, I am not a woman looking at a man carrying a corpse. I am that corpse. (Even if this is an idea I entertain for only a few seconds, preferring to be the 'someone else'.) And I will be that corpse for infinitely longer than I have ever been an individual woman with feelings and ideas and arms and legs, who sometimes looks at paintings. It's not me. But it will be me.

2.

Earlier, at Hal Foster's, we'd talked of Karl Ove Knausgård, the Norwegian author of a six-volume novel (or memoir?) called *My Struggle* (two volumes of which have been translated thus far). Everywhere I've gone this past year the talk, among bookish people, has been of this Norwegian. The first volume, *A Death in the Family*, minutely records the perfectly banal existence of 'Karl Ove', his unremarkable childhood, his troubles with girls, his adolescent attempts to buy beer for a New Year's Eve party (almost one hundred pages of that), and the death of his father.

The second, *A Man in Love*, renders a marriage in as much detail as any human can bear:

> What was going through her head?
>
> Oh, I knew. She was all alone with Vanja during the day, from when I went to my office until I returned, she felt lonely, and she had been looking forward so much to these two weeks. Some quiet days with her little family gathered round her, that was what she had been looking forward to. I, for my part, never looked forward to anything except the moment the office door closed behind me and I was alone and able to write.

As a whole these volumes work not by synecdoche or metaphor, beauty or drama, or even storytelling. What's notable is Karl Ove's ability, rare these days, to be fully present in and mindful of his own

377

existence. Every detail is put down without apparent vanity or decoration, as if the writing and the living are happening simultaneously. There shouldn't be anything remarkable about any of it except for the fact that it immerses you totally. You live his life with him.

Talking about him over dinner – like groupies discussing their favourite band – I discovered that although most people felt as strongly about their time spent under Karl Ove's skin as I had, we had a dissenter. An objection on the principle of boredom, which you sense Knausgård himself would not deny. Like Warhol, he makes no attempt to be interesting. But it's not the same kind of boredom Warhol celebrated, not that clean kind which, as Andy had it, makes 'the meaning go away', leaving you so much 'better and emptier'. Knausgård's boredom is baroque. It has many elaborations: the boredom of children's parties, of buying beers, of being married, writing, being oneself, dealing with one's family. It's a cathedral of boredom. And when you enter it, it looks a lot like the one you yourself are living in. (Especially true if, like Karl Ove, you happen to be a married writer. Such people are susceptible to the peculiar charms of Karl Ove.) It's a book that recognizes the tedious struggle of our daily lives and yet considers it nothing less than a tragedy that these lives, filled as they are not only with boredom but with fjords and cigarettes and works by Dürer, must all end in total annihilation.

But nothing happens! our dissenter cried. Still, a life filled with practically nothing, if you are fully present in and mindful of it, can be a beautiful struggle. In America we are perhaps more accustomed to art that enacts the boredom of life with a side order of that (by now) overfamiliar Warholian nihilism. I think of the similar-but-different maximalist narratives of the young writer Tao Lin, whose most recent novel, *Taipei*, is likewise committed to the blow-by-blow re-creation of everyday existence. That book – though occasionally unbearable to me as I read it – had, by the time I'd finished it, a cumulative effect, similar to the Knausgård.

Both exhaustively document a life: you don't simply 'identify' with the character, effectively you 'become' them. A narrative claustrophobia is at work, with no distance permitted between reader and protagonist. And if living with Tao Lin's Paul feels somewhat more relentless than living with Karl Ove, there is an element of geographical and historical luck in play: after all, Karl Ove has the built-in sublimity of fjords to console him, whereas Paul can claim only downtown Manhattan (with excursions to Brooklyn and, briefly, Taipei), the Internet and a sackload of prescription drugs.

Lin's work can be confounding, but isn't it a bit perverse to be angry at artists who deliver back to us the local details of our local reality? What's intolerable in *Taipei* is not the sentences (which are rather fine), it's the life Paul makes us live with him as we read. Both Lin and Knausgård eschew the solutions of minimalism and abstraction in interesting ways, opting instead for full immersion. Come with me, they seem to say, come into this life. If you can't beat us, join us, here, in the real. It might not be pretty – but this is life.

Would the premature corpsification of others concern us more if we were mindful of what it is to be a living human? That question is, for the sentimental humanist, the point at which aesthetics sidles up to politics. (If you believe they meet at all. Many people don't.) Concern over the premature corpsification of various types of beings – the poor, women, people of colour, homosexuals, animals – although consecrated in the legal sphere, usually emerges in the imaginary realm. First we become mindful – then we begin to mind. Of our mindlessness, meanwhile, we hear a lot these days; it's an accusation we constantly throw at each other and at ourselves.

It's claimed that Americans viewed twelve times as many Web pages about Miley Cyrus as about the gas attack in Syria. I read plenty about Miley Cyrus, on my iPhone, late at night. And you wake up and you hate yourself. My 'struggle'! The overweening absurdity of Karl Ove's title is a bad joke that keeps coming back to you as you try to construct a life worthy of an adult. How to be more present, more mindful? Of ourselves, of others? *For* others?

You need to build an ability to just be yourself and not be doing something. That's what the phones are taking away, the ability to just sit there . . . That's being a person . . . Because underneath everything in your life there is that thing, that empty – forever empty.

That's the comedian Louis C. K., practising his comedy-cum-art-cum-philosophy, reminding us that we'll all one day become corpses. His aim, in that skit, was to rid us of our smartphones, or at least get us to use the damn things a little less ('You never feel completely sad or completely happy, you just feel kinda satisfied with your products, and then you die'), and it went viral, and many people smiled sadly at it and thought how correct it was and how everybody (except them) should really maybe switch off their smartphones, and spend more time with live people offline because everybody (except them) was really going to die one day, and be dead for ever, and shouldn't a person live – truly live, a real life – while they're alive?

Meet Justin Bieber!

I'm not on Twitter but quite often I find myself thinking of Justin Bieber. It's not a sexual interest – at least, I don't think it is. It's more of a – bear with me – philosophical interest. I used to have a similar preoccupation with the teenage Michael Jackson. Basically: what's it like to *be* such a person? What does it feel like? Does it still feel like being a person? If you met Justin Bieber, would he be able to tell you?

When thinking about Bieber I like to envision him at a corporate meet-and-greet, organized by his record company. Passing two days in an empty stadium, positioned in front of the logo of the local radio station, experiencing himself as the sole and obsessive focus of an unending line of teenagers. Meeting and greeting, glad-handing and nodding, accepting professions of love from complete strangers: each one apparently sincere, each one essentially the same. With a fixed smile on his face he listens as they say the magic words, over and over: 'I can't believe I'm meeting Justin Bieber!' As if he were not a person at all, but a mountain range they had just climbed. This is Justin Bieber, the 'love object'. The idea of the love object: this is what interests me. It's a condition to which many people aspire, now more than ever. You can see why: so much love flows toward the love object. Why *would* we aspire to be doctors or teachers when we have before us the model of the love object? To walk into the world

and meet love, from everyone, everywhere – this is a rational dream.
By contrast, most of us enter the world and cannot be sure what
we will meet: perhaps resistance, perhaps indifference, perhaps
contempt. The moment of meeting is always unsure, fraught.
But for the love object there is a smooth certainty to all encounters.
This is because all meetings with others have in one sense
always already happened, for the love object is already known
and loved everywhere. He meets only those who feel they have
already met him, and already love him. Everyone Bieber meets is a
Belieber.

And yet – having watched this process so many times – we, the
public, know perfectly well that the love object is, more often than
not, a tragic figure. The love object 'lives the dream' (the dream that
everybody you meet says: 'I love you!') until the dream becomes
nightmare. Then the moment arrives when the love object himself
no longer wants to meet anyone. (Sometimes the aura surrounding
the love object fades first, but the result is the same.) The love object
withdraws. He is rarely seen in public and when he is, strange things
happen. What meetings he does have all seem to go awry: people get
punched, phones are stolen, babies are dangled out of windows,
drugs taken, cars crashed. His closest advisers begin to fear for him.
He is urged into many new and alarming kinds of meetings, with
therapists, drug counsellors, nutritionists, accountants. But these
meetings seem only to compound the problem: once again he is a
kind of object to be analysed, tweaked, examined. His advisers
despair. Is there nobody he could meet who could help?

Imagine a meeting: between Justin Bieber, global pop star, and
Martin Buber, long-dead Jewish philosopher. I know, I know. But in

my mind these two are destined to meet.* Buber had a lot to say about meeting-and-greeting, after all, although it's true that by 'meeting' Buber intended something more than a hug, a flashed peace-sign and a photo. He believed that to really meet someone involved entering an intimate, complex and precious state, a state we achieve only rarely. 'All real living is meeting,' he claimed. But by Buber's stringent measure not only does the Belieber in the signing queue never really meet Justin Bieber, most people rarely – if ever – meet their closest friends, mothers don't always meet their children, and many a husband has never met his wife, though he may sleep next to her every night. These and other peculiar ideas can be drawn from Buber's famous 1923 essay, *I and Thou*, a quasi-mystical work that asks what it really means to 'meet' another person in this world. Here is the opening premise, deceptively simple:

> To man the world is twofold, in accordance with his twofold attitude.
>
> The attitude of man is twofold, in accordance with the twofold nature of the primary words which he speaks.
>
> The primary words are not isolated words, but combined words.
> The one primary word is the combination *I-Thou.*
> The other primary word is the combination *I-It.*

I-Thou and *I-It*: two attitudes with which to meet the world. And it is when we meet the world with an *I-It* attitude, argues Buber, that we find ourselves in the realm of things. It is with an *I-It* attitude that

* Bieber and Buber are alternative spellings of the same German surname. Who am I to ignore these hints from the universe?

a man confronts the apparent 'content' of his life, meets the objects and ideas, nations and institutions, trees and cars, the sky and the sea. The world of things is always at his disposal. It is in this world that he is able to manipulate and control, order and create, decipher and destroy, and variously exercise his will. It is in this world that he spends all his time. Well – you might say – and what of it? You are suspicious, perhaps, that Buber is going to turn out to be one of these mystical types who wants to tell you that the world of things – the one that sustains forks and tax forms and cheese and Justin Bieber – is only an 'illusion'. But Buber is not one of those. He has one foot firmly planted on the ground. Buber defends the importance of the world of *It*. Aside from anything else, this is where the various achievements of man take place. It is also where all pain, poverty, cruelty and exploitation occur, none of which is ever illusory to those who suffer them. But still, Buber insists, we are twofold beings: 'In all the seriousness of truth, hear this: without *It* man cannot live. But he who lives with *It* alone is not a man.' For, alongside our relationship with things and ideas, we are also human beings who meet and form relations with other beings. This is the world of *I-Thou*. It concerns genuine meeting between persons, and is quite different:

> When I confront a human being as my *Thou* and speak the basic word *I-Thou* to him, then he is no thing among things nor does he consist of things. He is no longer He or She, a dot in the world grid of space and time, nor a condition to be experienced and described, a loose bundle of named qualities. Neighbourless and seamless, he is *Thou* and fills the firmament. Not as if there were nothing but he; but everything else lives in his light.

Other people, for Buber, are radically *other* – they are 'what is over and against us' – and as such cannot be reduced or assimilated, absorbed into our person or bent to our wills. They are not another item in our worldly list of things. Nor are they ever fully contained by our accounts of or experiences with them. And yet we are always, according to Buber, trying to turn the *I-Thou* relation into an *I-It*, a state of affairs which (refreshingly!) he finds perfectly natural, only to be expected. Buber sees that we must – if we want to live effectively in the world – call these others 'He' or 'She' or 'Justin Bieber' or 'Belieber', and that we will make use of them, and treat them as objects presented to our consciousness – even as tools for writing an essay. But when we are doing this sort of thing, Buber argues, we should at least be *aware* that this is what we are doing. We should recognize that we are back in the world of *I-It*, and the 'person' we imagine we are meeting is, in the final analysis, just another thing of the world to us, another object we have 'experienced'. Because it's by recognizing and naming our *I-It* relations that we will be better able to note and nurture the rare appearances of *I-Thou* in our lives:

> I do not experience the man to whom I say *Thou*. But I take my stand in relation to him, in the sanctity of the primary word. Only when I step out of it do I experience him once more. In the act of experience *Thou* is far away.

This is a bit perplexing; I need to unpack it a little for myself. And Bieber can be of help here if only because he is such an extreme instance of our experiences of other people that his example possesses an odd kind of purity, like an isolated sample laid out on a Petri dish.

So now I think again of a Belieber in the Justin Bieber signing queue. She is lining up for an experience, an experience which *even as it is happening* seems to be relegated to the past tense, as in: *I just held his hand, he just hugged me, I just met Justin Bieber* . . . Not only is this meeting always already a story, it only really exists as narrative. And it's because Bieber is Bieber that we can see this so clearly. It's obvious that a Belieber's only relation with the globally famous Bieber is as a piece of narrative to be told and retold – to herself, to other people – and that Bieber himself, in his human reality, is barely involved, almost unnecessary. It's easy to scorn the Beliebers for this, and yet we may also recognize elements of a Belieber's encounter with Justin Bieber in many of our own relations with perfectly unfamous people: with our sister-in-law or mother, with our friends or partners, with our colleagues, even with our own children. If we are honest with ourselves it is not often that we let these people 'fill the firmament'. Most of the time they present themselves simply as objects in our way, as examples of something, as annoyances and arguments, as assets that in some sense belong to us, or as the cause of – and explanation for – various elements of our own identities. But every now and then we do enter into an *I-Thou* relation with another person – as we never could with Bieber – and in those moments everything is different. Meeting Justin Bieber is nothing at all like looking into your father's eyes as he is dying, or having your grey and slimy baby placed, for the first time, on your chest. It is not like meeting up with your lover the day you realize you love her, nor is it like the moment you seem to meet yourself when your doctor sits across a desk from you and speaks aloud the dreaded diagnosis. That is not to say that all these moments are not also easily recounted as experiences, but while they are happening they are not quite experiences, they are *I-Thou* encounters with another being (or with one's own being), and they seem to exist only in the present moment. Because one of the vital ways we recognize an *I-Thou* relation, according to Buber, is the manner in which it seems almost to suspend time:

> The I of the primary word *I-It*, that is, the I faced by no *Thou*, but surrounded by a multitude of 'contents' has no present, only the past. Put in another way, in so far as man rests satisfied with the things that he experiences and uses, he lives in the past, and his moment has no present content.

I don't think it's possible to prove objectively any of what Buber is saying here; I can only apply it to the measure of my life, and yours. And I put it to you that when you meet someone you love, when you give birth, when you seem to encounter yourself in a moment of extreme physical peril* – something funny happens to time on these occasions. You are uniquely attentive to the present moment. You are aware of living in it.

All real living is meeting. But what most of us do, most of the time, feels more like 'presenting'. As in: I present myself, with all my individual qualities, to you, and you present yourself back. You experience the style of me, my identity. Subsequently, we have 'feelings' for each other. But even our 'feelings' – that most treasured aspect of our identities – are, to Buber, secondary in importance to our ability to enter into relation: 'Feelings are "entertained",' he writes, rather loftily. 'Love comes to pass. Feelings dwell in man; but man dwells in his love. That is not metaphor, but the actual truth.'

---

* To use the most commonly cited examples.

This, as Buber notes, is especially hard to comprehend '[i]f, like the modern man, you have learned to concern yourself wholly with your own feelings'. Feelings – or so we are told from childhood on – are what is naturally 'inside of us'; they are what make us special. They form our 'identity'. But Buber's problem with feelings is their conveniently hermetic nature. The thing about feelings is that they are, in the end, easily self-generated, easily celebrated, treasured and fetishized within oneself – just as easily sloughed off – and all this can be performed internally, without the least disturbance from another human soul. And (if you want to be cynical and a bit Marxist about it) they are also, in this late-capitalist society, a form of intimate distraction, slyly offered as compensation for the often brutal, mechanized and underpaid anonymity of our working lives. 'Feelings are "within",' writes Buber, 'where life is lived and man recovers from institutions.' Hey, girl, here's Justin Bieber! Stop worrying about unionizing! Have some feelings about him!

> Taking his stand in the shelter of the primary word of separation – which holds off the *I* and the *It* from one another – he has divided his life with his fellow-men into two tidily circled-off provinces, one of institutions and the other of feelings – the province of the *It* and the province of *I* [. . .] Neither of them knows man: institutions know only the specimen, feelings only the 'object'; neither knows the person, or mutual life.

I don't know about you but I find I want to resist Buber here. Because personally I am pretty attached to my own feelings (and the complex, fascinating personality they imply). Also, however much Buber may critique them, I can't seem to help but have them. But even if I can't accept Buber totally here, I do find him a useful correction to some of my worse instincts. Looking at my life through a Buber lens, for example, I see that it is quite possible that my feelings, as strong as they may be, may disclose no more of reality to me than is afforded by the outline of my own self-image. This is useful knowledge. Every day I am confronted by situations in which I must judge the reality or otherwise of a situation by way of my feelings about it (this is especially acute in marital arguments). But just because I feel something very strongly, does this make it true? Isn't it possible that in many cases where my feelings are strong I may indeed be *no different* to all those delusional girls in the Bieber signing queue, who have so many feelings for him, after all, so very many sincere, deep, excruciating feelings, which are, of course, what define their identity, what makes of each of them *Beliebers* . . .

Let's pause here for a musical interlude to consider the lyrics of Bieber's smash hit 'Boyfriend'.* They strike me as a fair example of the self-deceiving, twofold world most of us live in, most of the time. What are all young Bieber's songs about, in the end? Relationships. Wanting them, getting them, needing them, having them. In this sense Buber and Bieber are, again, rather close – not only in name but in spirit – for Buber's writing is likewise entirely preoccupied with relationships. And yet the world of Bieber – no matter how smoothly it masquerades as the world of *I-Thou* – is unmistakably the world of *I-It*. There is a sharp division, for example, between Bieber the 'boyfriend' and this anonymous girl he hopes to capture. Bieber being the one with all the feelings, all the desires. The girl, by contrast, seems a kind of thing, to be kept on his arm, like a watch or a bag. And as the song progresses Bieber does not seem to be entering – as Buber would

* Dear Reader – will you google them? Originally, they were included in the essay but it turns out that reproducing lyrics is incredibly expensive.

hope he might – 'a living mutual relation' with another person. No. He is listing all the things he could do for her and *to* her and all the things he himself has and could be. It is easy to take a dim view of Bieber's world of *I-It*, but as I say: isn't this in fact the world most of us live in, most of the time? Here is an individual with a strong will and plenty of ambition (he's going to take her places she ain't never been before), who also happens to be a generous person (he's got money he's interested in 'blowing'), not to mention a good-natured soul, of pacifist intention, apparently sincerely desirous of another person's happiness (he doesn't want to fight. He wants her shining brightly like a snow angel). This is not a bad guy per se. This is a guy operating pretty sympathetically in the world of *I-It*. He's even willing to change the kind of guy he is, as required. He certainly *feels* he is in a relationship with another human. But from Buber's point of view there are some problems. Many problems. First and foremost the monologic nature of the Bieber approach. He keeps saying, 'Hey girl, let me talk to you,' but he isn't really talking to or with her or with anyone – he's talking *at* a girl (who is every-where silent) while he slinks around to an R&B beat, now behind her, now at her ear, now sitting with her in a car, in that creepy pop version of man-splaining which is so inexplicably popular in the video charts (see also Justin Timberlake, Pharrell). In Buber's terms, the girl is merely *an experience Bieber is having*, but he has no real relation with her, and so she does not yet have any reality – she may as well be a figment of his imagination. Similarly, Bieber him-self – though he may be a very famous and popular individual – is still not yet a person:

Individuality makes its appearance by being differentiated from other individualities.

A person makes his appearance by entering into relation with other persons. The one is the spiritual form of natural detachment,* the other the spiritual form of natural solidarity of connection.

Like Bieber, we treasure our identities as individuals, and, like Bieber, work hard to differentiate ourselves. Like Bieber, we feel we are having relationships even if, much of the time, our relations with others seem to exist mainly in the stories we tell (to ourselves, to others). But what's the solution? From Buber's point of view a good place to start is moving from monologue to dialogue. Like, if Bieber's song was a duet? Then Bieber could be more like Socrates. Buber likes Socrates: 'How lovely and how fitting the sound of the lively and impressive *I* of Socrates! It is the *I* of endless dialogue . . . This *I* lived continually in the relation with man, which is bodied forth in dialogue. It never ceased to believe in the reality of men, and went out to meet them.' Recognizing the reality of other people – and having them recognize the reality of you – is at the heart of the matter. But this is easier said than done. Allowing another person to truly exist as a person – independent of your own fantasies, desires and feelings about them – proves to be, I have found, one of the more difficult things in the world to do. Surely especially difficult for Justin Bieber, who finds himself trapped by the fantasies of millions. And if Socrates is the model of a dialogic existence, to be as famous as Bieber, in the twenty-first century, is to live as pure monologue. I imagine even Socrates – with his boundless enthusiasm for meeting and greeting – would have found it hard to believe in the reality of others after spending two days in an empty stadium in Tokyo meeting

---

* It's also a spookily accurate definition of much of our online lives, seventy years before the Internet existed.

five thousand of them. Buber has a term for this phenomenon, he calls it 'the demonic *Thou*'. His own example is Napoleon: 'He was for millions the demonic *Thou*, the *Thou* that does not respond, that responds to *Thou* with *It*.' All cult leaders speak the demonic *Thou*, and there are many more Beliebers in the world right now than ever fought for Napoleon – though of course it cannot be said that Justin Bieber, troublesome tyke that he is, has ever massacred whole villages of Russian peasantry. His harmful acts – such as they are – are largely directed at himself. Drugs, D UIs, court appearances, racist outbursts, promises of early retirement . . . As if only by destroying the perfect love object of our creation can he get back to that half-forgotten, human person, who looked into the gaping maw of YouTube, all those years ago, and sang his little heart out.

Look, I may not be a Belieber – but nor do I want him deported to Canada. The overwhelming feeling I have when I consider fame on this scale is pity. I wouldn't wish the demonic *Thou* on my worst enemy:

> To him everything flames, but his fire is cold. To him a thousand sev-
> eral relations lead, but from him none. He shares in no reality, but in
> him immeasurable share is taken as though in a reality. He sees the
> beings around him, indeed, as machines, capable of various achieve-
> ments, which must be taken into account and utilized for the Cause.

To he who speaks the demonic *Thou* everyone and everything is to be utilized. ('Anne was a great girl. Hopefully she would have been a Belieber,' wrote Justin, in the guest book of the Anne Frank Museum.) Everything is an object, up to and including the self. As Buber has it: *He treats himself, too, as an It.* Now, I know that committed Beliebers feel that there is at least someone in this world with whom their hero can truly say *I-Thou*, and that this person is his on-off actress girlfriend, another globally famous young person called Selena Gomez. And perhaps he could, and perhaps she was – for a while. But the *I-Thou* relation is notoriously difficult to maintain – constantly under threat from the *I-It* – and I imagine that this proves especially true if you happen to be a very rich, lonely young man, about to lose the only mutual relation you ever came close to having, who is presently texting someone you love(d) as they try to break up with you (and gently suggest rehab):

'Enjoy life withOUT ME BITCH!!!! Fuck you!'
'Can't hear you over my cash, babe!'
'Come on. Don't tell me you don't miss this: [Insert 'dick pic' here.]'*

The demonic *Thou*, speaking loud and clear.

Postscript: It will be obvious to committed Beliebers that this essay was written around 2013, that is, before the release of Bieber's smash-hit album *Purpose* (on which I was delighted to find the *I-Thou* rearing its head more than once) and long before he announced on Instagram, during the spring of 2016, that he didn't want to do paid sign-and-greets any more because 'It filled [me] with so much of other people's spiritual energy that I end up so drained and unhappy.'

---

* Taken from a series of Bieber's texts to Gomez, leaked and posted to the Internet.

Love in the Gardens

Boboli, Florence

When my father was old and I was still young, I came into some money. Though it was money 'earned' for work done, it seemed, both to my father and me, no different than a win on the lottery. We looked at the contract more than once, checking and rechecking it, just like a lottery ticket, to ensure no mistake had been made. No mistake had been made. I was to be paid for writing a book. For a long time, neither of us could work out what to do about this new reality. My father kept on with his habit of tucking a ten- or twenty-pound note inside his letters to me. I took the rest of my family (my parents having separated long before) to a 'resort' back in the 'old country' (the Caribbean) where we rode around bored in golf carts, argued violently and lined up in grim silence to receive a preposterous amount of glistening fruit, the only black folk in line for the buffet.

It took a period of reflection before I realized that the money – though it may have arrived somewhat prematurely for me – had come at the right time for my father. A working life launched when he was thirteen, which had ended in penury, old age and divorce, might now, finally, find a soft landing. To this end, I moved Harvey from his shabby London flat to a cottage by the sea, and when the late spring came we thought not of Cornwall or Devon or the Lake District but of Europe.

Outrageous thought! Though not without precedent. The summer before I went to college, my father, in his scrupulous way, had worked out a budget that would allow the two of us to spend four days in Paris. Off we went. But it is not easy for a white man of almost seventy and a black girl of seventeen to go on a mini-break to Europe together; the smirks of strangers follow you everywhere. We did not like to linger in restaurants or in the breakfast room of our tiny hotel. Instead, on that first, exploratory trip, we found our pleasure in walking. Through the streets, through museums – but more than anywhere else, through gardens. No money has to be spent in a garden, and no awkward foreign conversation need be made, and no one thinks you odd or provincial if you consult your guidebook in front of a statue or a lake.

In public parks it is a little easier to feel you belong. I felt this instinctively as a teenager (and, thinking back, as a child on Hampstead Heath). Over the next few years, in college, I found myself attracted once more to gardens, this time intellectually. I wrote my final thesis on 'English Garden Poetry 1600–1900', putting special emphasis on the many ways in which 'work' and 'workers' are obscured in an English garden. Look at how the ha-ha replaces the fence or wall. See that solitary poetic hermit in his grotto, symbolic replacement for all those unpoetic men who dug the hole that created the artificial lake in the first place. The English lord looks out on his creation and sees just that – 'creation' – unspoiled by workers' cottages or beasts of burden. With a great deal of art he has made his garden imitate nature. The window from his Surrey bedroom reveals a view straight out of a classical pastoral, apparently untouched and yet exquisite, not unlike the hills of Tuscany he spied while on his Grand Tour.

Writing that essay, I became very interested in the notion of 'The Grand Tour'. I read the diaries of English men of means, accounts of their travels in Italy or Germany, and followed them as they looked at and acquired paintings and statues, walked through elaborate gardens, marvelled at all the marble, stood at the base of great ruins mulling the sublime futility of existence, and so on. Nice work if you can get it. During the Michaelmas break, I visited Harvey in his one-bedroom Kilburn box and thought: Why shouldn't my old man get a Grand Tour, too?

But when the opportunity arrived, I discovered that my father's interests lay more in France than in Italy. He liked the food and the cities and the look of the women. We wrangled a little, and I won: like all twenty-three-year-olds I was skilled at aligning any good deeds with my own pleasures (although we later went back to France). We booked for Florence. The hotel was called Porta Rossa. I understand it has recently undergone a transformation and now looks much like any other chic boutique hotel on the Continent, but when I went with Harvey it was a true *pensione*, unchanged since the nineteenth century.

Air came through windows – which we were under strict instructions to open only at night – and keys were heavy, key-shaped and attached to giant velvet tassels. The rooms themselves were wondrously large though almost entirely empty, featuring one uncomfortable bed with scratchy sheets, one creaking wardrobe, one wicker chair and a floor of dark red tile. No television, no mini-bar, no food. But you had only to look up at the ceiling, at the casually preserved remnant of some anonymous fresco, to feel what a stain it would be upon your person and nation even to think of walking down to the bellhop (no phone) to complain. True, like E. M. Forster's Lucy Honeychurch and Charlotte Bartlett, we did not have a room with a view – unless a patch of twelfth-century wall is a view – but I was at that point in life at which sharing a situation, albeit a poor one, with a fictional character was pleasure enough for me.

In the morning, we set out. We had the idea of reaching the Boboli Gardens. But many people set out from a Florence hotel with the hope of getting to a particular place – few ever get there. You step into a narrow alleyway, *cartina della città* in hand, walk confidently past the gelato place, struggle through the crowd at the mouth of the Ponte Vecchio, take a left, and find yourself in some godforsaken shady *vicolo* near a children's hospital, where the temperature is in the hundreds and someone keeps trying to sell you a rip-off Prada handbag. You look up pleadingly at the little putti babies. You take a right, a left, another right – here is the Duomo again. But you have already seen the Duomo. In Florence, wherever you try to get to, you end up at the Duomo, which seems to be constantly changing its location. The heat builds and the walls of the alleys feel very high; the thought of a green oasis is tantalizing but last time you remember seeing grass was that little strip in front of the train station. Will you ever see it again?

En route, we tried to amuse ourselves. Harvey, a talented amateur photographer, snapped pictures of beautiful women as they dashed from shade to shade. I, far less able, took a poor shot of a piece of ironic graffiti: *Welcome to Disneyland, Florence*. It got hotter. 'Where *are* we?' I asked my father. 'The Piazza of Fish,' he muttered, but then he was struck with fresh vision: 'I've a feeling we should have crossed that bridge.'

I remember this small geographical insight coming over us both as a revelation: there was, after all, a way out of this oppressively beautiful warren of streets, and it led to higher ground, height being the essential sensation of Boboli. Climbing toward it, we felt ourselves to be no longer British rats running around a medieval Italian maze – no, now we were heading up into the clear, entitled air of the Renaissance, to triumph over the ever-moving Duomo once and for all.

Through formal gardens we passed, each one more manicured and overdesigned than the next, our cameras hanging dumbly from our necks, for Boboli is a place that defeats framing. As an aesthetic experience it arrives pre-framed, and there's little joy to be had taking a picture of a series of diametric hedges. 'It's not much like an English garden, is it?' ventured Harvey, confronted by Bacchus sitting fatly on a turtle, his chubby penis pointed directly at our foreheads.

In one lake, Neptune stood naked about to stab a trident into a rock; in another, a fellow unknown to us reared up on his horse, as if a sea that had once parted for him now intended to swallow him whole. I remember no ducks or wandering fowl, not a leaf or pebble out of place. In Boboli you don't really escape the city for the country, nor are you allowed to forget for a moment the hours of labour required to shape a hedge into a shape that in no way resembles a hedge.

No, not like an English garden at all . . . though perhaps more honest in its intentions. It speaks of wealth and power without disguise. Boboli is Florence, echoed in nature. As a consequence of this, it is the only garden of which I can remember feeling a little shy. I would not have thought it possible to feel underdressed in a garden, but I did – we both did. Clumsy tourists dragging ourselves around a private fantasia. For though Boboli may be open to the public, it is still somehow the Medicis' park, and the feeling of trespassing never quite leaves you. It was a relief to find ourselves for a moment on an avenue of curved yew trees, shaded and discreet, where we were offered the possibility of respite, not only from the awful sun, but from the gleaming of monuments and the turrets of villas.

At the very peak we rested, and took far more photos of the red roofs of Florence than we had taken of the gardens themselves. 'Very grand, that was,' said my father a little later, when we had descended into a not-grand-at-all café to happily eat a baby cow covered in tuna sauce. Seeing his relief, I thought sadly of Charlotte Bartlett, and heard her grating voice echoing in my own mind: 'I feel that our tour together is hardly the success I had hoped. I might have known it would not do.'

Borghese, Rome

A little while after my father died, I moved to Rome. I was in mourning and it was winter, and the city was all stone and diagonal rain to me. I had no sense at all of it being a green place. I walked past the Spanish Steps into the wind without wondering where they led. With the spring, small patches of green revealed themselves: the ring of grass around the Castel Sant'Angelo; or the little walled garden off Via Nazionale, dotted with defunct fountains, one deep, waterless well, and covered in the scrawls of teenage lovers. *Raffaella – ti amo!* We would never have found these spots if not for the dog, who sniffed them out. One day in April, under a hedge in this walled garden, my husband led our pug to something more melancholy and curious than a pine cone: an empty Statue of Liberty costume, a tin of green spray paint, an empty bucket, an Indian immigrant's identity card.

It took us a while to discover the Villa Borghese. We lived on the other side of town, which is to say, less than fifteen minutes away, but of all the parochial spots in the world, Rome is one of the worst. Each *rione* is so charming and self-sufficient, you rarely feel the need to adventure beyond it. I should think we were in Monti a year before we crossed the river to explore the relative wilds of Trastevere. Once again, the dog provided impetus. By the summer she had helped pull us anxiously toward the Italian language, where we did our best to keep up with the chatter of the other dog owners we met in the walled garden, exchanging veterinary tips or boasting about bloodlines. (I never saw a mongrel dog in Rome. They all looked like they'd come straight out of the 'Breeds; Canine' section of the encyclopaedia.)

'*E dove possiamo correre con il nostro cane senza guinzaglio?*' I tried, and was rewarded, despite my grammar, with an avalanche of friendly yet almost totally incomprehensible information – verbs running into adjectives at high speed – yet from which we were, in the end, able to pluck a few nouns. The best place to run a dog off the lead was in a bourgeois villa. And where was this middle-class villa? Why, up the Spanish Steps! We'd see a villa and then a park. There would be museums and bicycles and lakes and a zoo, which is not called a zoo but a *bioparc*. *Che assurdo!* And yes, dogs, everywhere dogs. There is a special place for dogs!

The Borghese Gardens are shaped like a cartoon heart, though only a map reveals this: when inside, you walk its winding arterial paths without any sense of a formal plan, surprised here by a café, there by a lake, here by a museum or a film festival, by the head of Savonarola or a carousel or a wild splash of lavender. It is a lovely example of a truly public park. Wrested from the fists of a seventeenth-century cardinal and his descendants (who opened it to the public on Sundays and public holidays), it was delivered, in the twentieth century, into the hands of the people.

Like Hampstead Heath, like Central Park, it has wide avenues on which to promenade, and high grass in which to read and kiss, and children and dogs are welcome to run wild – though in both cases they are better dressed than their London and New York counterparts. Once we saw a borzoi in a yellow raincoat, yellow rain hat and four yellow booties. On Sundays you get little girls with a lot of froufrou curls and bows and underskirts, and boys in blazers and ties, like tiny CEOs of Fortune 500 companies.

At the spot we had been told about – where dogs may run without leads – things were more casual, though the Roman fetish for that British sartorial horror the Barbour jacket was everywhere in evidence. (*We are out in the open air, like an Englishman*, these jackets seem to say, each to the other, *exercising our dogs, as the English do*.) Towering Italian stone pines create a luxurious canine obstacle course; classy hounds chase each other in figures of eight while their owners laze about on a natural slope and settle in to watch people conduct their private lives in public.

It Happened in the Park is the English title of Vittorio de Sica's 1953 movie (in Italian it was simply *Villa Borghese*) and that's how it is: as if the doors of everybody's apartments have fallen off and left a clear view for any passing stranger to take in. In the six separate vignettes that make up that film, De Sica trumpets the glories of voyeurism while celebrating the power of the segue: his vision of a public park is of a journey without maps. In life, as in the film, one arrives with a very particular plan – a picnic in a precise spot, or a visit to the gallery – but the park is so full of random temptations and opportunities that it will always thwart your ambition to get from A to B. In one vignette, a couple of Roman prostitutes on the run from the law stumble across, and enter, a Miss Cinema beauty contest taking place in the park. Anyone can make it in the gardens of the Borghese.

It is this easy transition between high and low that is central to the charm of the place. It does not exclude. That all those stone busts of famous men should have their names clearly printed beneath, for example – well, it may be only a small matter of nineteenth-century taste, but what a difference it makes. No need to wander around nervously, ashamed of a lack of knowledge. Any housewife can walk right up to Leonardo da Vinci and think: *What girlish cheekbones! How weird he looks with that great beard!* Any working stiff can eat gelato in front of Archimedes, peer into his stone eyes and consider how much he looks like old Giancarlo from the post office. Harvey would have loved all that.

Inside the villa itself, the statuary shifts from pleasant to unequalled – while remaining entirely comprehensible to the casual shade-seeking visitor. What is the story of Apollo and Daphne if not a classic case of unrequited park-love? Bernini's masterwork repeats the main action of the gardens, where the boys watch the girls while the girls watch the boys who watch the girls go by. And having picked up my photographer father's habit of ogling the beautiful, I know, as Apollo did, how it can be painful to gaze upon a beautiful human who can never be yours.

To this agony of desire Bernini offers a solution – at least on the aesthetic plane – sublimely combining all the mismatched materials of a public park into one sculpture: human flesh, tree bark, marble. On Daphne's face you find the shock of transmogrification, but in Apollo's eyes I detect signs of relief. There is a kind of peace that comes with finally giving up the chase. For my father, who never

stopped desiring women who didn't want him, Daphne's absolute
refusal might have served as a moment of recognition. Sometimes
you just can't get the girl. Sometimes the girl would rather be a tree.

There is a sentimental season, early on in the process of mourning,
in which you believe that everything you happen to be doing or
seeing or eating, the departed person would also have loved to do or
see or eat, were he or she still here on earth. Harvey would have
loved this fried ball of rice. He would have loved the Pantheon.
He would have loved that Rossetti of a girl with her thick black
brows.

In the first season of mourning there is a tendency to overstate.
But still I feel certain that this was the garden that would have made
us both happy. It was a bittersweet thing to walk through it without
him, thinking of our last trip together, to crowded, expensive Venice,
which had not been much more successful than Florence. Why had
I never thought of Rome? Like me, he would have loved the glimpses
of the new arrivals: African families, Indian couples, Roma girls
hand in hand. Sitting for a picnic, unpacking foods that smelled
wonderfully of coriander – a herb most Roman grocers wouldn't
know from a weed.

Harvey and I knew from experience that it takes a while for
immigrants to believe a park is truly public and open to them: my
mother always used to complain, exaggerating somewhat (and not
without a little pride), that she was the only black woman to be seen
pushing a stroller through St James's Park in 1975. Sometimes a
generation of habitation is needed to create the necessary confidence;
to believe that this gate will open for you, too. In Italy, where so
many kinds of gates are closed to so many people, there is something
especially beautiful in the freedom of a garden.

For our two years in Rome, the Borghese Gardens became a

semi-regular haunt, the place most likely to drag us from our Monti stupor. And I always left the park reluctantly; it was not an easy transition to move from its pleasant chaos to the sometimes pedantic conventionality of the city. No, you can't have cheese on your *vongole*; no, this isn't the time for a cappuccino; yes, you can eat pizza on these steps but not near that fountain; in December we all go to India; in February we all ski in France; in September of course we go to New York. Everything Romans do is perfect and delightful, but it is sometimes annoying that they should insist on all doing the same things at exactly the same time. I think their argument is: given that all our habits are perfect and delightful, why would anyone stray from them?

I guess they have a point, but it is still a relief to escape into their gardens and eat food in any order while sitting in the grass and drinking a British amount of alcohol without anyone looking at you piteously. In a public Italian garden a Briton has all the things she loves about Italy – the sun, the food, the sky, the art, the sound of the language – without any of the inconvenient rules that attend their proper enjoyment. She is free to delight in that astounding country on her own slovenly terms. To think about her father and how he would have loved these oily *arancini* that she bought near the Pantheon (which he would also have loved). To watch the people come and go. And then perhaps go boating. And then perhaps fall asleep, a little drunk, in the grass.

When my father died I dashed to Rome, leaving a lot undone. I'd packed what little I found in his room in a box and abandoned it in my basement. Two years later, when I returned, I had to go through his things properly. There was not much, but there were some photos of trips we'd taken together in France and Italy. I think he got some pleasure from those holidays, but the photos have a sort of dutiful air to them, as if he's taking them to please me. He liked to get them blown up and sent to me in a large padded envelope, perfect as postcards and equally uninteresting.

The only sublime shot was taken in Carcassonne (his choice), where he quite uncharacteristically demanded a car stop so he could walk back a few yards to the edge of a sheer drop that gave on to a view of a valley. Here he took a magnificent panorama, of hills and dales and forests and fields, and a little thread of blue running through it all. He never sent me that one, but I found several copies of it among his things after he died, as if he didn't want me to know that the gardens he liked best were the wild ones.

The Shadow of Ideas

Se non è vero, è molto ben trovato

— Giordano Bruno

Piazza della Madonna dei Monti. There the morning sun gave us preferential treatment, casting the church and half the fountain into shadow, striking us instead at our usual table. I have my *integrale*, you have your *spremuta*, the dog is leaping at the waiters, and I am very proud of this little clutch of italicized Italian words. I am reading *La Repubblica*, very slowly, with a dictionary, but very proud. Sometimes people stop and speak to us in this Italian square, using the *tu* form, because we are young or youngish, or known to them or both. We live in Rome but I am a tourist. I never stop being one, particularly in the squares. I remained a tourist even in that little square, the one I burned down. Which fire was at the beginning, though in memory it comes at the end, and this is inconvenient, structurally. But my memories of our Italian squares are non-sequential, they jump from here to there, ignoring chronology. They are filed according to a variety of intimate systems — one of which involves the differing intensities of light — and so there is nothing to be done: we begin in Piazza della Madonna dei Monti, east of the river, not far from the Colosseum. You are reading the financial pages, like a local, whereas I am wondering about Vivaldi, like a tourist. I am aware that a performance of the *Four Seasons* is to happen in a basilica somewhere, at five thirty each weekday afternoon and twice on Saturday; I hate that I should know about it, but I do. Even if I don't pick up the soggy flyer, stained by coffee rings and sprinkled with tobacco shreds, I register the invitation, knowing that it's meant for the likes of me, for the ordinary tourist, although I am quick to agree with you when you say, 'No fucking way, those things are awful. Plus Vivaldi is awful.' You bent down to pour a little Pellegrino on the dog's panting face. The short waiter approached, the one without any beauty, though he was *furbo*, he watched everybody; we always left a euro to stay on his good side. He approached and the dog leapt up. I yanked her lead and pinned her stupid head between my ankles. In England this would be considered the right thing to do, but in that Italian square dogs were beloved and free to wander about by themselves, their leads trailing behind them, while their owners had coffee or bought a dress or whatever. The waiter looked with great sympathy at the dog; the dog had stopped being a tourist some time ago, now everybody pitied her for being stuck with us. He cleared the cups as we looked down at the table in silence. Once he had gone we could continue arguing in English. We didn't like to speak English in public. The fact we spoke English was for some reason a terrible secret no one in Rome must ever know.

'I just think we should go and see some music sometime.'

'Yeah, fine, but not bloody Vivaldi.'

It was 2007, or thereabouts. It was probably ten thirty in the morning. The day lay wide open before us. We would be almost fifty before we saw many more days like that one – but how were we to know that? We lived in pure possibility. The pound was strong. We were laying down memories – mainly of Italian squares – and I was filled with a kind of pre-emptive nostalgia. Why should we go to the basilica when we could do anything? We had no children, we were two youngish writers in an Italian square, we might walk perfectly unencumbered through the city, from square to square, never worrying about bottles of milk or the location of changing tables, as contented under an Italian sky as Keats ever was, more so, as we were both entirely free of tuberculosis. The dog was no handicap, we could take her anywhere, into churches, a butcher's, the post office, restaurants. We were free! In memory, freedom is obvious. In the present moment it's harder to appreciate, or recognize as a form of responsibility. Anyway, with my freedom I did very little, almost nothing. You, at least, read the financial news (and were consequently less surprised by what followed). I only walked from square to square, often mopey, even a little bored, oblivious, waiting for something to happen.

Now we move across town, further west. There goes the usual Vivaldi flyer, unpeeling itself from whichever basilica, blowing through the cobbled streets to Campo de' Fiori, and ending up, I was intending to write, 'slicked to the hem of Giordano Bruno's cloak', but Google images says I am a liar, or a tourist with an indifferent memory: Bruno stands on a plinth at least twelve feet in the air. I peeled it off the base, then, while you read the inscription.

'To Bruno' – you were translating – 'The century he predicted. Here is where the fire burned. Here,' you added. 'And over there.' You pointed to the square where we used to live, a few streets away, before I burned it down.

'But I survived my fire.'

'Well, to be fair, you weren't tied to a stake.'

'Giordano got lucky! I've got problems Giordano never had!'

'Of course.'

'Like what to do with the rest of my life.'

'Right, because Giordano had it easy compared to you. You've got *writer's block*. Whereas he was just burned at the stake for speaking truth to power.'

'Listen, it was all over for him in a couple of minutes. Existential ennui lasts for ever.'

Some time passed. Now we were in Venice, in Piazza San Marco, the water was rising. It was during the Biennale – everyone's fancy shoes were ruined. Rain pounded on the white decks of the yachts, rain slid off the basilicas. It rained until the square itself became a giant swimming pool, through which the international art crowd did wade. Cigarettes floated by, and empty bottles of Peroni, and wraps of cocaine, no doubt, and some sheikh's daughter. I took off my shoes and lifted my skirts, hugely pregnant, head-wrapped: I felt I was re-enacting ancient memories of a West African ancestor, heavy with child, crossing a river, except I was not seeking food or shelter or a dry place to give birth, I was just trying to get to a party on the other side of the canal, in the empty house of a banker. His son was having the party; it seemed to be happening without the banker's knowledge. We paused beneath the colonnades. Here, the previous day, we had paid twenty-one euro for orange juice, twelve of which turned out to be a music surcharge: someone nearby was playing a violin. And here, now, stood an artist, and her husband, a film-maker, they were also seeking shelter under the arches, they were also up to their ankles in water. We were all exactly the same age. Youngish. Not so young. The day before we had visited Il Giardino delle Vergini, a natural Italian square, a piazza-shaped hillock, covered with grass and fringed with flowers, to see the artist's installation, it was called *Eleven Heavy Things*. We stood behind a series of large white slabs – they looked like stone tablets – and each had a hole you could put your head through so that their inscriptions referred, at that moment, to you. We took turns standing on three empty plinths: *The Guilty One*, *The Guiltier One* or *The Guiltiest One*. It was an Italian square and we, the people, were the statuary. I put my head through a sign that read: *What I look like when I really mean it*. I put my head through a sign that read: *What I look like when I'm lying*. Now we stood with the artist herself in the colonnade, hiding from the rain, and discussed our time of life, the question of children, the rain, and the quay-side yachts that seemed bigger than I'd ever seen them, they looked like an invading force. And yet only nine months earlier, if memory served, Lehman had capsized. How could something so large go under, on the other side of the Atlantic, without sending even the slightest ripple this way? But these yachts were unperturbed. They looked like permanent installations.

The rain began to ease. We waded through San Marco and got on a vaporetto packed with art hipsters, heaving with linen tote bags. We looked back at the scene, at the square of Saint Mark, at the Tintoretto lights. Four hundred years earlier, Giordano Bruno, who had been lecturing abroad, found himself tempted back to Italy by an invitation: to teach his 'Art of Memory', right here in Venice. But when he arrived he was immediately betrayed, perhaps in this very square, and turned over to the Inquisition. You can find his memory techniques in a little book called *De umbrisidearum*, in which Bruno demonstrates how to memorize anything – long lists of facts, speeches, languages, histories – by attaching to whatever subject you want to recall certain referents of personal force, which he calls 'adjects'. An adject is simply a strong image that comes easily to your mind. It can come from life, from literature, nature, anywhere: 'Those things to make the heart pound,' he advises, 'having the power of something wondrous, frightening, pleasant, sad; a friend, an enemy, horrible, abominable, admirable, prodigious; things hoped for or which we are suspicious of, and all things that encroach powerfully on the inner emotions – bring these to bear.' Of course, Bruno was burned for more important heresies, but his memory system is especially interesting to me: heretical not only in content but also in form. For a Brunoesque memory bypasses collective official memory, and ignores chronology, and it's the opposite of ritual, which is the guise memory takes on within religion. It's a radically subjective way of remembering, in which the real and the fictional, the personal and the historical, can all be combined.

It was very foolish of Bruno to come back to Venice to talk about memory, at that fraught historical moment – but you can see exactly how it happened. Venice is beautiful, seductive. If someone invites you to the Biennale, for example, you can't resist it, you go for the beauty and get stuck. As we began to cross the canal I got a glimpse of that fancy hotel the art crowd favours, the Hotel Bauer, just off the square, where, a few nights earlier we had seen and heard a man holding up a bottle of vodka, laughing, announcing: 'Twenty minutes ago this was a hundred euro – now it's two hundred!' It was the summer of 2009. It was the last days of Rome. Except this time, as the empire fell, there remained a class of people who did not feel in any way weakened, on the contrary they appeared emboldened, engorged, stronger than ever. Next to me sat a young man who had heard what was said; I noticed him wince. We started talking. He was genuinely young, our knees were touching; there was a strange intensity to the way we spoke to each other, perhaps because we were from the same class and corner of London.

Conversation flowed and quickly became intimate. He told me that ten years earlier, still in his teens, unhappy at school, gay, isolated, he had become obsessed with contemporary art, he had no money at all but he knew that looking at art was all he wanted to do, and he sensed he had taste, or at least 'knew what he liked' and so began attending all the degree shows, going to anything free, befriending artists, especially artists who felt as he did at the time – abject, alone, out of place – and he became devoted to them, and many of them returned his affection, they became involved in each other's lives, and in the end people began to give him pieces, and for years he never sold a single one, even when these artists became world famous, he kept it all in his collection, hanging or installed in a tiny flat in Swiss Cottage. (Meanwhile the international contemporary art market boomed. Meanwhile a piece of contemporary art from a blue-chip gallery came to seem one of the safest investments in the world.) And when I did begin to sell some things, he said, I only ever sold to buy more, all I wanted was beauty, I just wanted beauty in my life, maybe it was all because of my older brother – he mentioned this as if it had only just occurred to him – my beloved brother, he took a single ecstasy pill and died, and yes, thinking about it maybe it was his death that made me want beauty so much, want it above all else, to really crave it, actually. The young man stopped talking and picked up his drink. We were drawn into the general conversation at the table and unfortunately I didn't get to speak to him again. I've been to a few art fairs since but that was the only real conversation about art I ever had at one.

In Piazza Navona, on a very hot day we sat on the iron barrier around a fountain, dipping the dog in the water, and watching the Guardia di Finanza chase a group of African bag-sellers past one

Bernini fountain, and then past the fountain we sat on, which was designed by Giacomo della Porta but to which Bernini made a late, great, addition. They were awfully fancy-looking, those guards: their uniforms were closely fitted and light grey, with belts and epaulettes, and they had little gold buttons and jaunty green berets and a gold medallion *on* the beret and you could tell that in their opinion none of this was even remotely funny. Off they went, in hot pursuit. They had sworn a holy oath to protect the brand purity of Prada and Fendi and Moschino and the rest, and defend their country's sacred right to produce overpriced leather goods. The guards never seemed to catch up with the Africans, but the sight of their chase through the city became as familiar to us as a priest mansplaining to a group of nuns or a taxi driver swearing at a cyclist. Having no purpose, as I have mentioned above, we tended to spend our days wandering from square to square, but these Africans – they ran. And on this occasion they ran right by us, and one came so close that his big fabric sack – made of a knotted bed sheet and filled with counterfeits – knocked my knee. I saw him look back to see what had almost upended him, and for a moment his profile came in line with the profile of Bernini's late edition, the Moor, who stands in a conch shell, in the centre of the fountain. It reminded me of one of those accidental acts of mirroring, between art and nature, of which Nabokov makes so much. The African ran on. The Moor stayed. I stayed, looking up at the Moor, admiring him. He is a Moor full of purpose, wrestling a big fish, every muscle alert and straining. Most people who pass him think he is Neptune, understandably, because of that fish, but no, in fact he is a Moor, not in the literal sense of being a Berber Muslim, he is one of those decorative Negroes, common in Renaissance art, and looking up at him I had a strange feeling. I saw myself as some kind of a decorative Moor, the kind

who does not need to wrestle dolphins or anything else, a Moor of
leisure, a Moor who lunches, a Moor who needn't run for her
livelihood through the public squares. A historically unprecedented
kind of Moor. A late-capitalism moor. A tourist Moor. The sort of
Moor who enters a public square not to protest or to march (or, in
an earlier age, to be hanged or sold) but simply to wander
about, without purpose. A Moor who has come to look at the art.
A Moor who sits on the lip of a fountain and asks herself: 'What,
if anything, is the purpose of the artist today?' A moor with the
luxury of doing that.

It was really a garden outside a pavilion but art had made a public
square of it. Sometimes art can do that. Elmgreen and Dragset, the
artist collaborators, ex-lovers, provocateurs, had taken over the
Danish and Nordic pavilions at the 53rd Venice Biennale, and
working as both artists and curators, had turned those two difficult
spaces into a pair of neighbouring, glamorous, modernist homes,
belonging to some unseen art collectors – gay collectors was the
explicit suggestion. The spaces were filled with beautiful *objets d'art*,
beautiful furniture, beautiful paintings and a beautiful young man,
of real flesh and blood, sitting naked in a tan Eames chair, wearing
noise-cancelling headphones and reading a book. And yet despite all
this beauty something was rotten in the state of Denmark. It was
summer 2009: something was rotten everywhere. The first clue was
a little stuffed white rat, up on its hind legs, on the second floor of
the house, looking down from a window. It was tiny, easy to miss,
like one of those cunning self-portraits it pleased Renaissance
masters to hide in this or that corner of their paintings. It was looking
down to the front yard, where a crowd had gathered, not for a
burning this time, but for a drowning, and we'd joined them, we

were pressed in with everybody else, around the obligatory water feature – which in this case was a swimming pool – and we gaped at the abject body of a rich white man, a collector, floating head down, dead in the water. A packet of Marlboro cigarettes and his fancy watch had sunk to the bottom. It was a suicide. You could tell that because he had left his shoes neatly on the side. It was the suicide of a whole culture. In the years since I have often thought of that crowd and of this very particular adject we shared. Clearly the unforgettable image might be connected to a series of similarly forceful adjects: Gatsby face down in his pool, poor Joe Gillis face down in the pool on Sunset Boulevard, Scarface bobbing in his own fountain . . . They all seem, to me, to be referents for the same subject: the end of a decadent age and the potential dawn of another. And that little rat? A buried image of the artist(s), quizzical at the window, examining the public space, wondering: What's next? Who or what shall we put on our pedestals and plinths? Who or what will we burn in our public squares? At least, that is what I choose to remember. Art can plant these kinds of false memories within us. It can outline the shadow of an idea. 'Our plan,' writes Giordano Bruno, 'is to pass on the art of the shadow of ideas, to lead you out from your sleeping nature; from error, misdirection and being led astray; from deficiencies of energy; to support and strengthen you, correct errors, achieve perfect results, and make you the emulation of industriousness.' Four centuries later it's hard to imagine an artist expressing such a plan so directly: the fashion is for indirection. And yet plans do surely still exist.

In Piazza Sforza Cesarini the problem was a halogen bulb, it was extremely hot and built into a bookcase. Perhaps the page of a book strayed over it, or the corner of a cushion, I'll never know. I was due

in New York the next morning, for a reading in Brooklyn, my bag
was packed, my dog was fed, my passport was in my back pocket,
and then a friend phoned and said, 'Why not come for one last
drink?', and I said yes, and thought, I'll leave the dog, no I'll take
the dog, no, I'll leave the dog, but the dog came on heavy with the
guilt trip and the sad eyes, so at the last minute I brought the dog
and lucky for the dog for otherwise she'd be dead. I went out, for
half an hour. You were in Washington, reading poetry aloud. You
say I burned the square down, but a person doesn't leave a halogen
light on for half an hour and expect an Italian square to burn down.
And I didn't burn the entire square, only one building, though it's
true that for two years afterwards, while they rebuilt the façades, the
square effectively disappeared, to be replaced by huge sheets painted
with a trompe l'œil, itself a sort of adject: a memory of the
square-as-it-once-had-been.

I didn't see the fire until I was quite far up the stone steps. Actually
even at the door I didn't see it, I only felt it: the heat and the smoke.
I got to the window of the communal hallway and searched my
memory for the word for fire. *Incendio!* I cried. (This is something
like leaning out a New York window and screaming: *Conflagration!*)
People looked up but nobody moved. The dog was screaming. I
opened our door to look for what might be saved. I reached out for
my laptop: burned my fingers, dropped it. But there was no novel in
there, anyway, only many photographs of the dog. In the background
I could see my clothes were already gone, and the suitcase that had
contained them, all books and family photographs, the phone, the
fridge, all furniture, every knife, fork and spoon. I understood at last
what it means to have money. By then it was seven years since I'd
had some money, but the day of the fire was the first time I
understood what it had done to me. The terror at the cashpoint, the

anxiety in the supermarket, the argument at the bank teller's desk, the furious family row because *someone* has left a light on, because *someone* thinks 'we have shares in the electricity company' (a catchphrase of my mother's; a powerful adject for me). All of that, the whole daily battle with money, was over. When money's scarce life is a daily emergency, everything is freighted with potential loss, you feel even the smallest misstep will destroy you. When there's money, it's different, even a real emergency never quite touches you, you're always shielded from risk. You are, in some sense, too big to fail. And when I looked at my life on fire I had a thought I don't believe any person in the history of my family – going back many generations on both sides – could ever have had or ever even think of having: *Everything lost can be replaced*. Yes, in the history of my clan it was an unprecedented thought. And what will happen, I thought, if my future children grow up with this idea, not as a revelation but as part and parcel of their natural inheritance? What if this idea were to be embedded in them at birth, like a genetic memory, which they then passed on to their children, who passed it to their children in turn, and onwards and upwards, into the next century, and beyond? These future descendants – what kind of people would they be? How would the world look to them? Would banking seem a good career choice to them? What would they choose to remember? What would they choose to forget?

I grabbed the real dog and ran downstairs. Outside was a very Roman scene. Everyone had gathered to watch an *incendio* in the public square, they were having a ball. The firemen were coming, but in no great hurry. The kindly waiters of Luigi's gave the dog water and tried to stop her screaming, but the dog was completely hysterical, she seemed aware of the loss of her digital archive and to be taking it personally. Finally the Vigili del Fuoco turned up in outfits almost as dashing as their friends' in the Guardia di Finanza. They put the fire out, established no one was dead or wounded, and when I asked what if anything was left they shook their heads sadly: '*Tutto distrutto.*' Our first, and last, Italian square. Ashes. I turned to the firemen. I begged to be let in. The firemen said no, no, it's not safe. I begged some more. The firemen looked at each other, sighed and said *va bene*. Only in Rome. As I climbed the stairs I remembered a line from an old Negro spiritual: 'God gave Noah the rainbow sign/No more water but the fire next time.' I entered the ruins of our apartment. I inhaled enough smoke to keep me coughing for several days. And they were right, it was all gone, your things, my things, your life, my life, it was our own little financial crash, that is, until I went round the corner and found your book still sitting there, it was in the laundry loft, that dark little corner where you worked – you'd had the foresight to print it all out on paper – and there it remained, on your chair (also preserved) under a picture of the Madonna, to whom, in respect of a miracle, the firemen took off their hats.

Find Your Beach

Across the way from our apartment – on Houston, I guess – there's a new wall ad. The site is forty feet high, twenty feet wide. It changes once or twice a year. Whatever's on that wall is my view: I look at it more than the sky or the new World Trade Center, more than the water towers, the passing cabs. It has a subliminal effect. Last semester it was a spot for high-end vodka, and while I wrangled children into their snowsuits, chock-full of domestic resentment, I'd find myself dreaming of cold Martinis.

Before that came an ad so high end I couldn't tell what it was for. There was no text – or none that I could see – and the visual was of a yellow firebird set upon a background of hellish red. It seemed a gnomic message, deliberately placed to drive a sleepless woman mad. Once, staring at it with a newborn in my arms, I saw another mother, in the tower opposite, holding her baby. It was 4 a.m. We stood there at our respective windows, separated by a hundred feet of expensive New York air.

The tower I live in is university accommodation; so is the tower opposite. The idea occurred that it was quite likely that the woman at the window also wrote books for a living, and, like me, was not writing anything right now. Maybe she was considering antidepressants. Maybe she was already on them. It was hard to tell. Certainly she had no way of viewing the ad in question, not without opening her window, jumping, and turning as she fell. I was her view. I was the ad for what she already had.

But that was all some time ago. Now the ad says: 'Find your beach.' The bottle of beer – it's an ad for beer – is very yellow and the background luxury-holiday-blue. It seems to me uniquely well placed, like a piece of commissioned public art in perfect sympathy with its urban site. The tone is pure Manhattan. Echoes can be found in the personal-growth section of the bookshop ('Find your happy'), and in exercise classes ('Find your soul'), and in the therapist's office ('Find your self'). I find it significant that there exists a more expansive, national version of this ad that runs in magazines, and on television.

In those cases photographic images are used, and the beach is real and seen in full. Sometimes the tag line is expanded, too: 'When life gives you limes . . . Find your beach.' But the wall I see from my window marks the entrance to Soho, a district that is home to media moguls, entertainment lawyers, every variety of celebrity, some students, as well as a vanishingly small subset of rent-controlled artists and academics.

Collectively we, the people of SoHo, consider ourselves pretty sophisticated consumers of media. You can't put a cheesy ad like that past us. And so the ad has been reduced to its essence – a yellow undulation against a field of blue – and painted directly on to the wall, in a bright Pop Art style. The mad men know that we know the Soho being referenced here: the SoHo of Roy Lichtenstein and Ivan Karp, the SoHo that came before Foot Locker, Sephora, Prada, frozen yogurt. That SoHo no longer exists, of course, but it's part of the reason we're all here, crowded on this narrow strip of a narrow island. Whoever placed this ad knows us well.

Find your beach. The construction is odd. A faintly threatening mixture of imperative and possessive forms, the transformation of a noun into a state of mind. Perhaps I'm reading too much into it. On the one hand it means, simply, 'Go out and discover what makes you happy.' Pursue happiness actively, as Americans believe it their right to do. And it's an ad for beer, which makes you happy in the special way of all intoxicants, by reshaping reality around a sensation you alone are having. So, even more precisely, the ad means: 'Go have a beer and let it make you happy.' Nothing strange there. Except beer used to be sold on the dream of communal fun: have a beer with a buddy, or lots of buddies. People crowded the frame, laughing and smiling. It was a lie about alcohol – as this ad is a lie about alcohol – but it was a different kind of lie, a wide-framed lie, including other people.

Here the focus is narrow, almost obsessive. Everything that is not absolutely necessary to your happiness has been removed from the visual horizon. The dream is not only of happiness, but of happiness conceived in perfect isolation. Find your beach in the middle of the city. Find your beach no matter what else is happening. Do not be distracted from finding your beach. Find your beach even if – as in the case of this wall painting – it is not actually there. Create this beach inside yourself. Carry it with you wherever you go. The pursuit of happiness has always seemed to me a somewhat heavy American burden, but in Manhattan it is conceived as a peculiar form of duty.

In an exercise class recently the instructor shouted at me, at all of us: 'Don't let your mind set limits that aren't really there.' You'll find this attitude all over the island. It is encouraged and reflected in the popular culture, especially the movies, so many of which, after all, begin their creative lives here, in Manhattan. According to the movies it's only our own limited brains that are keeping us from happiness. In the future we will take a pill to make us limitless (and ideal citizens of Manhattan), or we will, like Scarlett Johansson in *Lucy*, use a hundred per cent of our brain's capacity instead of the mythic ten. In these formulations the world as it is has no real claim on us. Our happiness, our miseries, our beaches, or our blasted heaths – they are all within our own power to create, or destroy. On Tina Fey's television show *30 Rock*, Jack Donaghy – the consummate citizen of this new Manhattan – deals with problems by crushing them with his 'mind vise'.

The beach is always there: you just have to conceive of it. It follows that those who fail to find their beach are, in the final analysis, mentally fragile; in Manhattan terms, simply weak. Jack Donaghy's verbal swordplay with Liz Lemon was a comic rendering of the various things many citizens of Manhattan have come to regard as fatal weakness: childlessness, obesity, poverty. To find your beach you have to be ruthless. Manhattan is for the hard-bodied, the hard-minded, the multitasker, the alpha mamas and papas. A perfect place for self-empowerment – as long as you're pretty empowered to begin with. As long as you're one of these people who simply do not allow anything – not even reality – to impinge upon that clear field of blue.

There is a kind of individualism so stark that it seems to dovetail with an existentialist creed: Manhattan is right at that crossroads. You are pure potential in Manhattan, limitless, you are making yourself every day. When I am in England each summer, it's the opposite: all I see are the limits of my life. The brain that puts a hairbrush in the fridge, the leg that radiates pain from the hip to the toe, the lovely children who eat all my time, the books unread and unwritten.

And casting a shadow over it all is what Philip Larkin called 'extinction's alp', no longer a stable peak in a distance, finally becoming rising ground. In England even at the actual beach I cannot find my beach. I look out at the freezing water, at the families squeezed into ill-fitting wetsuits, huddled behind windbreakers, approaching a day at the beach with the kind of stoicism once conjured for things like the Battle of Britain, and all I can think is what funny, limited creatures we are, subject to every wind and wave, building castles in the sand that will only be knocked down by the generation coming up beneath us.

When I land at JFK, everything changes. For the first few days it is a shock: I have to get used to old New York ladies beside themselves with fury that I have stopped their smooth elevator journey and got in with some children. I have to remember not to pause while walking in the street – or during any fluid-moving city interaction – unless I want to utterly exasperate the person behind me. Each man and woman in this town is in pursuit of his or her beach and God help you if you get in their way. I suppose it should follow that I am happier in pragmatic England than idealist Manhattan, but I can't honestly say that this is so. You don't come to live here unless the delusion of a reality shaped around your own desires isn't a strong aspect of your personality. 'A reality shaped around your own desires' – there is something sociopathic in that ambition.

It is also a fair description of what it is to write fiction. And to live in a city where everyone has essentially the same tunnel vision and obsessive focus as a novelist is to disguise your own sociopathy among the herd. Objectively all the same limits are upon me in Manhattan as they are in England. I walk a ten-block radius every day, constrained in all the usual ways by domestic life, reduced to writing about whatever is right in front of my nose. But the fact remains that here I *do* write, the work gets done.

Even if my Manhattan productivity is powered by a sociopathic illusion of my own limitlessness, I'm thankful for it, at least when I'm writing. There's a reason so many writers once lived here, beyond the convenient laundromats and the take-out food, the libraries and cafés. We have always worked off the energy generated by this town, the money-making and tower-building as much as the street art and underground cultures. Now the energy is different: the underground has almost entirely disappeared. (You hope there are still young artists in Washington Heights, in the Barrio, or Stuyvesant Town, but how much longer can they hang on?) A twisted kind of energy radiates instead off the soulcycling mothers and marathon-running octogenarians, the entertainment lawyers glued to their iPhones and the moguls building five 'individualized' condo townhouses where once there was a hospital.

It's not a pretty energy, but it still runs what's left of the show. I contribute to it. I ride a stationary bike like the rest of them. And then I despair when Shakespeare and Co. closes in favour of another Foot Locker. There's no way to be in good faith on this island any more. You have to crush so many things with your 'mind vise' just to get through the day. Which seems to me another aspect of the ad outside my window: wilful intoxication. Or to put it more snappily: 'You don't have to be high to live here, but it helps.'

Finally the greatest thing about Manhattan is the worst thing about Manhattan: self-actualization. Here you will be free to stretch yourself to your limit, to find the beach that is yours alone. But sooner or later you will be sitting on that beach wondering what comes next. I can see my own beach ahead now, as the children grow, as the practical limits fade; I see afresh the huge privilege of my position; it reclarifies itself. Under the protection of a university I live on one of the most privileged strips of built-up beach in the world, among people who believe they have no limits and who push me, by their very proximity, into the same useful delusion, now and then.

It is such a good town in which to work and work. You can find your beach here, find it falsely, but convincingly, still thinking of Manhattan as an isle of writers and artists – of downtown underground wildlings and uptown intellectuals – against all evidence to the contrary. Oh, you still see them occasionally here and there, but unless they are under the protection of a university – or have sold that TV show – they are all of them, every single last one of them, in Brooklyn.

Joy

It might be useful to distinguish between pleasure and joy. But maybe everybody does this very easily, all the time, and only I am confused. A lot of people seem to feel that joy is only the most intense version of pleasure, arrived at by the same road – you simply have to go a little further down the track. That has not been my experience. And if you asked me if I wanted more joyful experiences in my life, I wouldn't be at all sure I did, exactly because it proves such a difficult emotion to manage. It's not at all obvious to me how we should make an accommodation between joy and the rest of our everyday lives.

Perhaps the first thing to say is that I experience at least a little pleasure every day. I wonder if this is more than the usual amount? It was the same even in childhood, when most people are miserable. I don't think this is because so many wonderful things happen to me but rather that the small things go a long way. I seem to get more than the ordinary satisfaction out of food, for example – any old food. An egg sandwich from one of these grimy food vans on Washington Square has the genuine power to turn my day around. Whatever is put in front of me, foodwise, will usually get a five-star review.

You'd think that people would like to cook for, or eat with, me – in fact I'm told it's boring. Where there is no discernment there can be no awareness of expertise or gratitude for special effort. 'Don't say that was delicious,' my husband warns. 'You say everything's delicious.' 'But it was delicious.' It drives him crazy. All day long I can look forward to a popsicle. The persistent anxiety that fills the rest of my life is calmed for as long as I have the flavour of something good in my mouth. And though it's true that when the flavour is finished the anxiety returns, we do not have so many reliable sources of pleasure in this life as to turn our nose up at one that is so readily available, especially here in America. A pineapple popsicle. Even the great anxiety of writing can be stilled for the eight minutes it takes to eat a pineapple popsicle.

My other source of daily pleasure is – but I wish I had a better way of putting it – 'other people's faces'. A red-headed girl, with a marvellous large nose she probably hates, and green eyes and that sun-shy complexion composed more of freckles than skin. Or a heavyset grown man, smoking a cigarette in the rain, with a soggy moustache, combined with a surprise – the keen eyes, snub nose and cherub mouth of his own eight-year-old self. Upon leaving the library at the end of the day I will walk a little more quickly to the apartment to tell my husband about an angular, cat-eyed teenager, in skinny jeans and stacked-heel boots, a perfectly ordinary grey sweatshirt, last night's make-up, and a silky Pocahontas wig slightly askew over his Afro. He was sashaying down the street, plaits flying, using the whole of Broadway as his personal catwalk. 'Miss Thang, but off duty.' I add this for clarity, but my husband nods a little impatiently; there was no need for the addition. My husband is also a professional gawker.

The advice one finds in ladies' magazines is usually to be feared, but there is something in that old chestnut: 'shared interests'. It *does* help. I like to hear about the Chinese girl he saw in the hall, carrying

428

a large medical textbook, so beautiful she looked like an illustration. Or the tall Kenyan in the elevator whose elongated physical elegance reduced every other nearby body to the shrunken, gnarly status of a troll. Usually I will not have seen these people – my husband works on the eighth floor of the library, I work on the fifth – but simply hearing them described can be almost as much a pleasure as encountering them myself. More pleasurable still is when we re-create the walks or gestures or voices of these strangers, or whole conversations – between two people in the queue for the ATM, or two students on a bench near the fountain.

And then there are all the many things that the dog does and says, entirely anthropomorphized and usually offensive, which express the universe of things we ourselves cannot do or say, to each other or to other people. 'You're being the dog,' our child said recently, surprising us. She is almost three and all our private languages are losing their privacy and becoming known to her. Of course, we knew she would eventually become fully conscious, and that before this happened we would have to give up arguing, smoking, eating meat, using the Internet, talking about other people's faces, and voicing the dog, but now the time has come, she is fully aware, and we find ourselves unable to change. 'Stop being the dog,' she said, 'it's very silly,' and for the first time in eight years we looked at the dog and were ashamed.

Occasionally the child, too, is a pleasure, though mostly she is a joy, which means in fact she gives us not much pleasure at all but rather that strange admixture of terror, pain and delight that I have come to recognize as joy, and now must find some way to live with daily. This is a new problem. Until quite recently I had known joy only five times in my life, perhaps six, and each time tried to forget it soon after it happened, out of the fear that the memory of it would dement and destroy everything else.

Let's call it six. Three of those times I was in love, but only once was the love viable, or likely to bring me any pleasure in the long run. Twice I was on drugs – of quite different kinds. Once I was in water, once on a train, once sitting on a high wall, once on a high hill, once in a nightclub, and once in a hospital bed. It is hard to arrive at generalities in the face of such a small and varied collection of data. The uncertain item is the nightclub, and because it was essentially a communal experience I feel I can open the question out to the floor. I am addressing this to my fellow Britons in particular. Fellow Britons! Those of you, that is, who were fortunate enough to take the first generation of the amphetamine ecstasy and yet experience none of the adverse, occasionally lethal reactions we now know others suffered – yes, for you people I have a question. Was that joy?

I am especially interested to hear from anyone who happened to be in the Fabric club, near the old Smithfield meat market, on a night sometime in the year 1999 (I'm sorry I can't be more specific) when the DJ mixed 'Can I Kick It?' and then 'Smells Like Teen Spirit' into the deep-house track he had been seeming to play exclusively for the previous four hours. I myself was wandering out of the cavernous unisex (!) toilets, wishing I could find my friend Sarah, or if not her, my friend Warren, or if not him, anyone who would take pity on a girl who had taken and was about to come up on ecstasy who had lost everyone and everything, including her handbag. I stumbled back into the fray.

Most of the men were topless, and most of the women, like me, wore strange aprons, fashionable at the time, that covered just the front of one's torso, and only remained decent by means of a few weak-looking strings tied in dainty bows behind. I pushed through this crowd of sweaty bare backs, despairing, wondering where in a super-club one might bed down for the night (the stairs? the fire exit?). But everything I tried to look at quickly shattered and arranged itself in a series of patterned fragments, as if I were living in a kaleidoscope. Where was I trying to get to anyway? There was no longer any 'bar' or 'chill-out zone' – there was only dance floor. All was dance floor. Everybody danced. I stood still, oppressed on all sides by dancing, quite sure I was about to go out of my mind.

Then suddenly I could hear Q-Tip – blessed Q-Tip! – not a synthesizer, not a vocoder, but Q-Tip, with his human voice, rapping over a human beat. And the top of my skull opened to let human Q-Tip in, and a rail-thin man with enormous eyes reached across a sea of bodies for my hand. He kept asking me the same thing over and over: *You feeling it?* I was. My ridiculous heels were killing me, I was terrified I might die, yet I felt simultaneously overwhelmed with delight that 'Can I Kick It?' should happen to be playing at this precise moment in the history of the world, and was now morphing into 'Smells Like Teen Spirit'. I took the man's hand. The top of my head flew away. We danced and danced. We gave ourselves up to joy.

Years later, while listening to a song called 'Weak Become Heroes' by the British musicians the Streets I found this experience almost perfectly re-created in rhyme, and realized that just as most American children alive in 1969 saw the moon landings, nearly every Briton between sixteen and thirty in the nineties met some version of the skinny pill head I came across that night in Fabric. The name the Streets gives him is 'European Bob'. I suspect he is an archetypal figure of my generation. The character Super Hans in the British TV comedy *Peep Show* is another example of the breed, though it might be more accurate to say Super Hans is European Bob in 'old' age (forty). I don't remember the name of my particular pill head, but will call him Smiley. He was one of these strangers you met exclusively on dance floors, or else on a beach in Ibiza. They tended to have inexplicable nicknames, no home or family you could ever identify, a limitless capacity for drug-taking and a universal feeling of goodwill toward all men and women, no matter their colour, creed or state of inebriation.

Their most endearing quality was their generosity. For the length of one night Smiley would do anything at all for you. Find you a cab, walk miles through the early-morning streets looking for food, hold your hair as you threw up, and listen to you complain at great length about your parents and friends – agreeing with all your grievances – though every soul involved in these disputes was completely unknown to him. Contrary to your initial suspicions Smiley did not want to sleep with you, rob you, or con you in any way. It was simply intensely important to him that you had a good time, tonight, with him. 'How you feeling?' was Smiley's perennial question. 'You feeling it yet? I'm feeling it. You feeling it yet?' And that *you* should feel it seemed almost more important to him than that *he* should.

Was that joy? Probably not. But it mimicked joy's conditions pretty well. It included, in minor form, the great struggle that tends to precede joy, and the feeling – once one is 'in' joy – that the experiencing subject has somehow 'entered' the emotion, and disappeared. I 'have' pleasure, it is a feeling I want to experience and own. A beach holiday is a pleasure. A new dress is a pleasure. But on that dance floor I *was* joy, or some small piece of joy, with all these other hundreds of people who were also a part of joy.

The Smileys, in their way, must have recognized the vital difference; it would explain their great concern with other people's experiences. For as long as that high lasted, they seemed to pass beyond their own egos. And it might really have been joy if the next morning didn't always arrive. I don't just mean the deathly headache, the blurred vision and the stomach cramps. What really destroyed the possibility that this had been joy was the replaying in one's mind of the actual events of the previous night, and the brutal recognition that every moment of sublimity – every conversation that had seemed to touch upon the meaning of life, every tune that had appeared a masterwork – had no substance whatsoever now, here, in the harsh light of the morning. The final indignity came when you dragged yourself finally from your bed and went into the living room. There, on your mother's sofa – in the place of that jester spirit-animal saviour person you thought you'd met last night – someone had left a crushingly boring skinny pill head, already smoking a joint, who wanted to borrow twenty quid for a cab.

It wasn't all a waste of time, though. At the neural level, such experiences gave you a clue about what joy not-under-the-influence would feel like. Helped you learn to recognize joy, when it arrived. I suppose a neuroscientist could explain in very clear terms why the moment after giving birth can feel ecstatic, or swimming in a Welsh mountain lake with somebody dear to you. Perhaps the same synapses that ecstasy falsely twanged are twanged authentically by fresh water, certain epidurals and oxytocin. And if, while sitting on a high hill in the south of France, someone who has access to a phone comes dashing up the slope to inform you that two years of tension, tedious study and academic anxiety have not been in vain – perhaps again these same synapses or whatever they are do their happy dance.

We certainly don't need to be neuroscientists to know that wild romantic crushes – especially if they are fraught with danger – do something ecstatic to our brains, though like the pills that share the name, horror and disappointment are usually not far behind. When my wild crush came, we wandered around a museum for so long it closed without us noticing; stuck in the grounds we climbed a high wall and, finding it higher on its other side, considered our options: broken ankles or a long night sleeping on a stone lion. In the end a passer-by helped us down, and things turned prosaic and, after a few months, fizzled out. What looked like love had just been teen spirit. But what a wonderful thing, to sit on a high wall, dizzy with joy, and think nothing of breaking your ankles.

Real love came much later. It lay at the end of a long and arduous road, and up to the very last moment I had been convinced it wouldn't happen. I was so surprised by its arrival, so unprepared, that on the day it arrived I had already arranged for us to visit the Holocaust museum at Auschwitz. You were holding my feet on the train to the bus that would take us there. We were heading toward all that makes life intolerable, feeling the only thing that makes it worthwhile. That was joy. But it's no good thinking about or discussing it. It has no place next to the furious argument about who cleaned the house or picked up the child. It is irrelevant when sitting peacefully, watching an old movie, or doing an impression of two old ladies in a shop, or as I eat a popsicle while you scowl at me, or when working on different floors of the library. It doesn't fit with the everyday. The thing no one ever tells you about joy is that it has very little real pleasure in it. And yet if it hadn't happened at all, at least once, how would we live?

A final thought: sometimes joy multiplies itself dangerously. Children are the infamous example. Isn't it bad enough that the beloved, with whom you have experienced genuine joy, will eventually be lost to you? Why add to this nightmare the child, whose loss, if it ever happened, would mean nothing less than your total annihilation? It should be noted that an equally dangerous joy, for many people, is the dog or the cat, relationships with animals being in some sense intensified by guaranteed finitude. You hope to leave this world before your child. You are quite certain your dog will leave before you do. Joy is such a human madness.

The writer Julian Barnes, considering mourning, once said, 'It hurts just as much as it is worth.' In fact, it was a friend of his who wrote the line in a letter of condolence, and Julian told it to my husband, who told it to me. For months afterwards these words stuck with both of us, so clear and so brutal. *It hurts just as much as it is worth*. What an arrangement. Why would anyone accept such a crazy deal? Surely if we were sane and reasonable we would every time choose a pleasure over a joy, as animals themselves sensibly do. The end of a pleasure brings no great harm to anyone, after all, and can always be replaced with another of more or less equal worth.

AFTERWORD

Most of the essays in this book were written for Bob Silvers, David Remnick and Deborah Treisman. I thank them for their encouragement and support. I'm lucky to have many editors and early readers: thank you to Cressida Leyshon, Simon Prosser, Georgia Garrett, Ann Godoff, Darryl Pinckney, Nikita Lalwani, Hilton Als, my ex-assistant, Devin Jacobsen, and my present one, Porter Yelton. Thank you to Gemma Sieff for thinking to hire me for a while at *Harper's*. Thank you, Catie Marron, for asking for something about squares and accepting something about circles. Thank you to Christopher Sweet for commissioning some thoughts on Billie. Special thanks to Devorah Baum, early reader, friend, and cleverest woman in London. Nick: *grazie infinite* for the title, the early reads, the edits, articles, links, books, ideas – and all the rest.

PICTURE CREDITS

p. 165 Billie Holiday on Broad Street in front of Sugar Hill with her pet chihuahua, Pepi; 18 April 1957, Newark, NJ. Photograph by Jerry Dantzic © 2017 Jerry Dantzic Archives. All Rights Reserved.

p. 174 Balthasar Denner: *Alte Frau*, 1721. Reproduced by kind permission of KHM-Museumsverband.

p. 182 Mark Bradford, *Niagara*, 2005. Video, colour, no sound, 3.17 min.

p. 202 Sarah Sze: *Centrifuge*, 2017. Mixed media, mirrors, wood, bamboo, stainless steel, archival inkjet prints, video projectors, ceramic, acrylic paint, salt. Dimensions variable. Courtesy of the artist, Tanya Bonakdar Gallery and Victoria Miro Gallery. © Sarah Sze.

p. 365 Harvey Smith: *The Family is a Violent Event*. Used by permission of the Smith estate.

p. 367 Luca Signorelli: *Nude Man from the Back Carrying a Corpse on His Shoulders*. Paris, Louvre (Cabinet des Dessins). © 2017. Photo: Scala, Florence.

p. 419 Elmgreen and Dragset: *Death of a Collector*, 2009. Photo: Anders Sune Berg. Courtesy: Colección Helga de Alvear, Madrid/Cáceres.

ACKNOWLEDGEMENTS

The essays in this collection were first published in the journals and books mentioned below, and any works reviewed in these essays are also included.

Part 1: In the World

North-west London Blues
(*New York Review of Books*, 2 June 2012)

Elegy on a Country's Seasons
(*New York Review of Books*, 3 April 2014)

Fences: A Brexit Diary
(*New York Review of Books*, 18 August 2016)

On Optimism and Despair
(*New York Review of Books*, 22 December 2016)

Part II: In the Audience

Generation Why?
(*New York Review of Books*, 25 November 2010)
  The Social Network by Aaron Sorkin (2010)

The House That Hova Built
(*The New York Times*, 6 September 2012)
'7 Minute Freestyle' by Big L
'Renegade', 'Success', 'Izzo', 'Never Change', 'Gotta Have It',
'Murder to Excellence', 'Who Gon Stop Me,' 'Dead Presidents
II' and 'Blueprint (Momma Loves Me)' by Jay-Z

Brother from Another Mother
(*New Yorker*, 23 February 2015)
'Sad Fitty Cent' (2009) and 'Obama's Anger Translator' (2012)
by Keegan-Michael Key and Jordan Peele for MADtv on
Comedy Central
'Lines Written a Few Miles above Tintern Abbey' from *Lyrical
Ballads, with Other Poems* by William Wordsworth (1800)

Some Notes on Attunement
(*New Yorker*, 17 December 2012)
Fear and Trembling by Søren Kierkegaard (1843)
'A Conversation with Joni Mitchell' words from Joni Mitchell
interviewed by Jody Denberg on KGSR-FM (1998)

Windows on the Will: *Anomalisa*
(*New York Review of Books*, 10 March 2016)
Voiceover at *The Polar Express 4-D Experience*, Central Park Zoo,
New York City
On the Suffering of the World by Arthur Schopenhauer (1850)
Being John Malkovich by Charlie Kaufman (2000)
Anomalisa by Charlie Kaufman (2015)
Lakmé by Léo Delibes (1883)

Dance Lessons for Writers
(*Guardian*, 29 October 2016)
Blood Memory by Martha Graham (1972)

Part III: In the Gallery

Killing Orson Welles at Midnight
(*New York Review of Books*, 28 April 2011)
   'Morning Song' from *Ariel* by Sylvia Plath (1965)
   Against Interpretation by Susan Sontag (1964)

Flaming June
(*Sotheby's Magazine*)

'Crazy They Call Me': On Looking at Jerry Dantzic's photos of
   Billie Holiday
(first published as an Introduction to *Jerry Dantzic: Billie Holiday at
   Sugar Hill* in April 2016, Thames & *Hudson*)
   'Take Back Your Mink' from *Guys and Dolls* by Frank Loesser (1950)

Alte Frau
(January 2017)
   Ways of Seeing by John Berger (1972)

Mark Bradford's *Niagara*
(first published in a Venice Biennale catalogue titled *Mark Bradford:
   Tomorrow*, in June 2017, GRM & Co.)
   'Marilyn Lets Her Hair Down About Being Famous' by Richard
      Meryman, *LIFE* magazine (1962)
   Interview with Mark Bradford (2009)

A Bird of Few Words: Narrative Mysteries in the Paintings of
   Lynette Yiadom-Boakye
(*New Yorker*, 19 June 2017)
   Interview with Lynette Yiadom-Boakye from *TimeOut New York*
      (2017)

'Plans of the Night', 'In Conversation' and 'The Meaning of Restraint' from *Lynette Yiadom-Boakye* with contributions by Naomi Beckwith, Donatien Grau, Jennifer Higgie and Lynette Yiadom-Boakye (2014)

The Tattered Ruins of the Map: On Sarah Sze's *Centrifuge*
(first published in the catalogue accompanying the work *Centrifuge* by Sarah Sze, a site-specific installation commissioned by Haus der Kunst in Munich for the 2017 edition of *Der Öffentlichkeit – von den Freunden Haus der Kunst*)

Getting In and Out
(*Harper's*, July 2017)
'Theme for English B' from *Collected* Poems by Langston Hughes (1994)
I Am Not Your Negro by James Baldwin and Raoul Peck (2016)
Pnin by Vladimir Nabokov (1957)

Part IV: On the bookshelf

Crash by J. G. Ballard
(first published as an introduction to the reissue of *Crash*, 4th Estate, 2014).
Crash by J. G. Ballard (1973)
Manifesto of Futurism by Filippo Tommaso Marinetti (1909)

The Buddha of Suburbia by Hanif Kureishi
(first published as an introduction to *The Buddha of Suburbia*, Faber and Faber Ltd, 2015)
The Buddha of Suburbia by Hanif Kureishi (1990)

Notes on *NW*
(*Guardian*, 1 August 2013)

Acknowledgements

The *Harper's* Columns
(*Harper's*, March–August 2011)

'On Harlem, Hatred and Javier'

Harlem is Nowhere by Sharifa Rhodes-Pitts (2011)
My Prizes by Thomas Bernhard (2011)
While the Women are Sleeping by Javier Marías (2010)
The Immortalization Commission by John Gray (2011)
Anticipations of the Reaction of Mechanical and Scientific Progress upon Human Life and Thought by H. G. Wells (1901)
Wait for Me! by Deborah Cavendish, Duchess of Devonshire (2010)
Autoportrait by Édouard Levé and Lorin Stein (2012)
Suicide by Édouard Levé (2008)
Seven Years by Peter Stamm (2010)

'Paula Fox and Geoff Dyer'

News from the World by Paula Fox (2011)
A Room with a View by E. M. Forster (1908)
Otherwise Known as the Human Condition by Geoff Dyer (2011)
'In Time of War' by W. H. Auden, from *Journey to a War* by W. H. Auden and Christopher Isherwood (1939)

'Two Legs Bad, Six Legs Good – Sontag Worse!'

Am I a Redundant Human Being? by Mela Hartwig, trans. Kerri A. Pierce (2010)
Sex on Six Legs by Marlene Zuk (2011)

'A St Aubyn Summer'

At Last by Edward St Aubyn (2011)

Acknowledgements

'On Island Life and Mother Love'

> *The Dead Yard* by Ian Thomson (2009)
> *Caucasia* (1998) and *You Are Free* (2011) by Danzy Senna

'On Wild Girls, Cruel Birds – and Rimbaud!'

> *The Wild Girls* by Ursula K. Le Guin (2011)
> *Three to See the King* (2001) and *A Cruel Bird Came to the Nest and Looked In* (2011) by Magnus Mills
> *A Season in Hell* by Arthur Rimbaud (1873)
> *Rimbaud in Java* by Jamie James (2011)

The Inaugural Newark Lecture: 'The I Who Is Not Me' (Zadie Smith, 2017; inaugural Philip Roth Lecture at the Newark Public Library, 27 October 2016)

> *Speak, Memory* by Vladimir Nabokov (1951)
> 'The Choice' by W. B. Yeats, from *The Collected Poems of W. B. Yeats* (2000)

Part V: Feel Free

Life-writing
(*Rookie* Magazine, 2 June 2015)

The Bathroom
(Zadie Smith, 2017)

Man versus Corpse
(*New York Review of Books*, 5 December 2013)

> *The Return of the Real* by Hal Foster (1996)

Acknowledgements

Meet Justin Bieber!
(Zadie Smith, 2017)

Love in the Gardens
(*New York Review of Books*, 7 November 2013)
  A Room with a View by E. M. Forster (1908)
  'Music to Watch Girls By' by Tony Velona (1966)

The Shadow of Ideas
(Zadie Smith, 2017)

Find Your Beach
(*New York Review of Books*, 23 October 2014)

Joy
(*New York Review of Books*, 10 January 2013)
  De Umbris Idearum by Giordano Bruno (1582)

Every effort has been made to trace copyright holders and to obtain their permission for the use of copyright material. The publisher apologizes for any errors or omissions and would be grateful to be notified of any corrections that should be incorporated in future editions of this book.

INDEX

Page references in *italic* indicate illustrations.

445